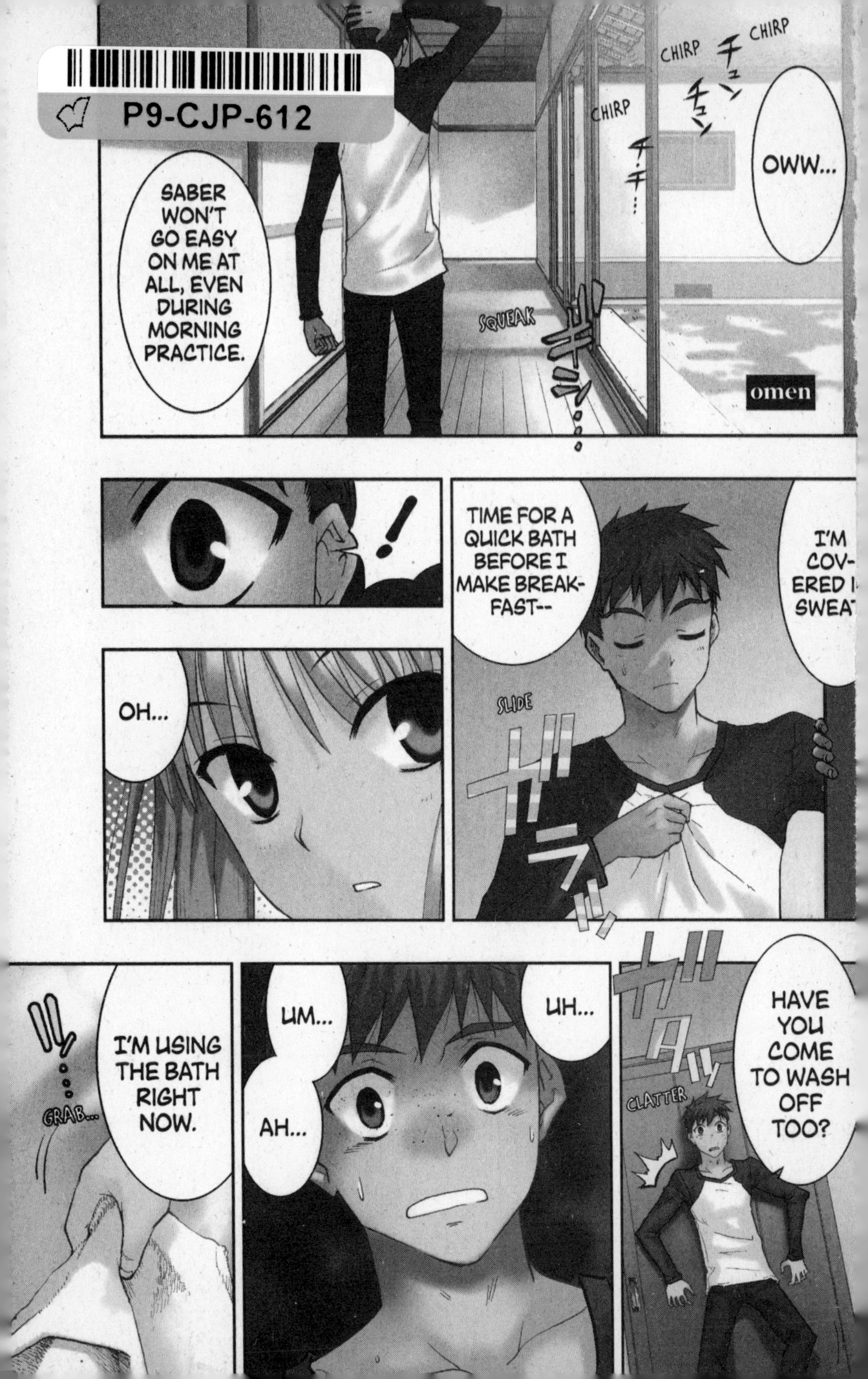
omen
CHIRP
CHIRP
CHIRP
OWW...
SQUEAK
SABER WON'T GO EASY ON ME AT ALL, EVEN DURING MORNING PRACTICE.
I'M COV- ERED I SWEA
TIME FOR A QUICK BATH BEFORE I MAKE BREAK- FAST--
SLIDE
!
OH...
HAVE YOU COME TO WASH OFF TOO?
CLATTER
UH...
UM...
AH...
I'M USING THE BATH RIGHT NOW.
GRAB...

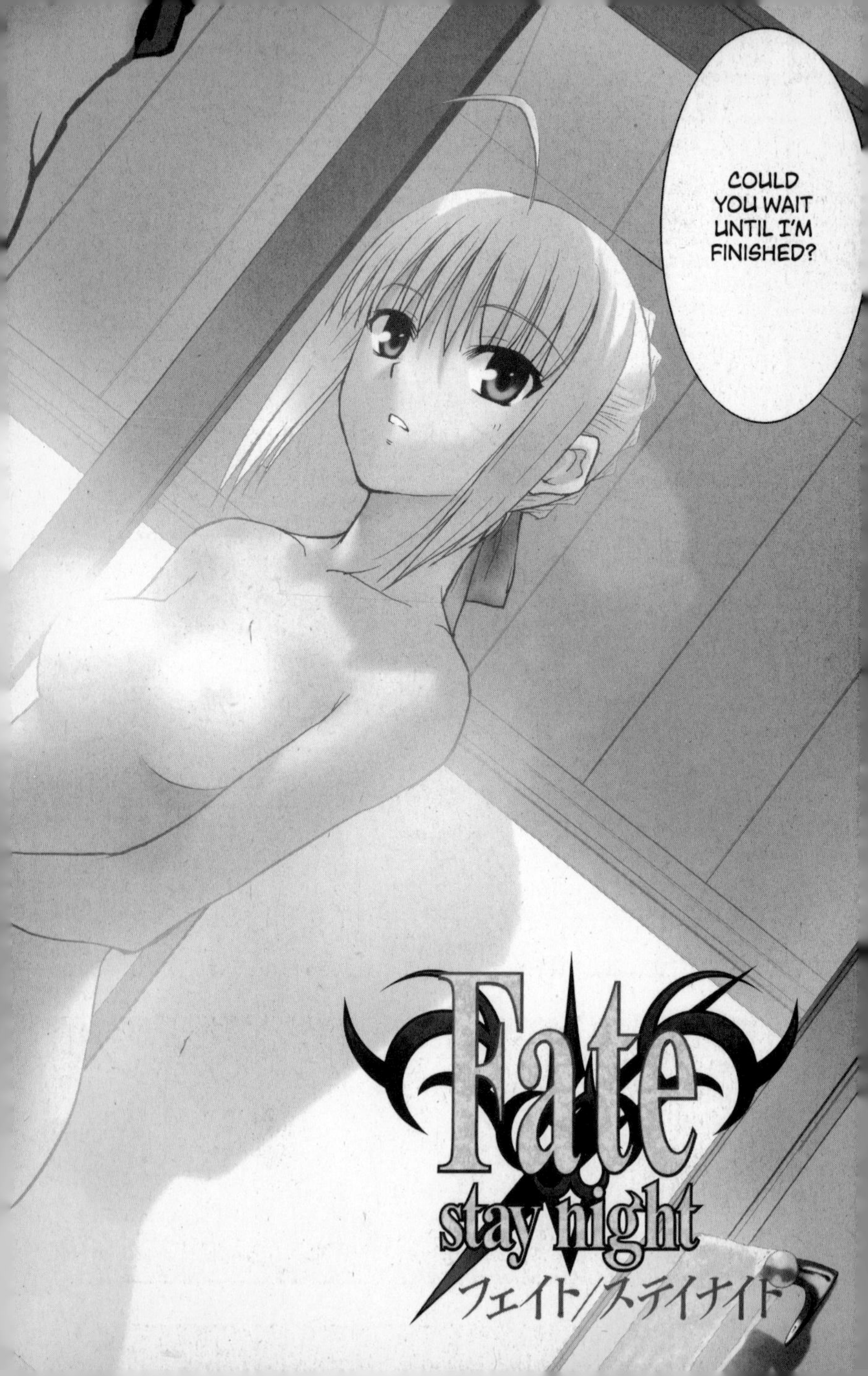
COULD YOU WAIT UNTIL I'M FINISHED?
Fate stay night
フェイト/ステイナイト

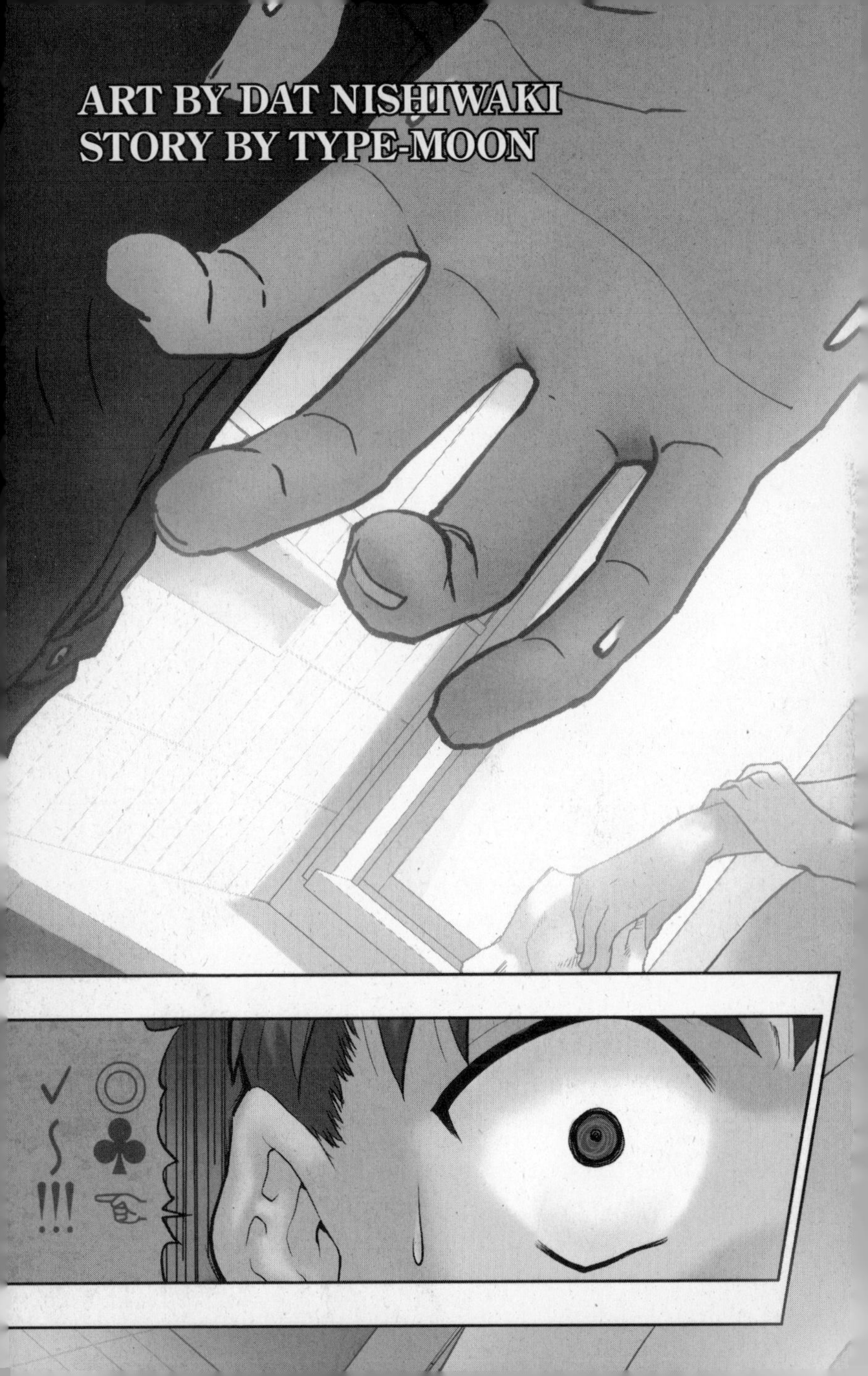
ART BY DAT NISHIWAKI
STORY BY TYPE-MOON
!!!

Fate
stay night ◇5◇
フェイト/ステイナイト

Fate
stay night
フェイト/ステイナイト

VOLUME 5

ART BY DAT NISHIWAKI
STORY BY TYPE-MOON

HAMBURG // LONDON // LOS ANGELES // TOKYO

Fate/Stay Night Volume 5
Story by TYPE-MOON
Art By Dat Nishiwaki

Translation - Lori Riser
English Adaptation - Peter Ahlstrom
Retouch and Lettering - Star Print Brokers
Production Artist - Rui Kyo
Copy Editor - Daniella Orihuela-Gruber
Graphic Designer - Louis Csontos

Editor - Lillian Diaz-Przybyl
Print Production Manager - Lucas Rivera
Managing Editor - Vy Nguyen
Senior Designer - Louis Csontos
Art Director - Al-Insan Lashley
Director of Sales and Manufacturing - Allyson De Simone
Associate Publisher - Marco F. Pavia
President and C.O.O. - John Parker
C.E.O. and Chief Creative Officer - Stu Levy

A 🐸 TOKYOPOP® Manga

TOKYOPOP and 🐸 are trademarks or registered trademarks of TOKYOPOP Inc.

TOKYOPOP Inc.
5900 Wilshire Blvd. Suite 2000
Los Angeles, CA 90036

E-mail: info@TOKYOPOP.com
Come visit us online at www.TOKYOPOP.com

Fate/stay night Volume 5
© 2007 Dat NISHIWAKI© TYPE-MOON
First published in Japan in 2007 by KADOKAWA SHOTEN
PUBLISHING CO., LTD., Tokyo. English translation rights
arranged with KADOKAWA SHOTEN PUBLISHING CO., LTD.,
Tokyo
English text copyright © 2009 TOKYOPOP Inc.

ISBN: 978-1-4278-1303-9

First TOKYOPOP printing: October 2009
10 9 8 7 6 5 4 3 2 1
Printed in the USA

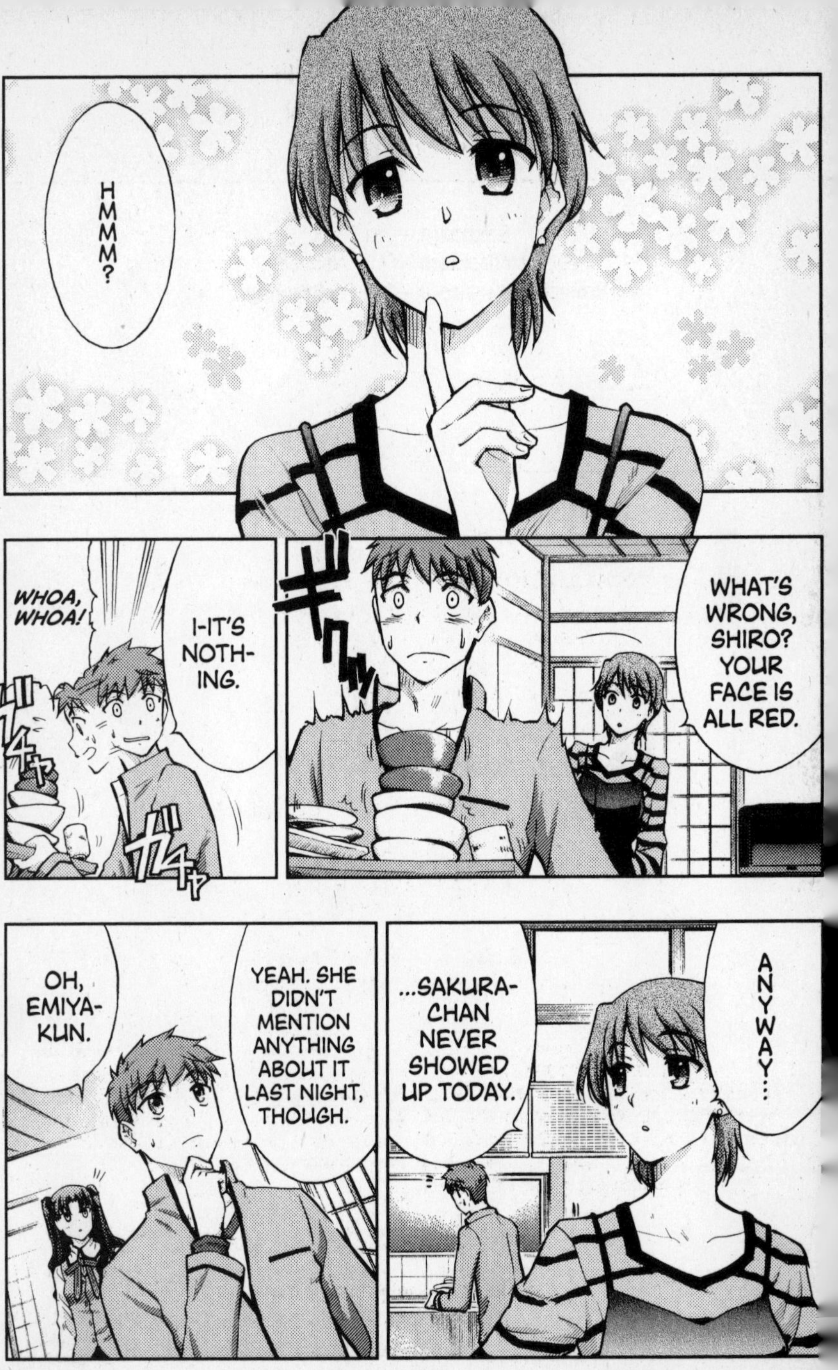
HMMM?
WHAT'S WRONG, SHIRO? YOUR FACE IS ALL RED.
I-IT'S NOTHING.
WHOA, WHOA!
ANYWAY...
...SAKURA-CHAN NEVER SHOWED UP TODAY.
YEAH. SHE DIDN'T MENTION ANYTHING ABOUT IT LAST NIGHT, THOUGH.
OH, EMIYA-KUN.

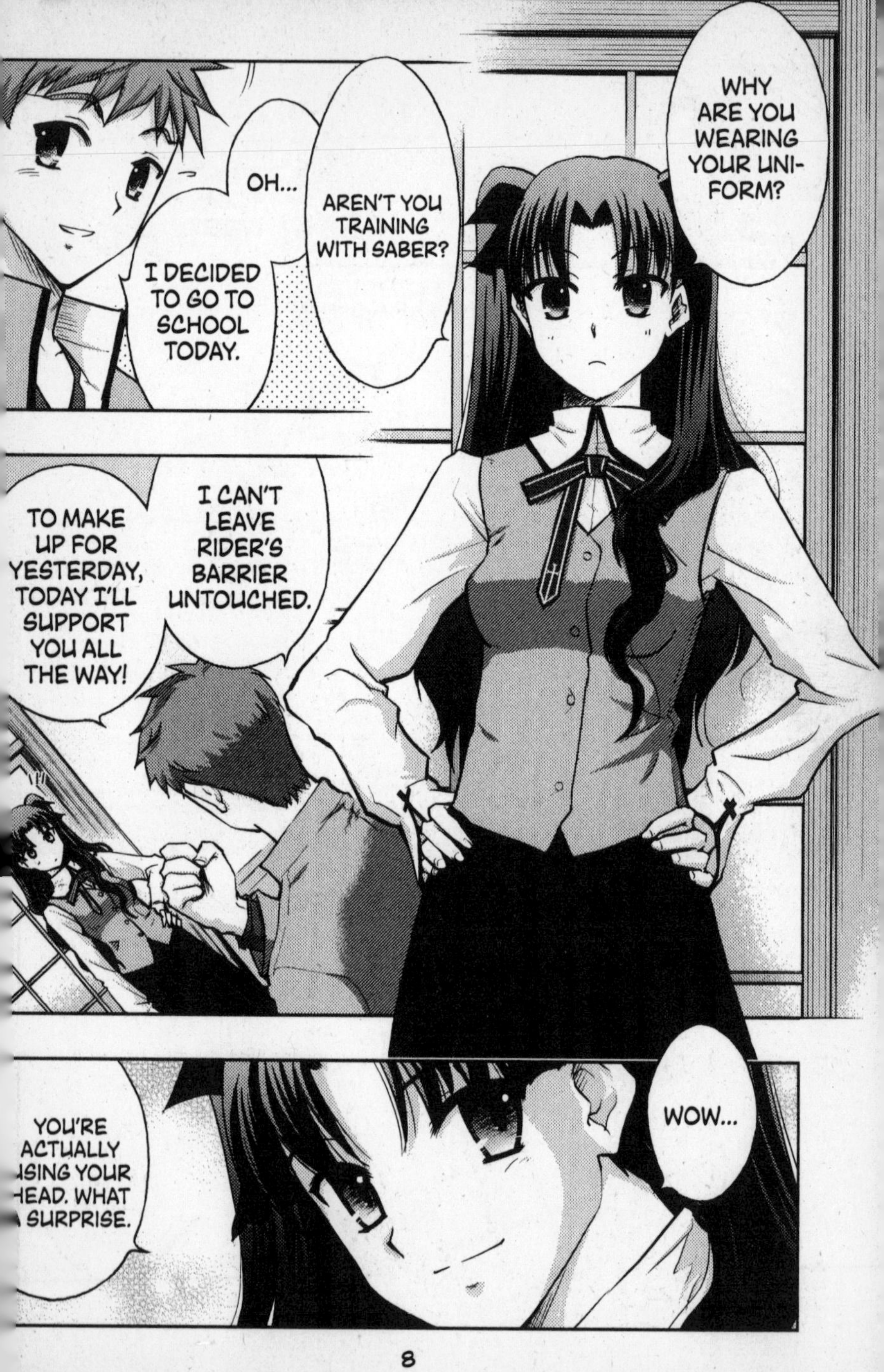
WHY ARE YOU WEARING YOUR UNI-FORM?
AREN'T YOU TRAINING WITH SABER?
OH...
I DECIDED TO GO TO SCHOOL TODAY.
I CAN'T LEAVE RIDER'S BARRIER UNTOUCHED.
TO MAKE UP FOR YESTERDAY, TODAY I'LL SUPPORT YOU ALL THE WAY!
WOW...
YOU'RE ACTUALLY USING YOUR HEAD. WHAT A SURPRISE.

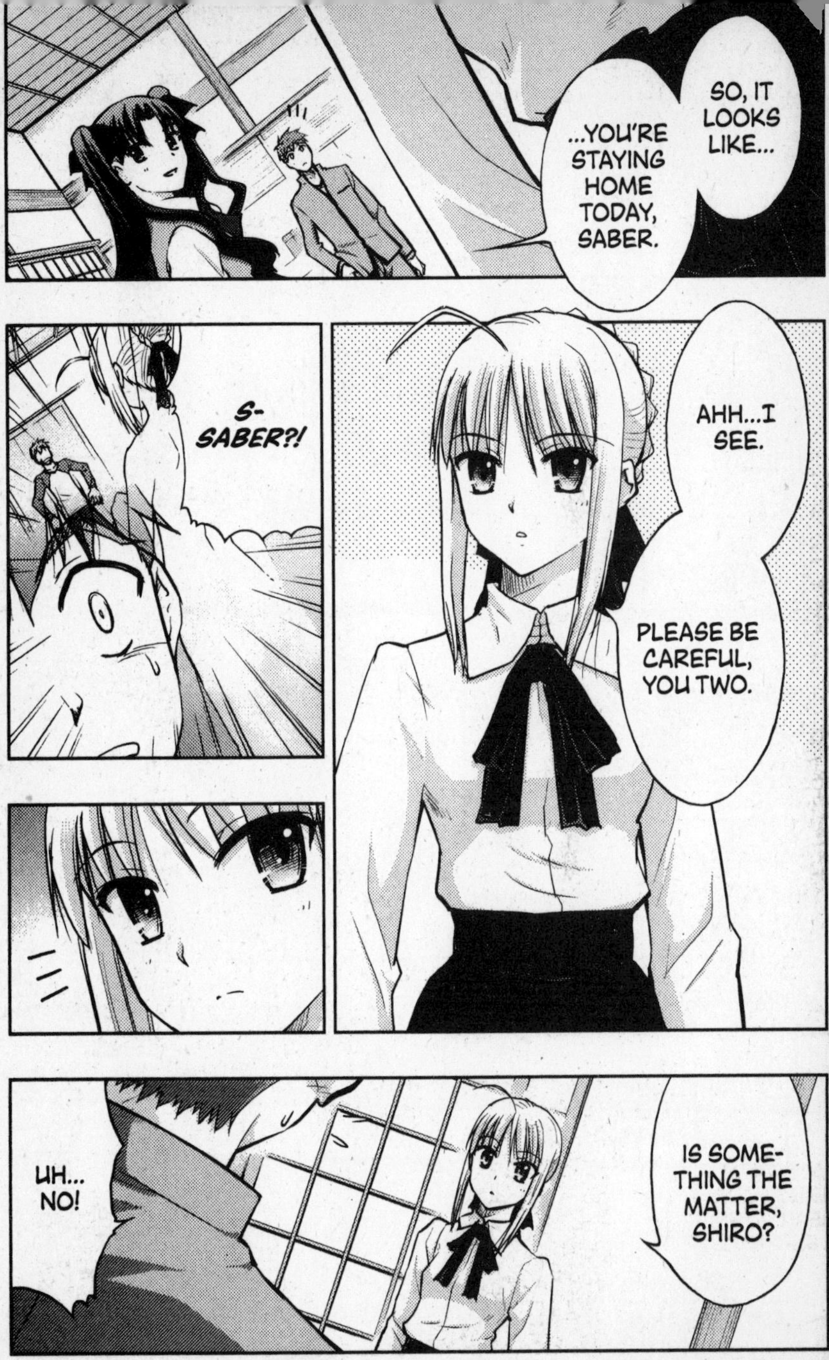
SO, IT LOOKS LIKE...
...YOU'RE STAYING HOME TODAY, SABER.
AHH...I SEE.
PLEASE BE CAREFUL, YOU TWO.
S-SABER?!
IS SOME-THING THE MATTER, SHIRO?
UH... NO!

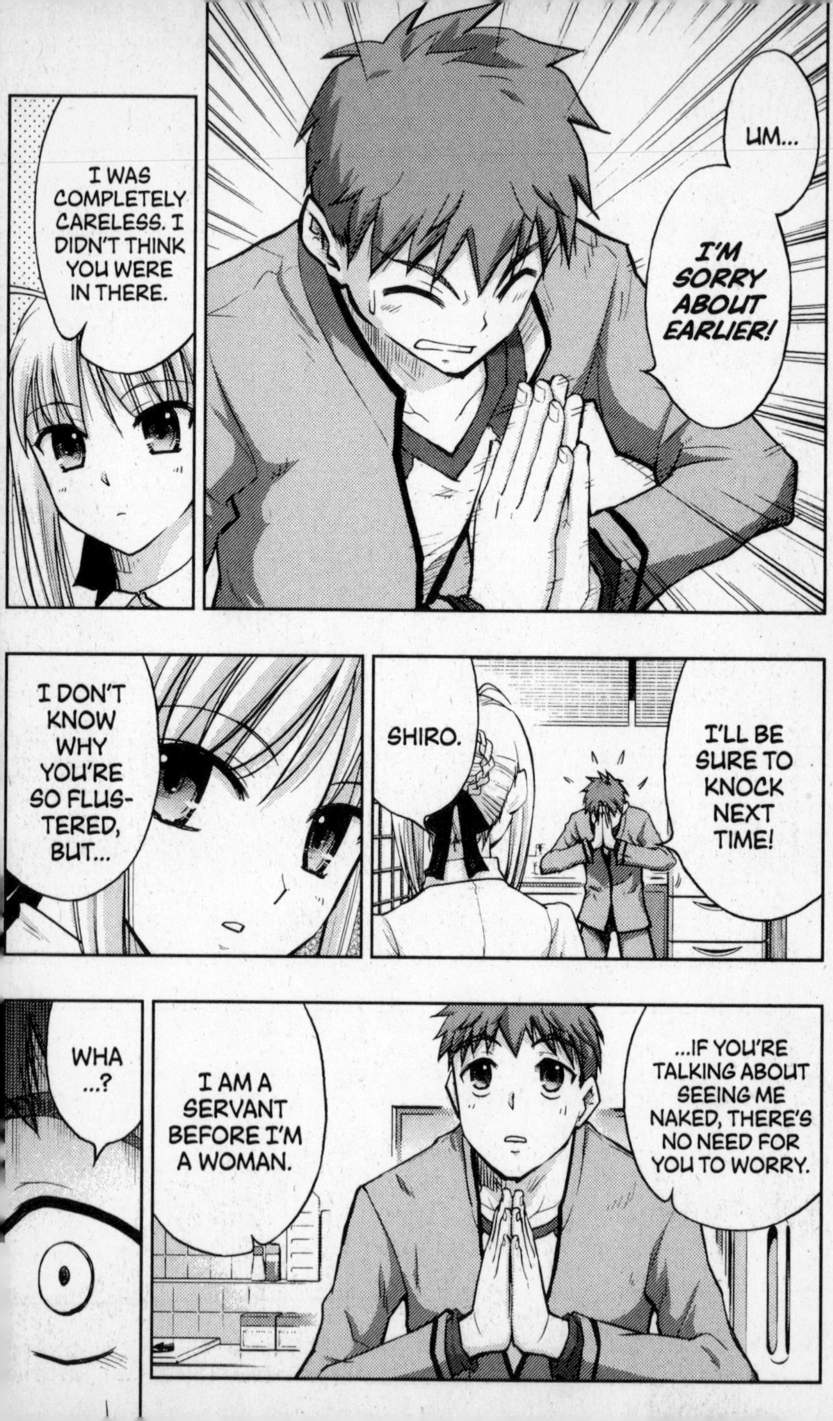
UM...
I'M SORRY ABOUT EARLIER!
I WAS COMPLETELY CARELESS. I DIDN'T THINK YOU WERE IN THERE.
I'LL BE SURE TO KNOCK NEXT TIME!
SHIRO.
I DON'T KNOW WHY YOU'RE SO FLUS-TERED, BUT...
...IF YOU'RE TALKING ABOUT SEEING ME NAKED, THERE'S NO NEED FOR YOU TO WORRY.
I AM A SERVANT BEFORE I'M A WOMAN.
WHA ...?

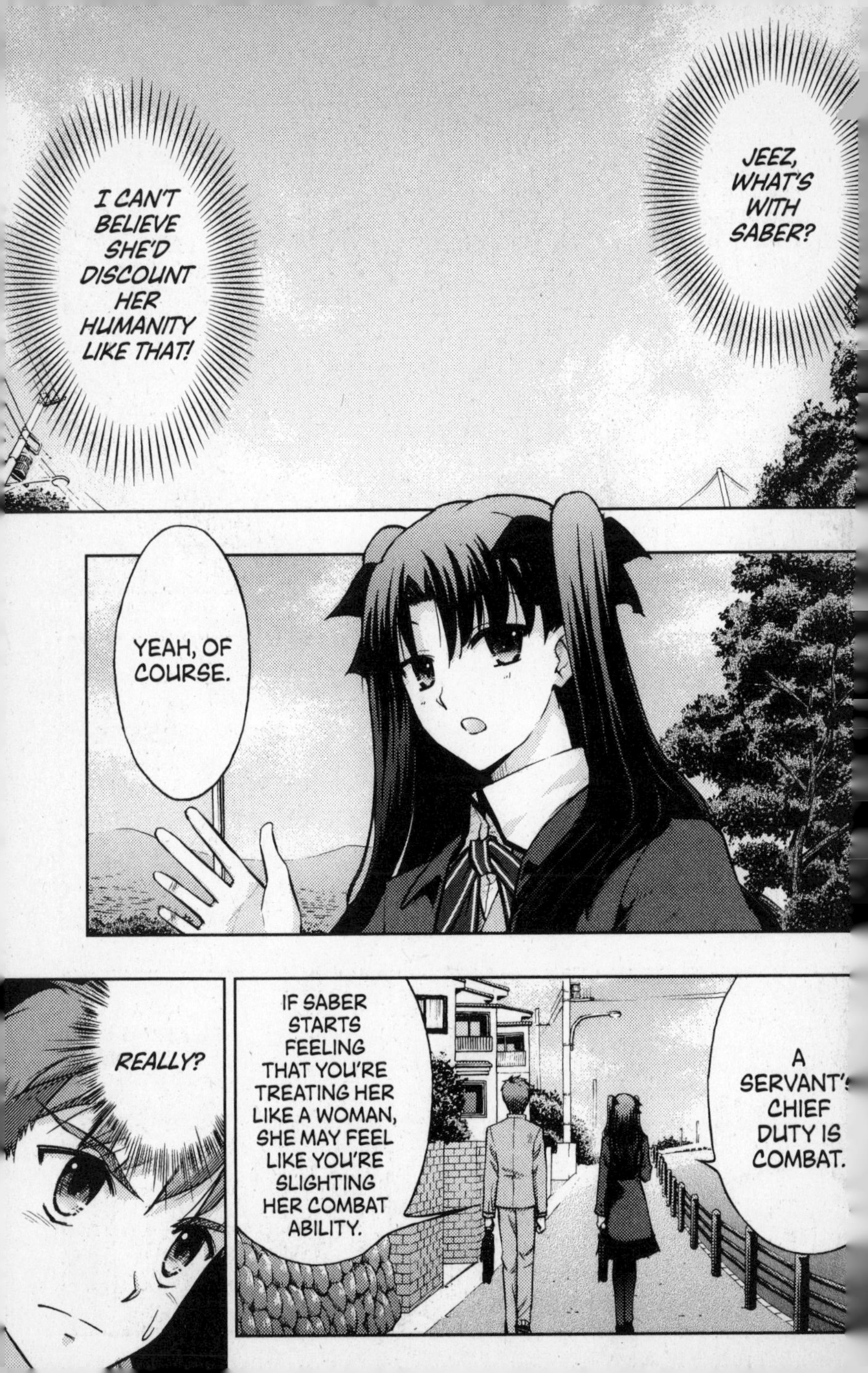
JEEZ, WHAT'S WITH SABER?
I CAN'T BELIEVE SHE'D DISCOUNT HER HUMANITY LIKE THAT!
YEAH, OF COURSE.
A SERVANT'S CHIEF DUTY IS COMBAT.
IF SABER STARTS FEELING THAT YOU'RE TREATING HER LIKE A WOMAN, SHE MAY FEEL LIKE YOU'RE SLIGHTING HER COMBAT ABILITY.
REALLY?

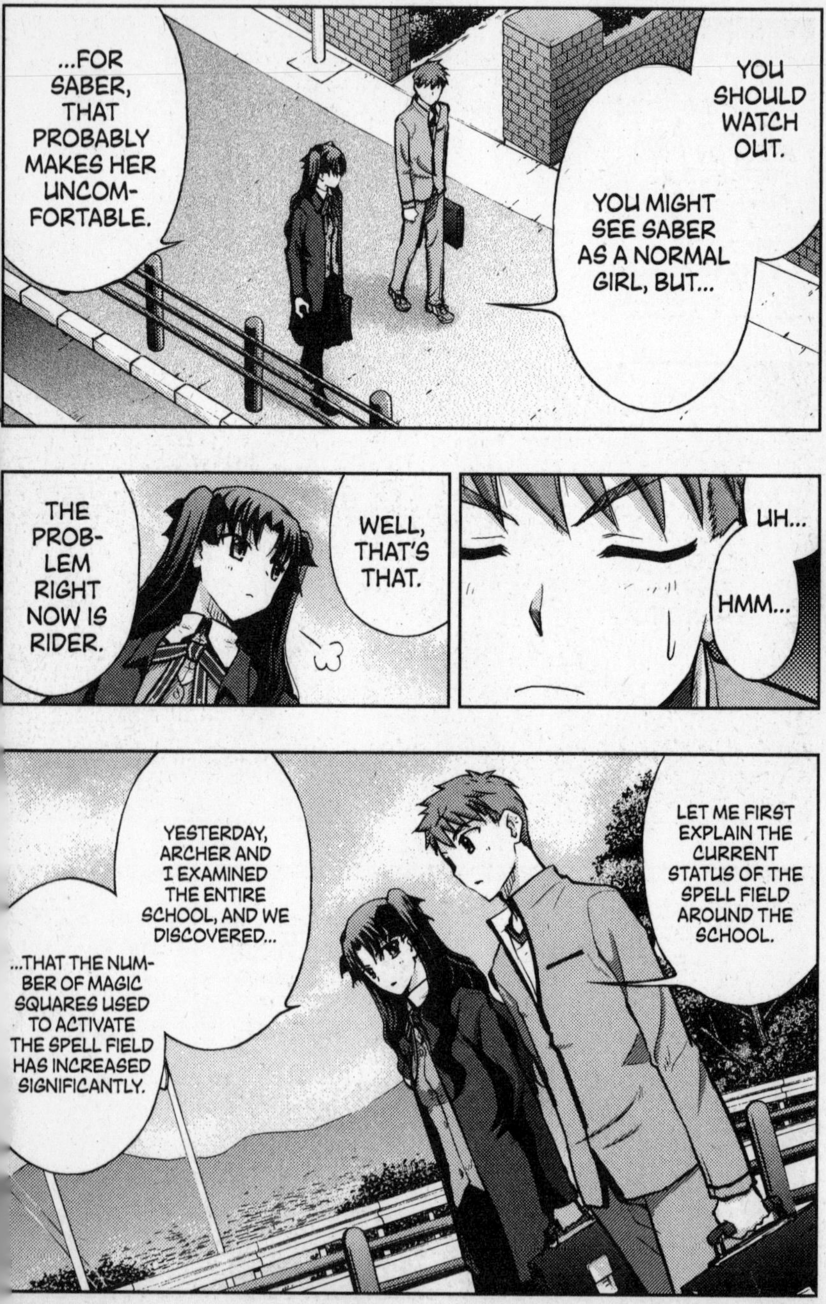
YOU SHOULD WATCH OUT.
YOU MIGHT SEE SABER AS A NORMAL GIRL, BUT...
...FOR SABER, THAT PROBABLY MAKES HER UNCOM-FORTABLE.
UH...
HMM...
WELL, THAT'S THAT.
THE PROB-LEM RIGHT NOW IS RIDER.
LET ME FIRST EXPLAIN THE CURRENT STATUS OF THE SPELL FIELD AROUND THE SCHOOL.
YESTERDAY, ARCHER AND I EXAMINED THE ENTIRE SCHOOL, AND WE DISCOVERED...
...THAT THE NUM-BER OF MAGIC SQUARES USED TO ACTIVATE THE SPELL FIELD HAS INCREASED SIGNIFICANTLY.

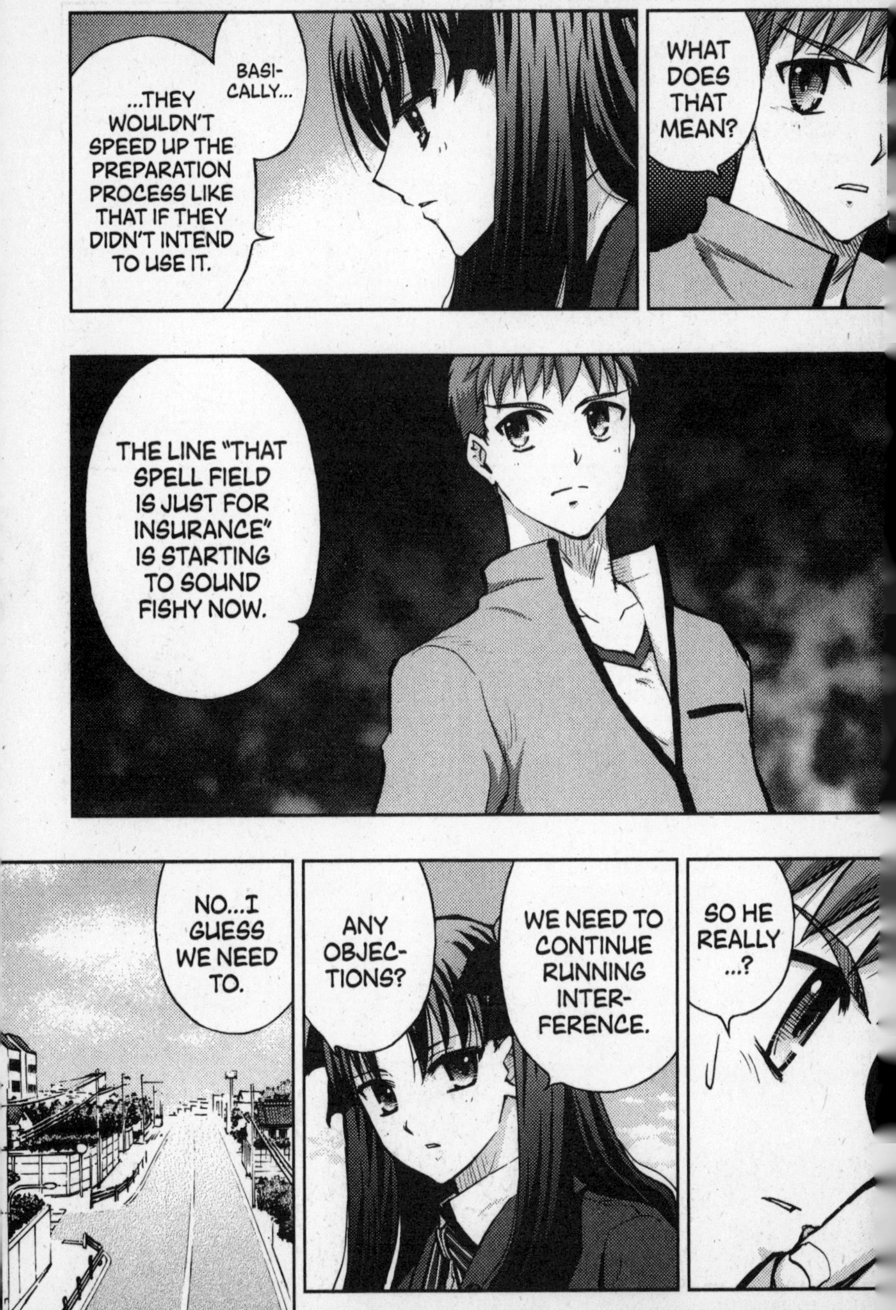
WHAT DOES THAT MEAN?
BASICALLY...
...THEY WOULDN'T SPEED UP THE PREPARATION PROCESS LIKE THAT IF THEY DIDN'T INTEND TO USE IT.
THE LINE "THAT SPELL FIELD IS JUST FOR INSURANCE" IS STARTING TO SOUND FISHY NOW.
SO HE REALLY ...?
WE NEED TO CONTINUE RUNNING INTERFERENCE.
ANY OBJECTIONS?
NO...I GUESS WE NEED TO.

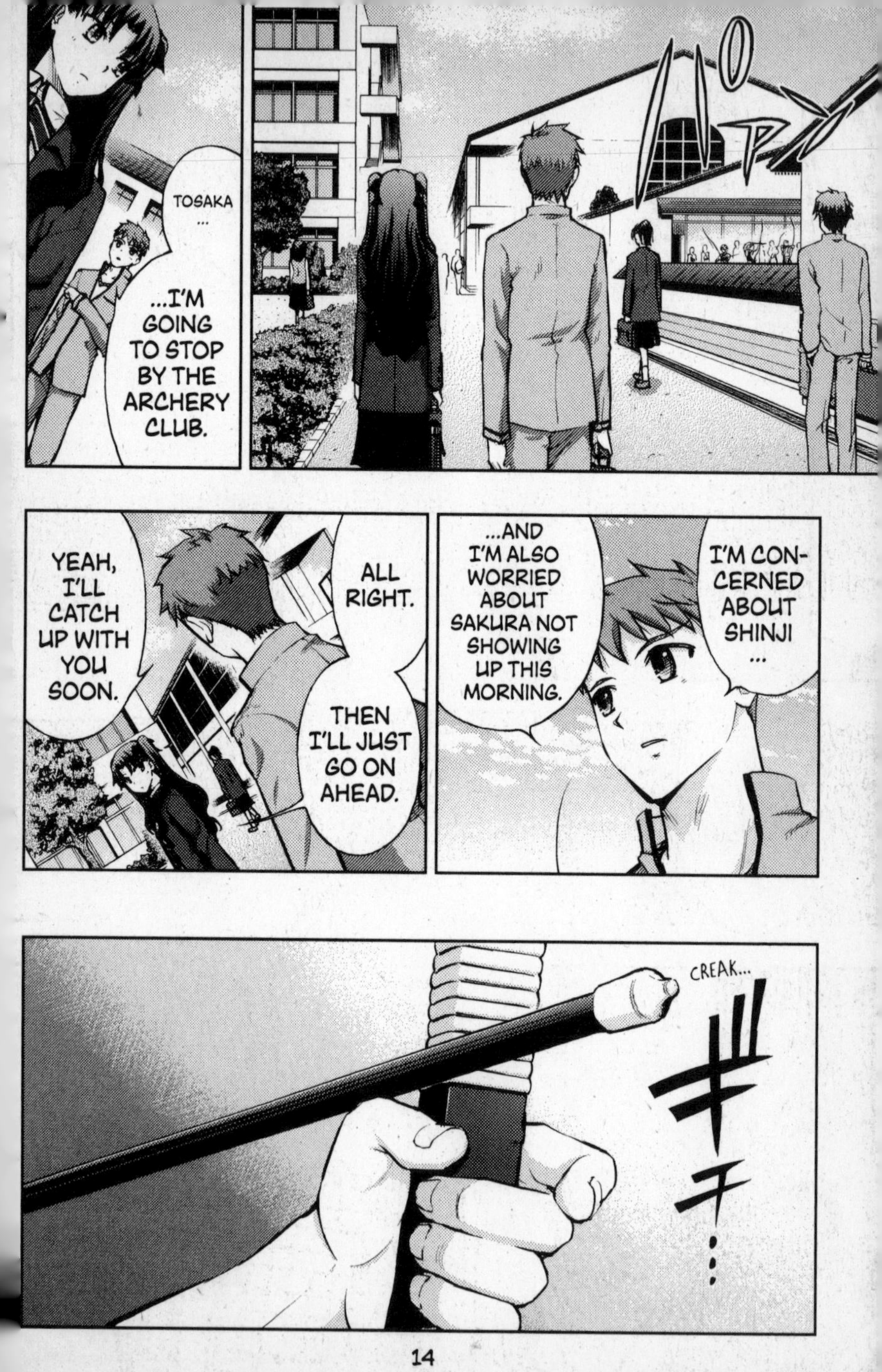
TOSAKA ...
...I'M GOING TO STOP BY THE ARCHERY CLUB.
I'M CON-CERNED ABOUT SHINJI ...
...AND I'M ALSO WORRIED ABOUT SAKURA NOT SHOWING UP THIS MORNING.
ALL RIGHT.
THEN I'LL JUST GO ON AHEAD.
YEAH, I'LL CATCH UP WITH YOU SOON.
CREAK...
ギチ…

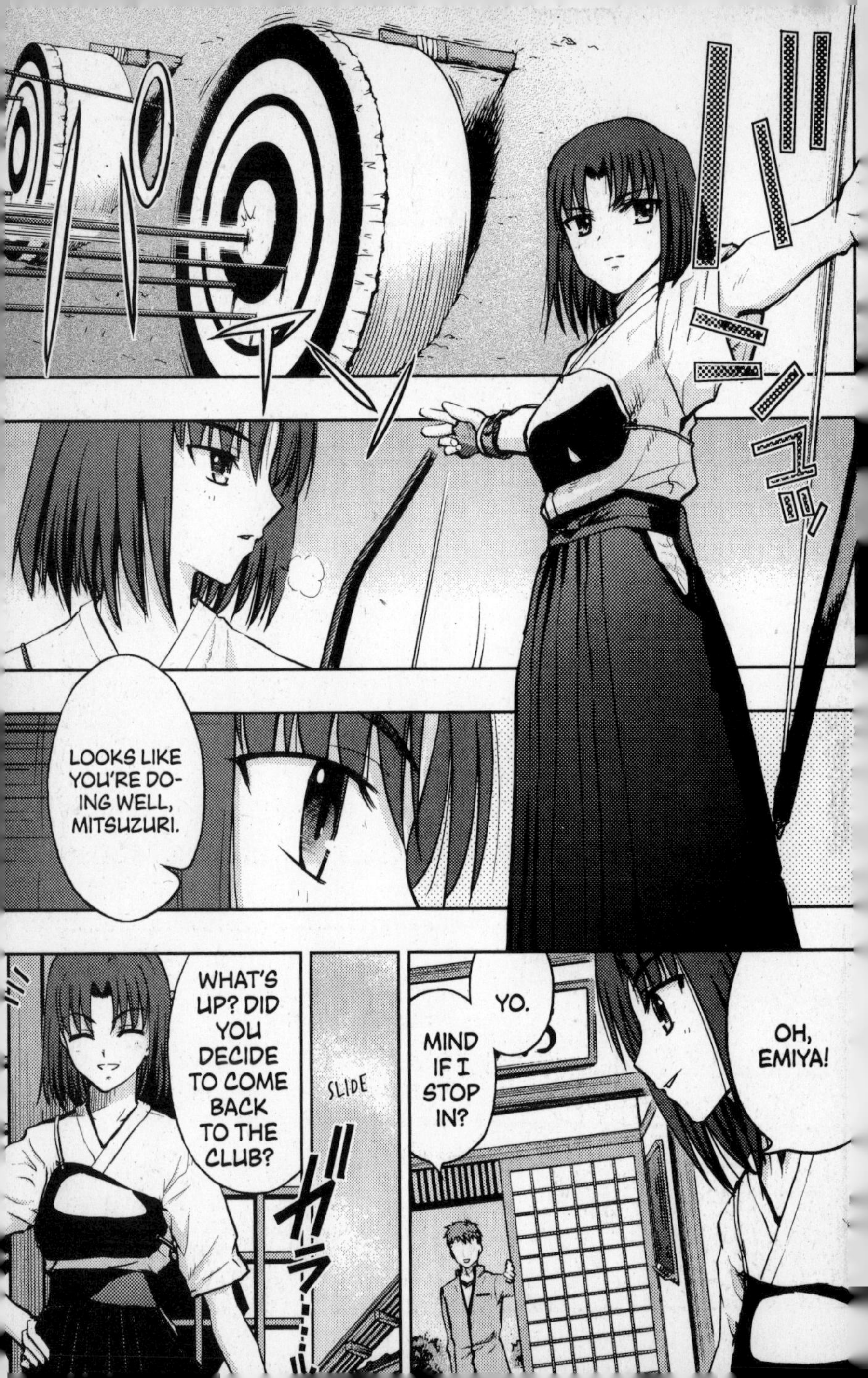
LOOKS LIKE YOU'RE DO-ING WELL, MITSUZURI.
OH, EMIYA!
YO.
MIND IF I STOP IN?
SLIDE
WHAT'S UP? DID YOU DECIDE TO COME BACK TO THE CLUB?

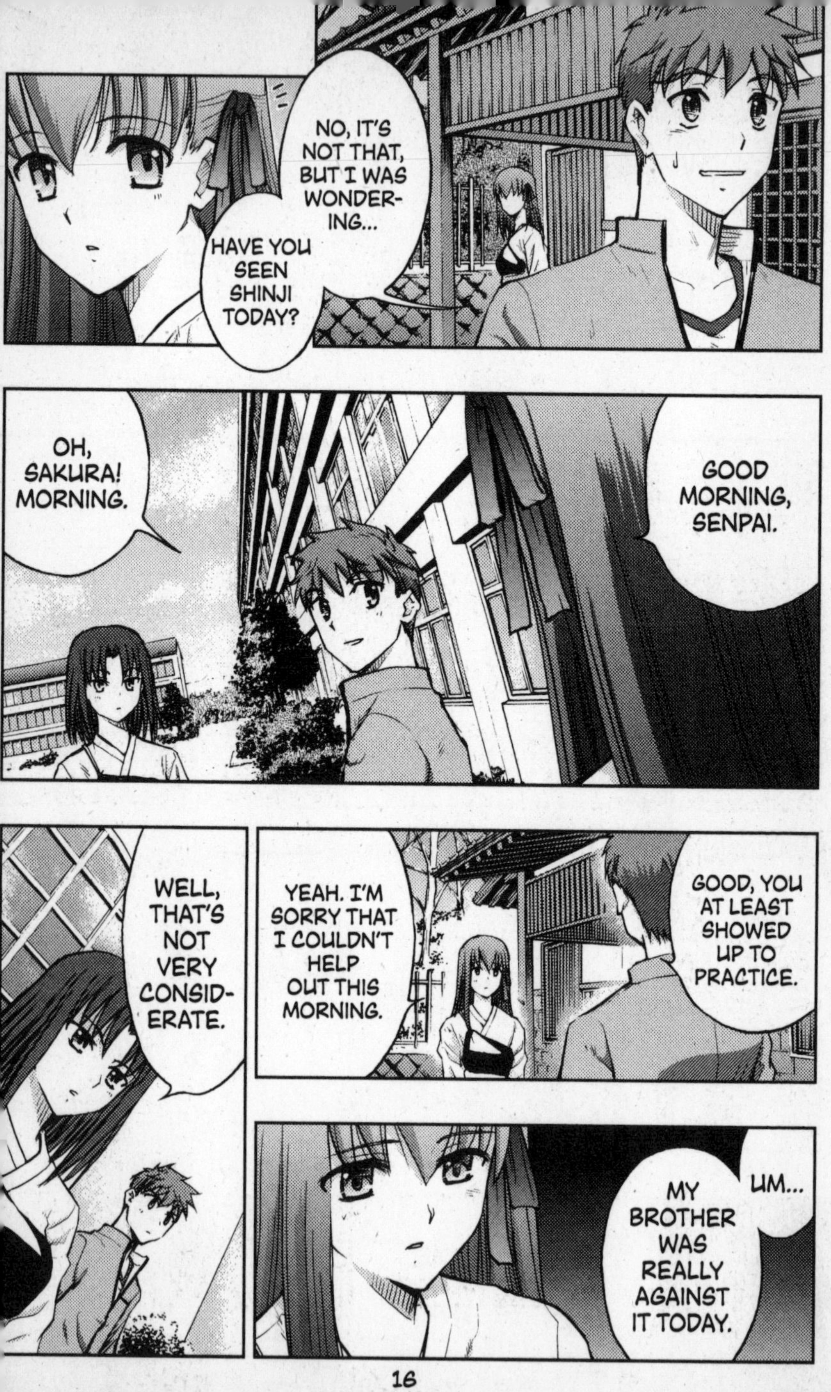
NO, IT'S NOT THAT, BUT I WAS WONDERING...
HAVE YOU SEEN SHINJI TODAY?
GOOD MORNING, SENPAI.
OH, SAKURA! MORNING.
GOOD, YOU AT LEAST SHOWED UP TO PRACTICE.
YEAH. I'M SORRY THAT I COULDN'T HELP OUT THIS MORNING.
UM...
MY BROTHER WAS REALLY AGAINST IT TODAY.
WELL, THAT'S NOT VERY CONSIDERATE.

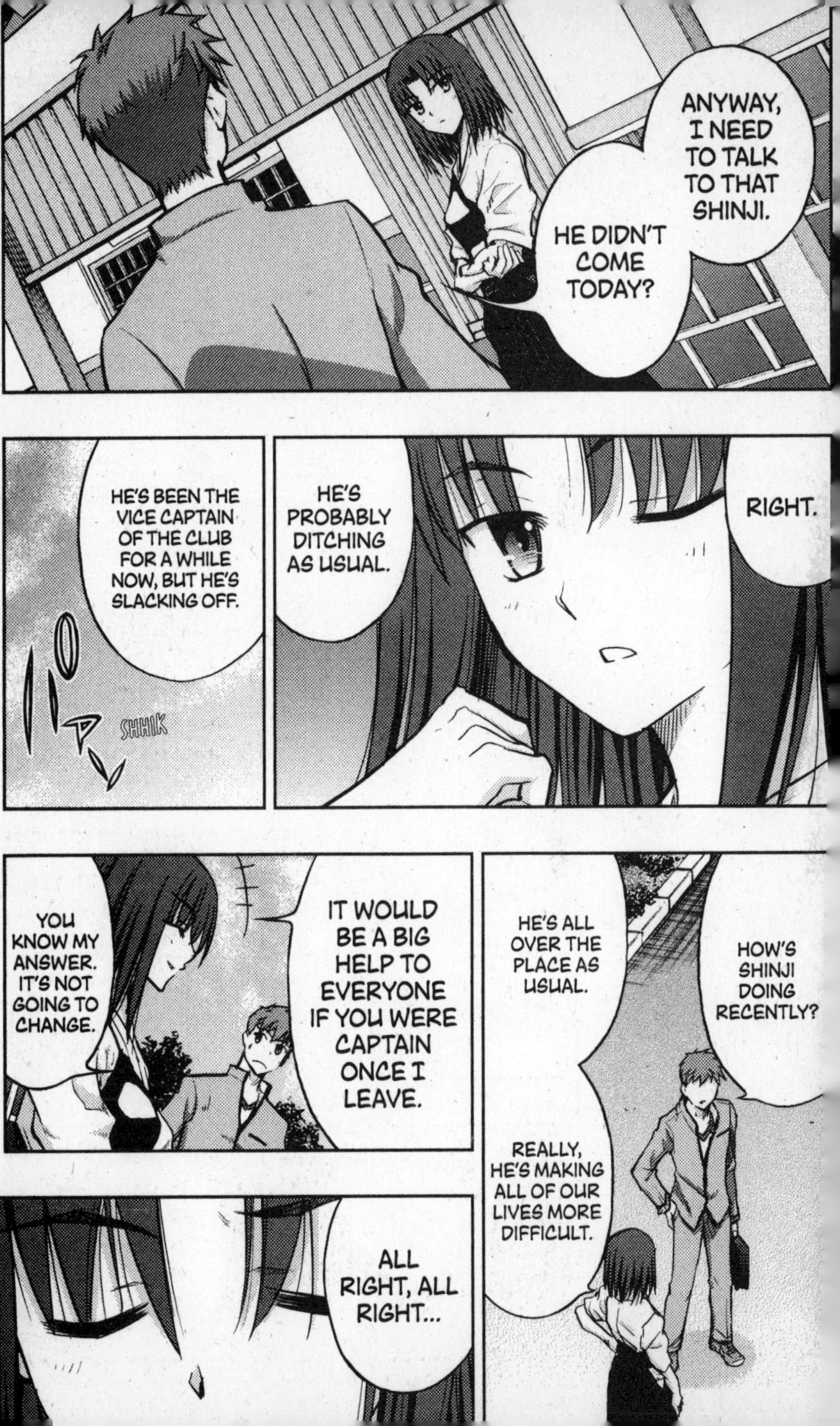
ANYWAY, I NEED TO TALK TO THAT SHINJI.
HE DIDN'T COME TODAY?
RIGHT.
HE'S PROBABLY DITCHING AS USUAL.
HE'S BEEN THE VICE CAPTAIN OF THE CLUB FOR A WHILE NOW, BUT HE'S SLACKING OFF.
SHHIK
HOW'S SHINJI DOING RECENTLY?
HE'S ALL OVER THE PLACE AS USUAL.
REALLY, HE'S MAKING ALL OF OUR LIVES MORE DIFFICULT.
IT WOULD BE A BIG HELP TO EVERYONE IF YOU WERE CAPTAIN ONCE I LEAVE.
YOU KNOW MY ANSWER. IT'S NOT GOING TO CHANGE.
ALL RIGHT, ALL RIGHT...

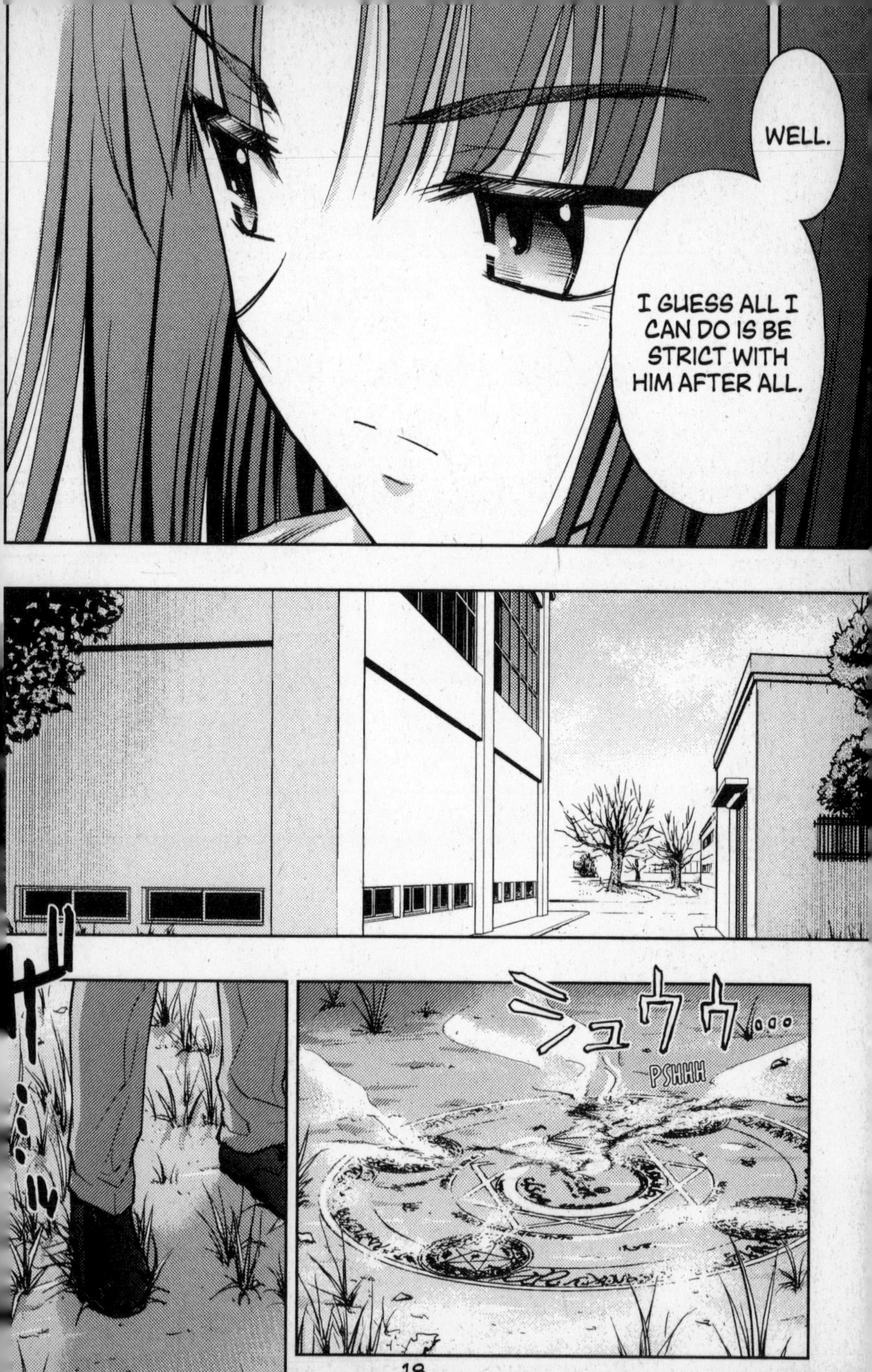
WELL.
I GUESS ALL I CAN DO IS BE STRICT WITH HIM AFTER ALL.
シュウウ...
PSHHH
ザ……ッ

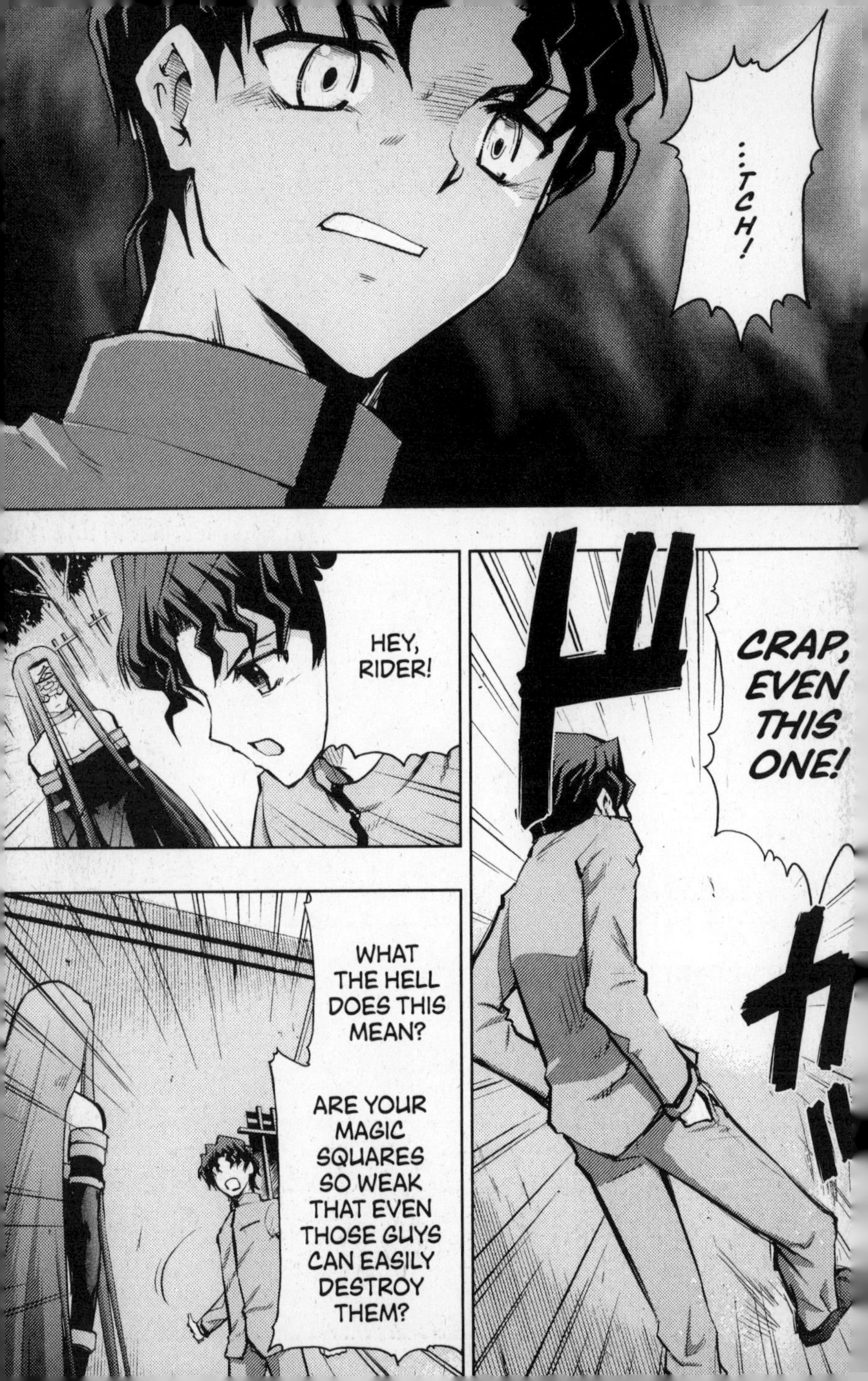
...TCH!
CRAP, EVEN THIS ONE!
HEY, RIDER!
WHAT THE HELL DOES THIS MEAN?
ARE YOUR MAGIC SQUARES SO WEAK THAT EVEN THOSE GUYS CAN EASILY DESTROY THEM?

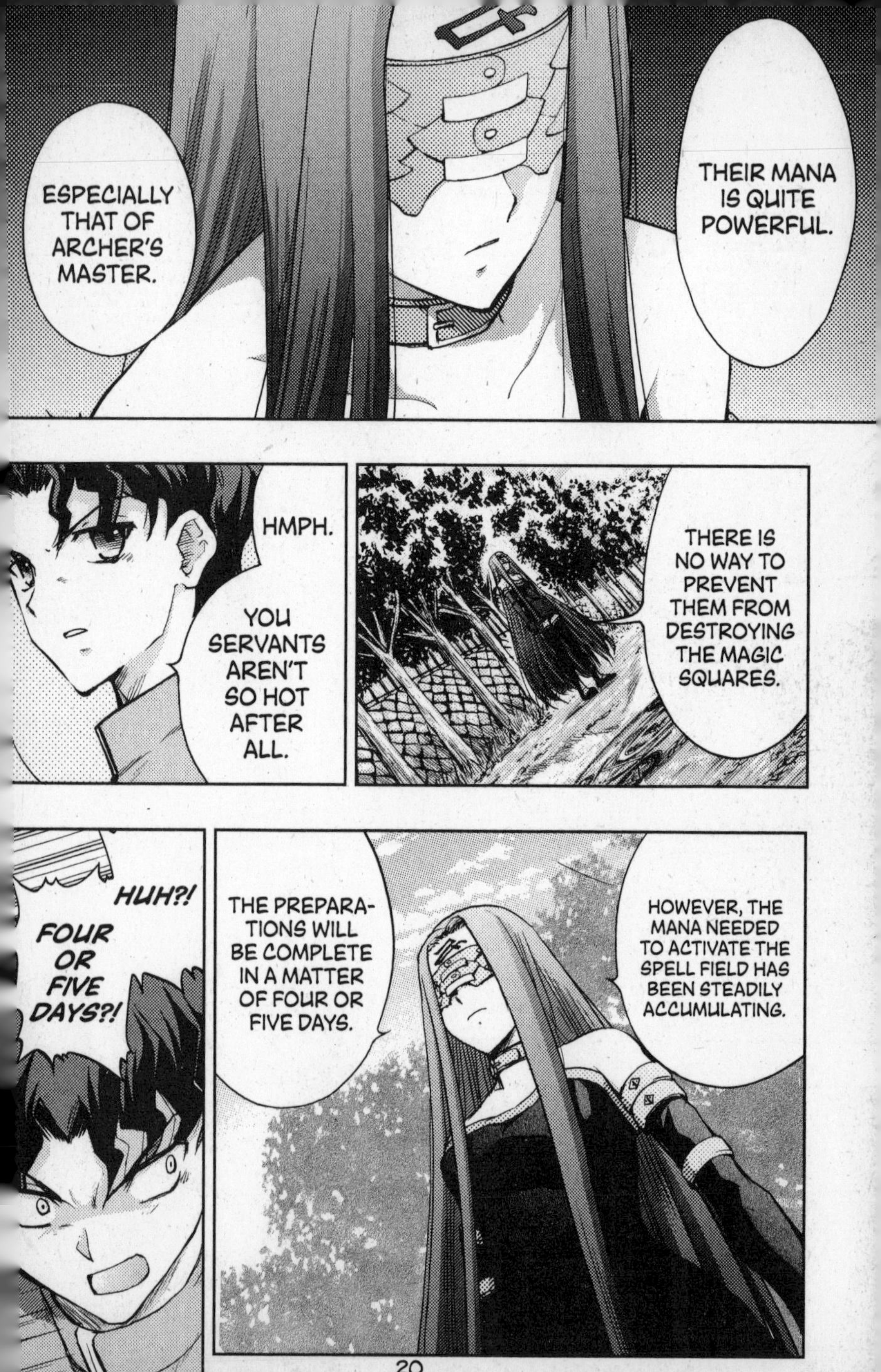
THEIR MANA IS QUITE POWERFUL.
ESPECIALLY THAT OF ARCHER'S MASTER.
THERE IS NO WAY TO PREVENT THEM FROM DESTROYING THE MAGIC SQUARES.
HMPH.
YOU SERVANTS AREN'T SO HOT AFTER ALL.
HOWEVER, THE MANA NEEDED TO ACTIVATE THE SPELL FIELD HAS BEEN STEADILY ACCUMULATING.
THE PREPARATIONS WILL BE COMPLETE IN A MATTER OF FOUR OR FIVE DAYS.
HUH?!
FOUR OR FIVE DAYS?!

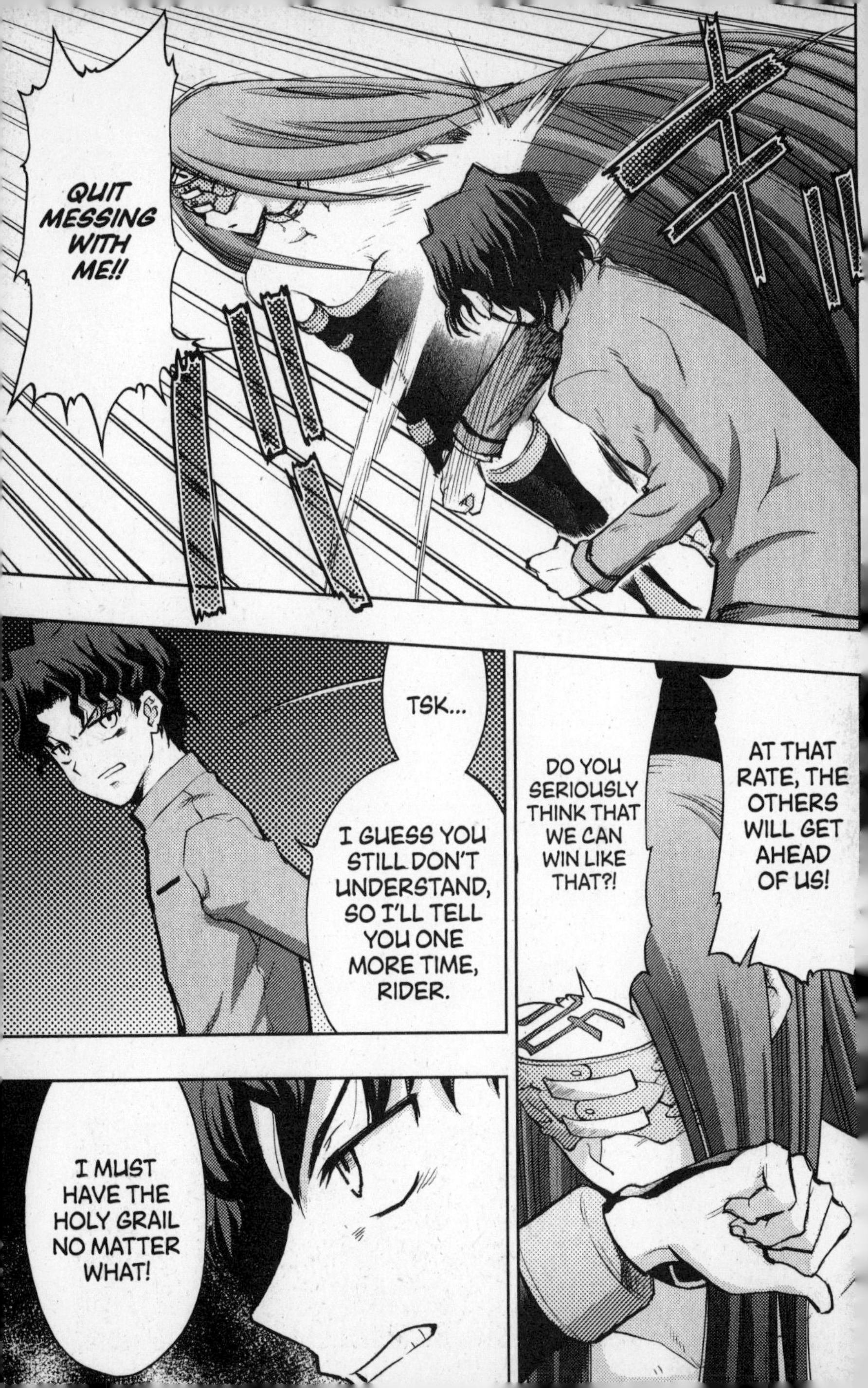
QUIT MESSING WITH ME!!
AT THAT RATE, THE OTHERS WILL GET AHEAD OF US!
DO YOU SERIOUSLY THINK THAT WE CAN WIN LIKE THAT?!
TSK...
I GUESS YOU STILL DON'T UNDERSTAND, SO I'LL TELL YOU ONE MORE TIME, RIDER.
I MUST HAVE THE HOLY GRAIL NO MATTER WHAT!

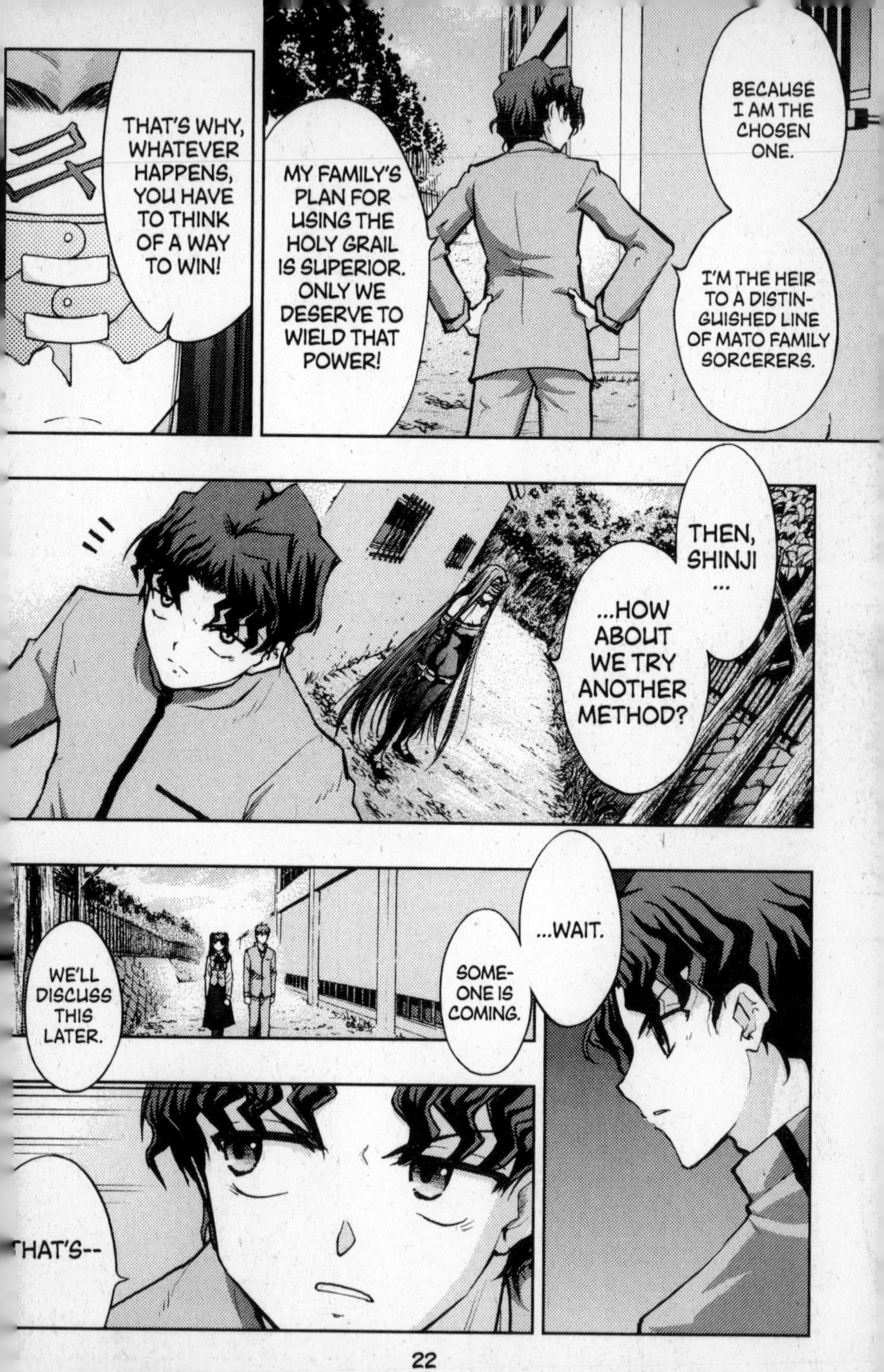
BECAUSE I AM THE CHOSEN ONE.
I'M THE HEIR TO A DISTIN-GUISHED LINE OF MATO FAMILY SORCERERS.
MY FAMILY'S PLAN FOR USING THE HOLY GRAIL IS SUPERIOR. ONLY WE DESERVE TO WIELD THAT POWER!
THAT'S WHY, WHATEVER HAPPENS, YOU HAVE TO THINK OF A WAY TO WIN!
THEN, SHINJI ...
...HOW ABOUT WE TRY ANOTHER METHOD?
...WAIT.
SOME-ONE IS COMING.
WE'LL DISCUSS THIS LATER.
THAT'S--

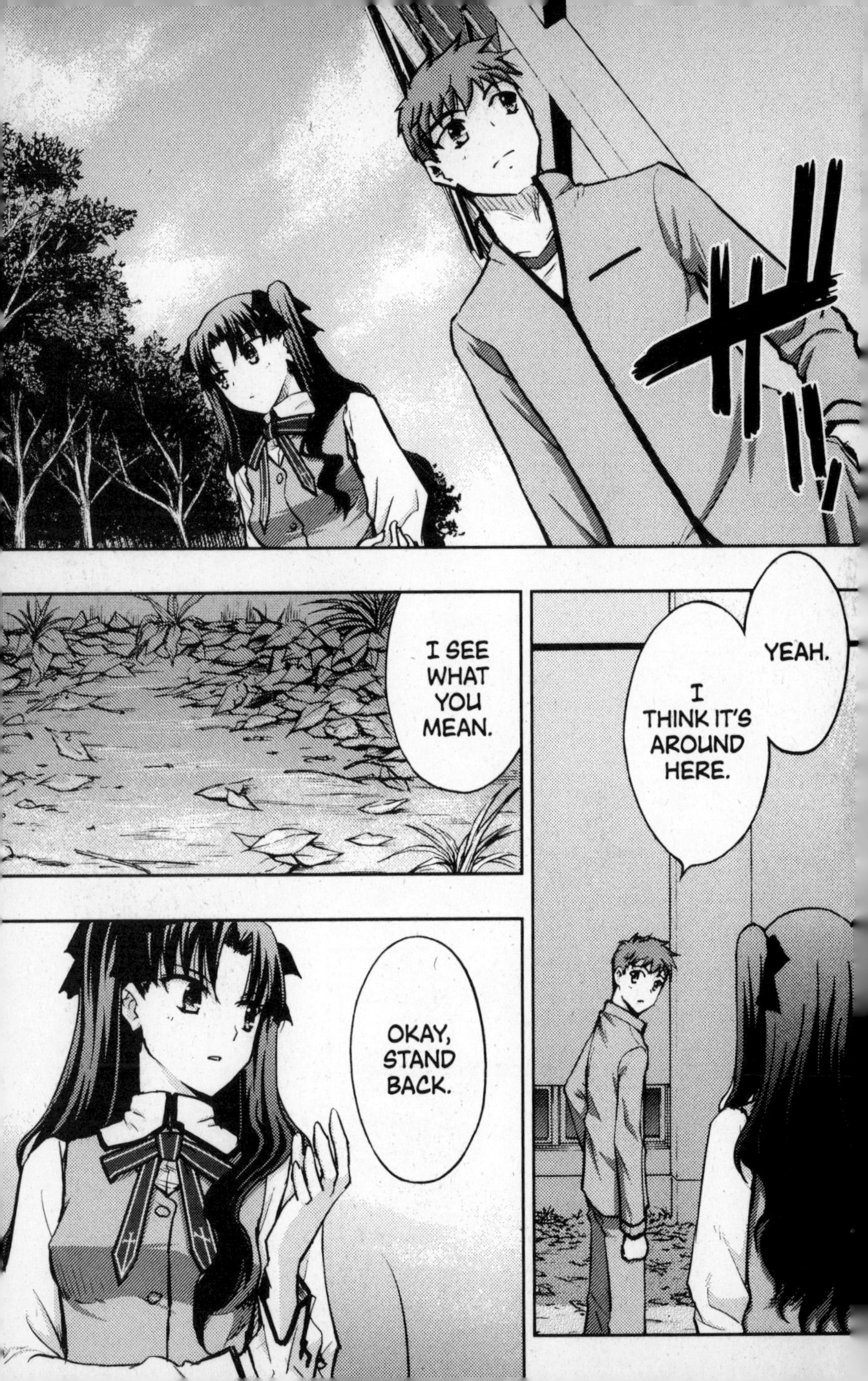
YEAH.
I THINK IT'S AROUND HERE.
I SEE WHAT YOU MEAN.
OKAY, STAND BACK.

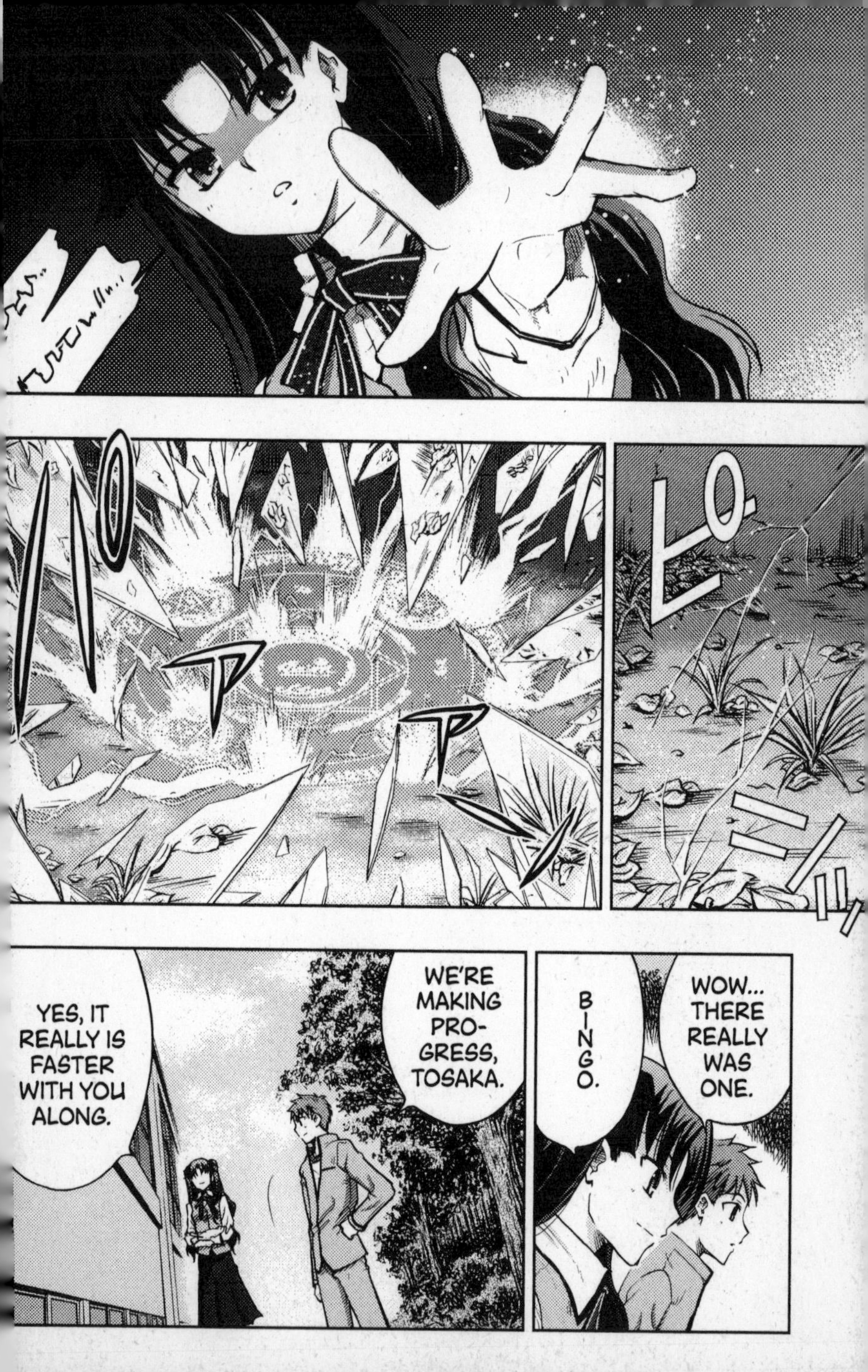
WOW... THERE REALLY WAS ONE.
BINGO.
WE'RE MAKING PRO-GRESS, TOSAKA.
YES, IT REALLY IS FASTER WITH YOU ALONG.

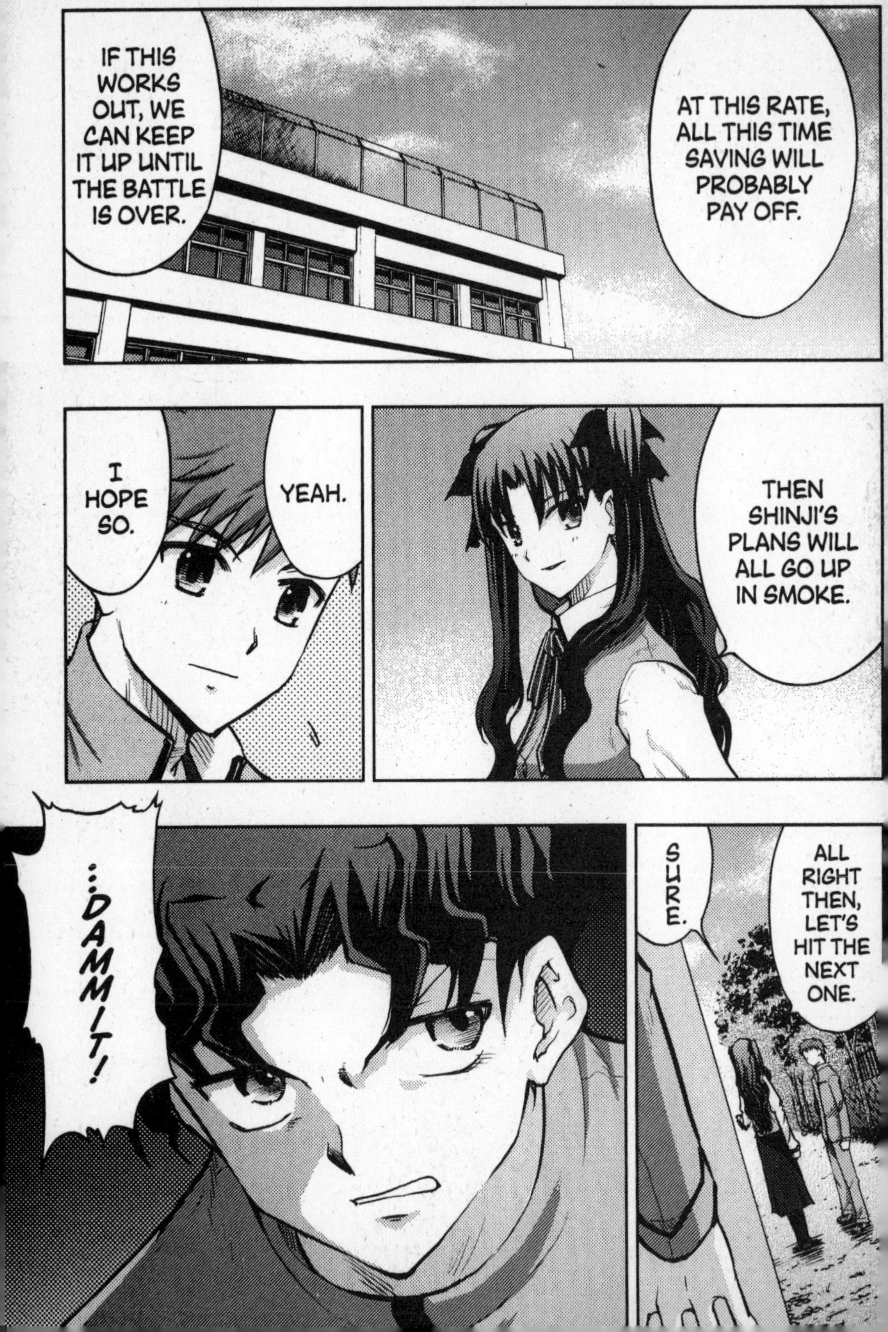
AT THIS RATE, ALL THIS TIME SAVING WILL PROBABLY PAY OFF.
IF THIS WORKS OUT, WE CAN KEEP IT UP UNTIL THE BATTLE IS OVER.
THEN SHINJI'S PLANS WILL ALL GO UP IN SMOKE.
YEAH.
I HOPE SO.
ALL RIGHT THEN, LET'S HIT THE NEXT ONE.
SURE.
...DAMMIT!

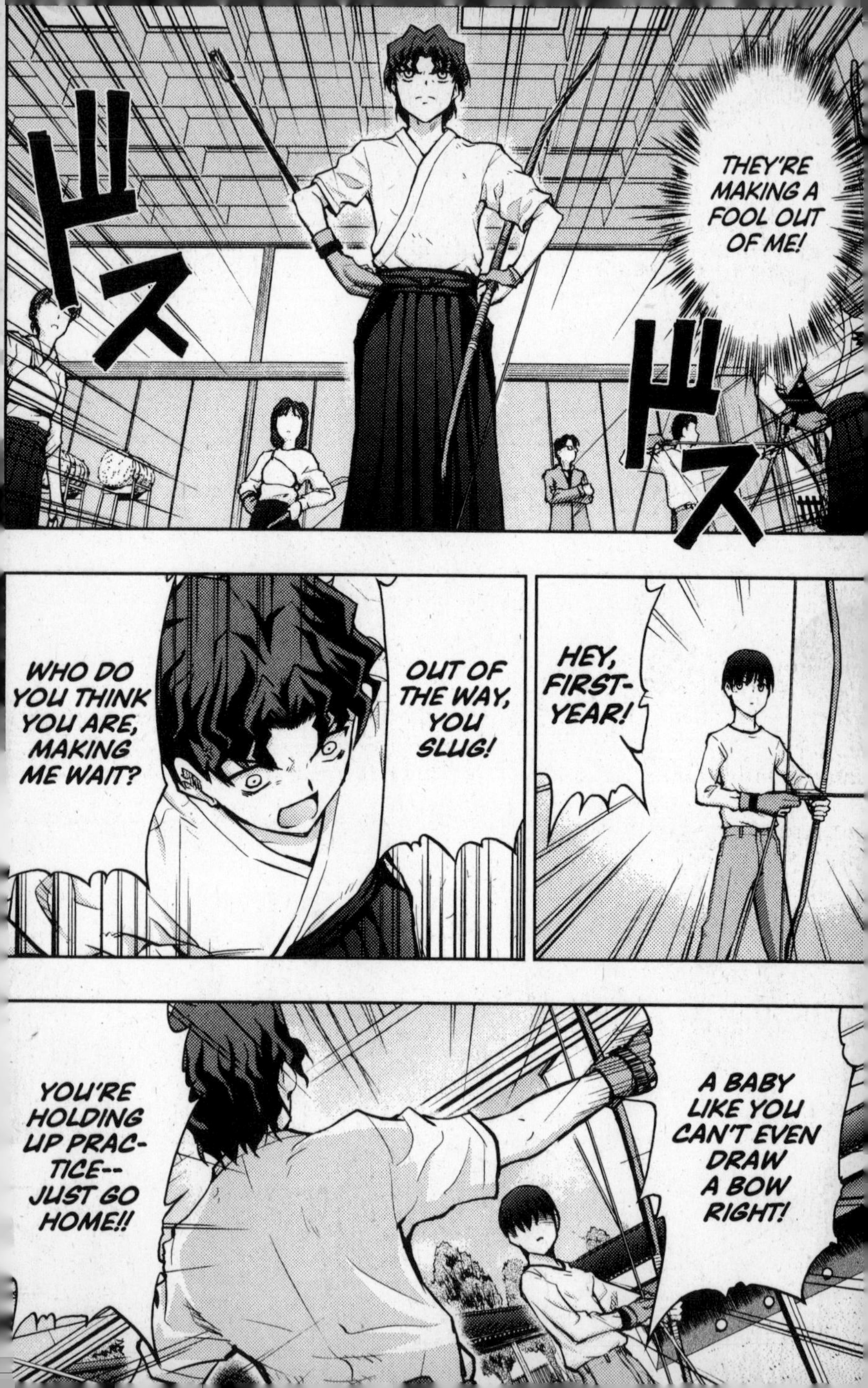
THEY'RE MAKING A FOOL OUT OF ME!
ドス
ドス
HEY, FIRST-YEAR!
OUT OF THE WAY, YOU SLUG!
WHO DO YOU THINK YOU ARE, MAKING ME WAIT?
A BABY LIKE YOU CAN'T EVEN DRAW A BOW RIGHT!
YOU'RE HOLDING UP PRAC-TICE-- JUST GO HOME!!

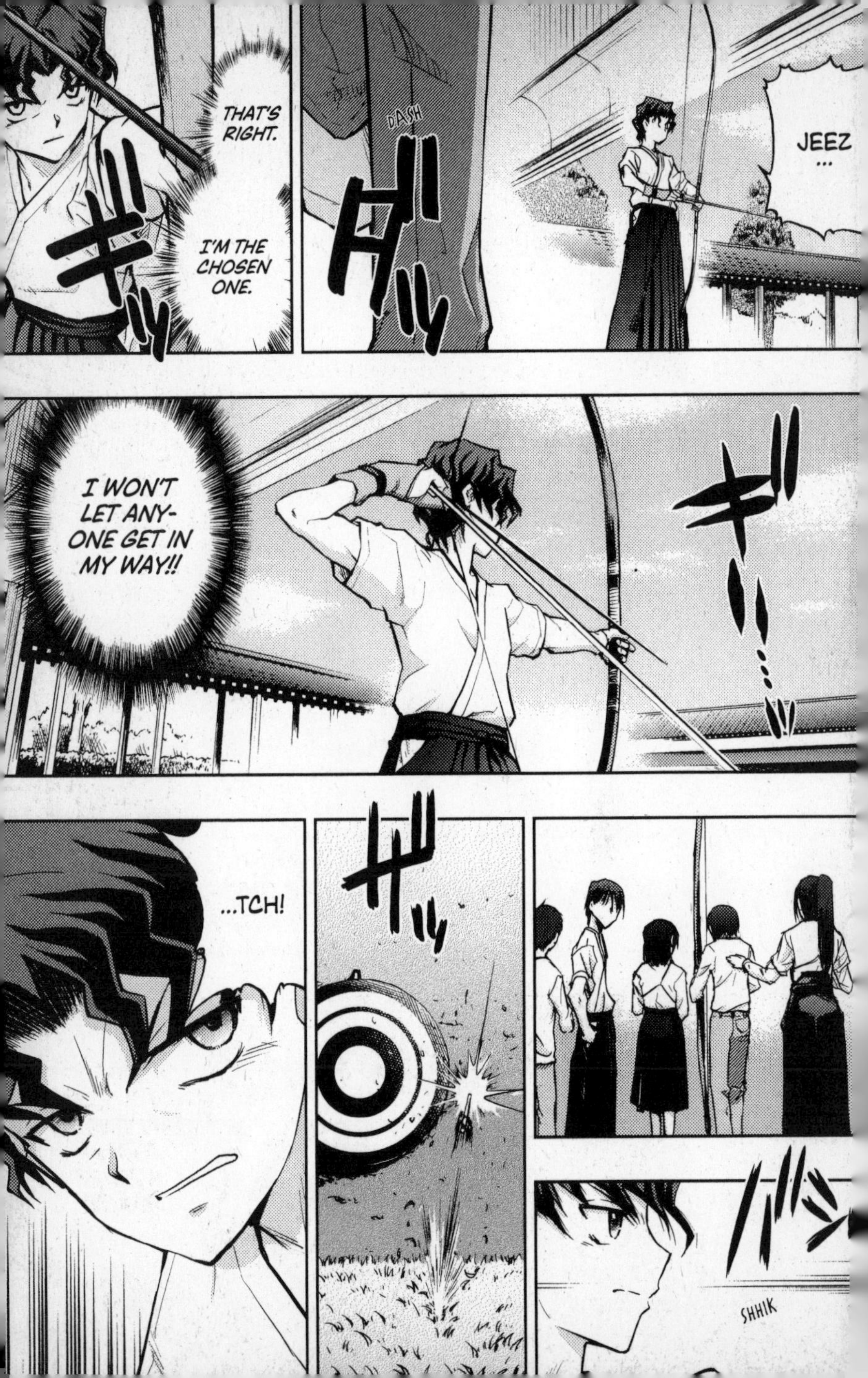
JEEZ ...
DASH
THAT'S RIGHT.
I'M THE CHOSEN ONE.
I WON'T LET ANY-ONE GET IN MY WAY!!
SHHIK
...TCH!

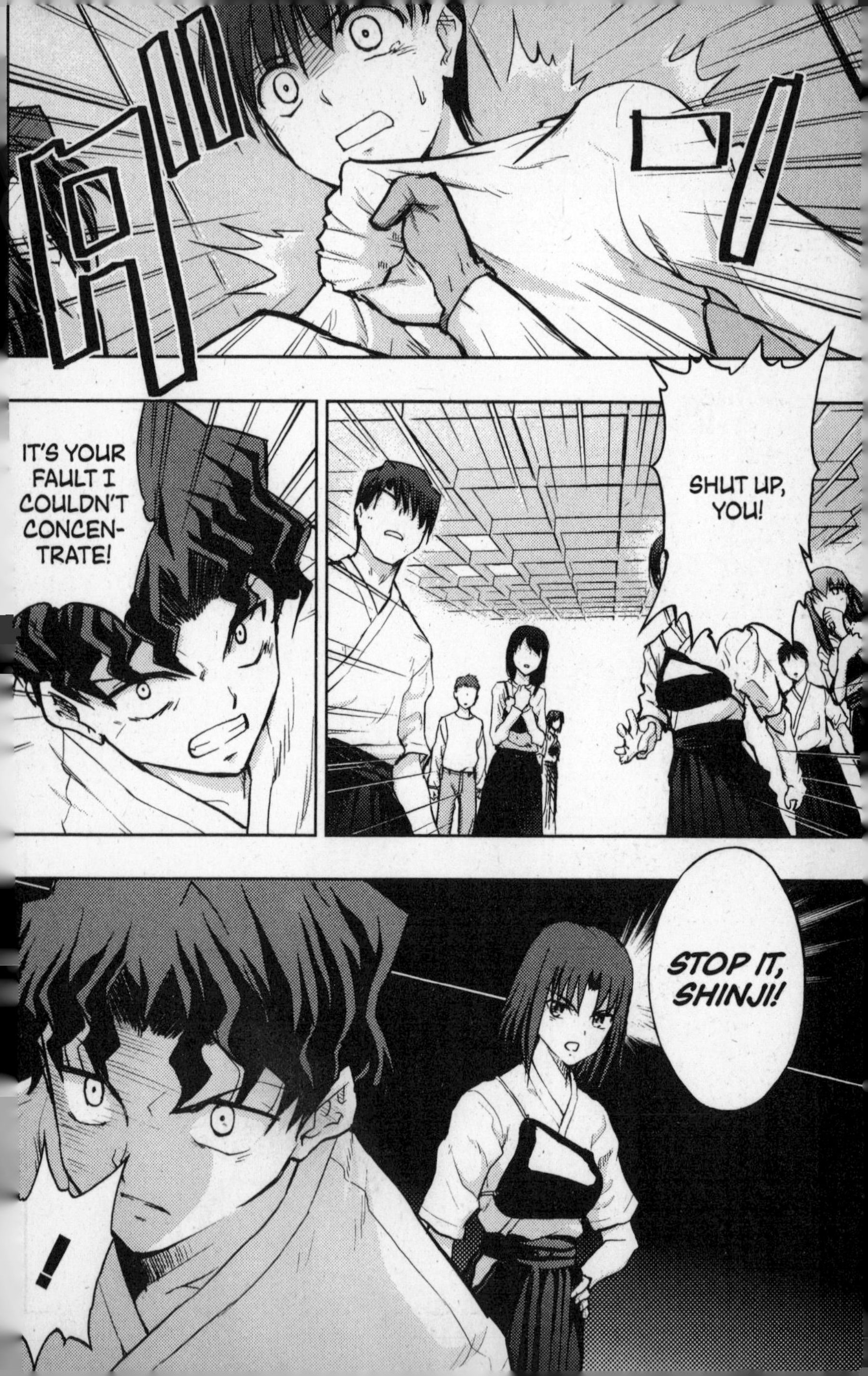
SHUT UP, YOU!
IT'S YOUR FAULT I COULDN'T CONCENTRATE!
STOP IT, SHINJI!
!

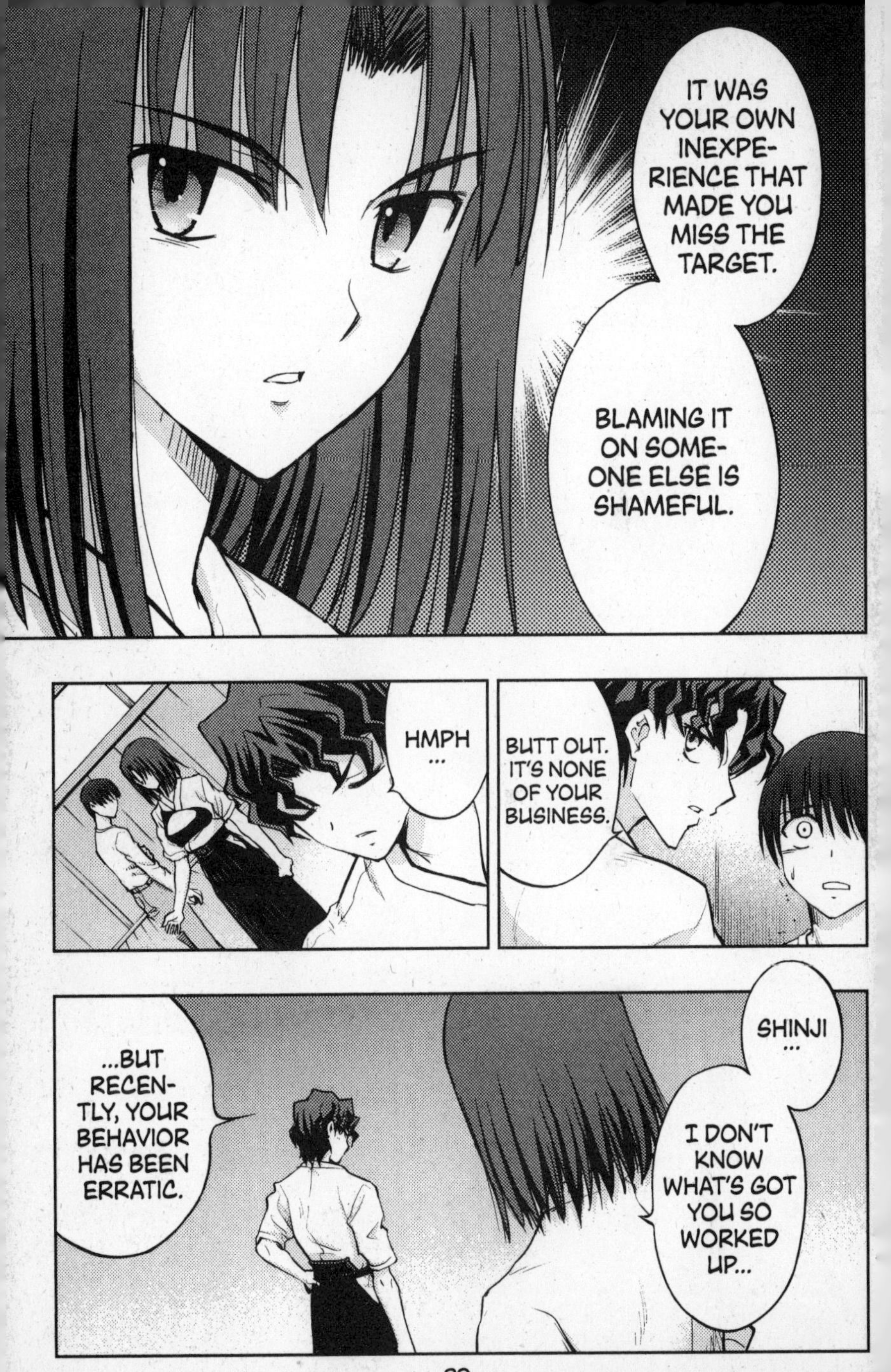
IT WAS YOUR OWN INEXPE-RIENCE THAT MADE YOU MISS THE TARGET.
BLAMING IT ON SOME-ONE ELSE IS SHAMEFUL.
BUTT OUT. IT'S NONE OF YOUR BUSINESS.
HMPH ...
SHINJI ...
I DON'T KNOW WHAT'S GOT YOU SO WORKED UP...
...BUT RECEN-TLY, YOUR BEHAVIOR HAS BEEN ERRATIC.

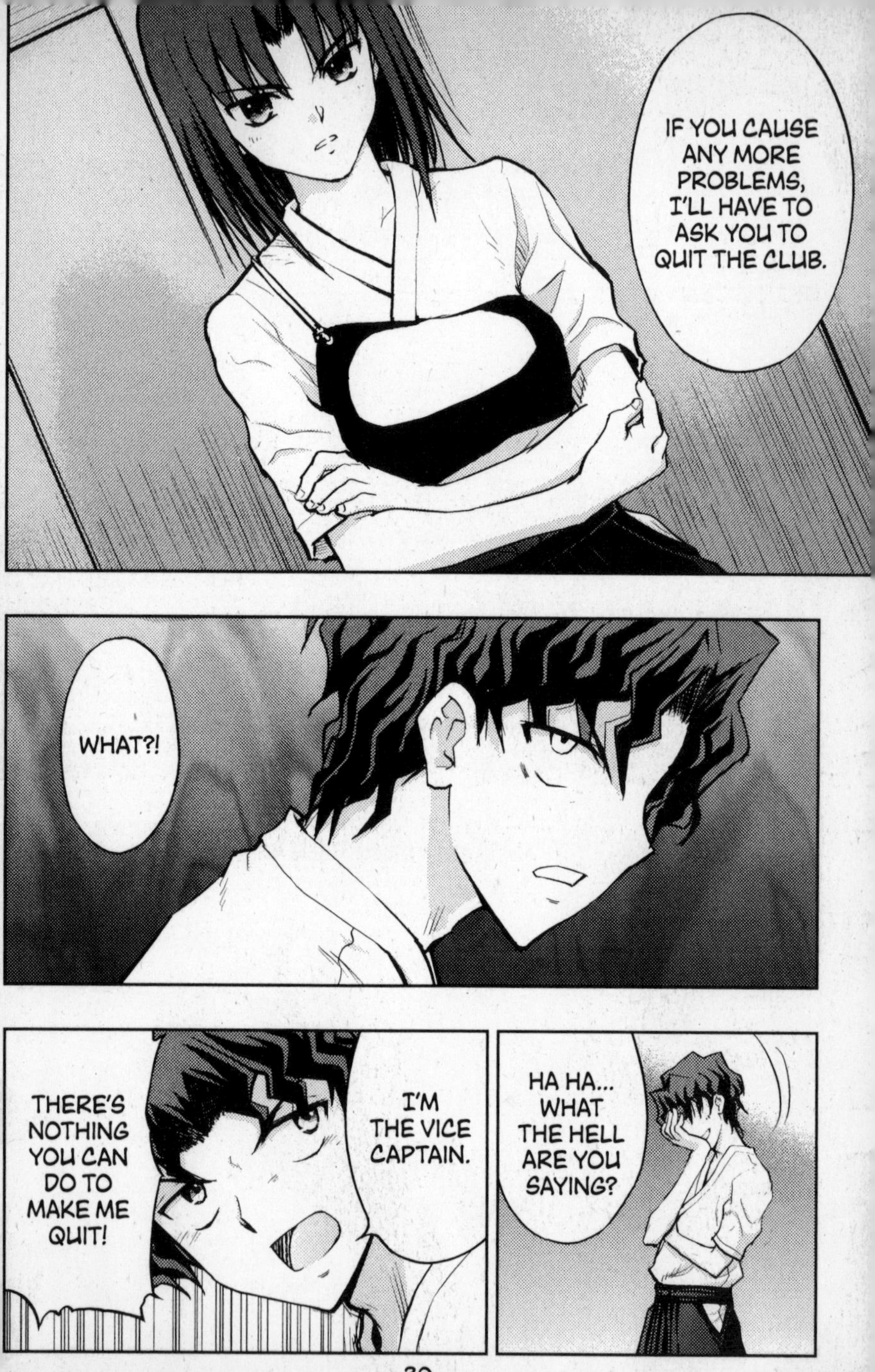
IF YOU CAUSE ANY MORE PROBLEMS, I'LL HAVE TO ASK YOU TO QUIT THE CLUB.
WHAT?!
HA HA... WHAT THE HELL ARE YOU SAYING?
I'M THE VICE CAPTAIN.
THERE'S NOTHING YOU CAN DO TO MAKE ME QUIT!

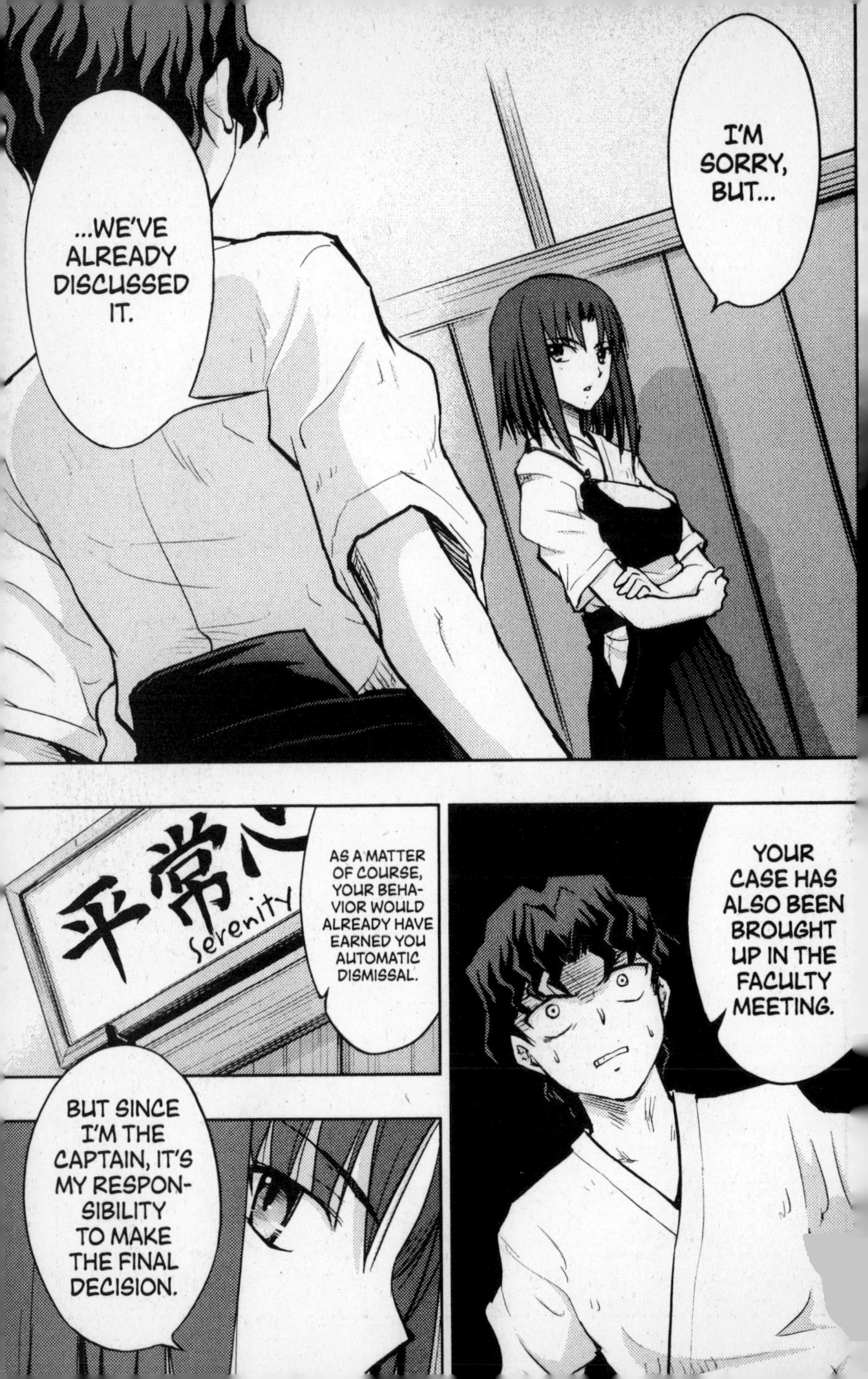
I'M SORRY, BUT...
...WE'VE ALREADY DISCUSSED IT.
YOUR CASE HAS ALSO BEEN BROUGHT UP IN THE FACULTY MEETING.
平常
serenity
AS A MATTER OF COURSE, YOUR BEHA- VIOR WOULD ALREADY HAVE EARNED YOU AUTOMATIC DISMISSAL.
BUT SINCE I'M THE CAPTAIN, IT'S MY RESPON- SIBILITY TO MAKE THE FINAL DECISION.

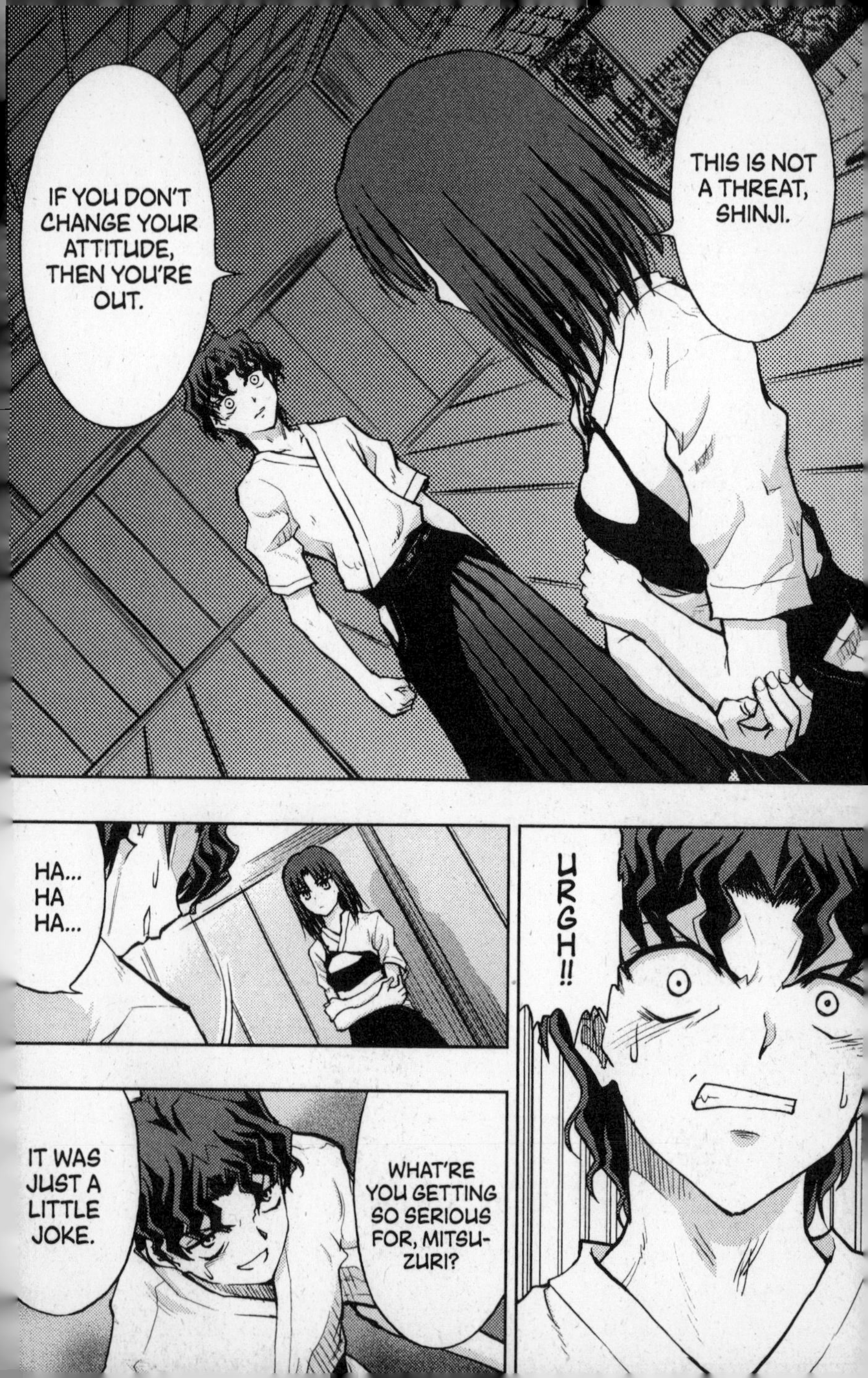
THIS IS NOT A THREAT, SHINJI.
IF YOU DON'T CHANGE YOUR ATTITUDE, THEN YOU'RE OUT.
URGH!!
HA... HA HA...
WHAT'RE YOU GETTING SO SERIOUS FOR, MITSU-ZURI?
IT WAS JUST A LITTLE JOKE.

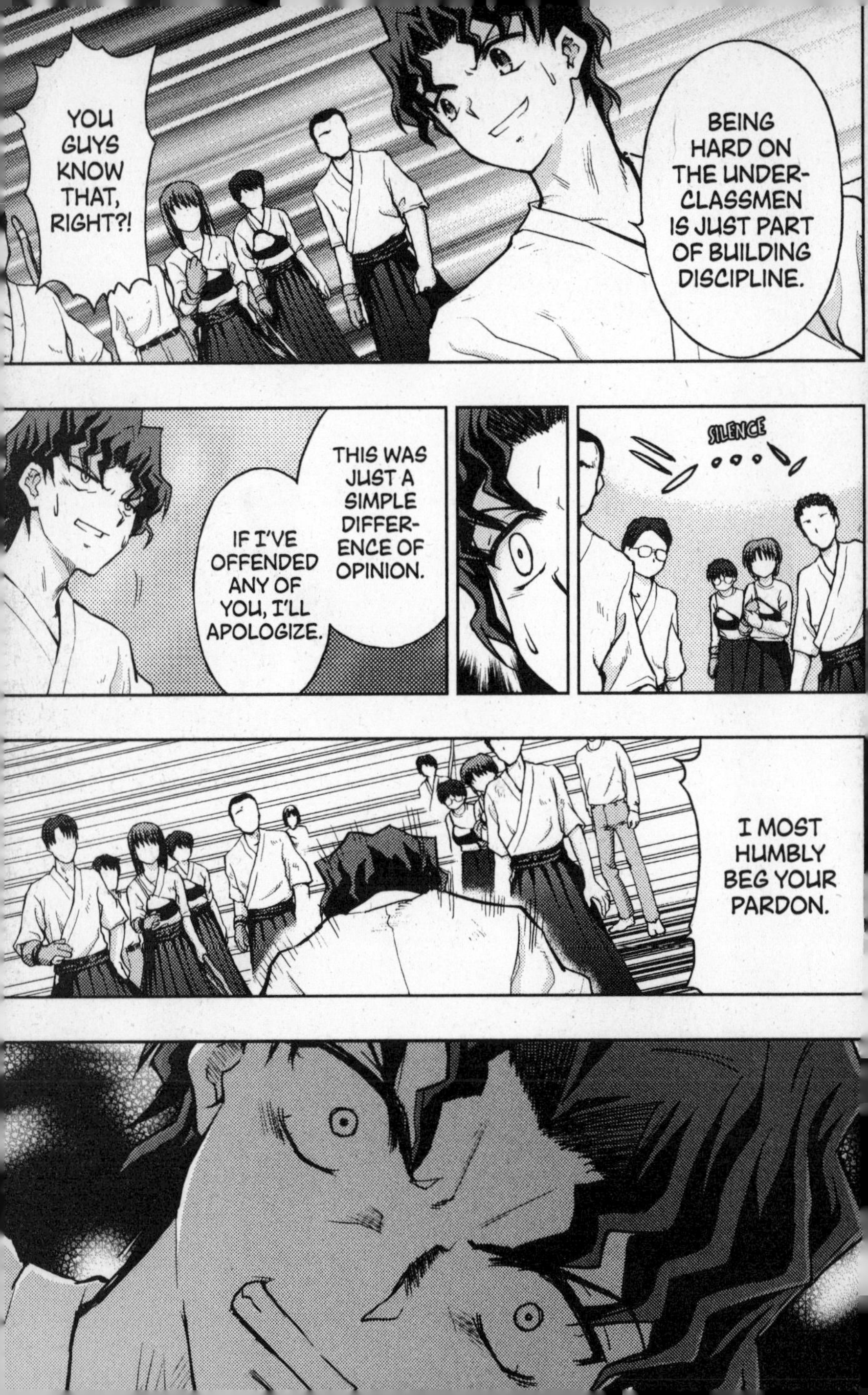
BEING HARD ON THE UNDER-CLASSMEN IS JUST PART OF BUILDING DISCIPLINE.
YOU GUYS KNOW THAT, RIGHT?!
SILENCE
...
THIS WAS JUST A SIMPLE DIFFER-ENCE OF OPINION.
IF I'VE OFFENDED ANY OF YOU, I'LL APOLOGIZE.
I MOST HUMBLY BEG YOUR PARDON.

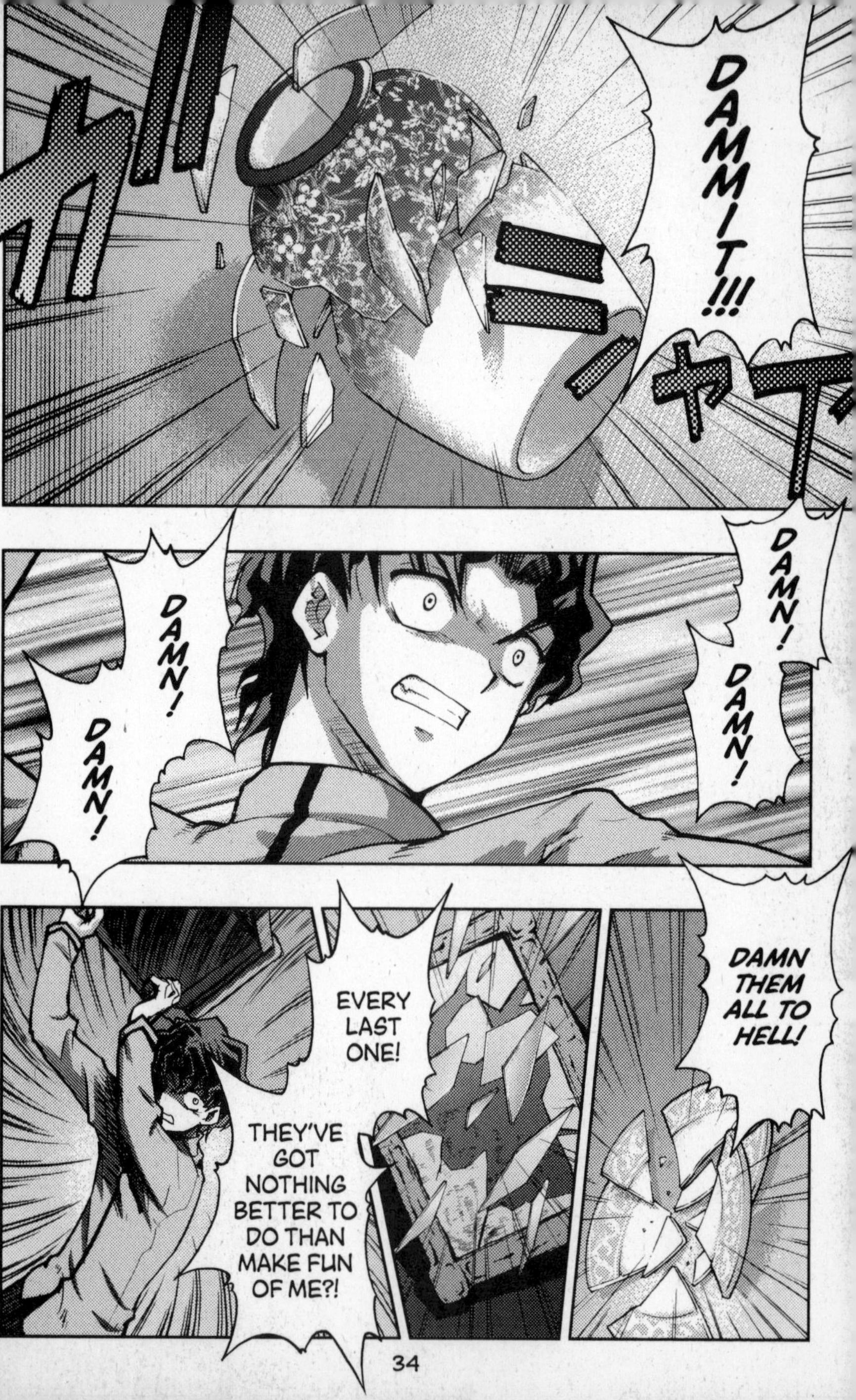
DAMMIT!!!
DAMN! DAMN!
DAMN! DAMN!
DAMN THEM ALL TO HELL!
EVERY LAST ONE!
THEY'VE GOT NOTHING BETTER TO DO THAN MAKE FUN OF ME?!

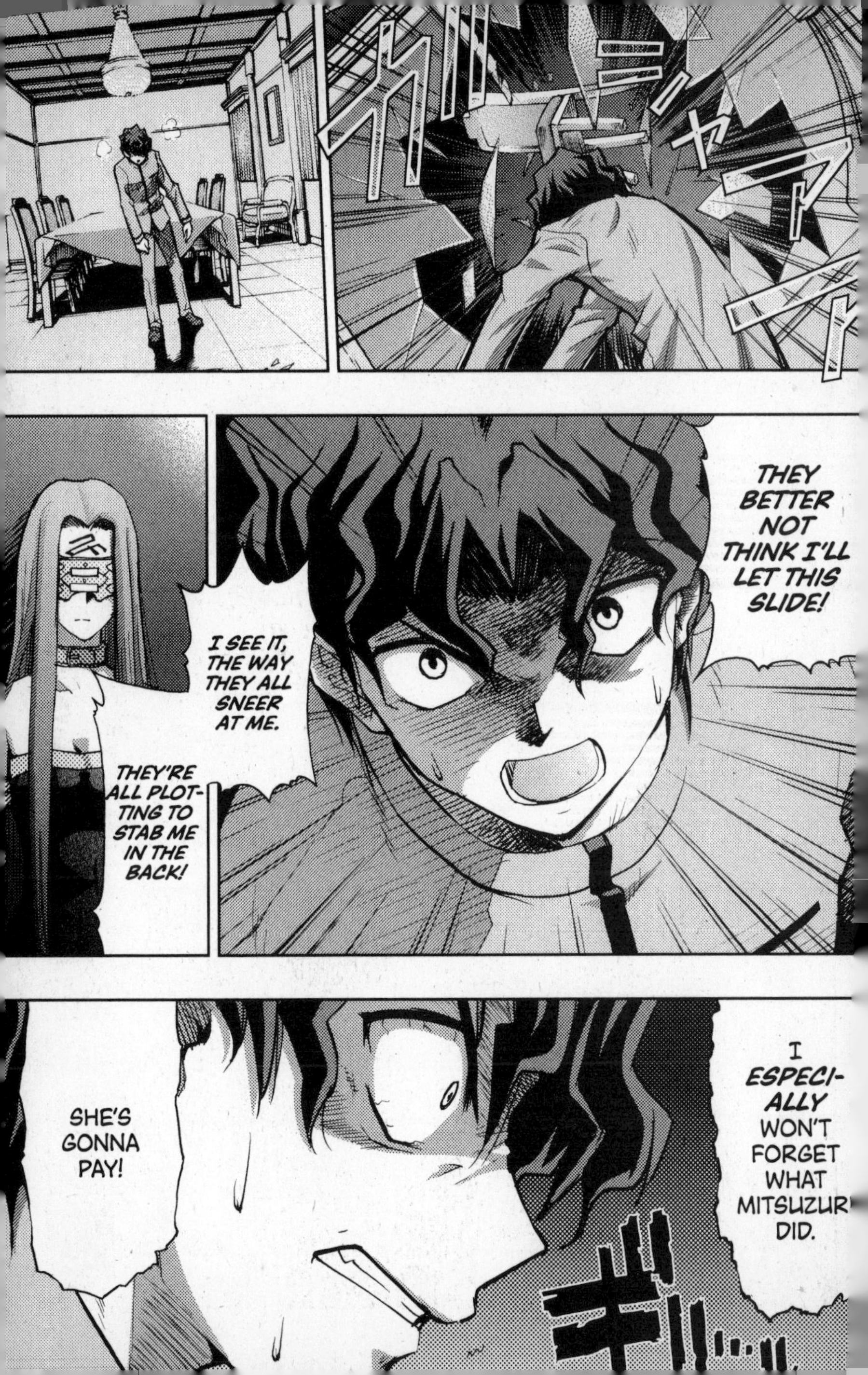
THEY BETTER NOT THINK I'LL LET THIS SLIDE!
I SEE IT, THE WAY THEY ALL SNEER AT ME.
THEY'RE ALL PLOT-TING TO STAB ME IN THE BACK!
I ESPECI-ALLY WON'T FORGET WHAT MITSUZURI DID.
SHE'S GONNA PAY!

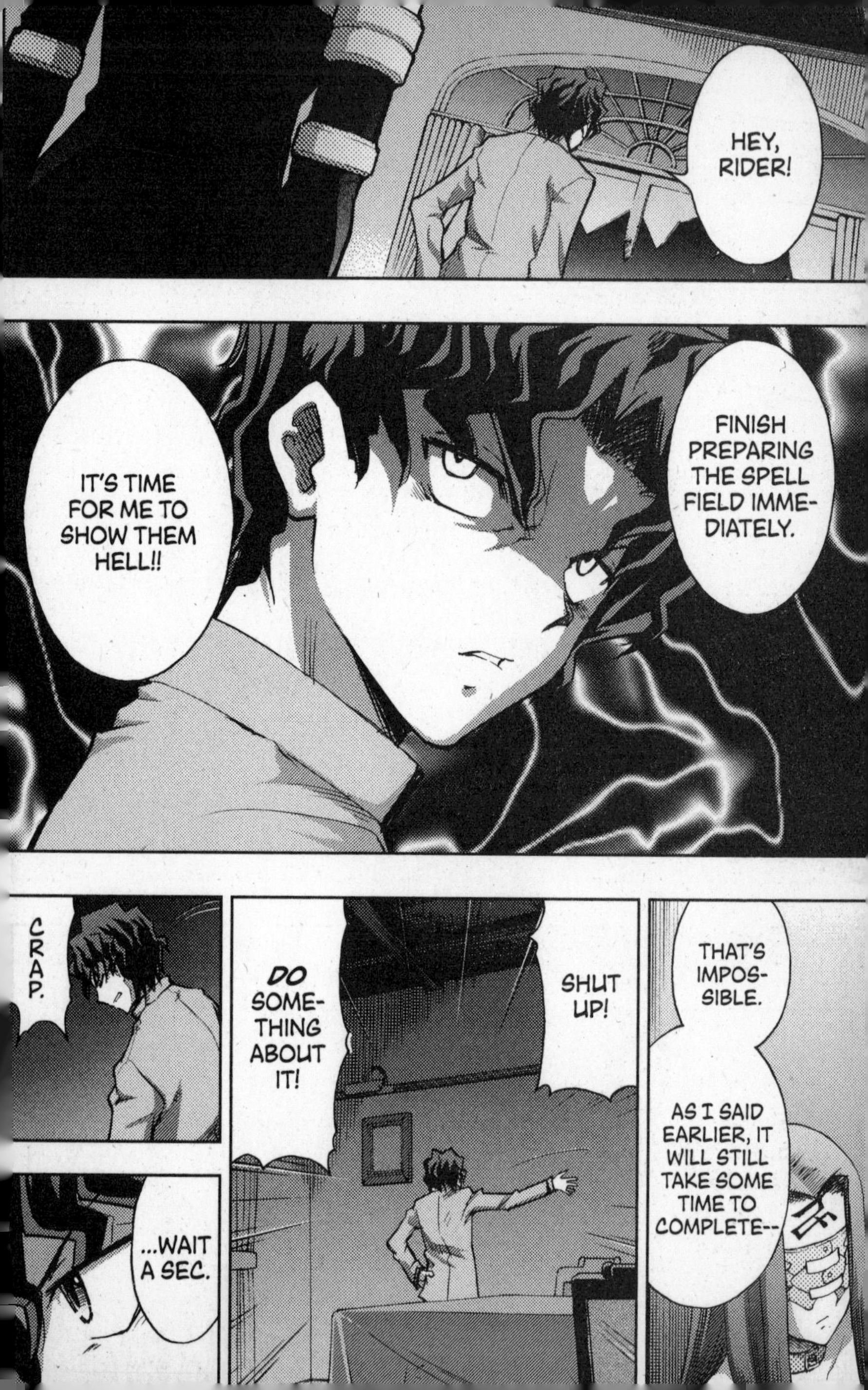
HEY, RIDER!
FINISH PREPARING THE SPELL FIELD IMME-DIATELY.
IT'S TIME FOR ME TO SHOW THEM HELL!!
THAT'S IMPOS-SIBLE.
AS I SAID EARLIER, IT WILL STILL TAKE SOME TIME TO COMPLETE--
SHUT UP!
DO SOME-THING ABOUT IT!
CRAP.
...WAIT A SEC.

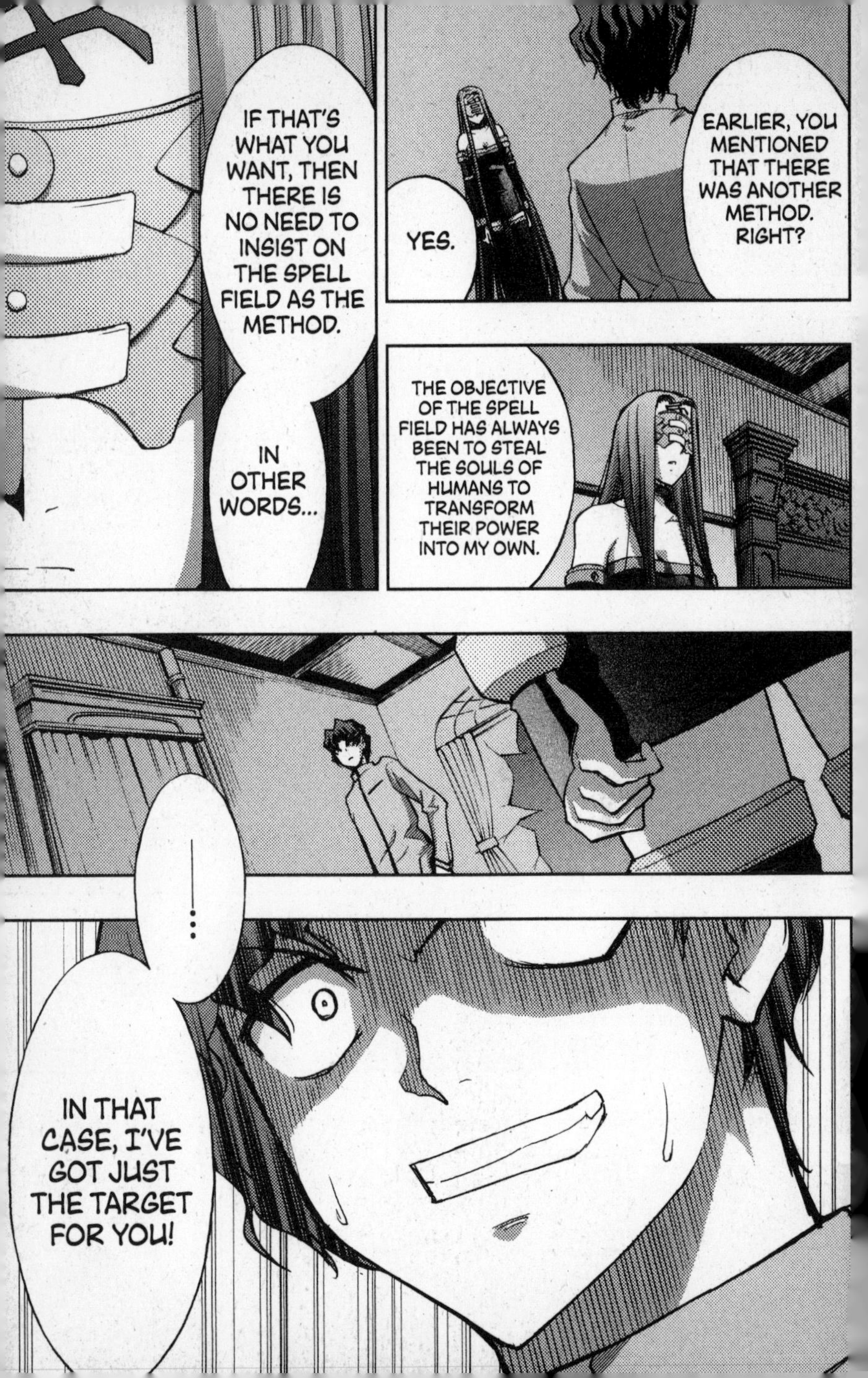
EARLIER, YOU MENTIONED THAT THERE WAS ANOTHER METHOD. RIGHT?
YES.
THE OBJECTIVE OF THE SPELL FIELD HAS ALWAYS BEEN TO STEAL THE SOULS OF HUMANS TO TRANSFORM THEIR POWER INTO MY OWN.
IF THAT'S WHAT YOU WANT, THEN THERE IS NO NEED TO INSIST ON THE SPELL FIELD AS THE METHOD.
IN OTHER WORDS...
—...
IN THAT CASE, I'VE GOT JUST THE TARGET FOR YOU!

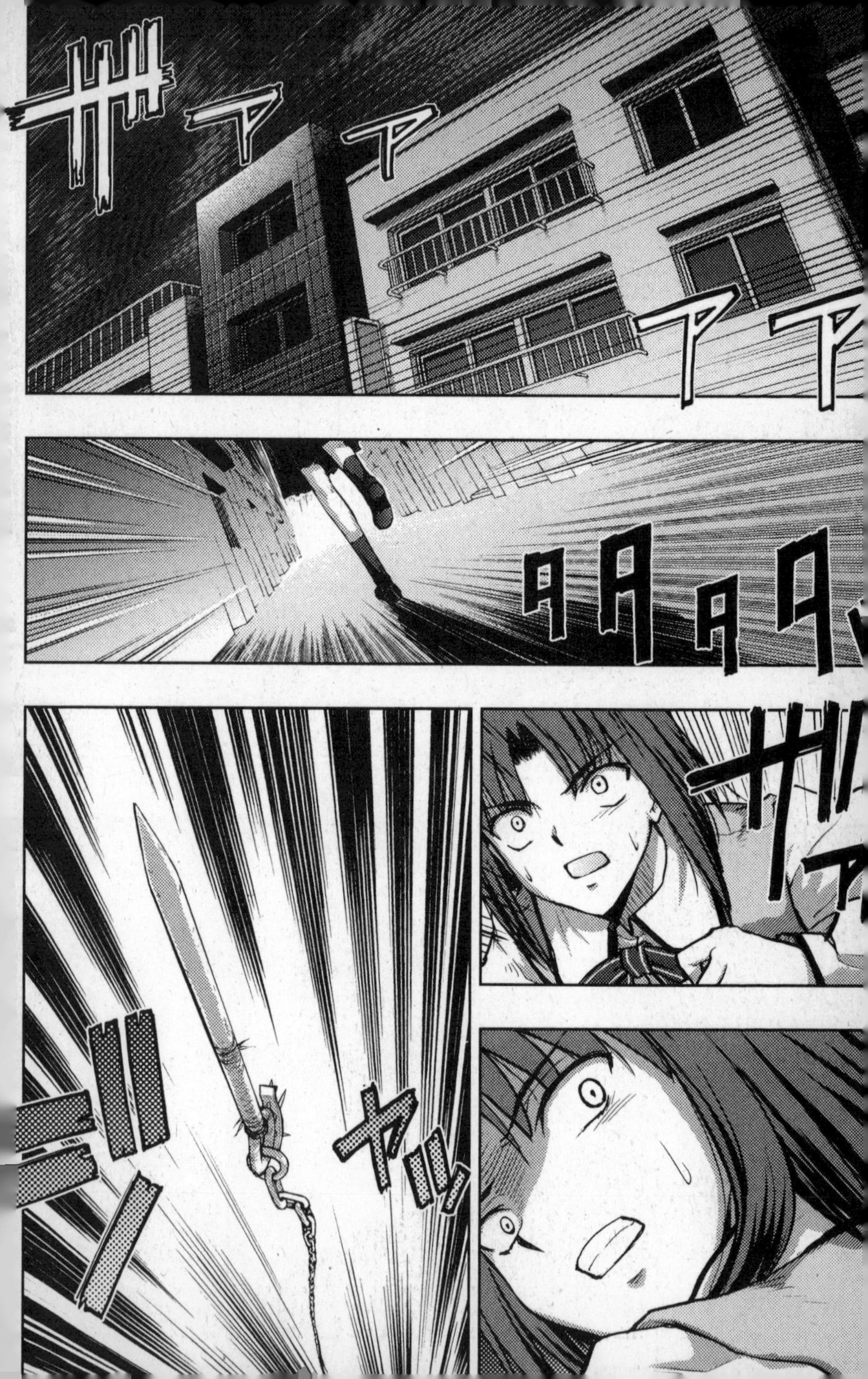
ザァァァァ
タタタタッ
ザァ
ジャッ

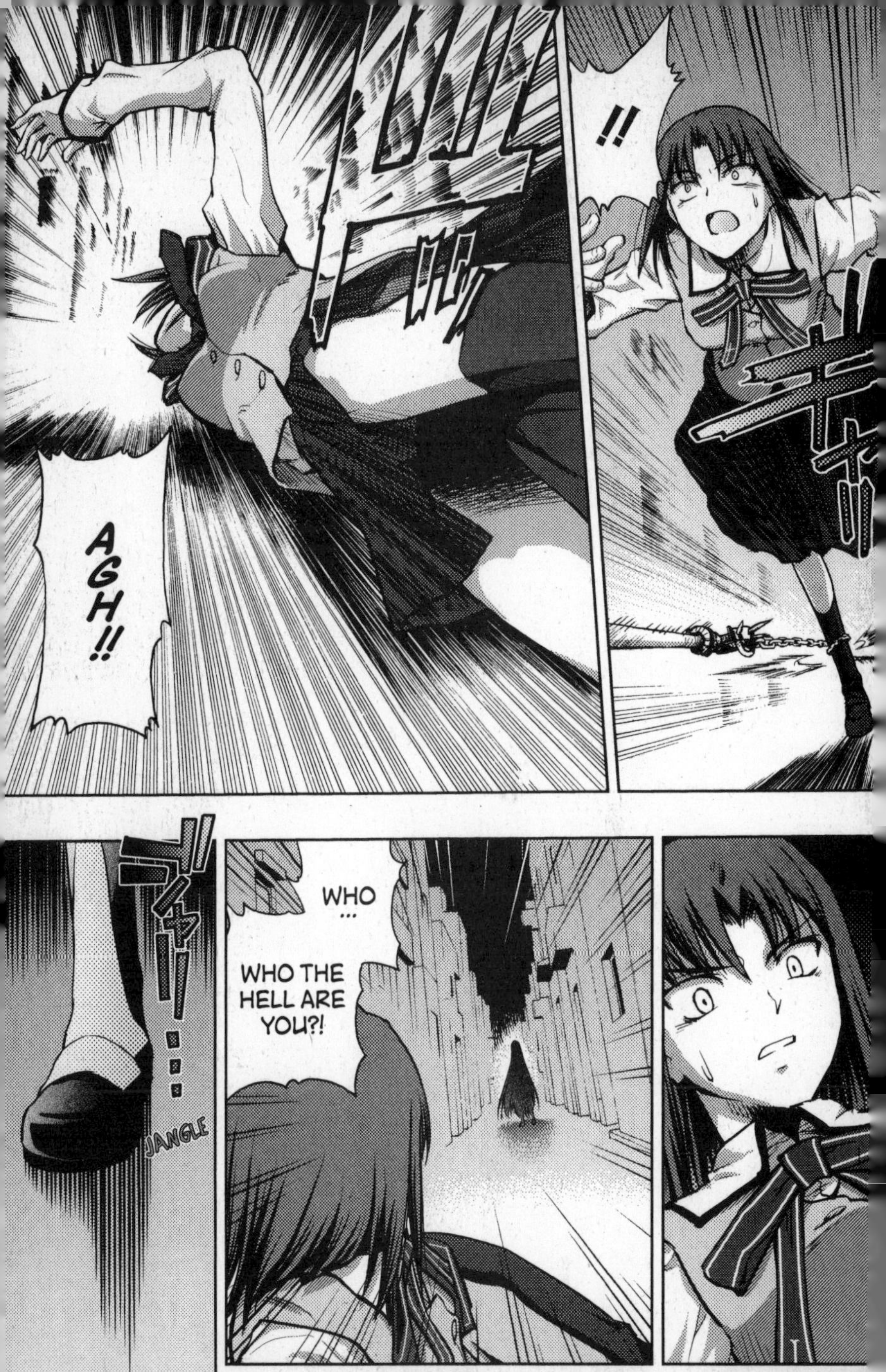
!!
AGH!!
WHO ...
WHO THE HELL ARE YOU?!
JANGLE

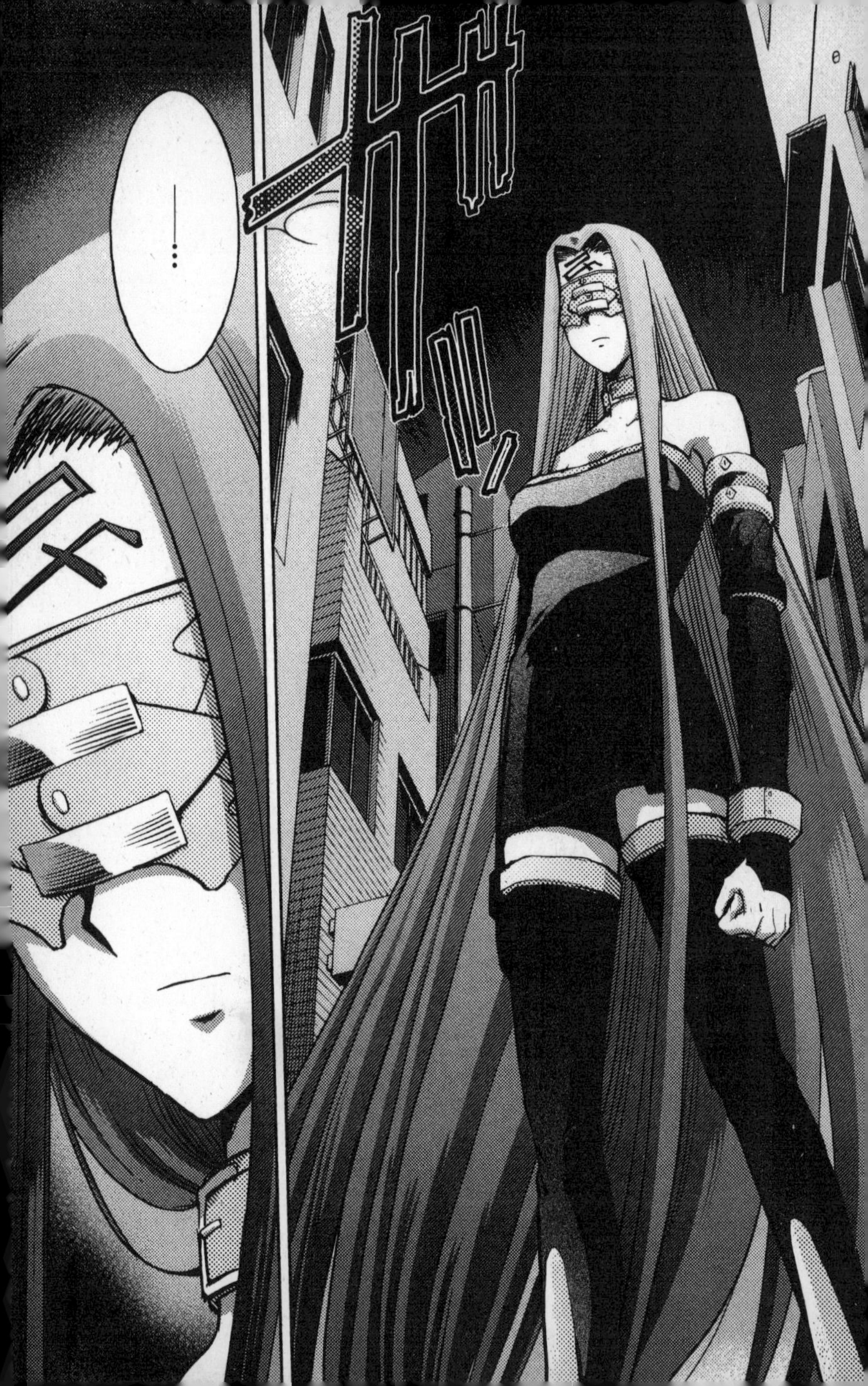
...

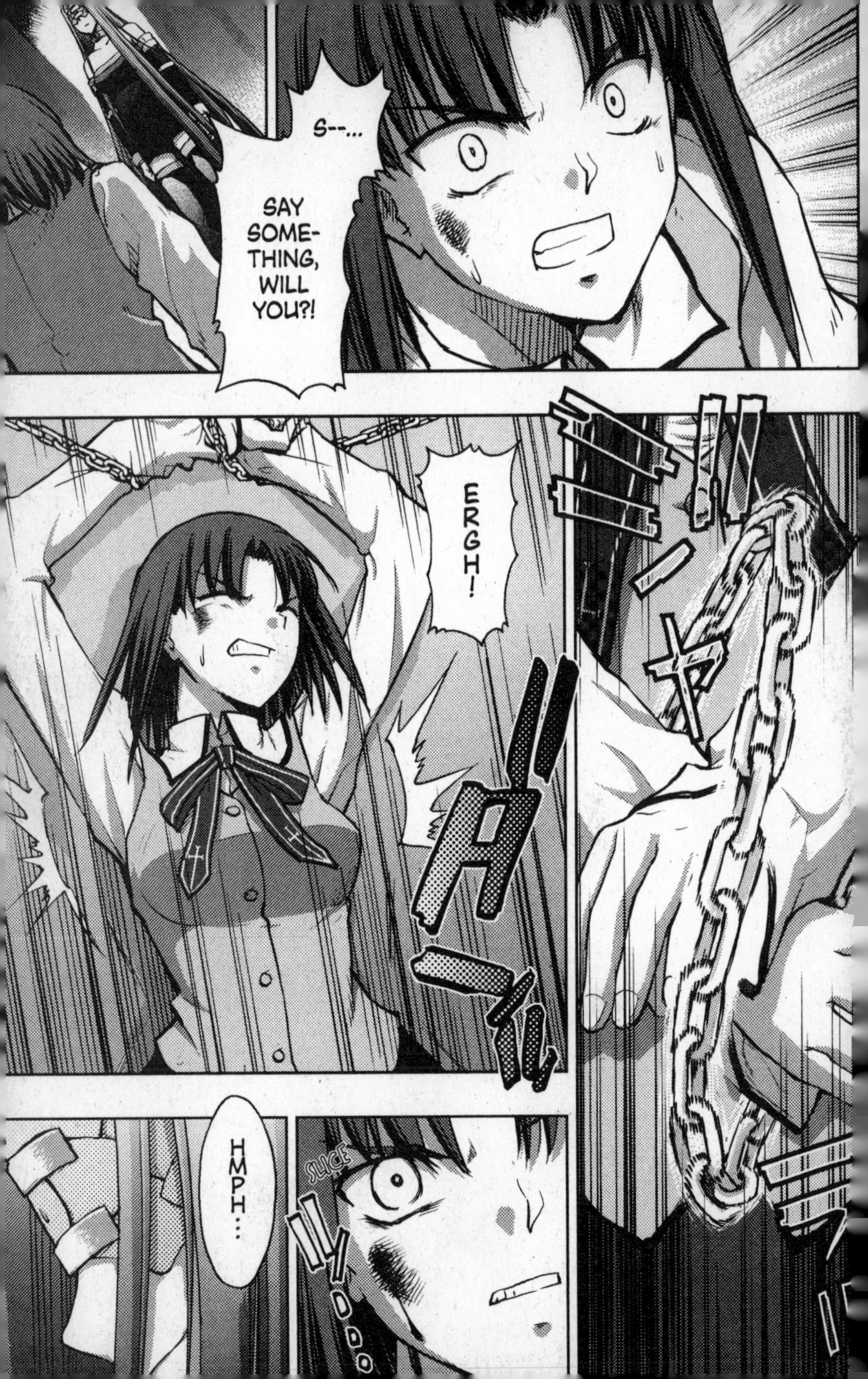
S--...
SAY SOME-THING, WILL YOU?!
ERGH!
SLICE
HMPH...

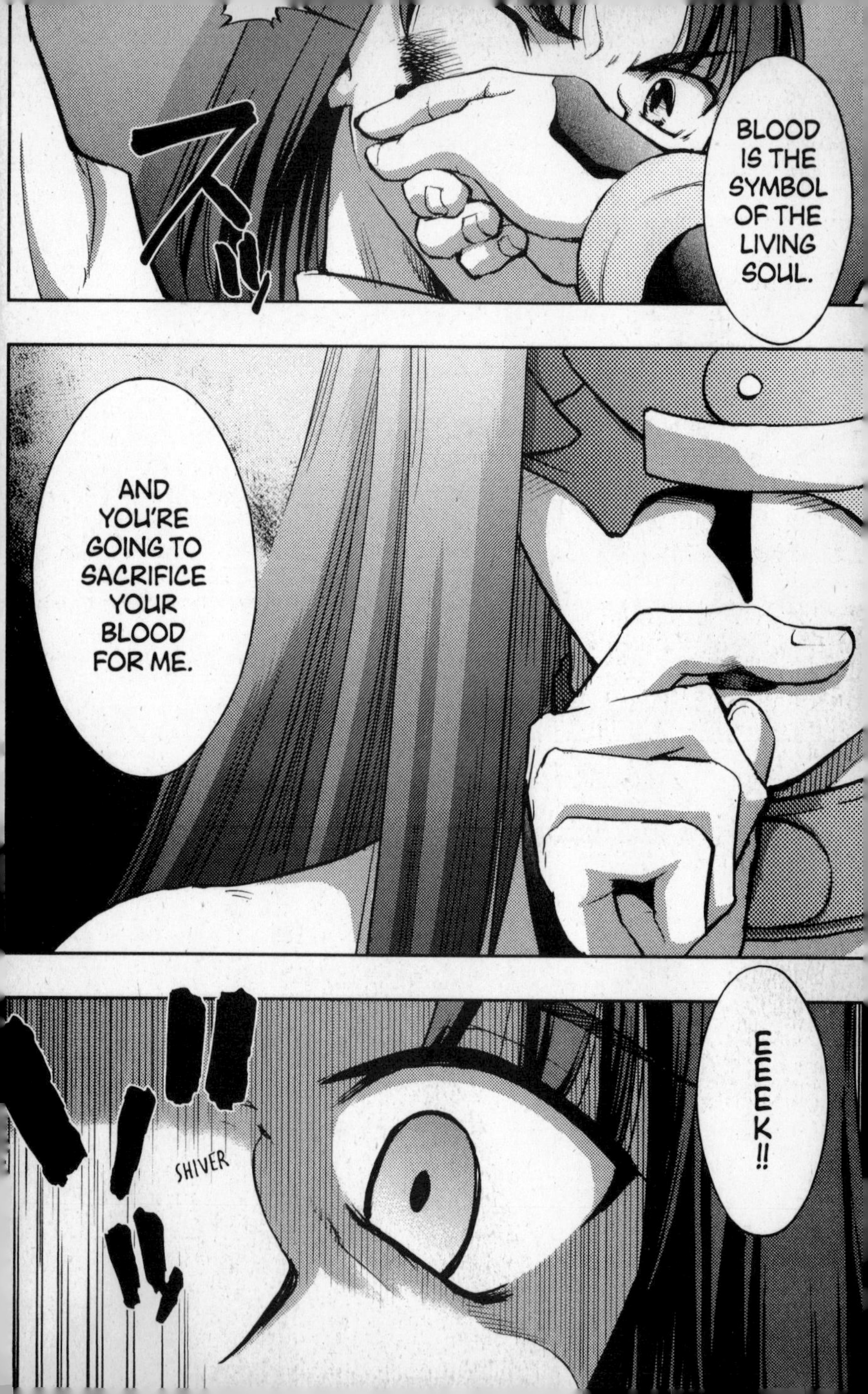
BLOOD IS THE SYMBOL OF THE LIVING SOUL.
ス
AND YOU'RE GOING TO SACRIFICE YOUR BLOOD FOR ME.
EEEK!!
SHIVER

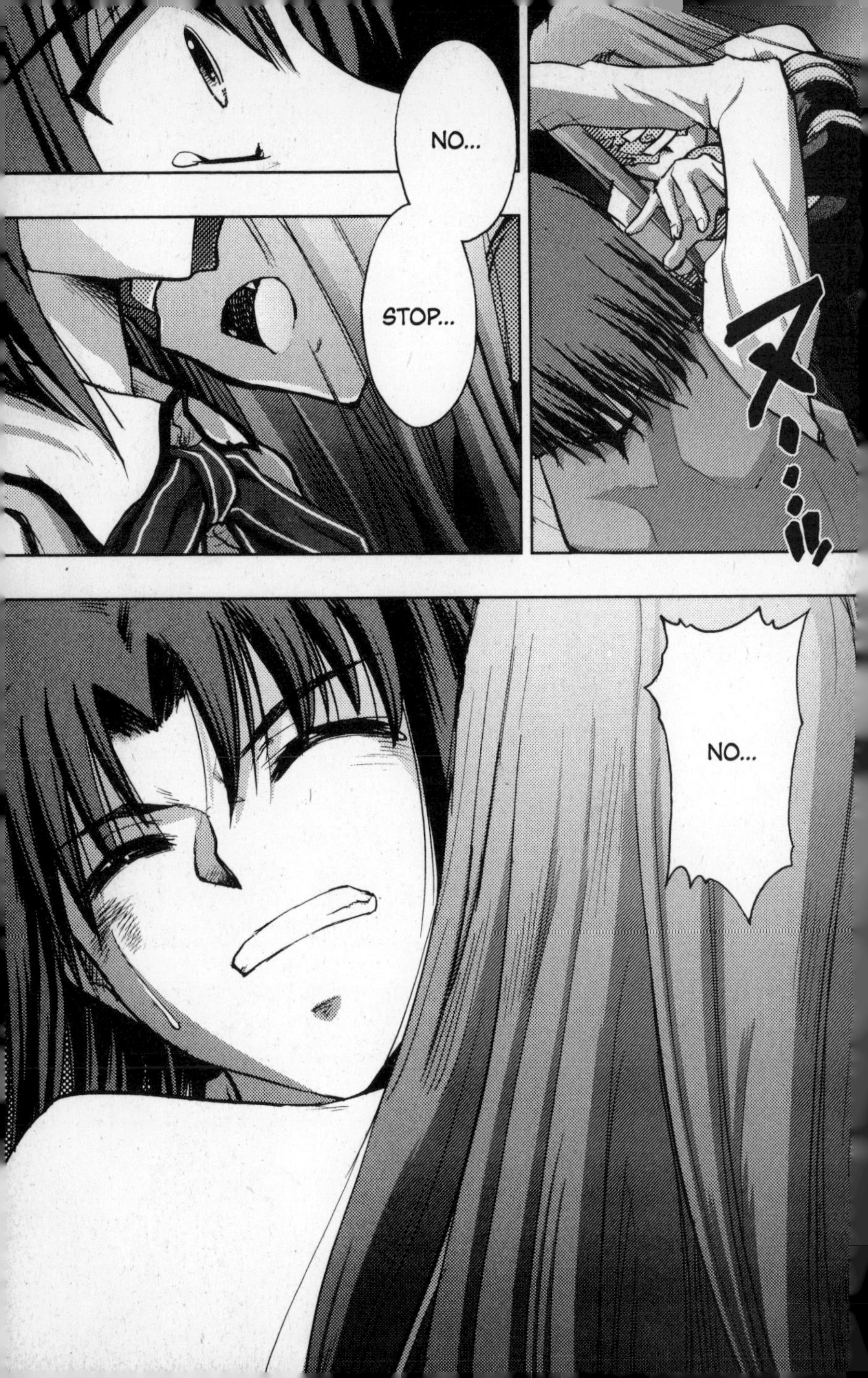
NO...
STOP...
NO...

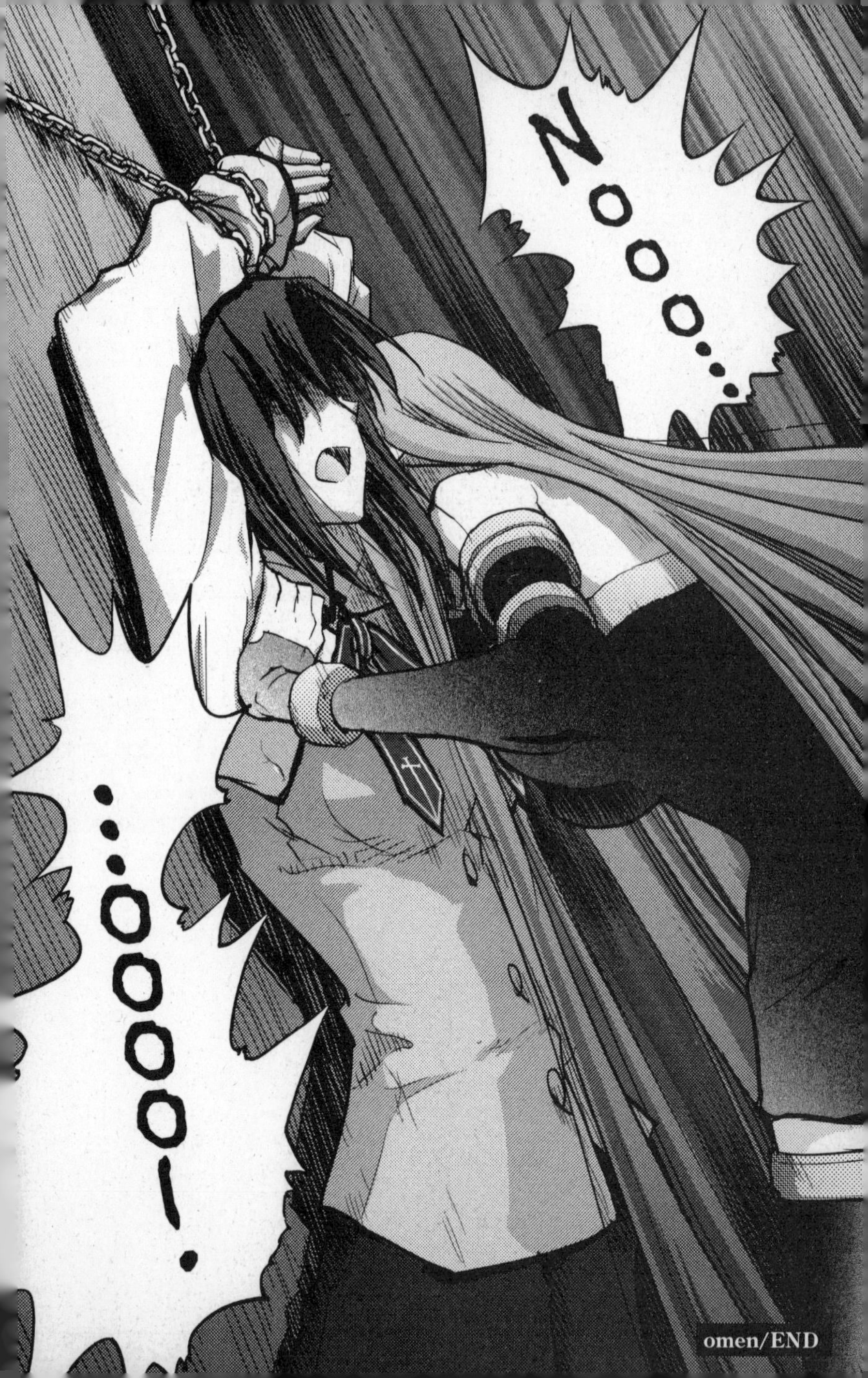
NOOO...
...OOOO!
omen/END

Fate
stay night

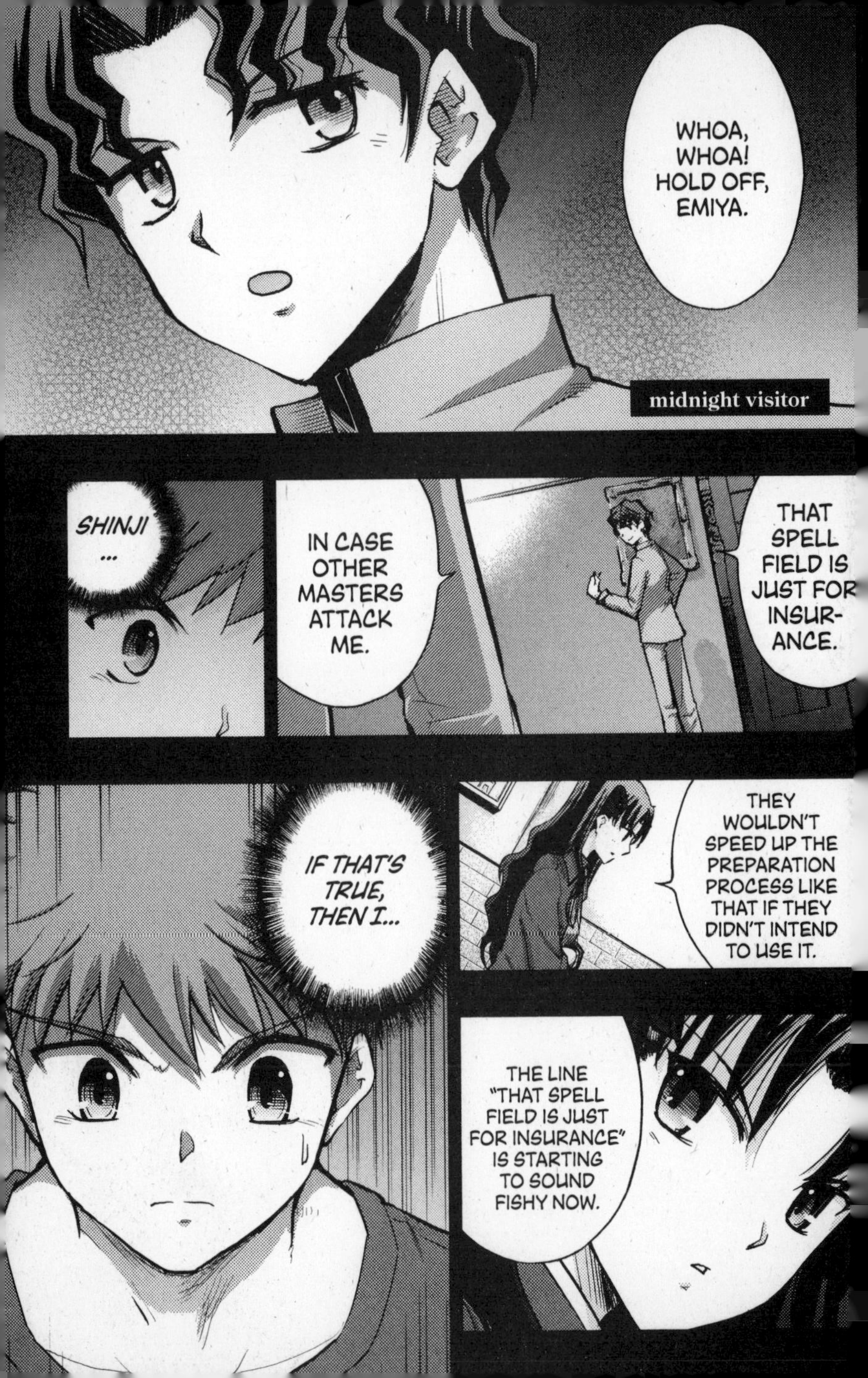
WHOA, WHOA! HOLD OFF, EMIYA.
midnight visitor
THAT SPELL FIELD IS JUST FOR INSUR-ANCE.
IN CASE OTHER MASTERS ATTACK ME.
SHINJI ...
THEY WOULDN'T SPEED UP THE PREPARATION PROCESS LIKE THAT IF THEY DIDN'T INTEND TO USE IT.
THE LINE "THAT SPELL FIELD IS JUST FOR INSURANCE" IS STARTING TO SOUND FISHY NOW.
IF THAT'S TRUE, THEN I...

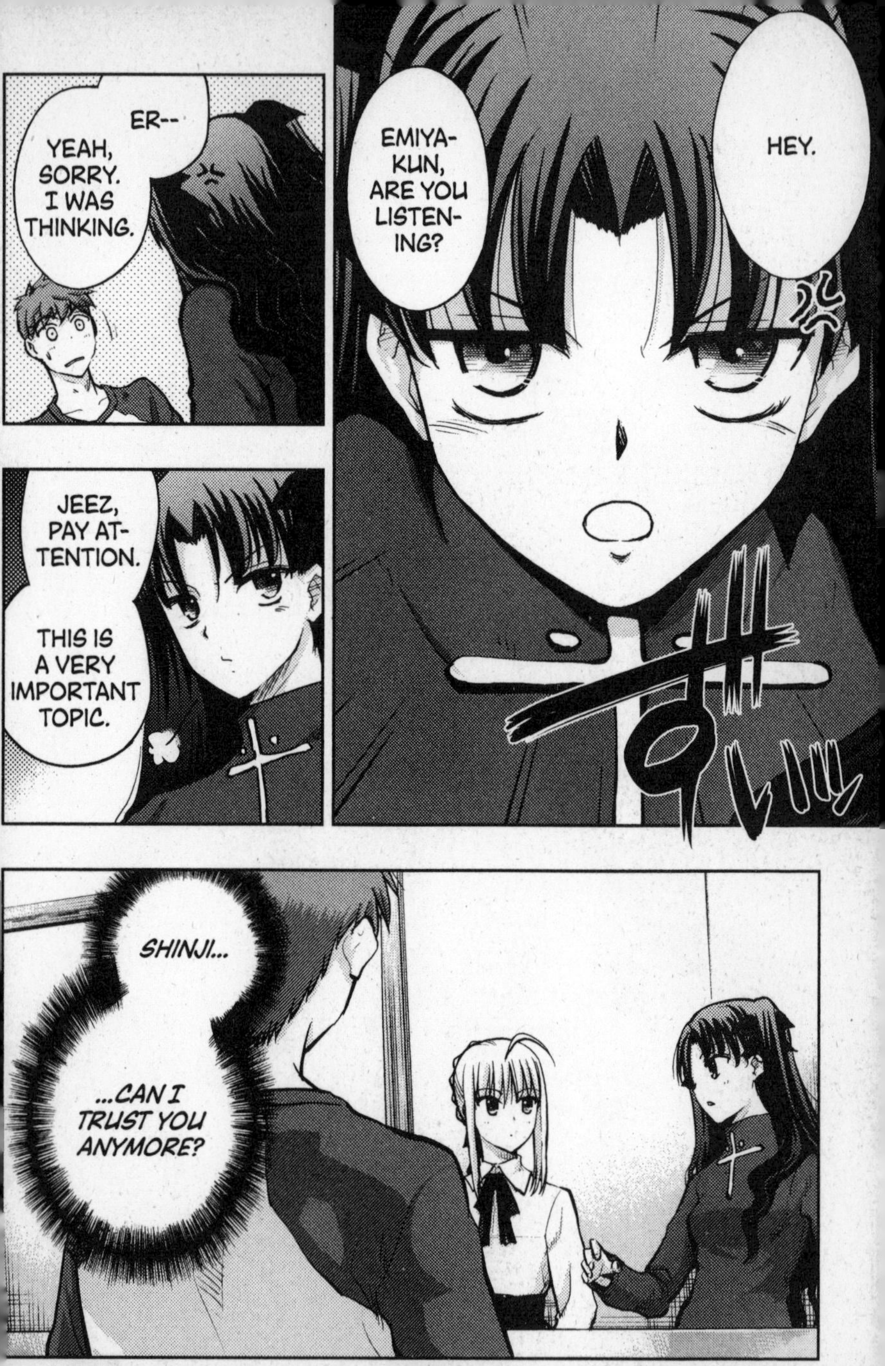
HEY.
EMIYA-KUN, ARE YOU LISTENING?
ER--
YEAH, SORRY. I WAS THINKING.
JEEZ, PAY ATTENTION.
THIS IS A VERY IMPORTANT TOPIC.
SHINJI...
...CAN I TRUST YOU ANYMORE?

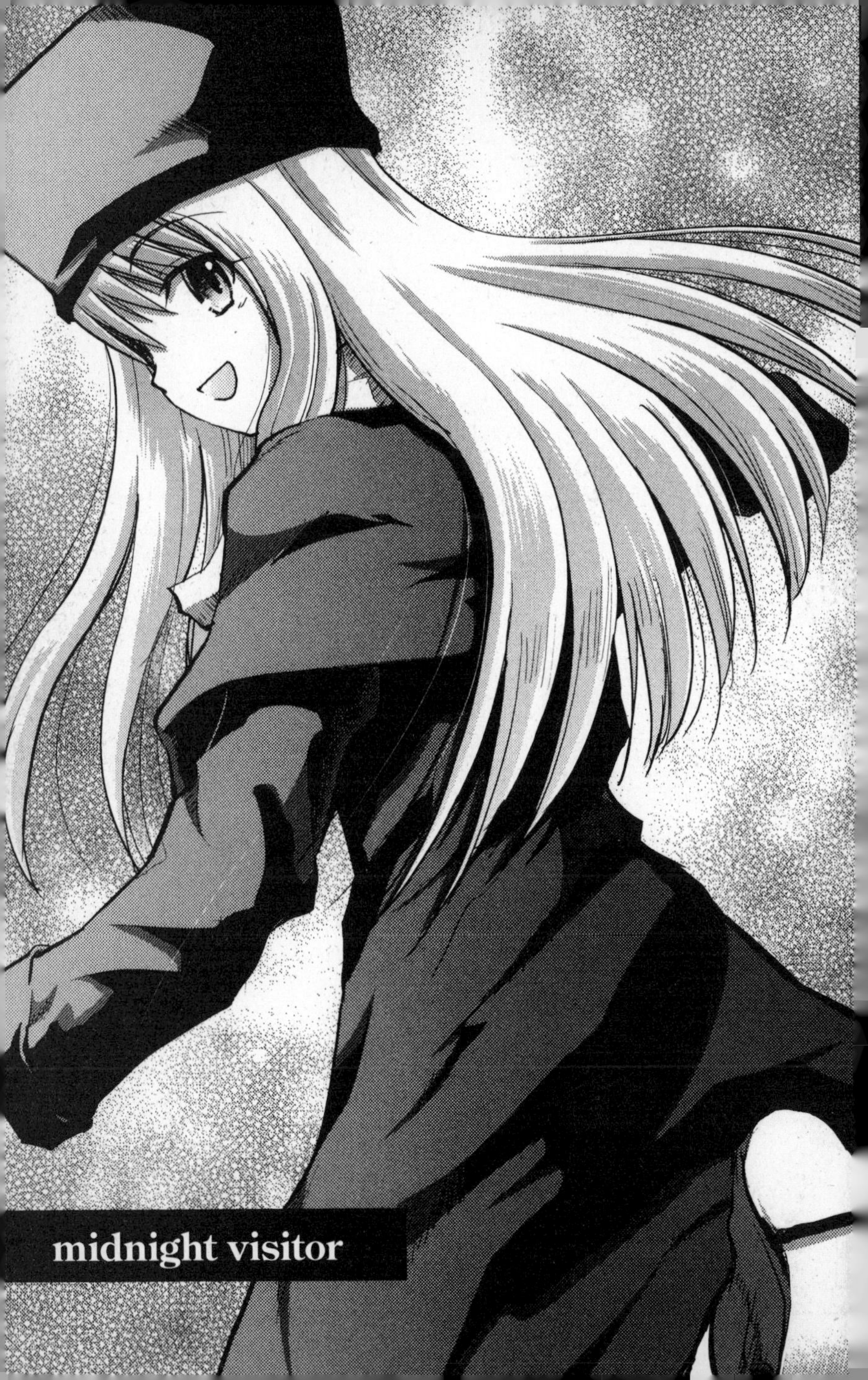
midnight visitor

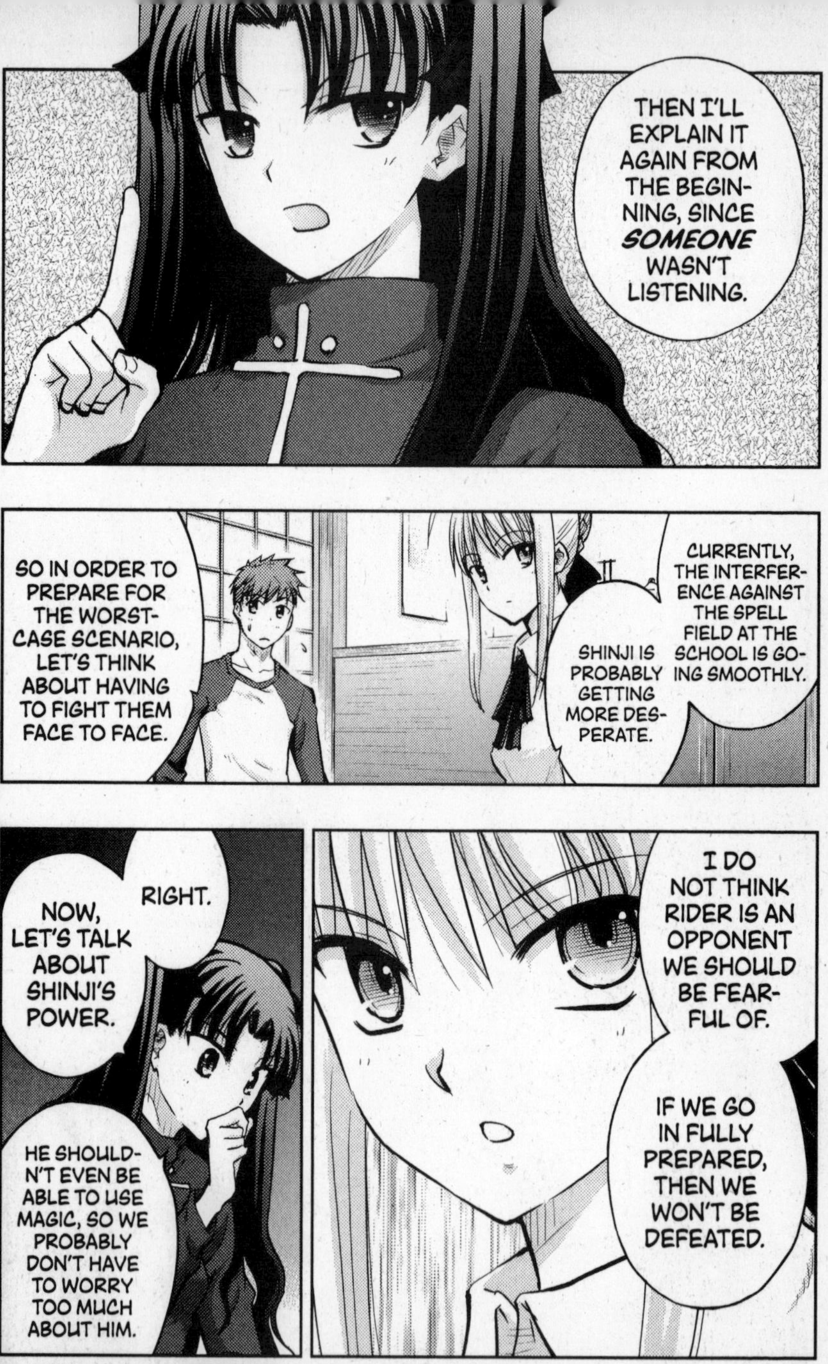
THEN I'LL EXPLAIN IT AGAIN FROM THE BEGIN-NING, SINCE *SOMEONE* WASN'T LISTENING.
CURRENTLY, THE INTERFER-ENCE AGAINST THE SPELL FIELD AT THE SCHOOL IS GO-ING SMOOTHLY.
SHINJI IS PROBABLY GETTING MORE DES-PERATE.
SO IN ORDER TO PREPARE FOR THE WORST-CASE SCENARIO, LET'S THINK ABOUT HAVING TO FIGHT THEM FACE TO FACE.
I DO NOT THINK RIDER IS AN OPPONENT WE SHOULD BE FEAR-FUL OF.
IF WE GO IN FULLY PREPARED, THEN WE WON'T BE DEFEATED.
RIGHT.
NOW, LET'S TALK ABOUT SHINJI'S POWER.
HE SHOULD-N'T EVEN BE ABLE TO USE MAGIC, SO WE PROBABLY DON'T HAVE TO WORRY TOO MUCH ABOUT HIM.

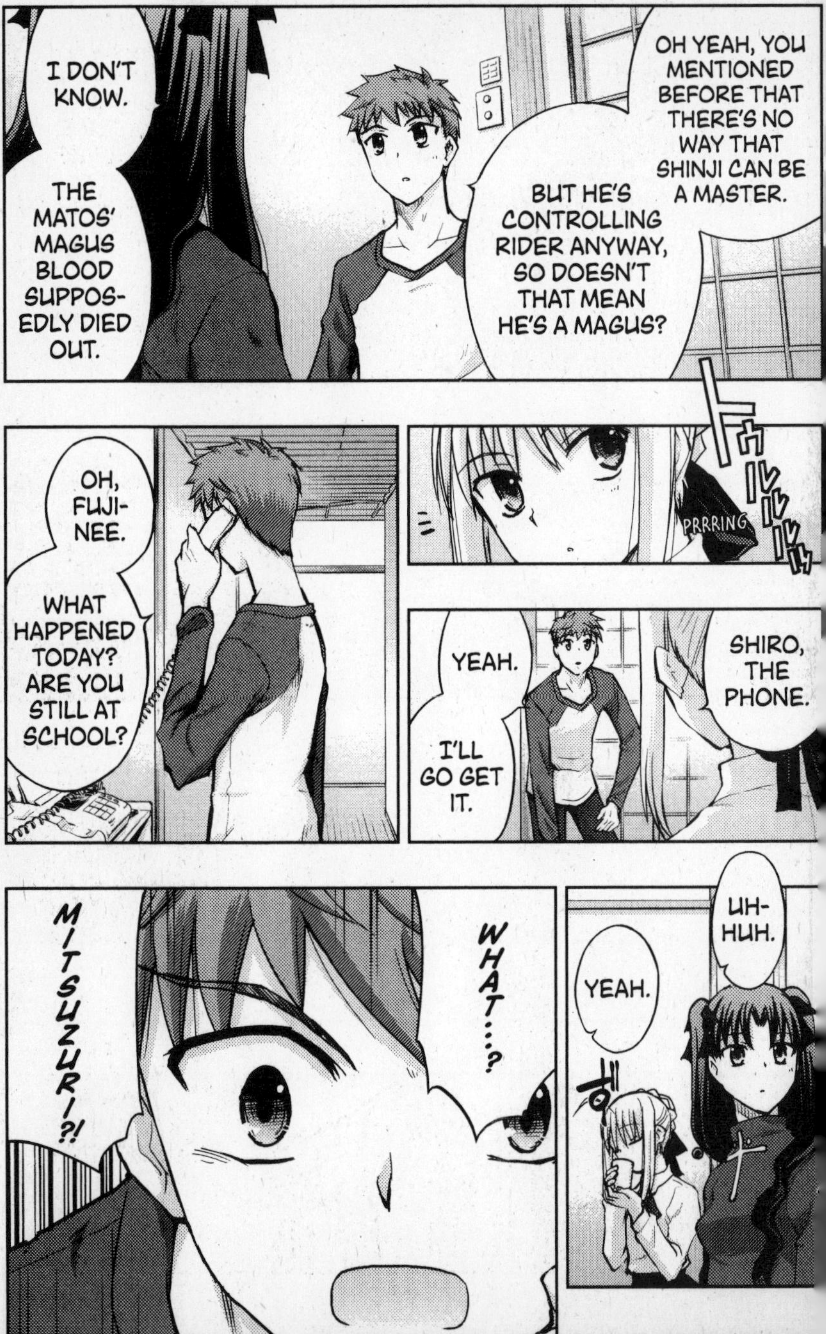
OH YEAH, YOU MENTIONED BEFORE THAT THERE'S NO WAY THAT SHINJI CAN BE A MASTER.
BUT HE'S CONTROLLING RIDER ANYWAY, SO DOESN'T THAT MEAN HE'S A MAGUS?
I DON'T KNOW.
THE MATOS' MAGUS BLOOD SUPPOS-EDLY DIED OUT.
PRRRING
SHIRO, THE PHONE.
YEAH.
I'LL GO GET IT.
OH, FUJI-NEE.
WHAT HAPPENED TODAY? ARE YOU STILL AT SCHOOL?
UH-HUH.
YEAH.
WHAT...?
MITSUZURI?!

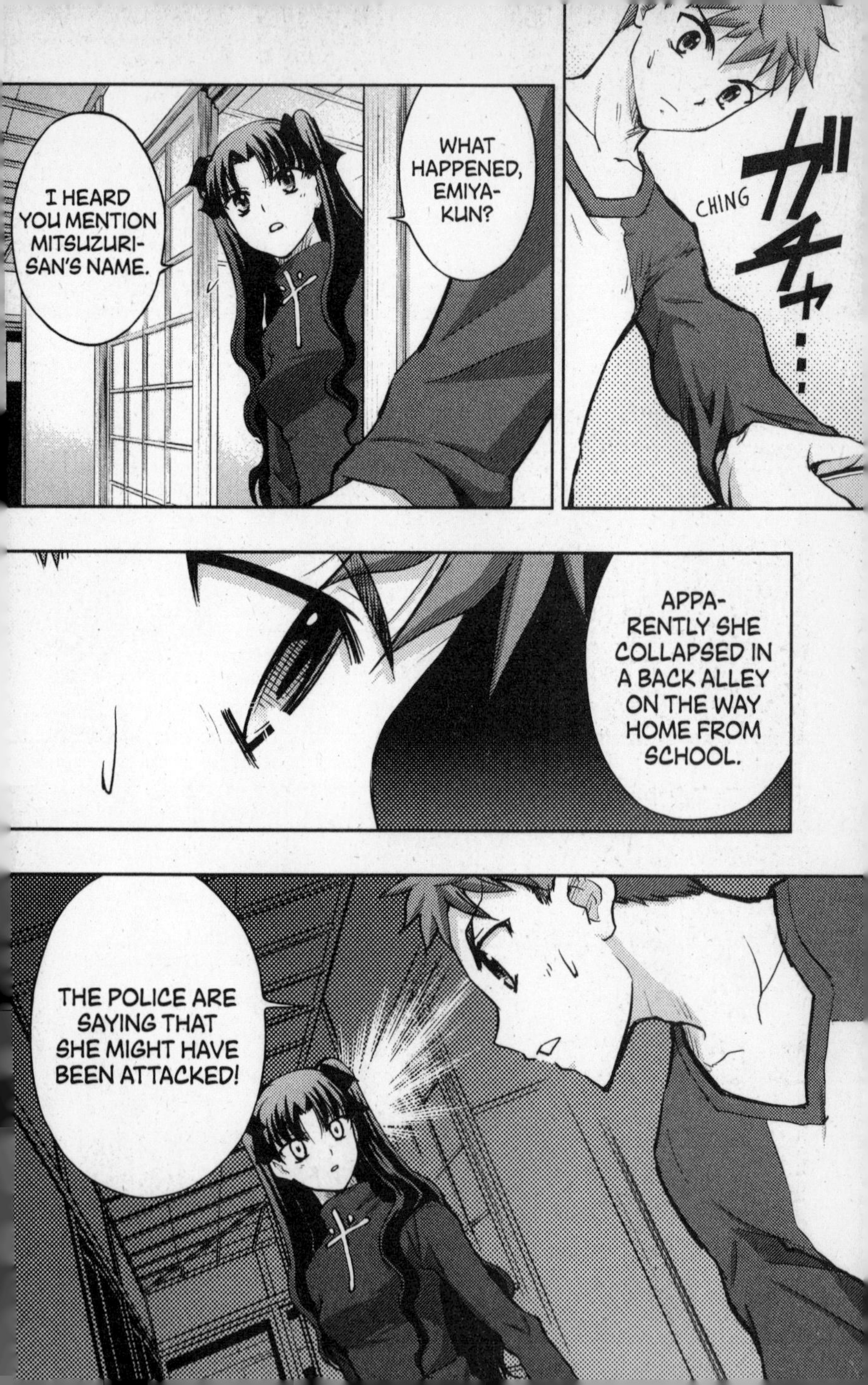
ガチャ…
CHING
WHAT HAPPENED, EMIYA-KUN?
I HEARD YOU MENTION MITSUZURI-SAN'S NAME.
APPARENTLY SHE COLLAPSED IN A BACK ALLEY ON THE WAY HOME FROM SCHOOL.
THE POLICE ARE SAYING THAT SHE MIGHT HAVE BEEN ATTACKED!

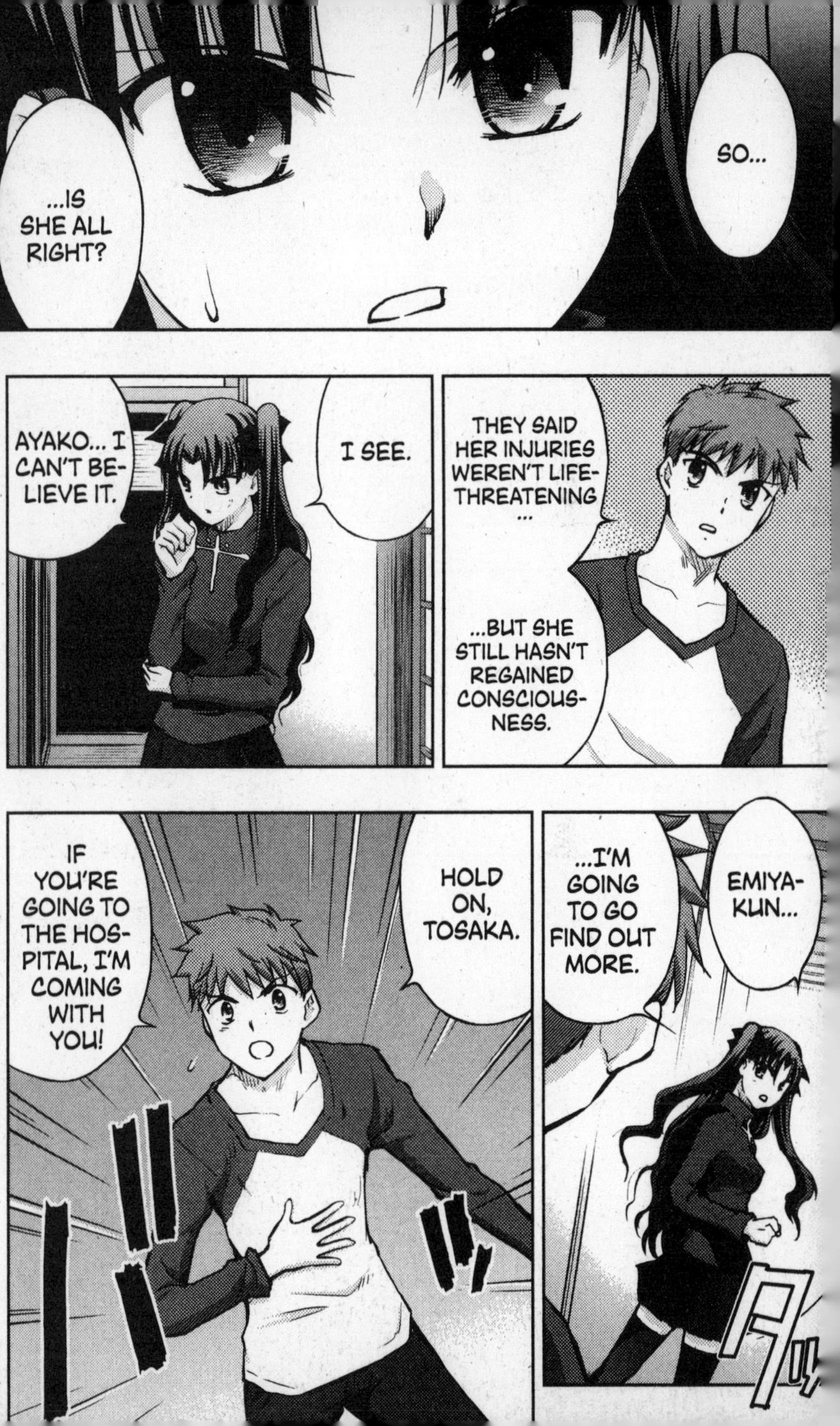
SO...
...IS SHE ALL RIGHT?
THEY SAID HER INJURIES WEREN'T LIFE-THREATENING ...
...BUT SHE STILL HASN'T REGAINED CONSCIOUSNESS.
I SEE.
AYAKO... I CAN'T BELIEVE IT.
EMIYA-KUN...
...I'M GOING TO GO FIND OUT MORE.
HOLD ON, TOSAKA.
IF YOU'RE GOING TO THE HOSPITAL, I'M COMING WITH YOU!

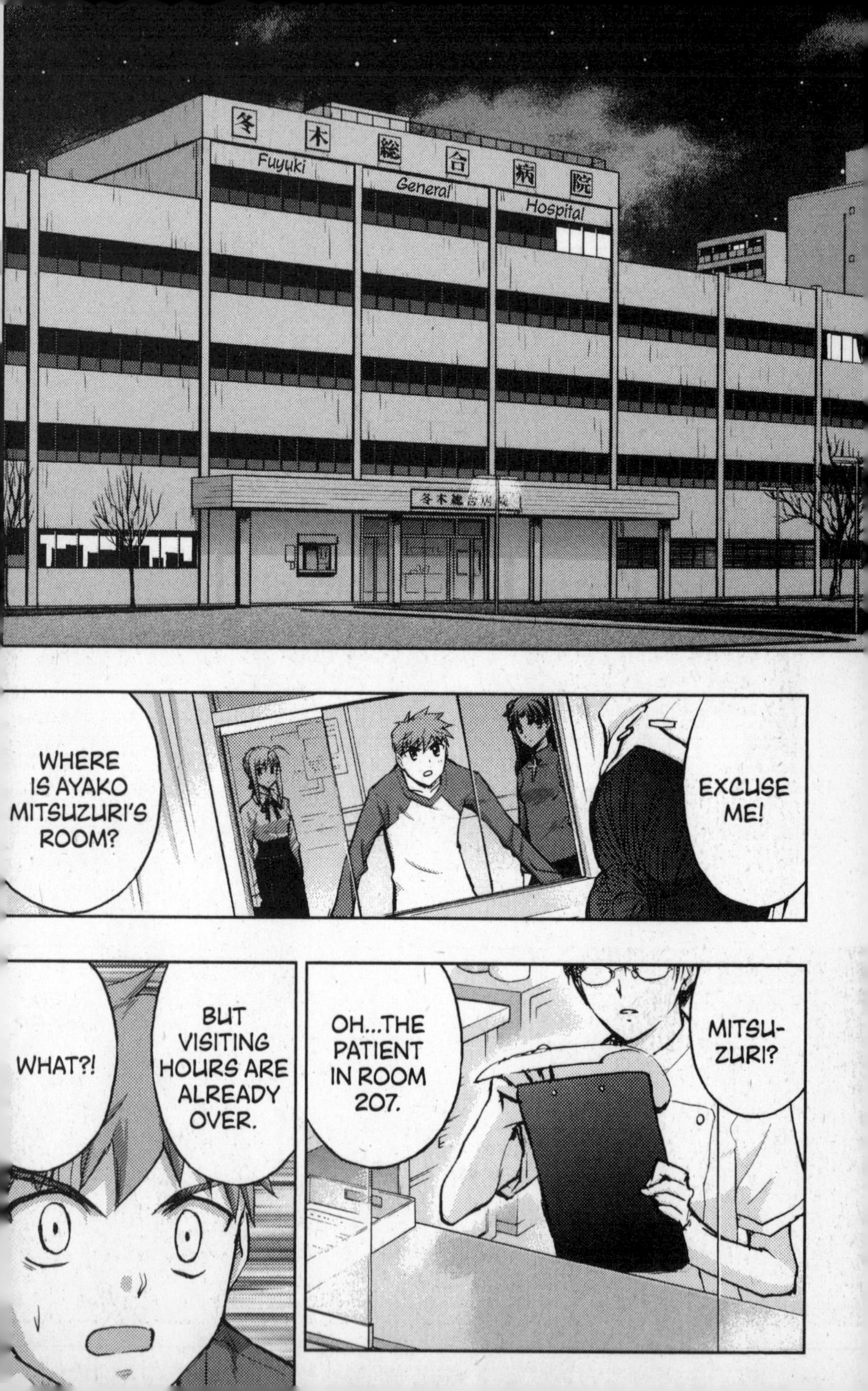
冬木総合病院
Fuyuki General Hospital
EXCUSE ME!
WHERE IS AYAKO MITSUZURI'S ROOM?
MITSU-ZURI?
OH...THE PATIENT IN ROOM 207.
BUT VISITING HOURS ARE ALREADY OVER.
WHAT?!

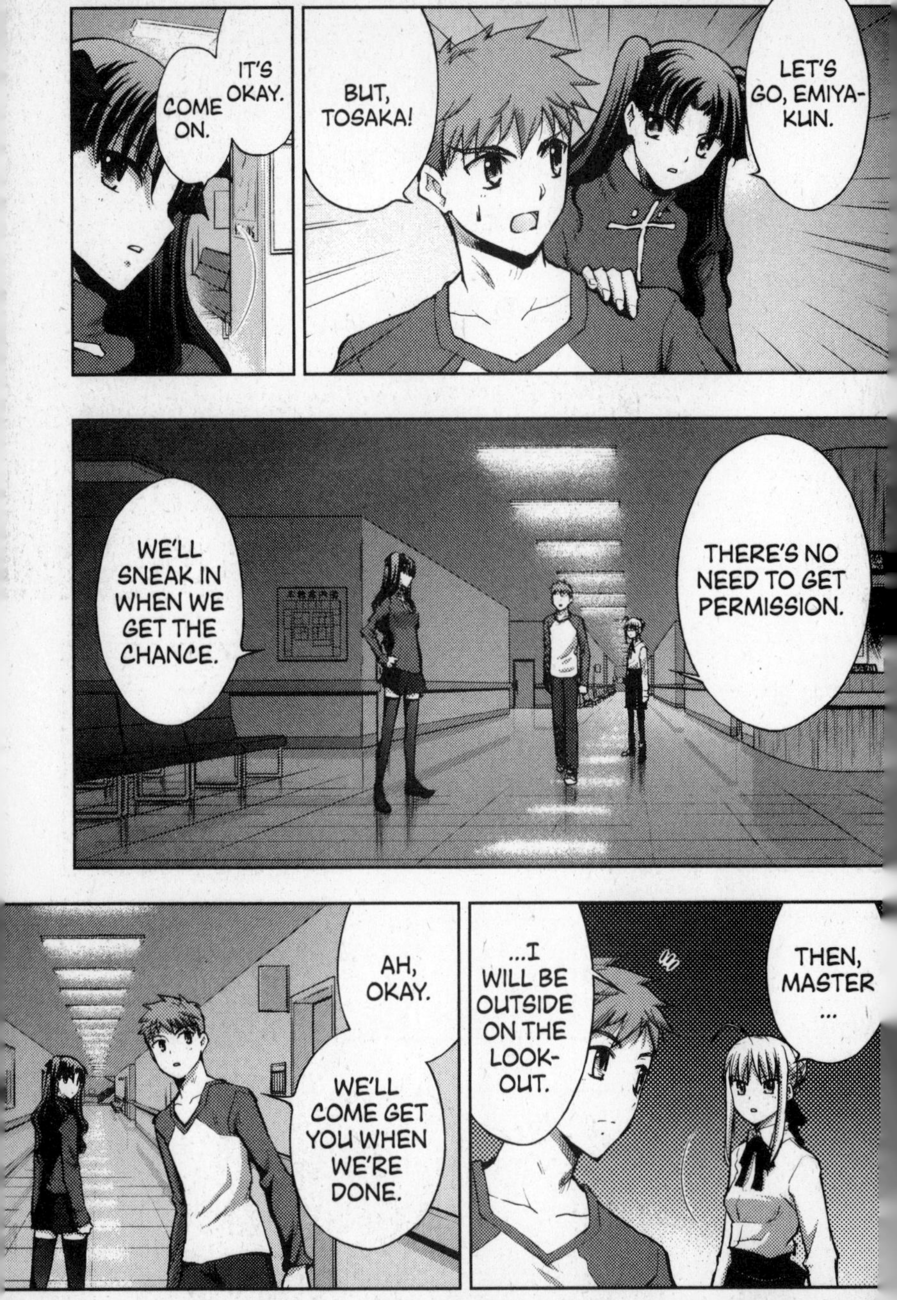
LET'S GO, EMIYA-KUN.
BUT, TOSAKA!
IT'S OKAY.
COME ON.
THERE'S NO NEED TO GET PERMISSION.
WE'LL SNEAK IN WHEN WE GET THE CHANCE.
THEN, MASTER ...
...I WILL BE OUTSIDE ON THE LOOK-OUT.
AH, OKAY.
WE'LL COME GET YOU WHEN WE'RE DONE.

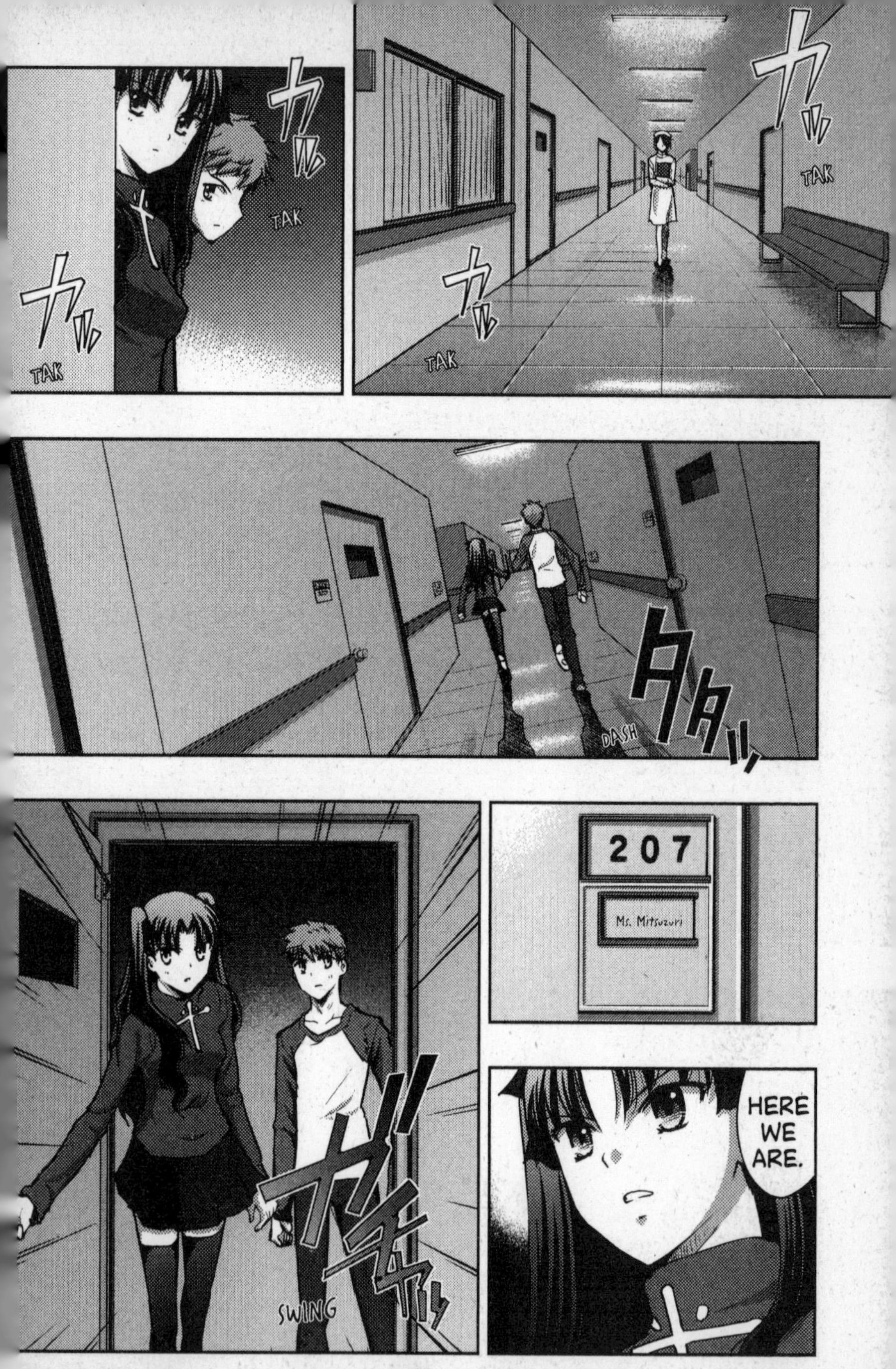
TAK
TAK
TAK
DASH
207
Ms. Mitsuzuri
HERE WE ARE.
SWING

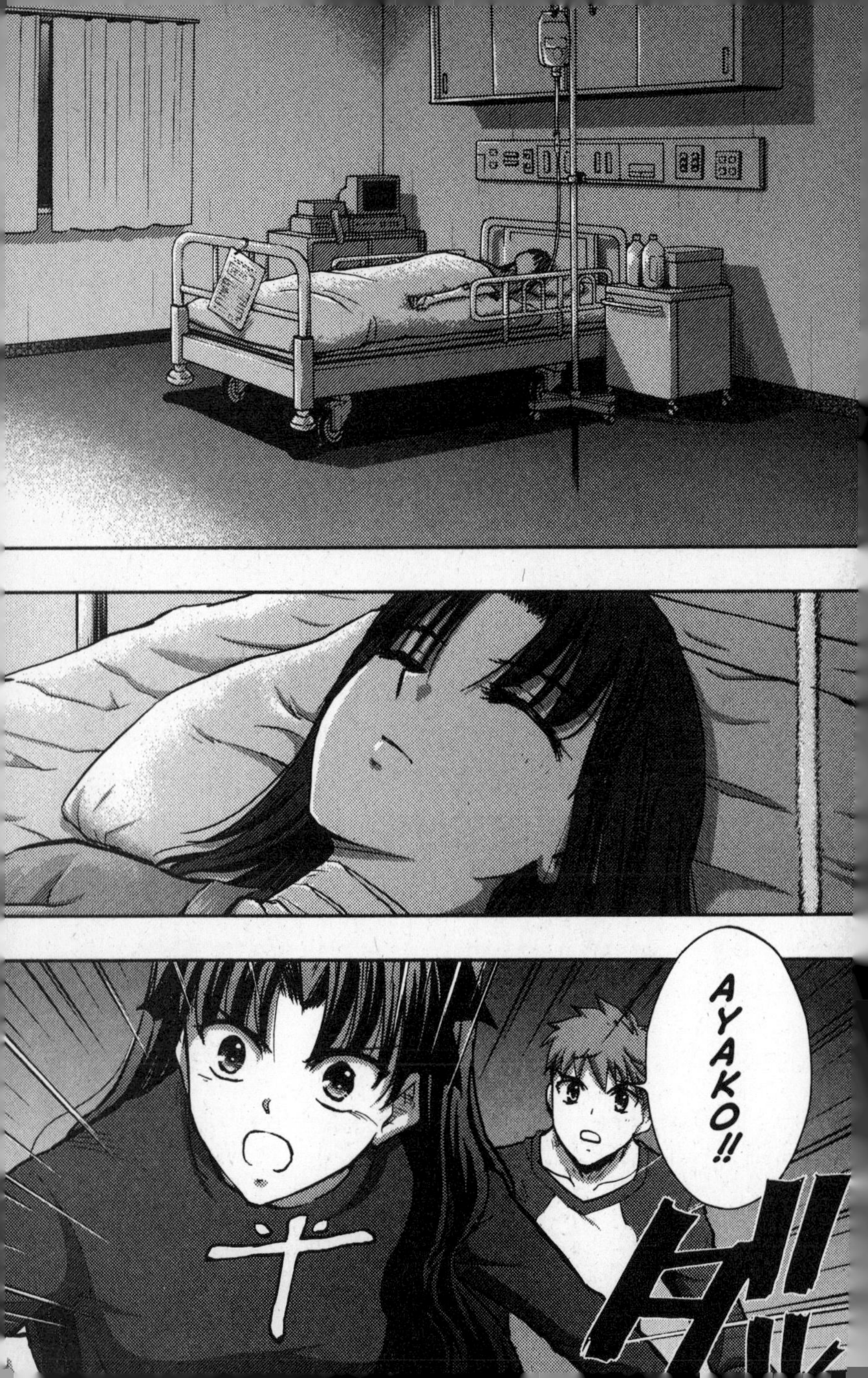
AYAKO!!

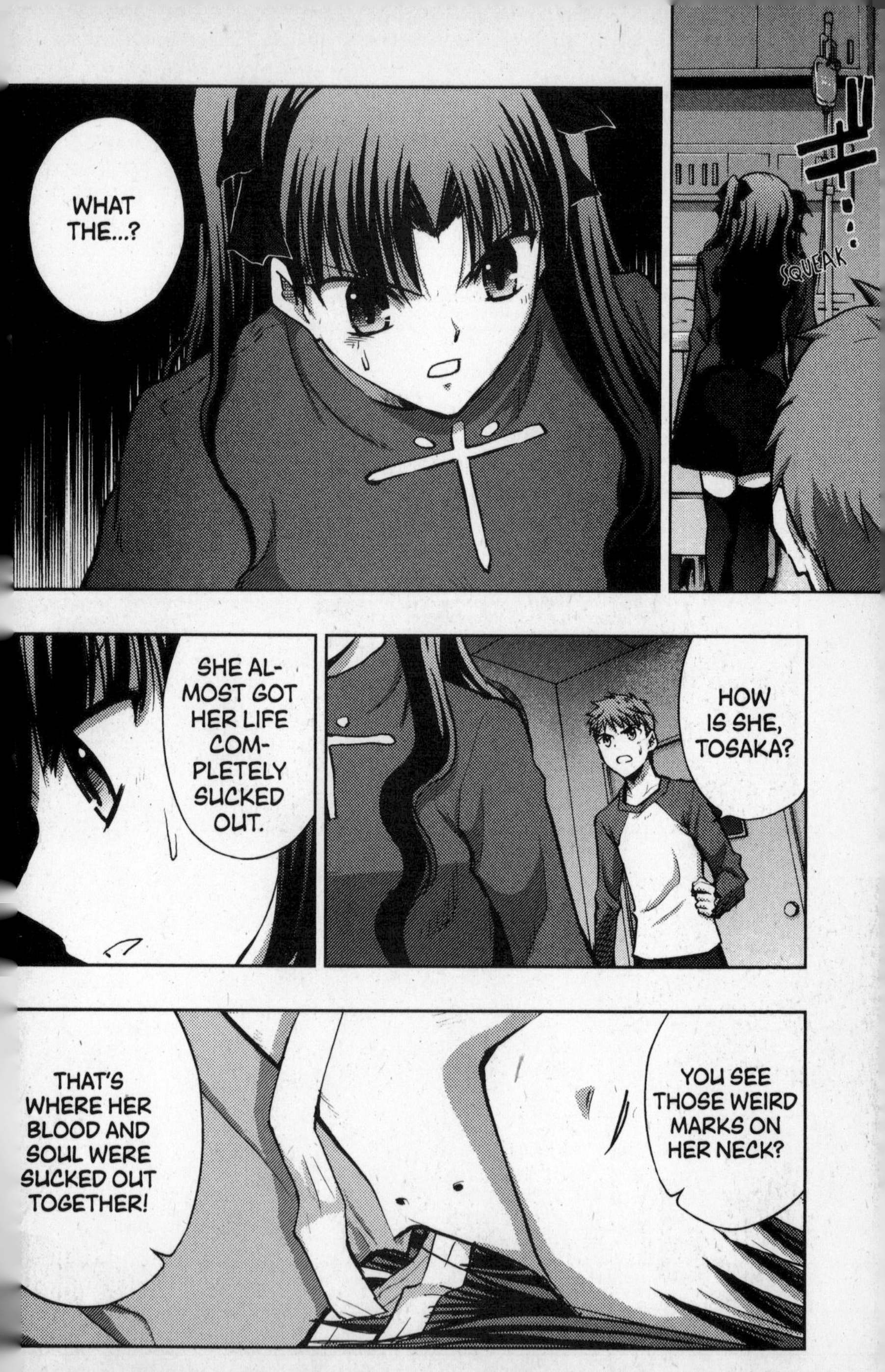
SQUEAK
WHAT THE...?
HOW IS SHE, TOSAKA?
SHE AL-MOST GOT HER LIFE COM-PLETELY SUCKED OUT.
YOU SEE THOSE WEIRD MARKS ON HER NECK?
THAT'S WHERE HER BLOOD AND SOUL WERE SUCKED OUT TOGETHER!

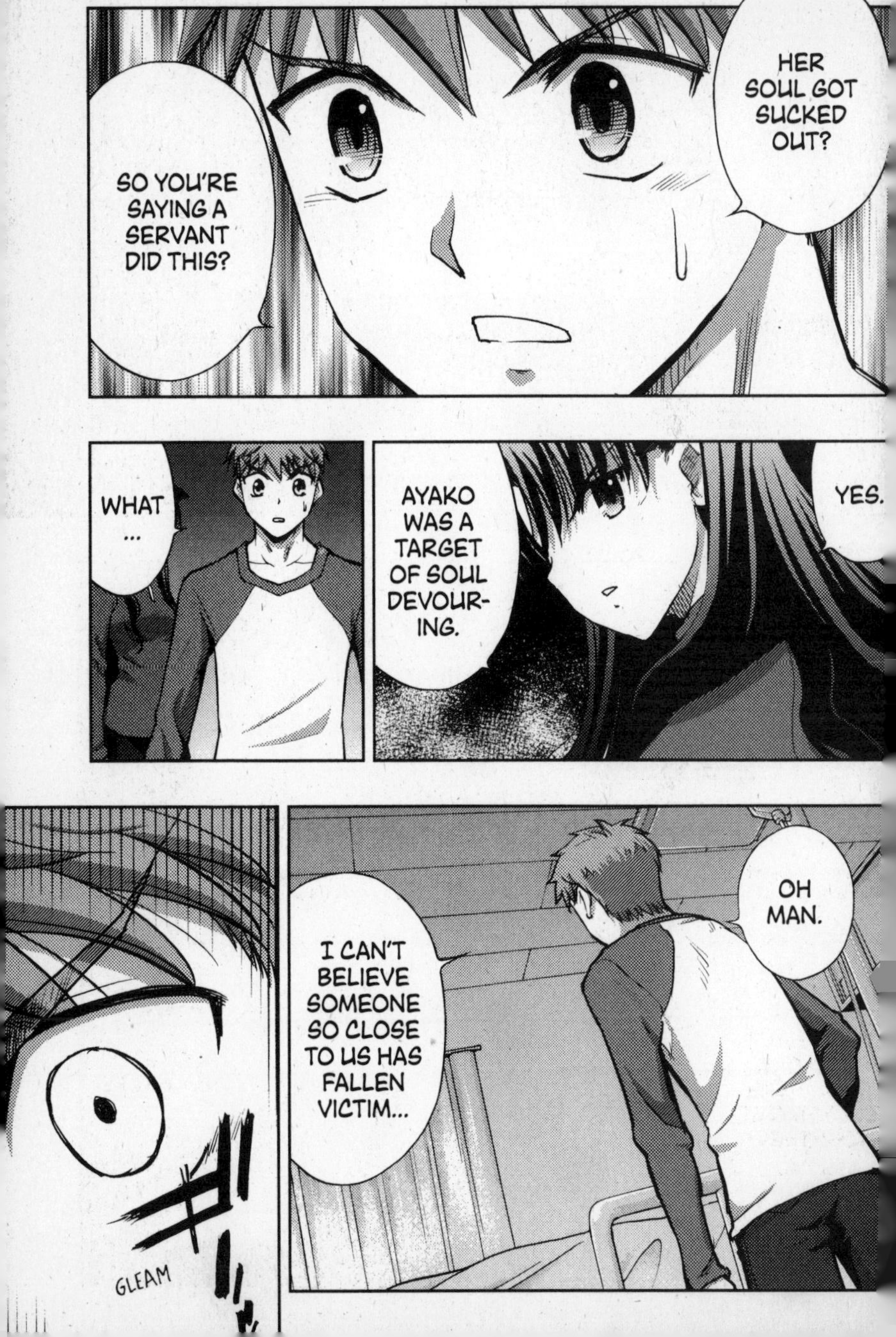
HER SOUL GOT SUCKED OUT?
SO YOU'RE SAYING A SERVANT DID THIS?
YES.
AYAKO WAS A TARGET OF SOUL DEVOUR-ING.
WHAT ...
OH MAN.
I CAN'T BELIEVE SOMEONE SO CLOSE TO US HAS FALLEN VICTIM...
GLEAM

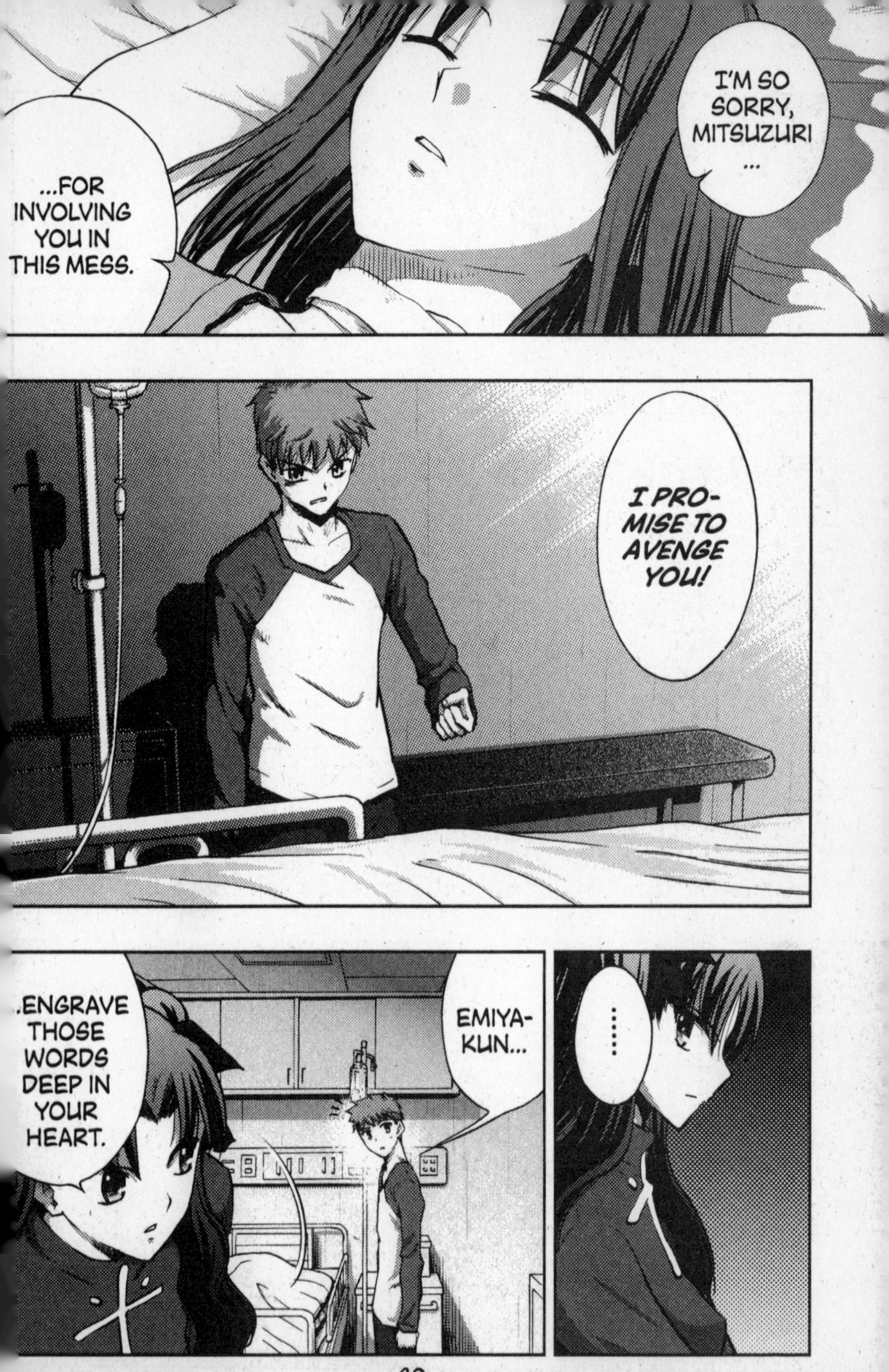
I'M SO SORRY, MITSUZURI ...
...FOR INVOLVING YOU IN THIS MESS.
I PROMISE TO AVENGE YOU!
......
EMIYA-KUN...
.ENGRAVE THOSE WORDS DEEP IN YOUR HEART.

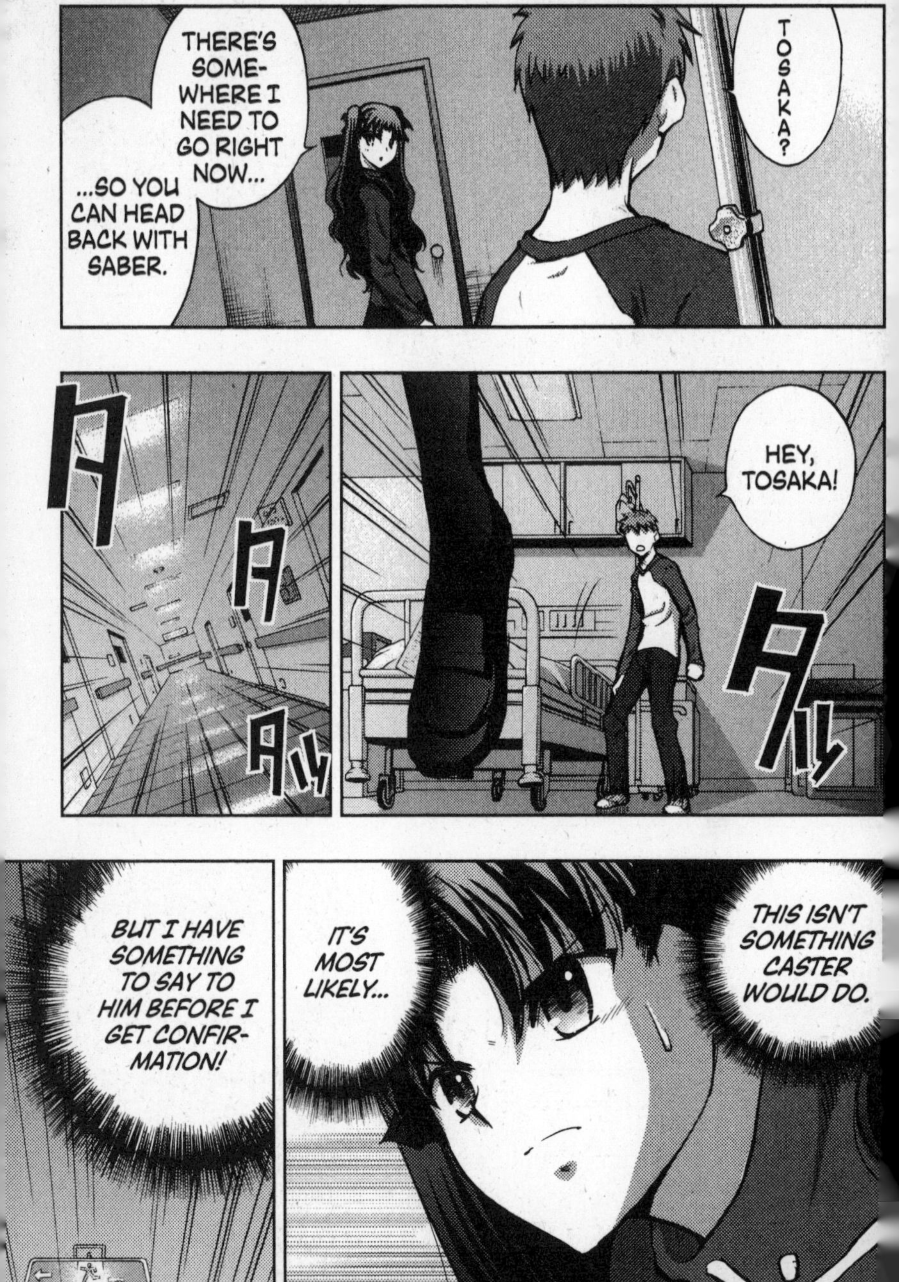
TOSAKA?
THERE'S SOMEWHERE I NEED TO GO RIGHT NOW...
...SO YOU CAN HEAD BACK WITH SABER.
HEY, TOSAKA!
タッ
タ
タ
タッ
THIS ISN'T SOMETHING CASTER WOULD DO.
IT'S MOST LIKELY...
BUT I HAVE SOMETHING TO SAY TO HIM BEFORE I GET CONFIRMATION!

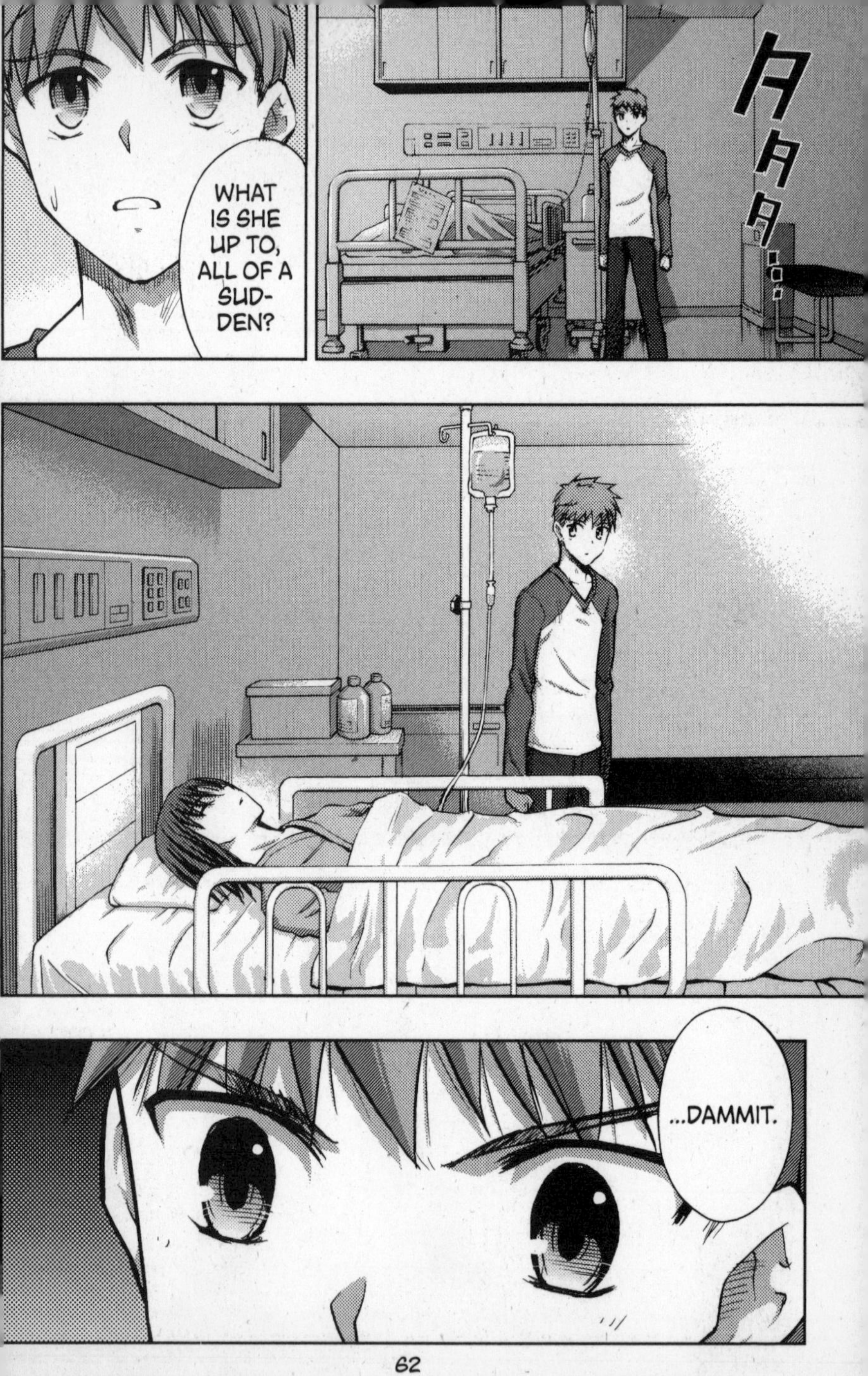
タタタ…
WHAT IS SHE UP TO, ALL OF A SUD-DEN?
...DAMMIT.

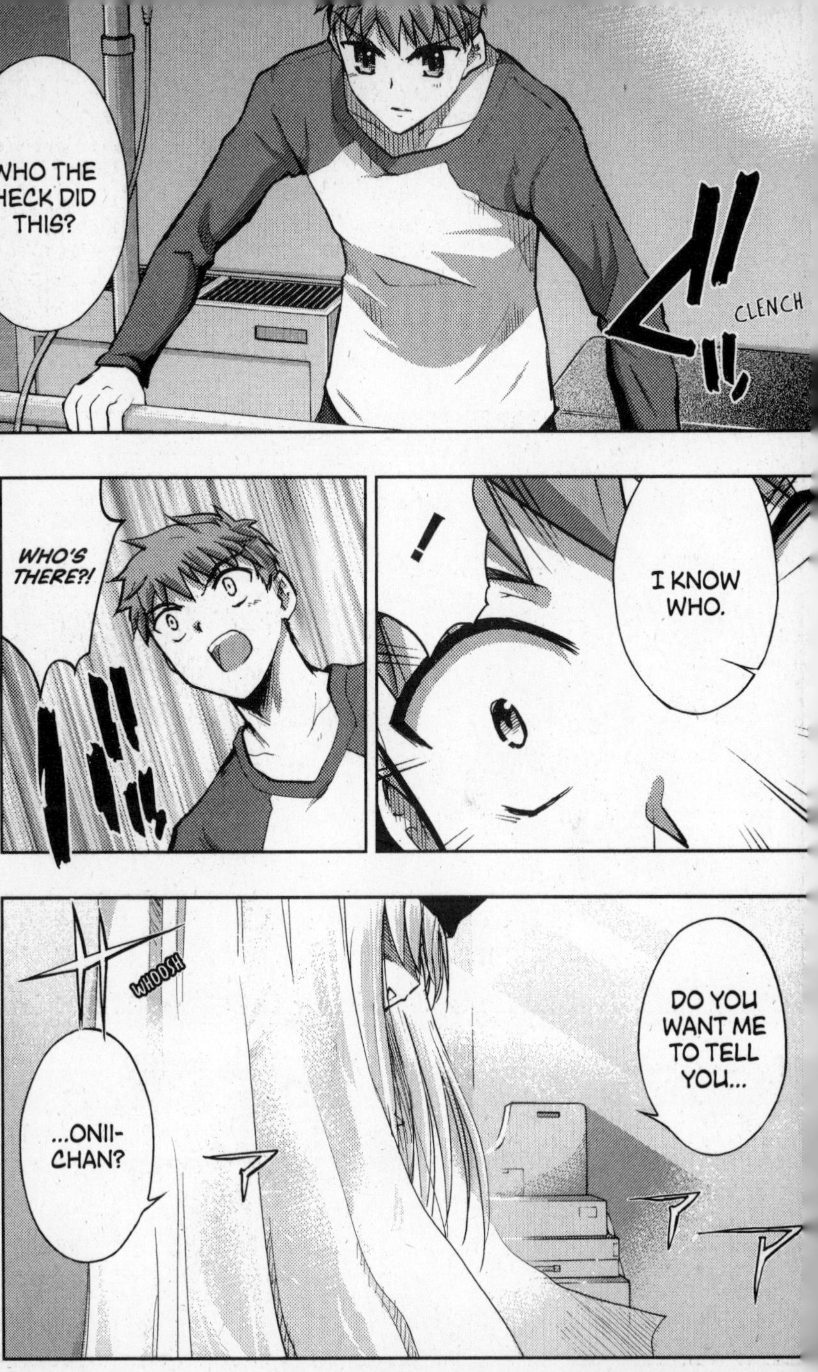
WHO THE HECK DID THIS?
CLENCH
!
I KNOW WHO.
WHO'S THERE?!
DO YOU WANT ME TO TELL YOU...
WHOOSH
...ONII-CHAN?

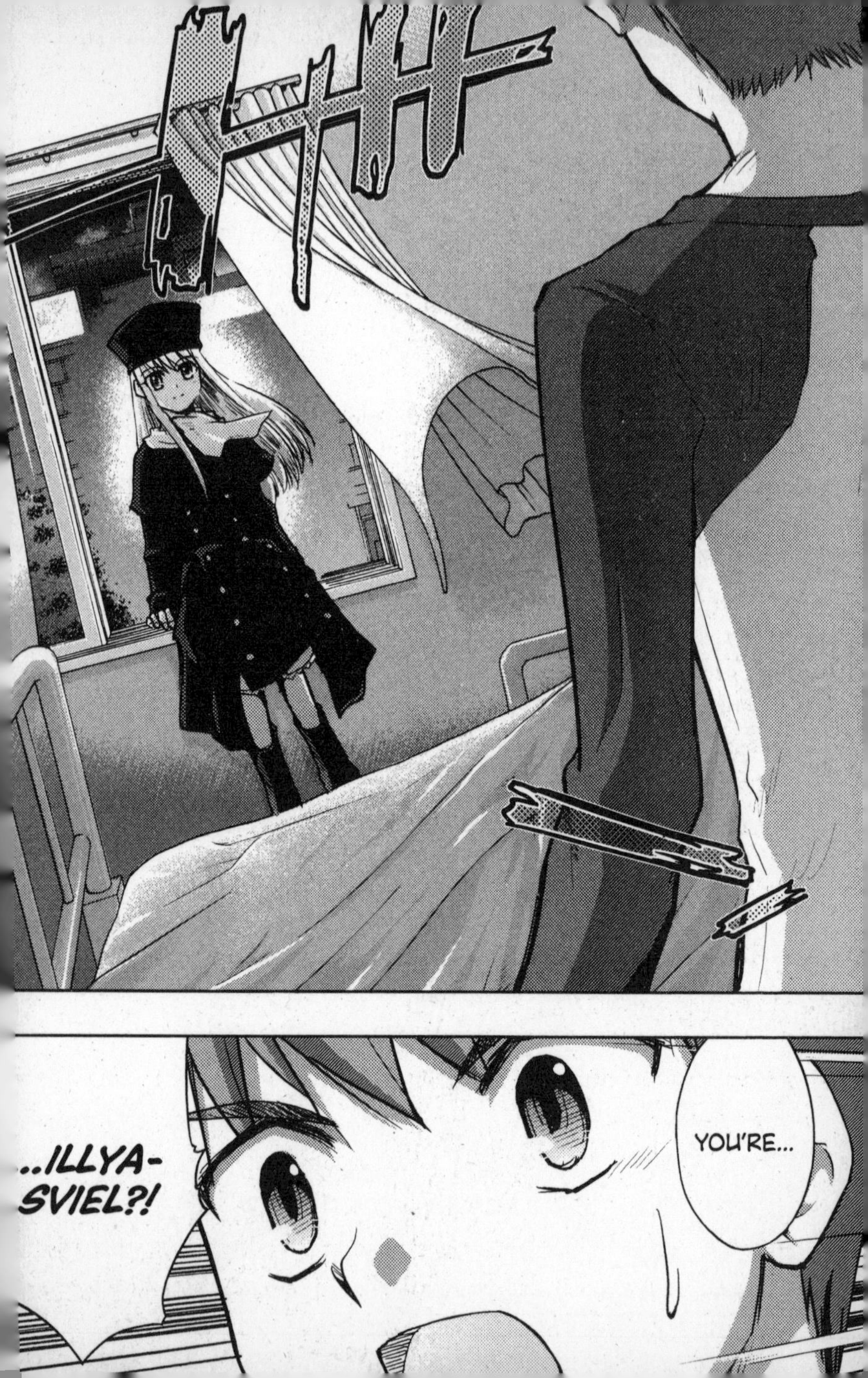
YOU'RE...
...ILLYA-SVIEL?!

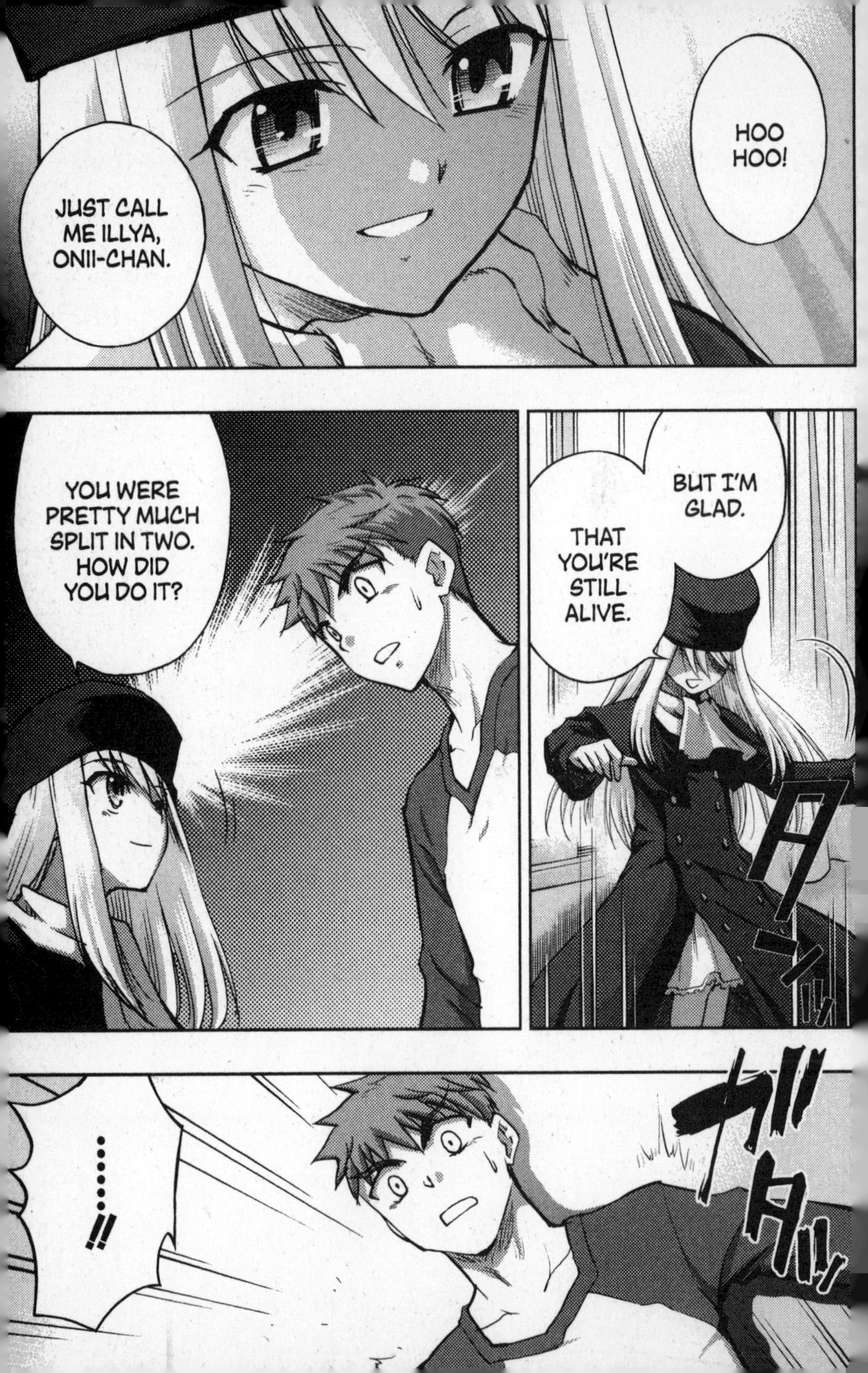
HOO HOO!
JUST CALL ME ILLYA, ONII-CHAN.
BUT I'M GLAD.
THAT YOU'RE STILL ALIVE.
YOU WERE PRETTY MUCH SPLIT IN TWO. HOW DID YOU DO IT?
......!!

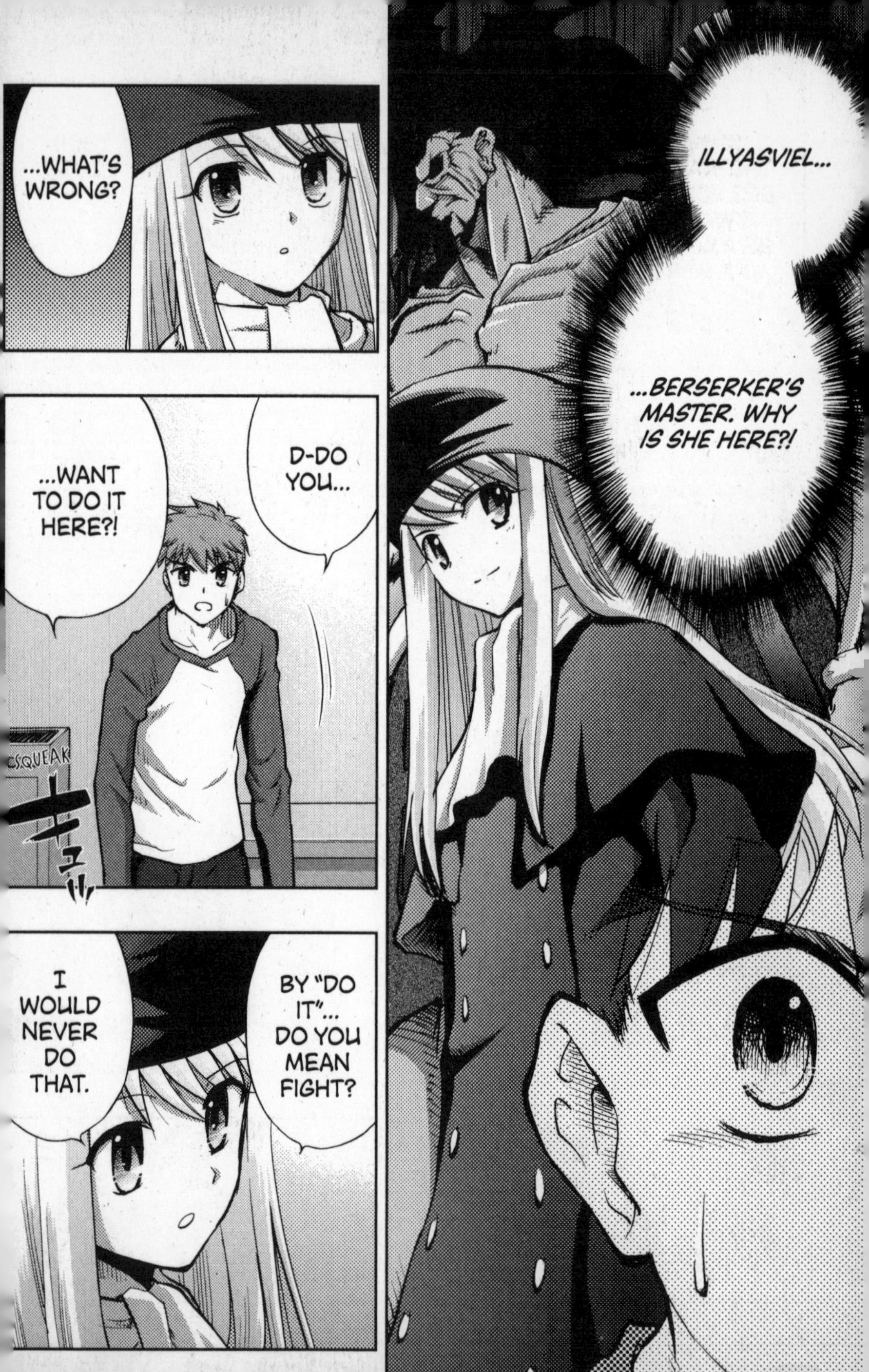
ILLYASVIEL...
...BERSERKER'S MASTER. WHY IS SHE HERE?!
...WHAT'S WRONG?
D-DO YOU...
...WANT TO DO IT HERE?!
SQUEAK
BY "DO IT"... DO YOU MEAN FIGHT?
I WOULD NEVER DO THAT.

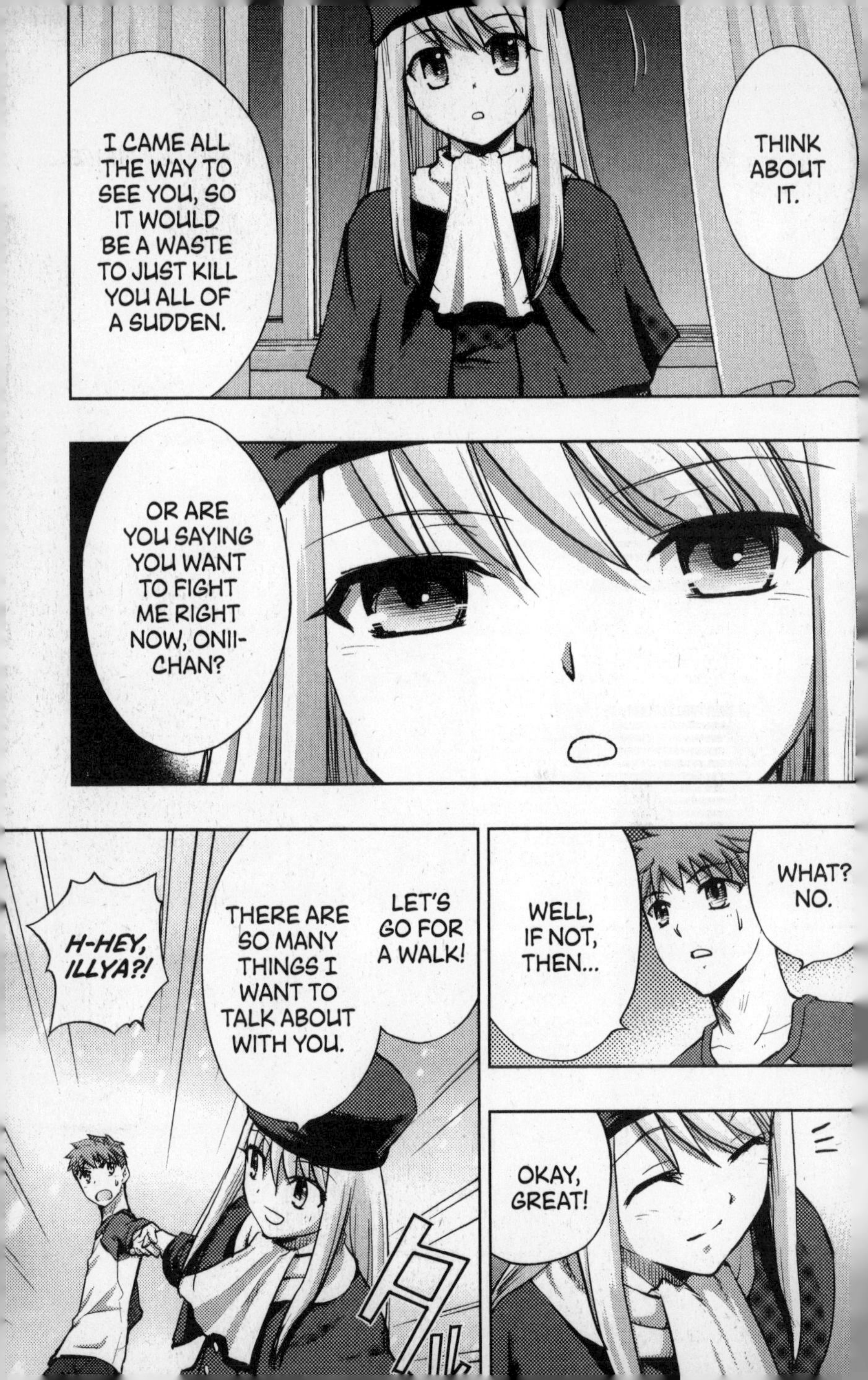
THINK ABOUT IT.
I CAME ALL THE WAY TO SEE YOU, SO IT WOULD BE A WASTE TO JUST KILL YOU ALL OF A SUDDEN.
OR ARE YOU SAYING YOU WANT TO FIGHT ME RIGHT NOW, ONII-CHAN?
WHAT? NO.
WELL, IF NOT, THEN...
OKAY, GREAT!
LET'S GO FOR A WALK!
THERE ARE SO MANY THINGS I WANT TO TALK ABOUT WITH YOU.
H-HEY, ILLYA?!

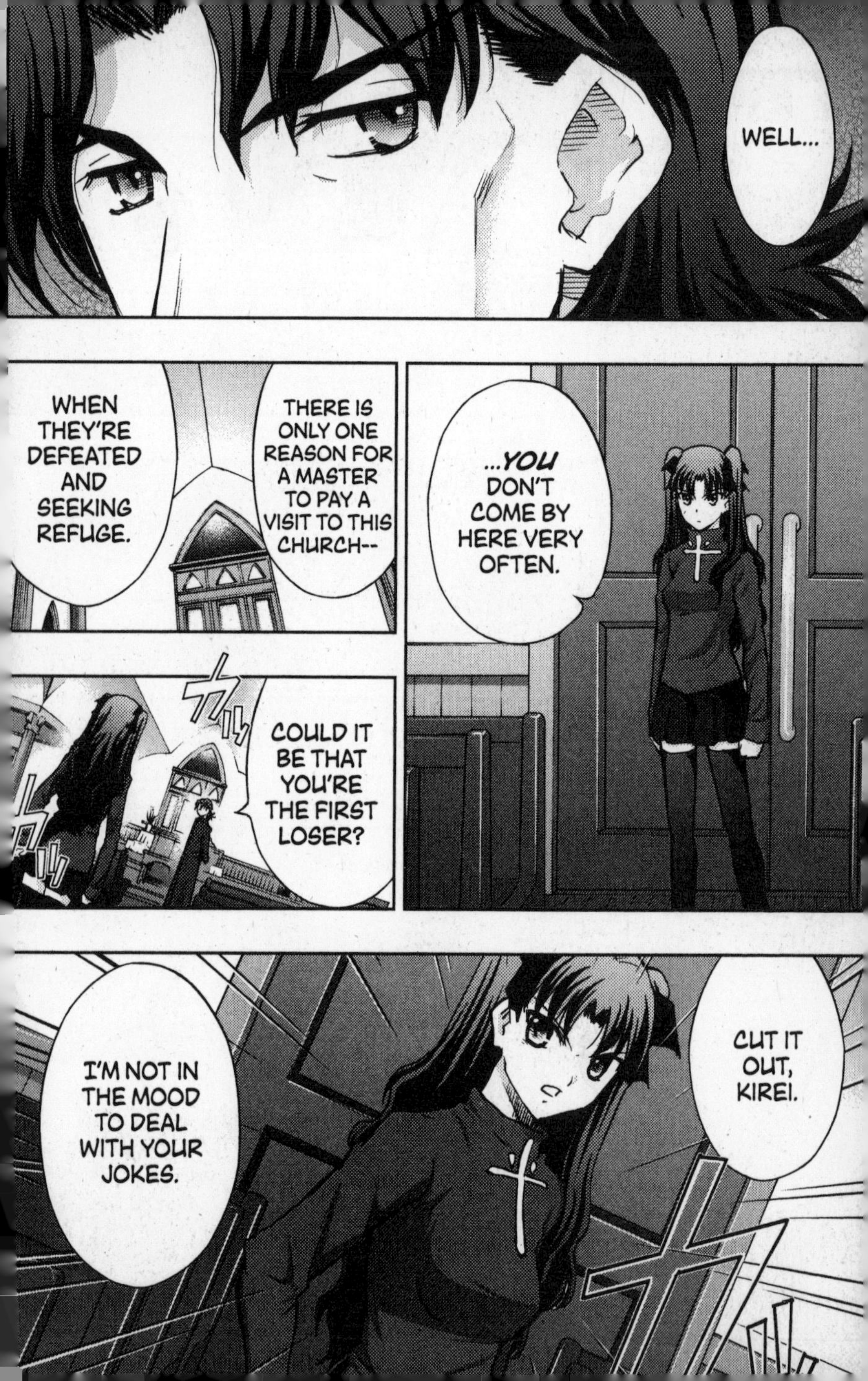
WELL...
...*YOU* DON'T COME BY HERE VERY OFTEN.
THERE IS ONLY ONE REASON FOR A MASTER TO PAY A VISIT TO THIS CHURCH--
WHEN THEY'RE DEFEATED AND SEEKING REFUGE.
COULD IT BE THAT YOU'RE THE FIRST LOSER?
CUT IT OUT, KIREI.
I'M NOT IN THE MOOD TO DEAL WITH YOUR JOKES.

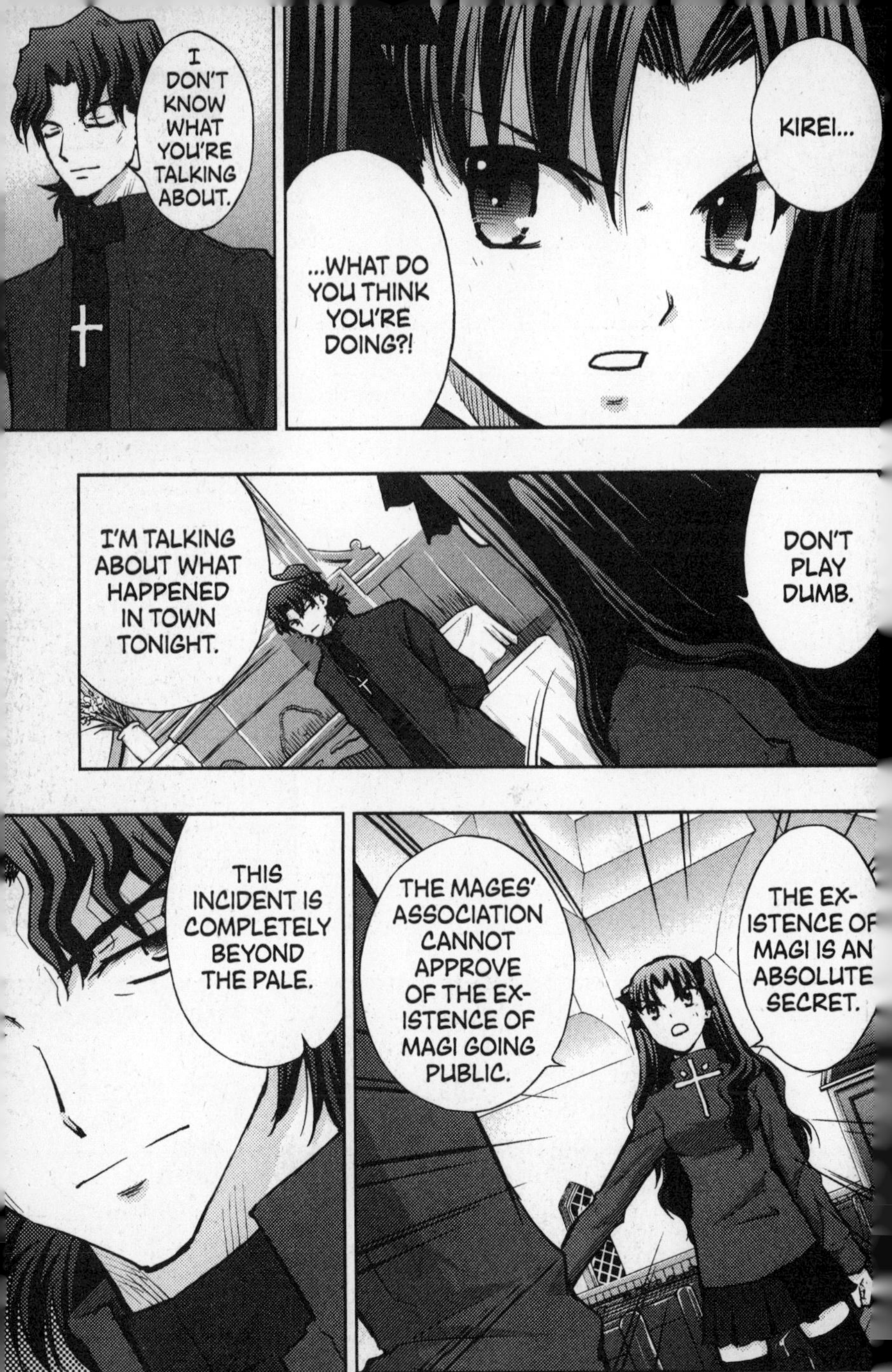
KIREI...
...WHAT DO YOU THINK YOU'RE DOING?!
I DON'T KNOW WHAT YOU'RE TALKING ABOUT.
DON'T PLAY DUMB.
I'M TALKING ABOUT WHAT HAPPENED IN TOWN TONIGHT.
THE EXISTENCE OF MAGI IS AN ABSOLUTE SECRET.
THE MAGES' ASSOCIATION CANNOT APPROVE OF THE EXISTENCE OF MAGI GOING PUBLIC.
THIS INCIDENT IS COMPLETELY BEYOND THE PALE.

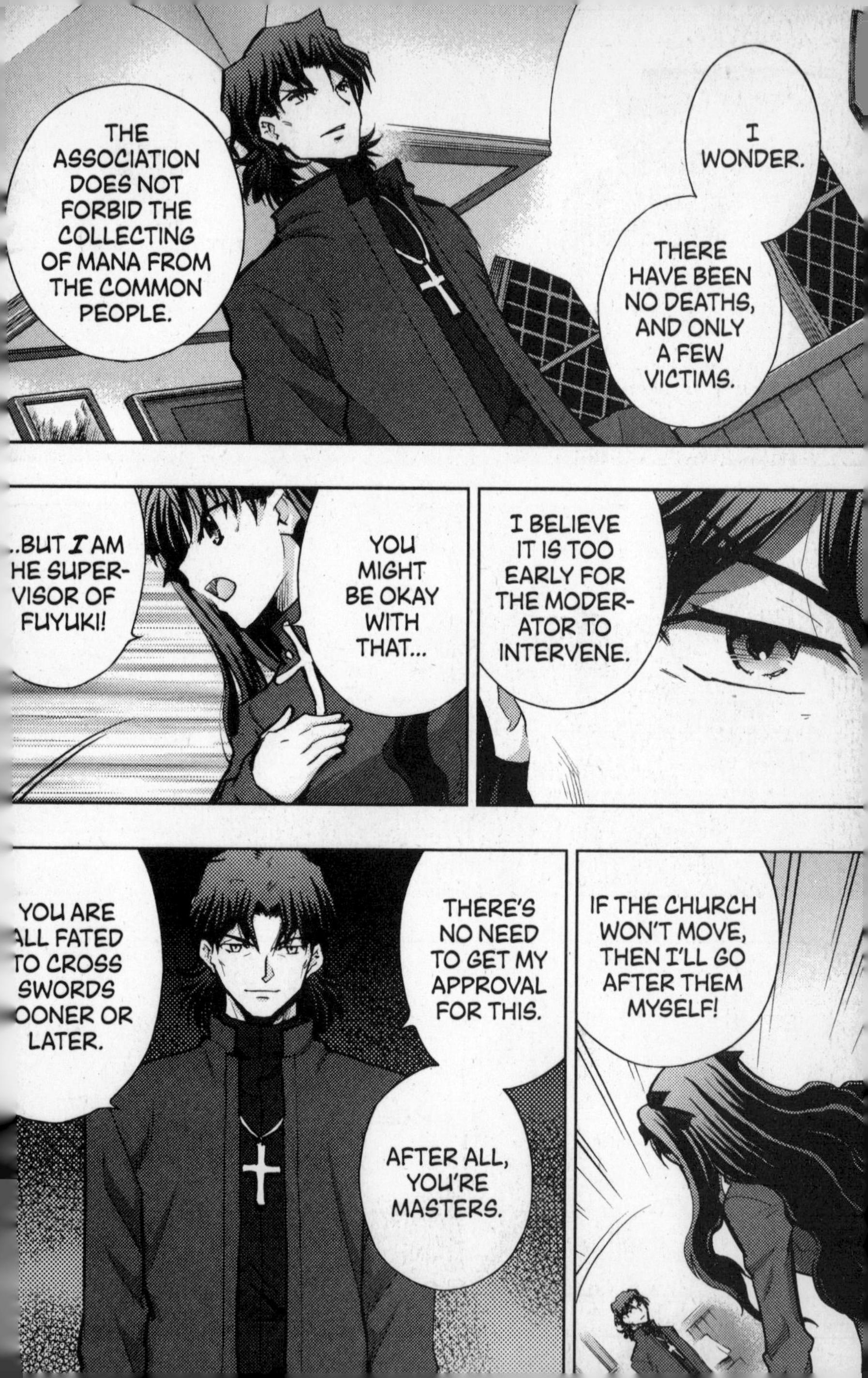
I WONDER.
THERE HAVE BEEN NO DEATHS, AND ONLY A FEW VICTIMS.
THE ASSOCIATION DOES NOT FORBID THE COLLECTING OF MANA FROM THE COMMON PEOPLE.
I BELIEVE IT IS TOO EARLY FOR THE MODER-ATOR TO INTERVENE.
YOU MIGHT BE OKAY WITH THAT...
..BUT I AM HE SUPER-VISOR OF FUYUKI!
IF THE CHURCH WON'T MOVE, THEN I'LL GO AFTER THEM MYSELF!
THERE'S NO NEED TO GET MY APPROVAL FOR THIS.
AFTER ALL, YOU'RE MASTERS.
YOU ARE LL FATED TO CROSS SWORDS OONER OR LATER.

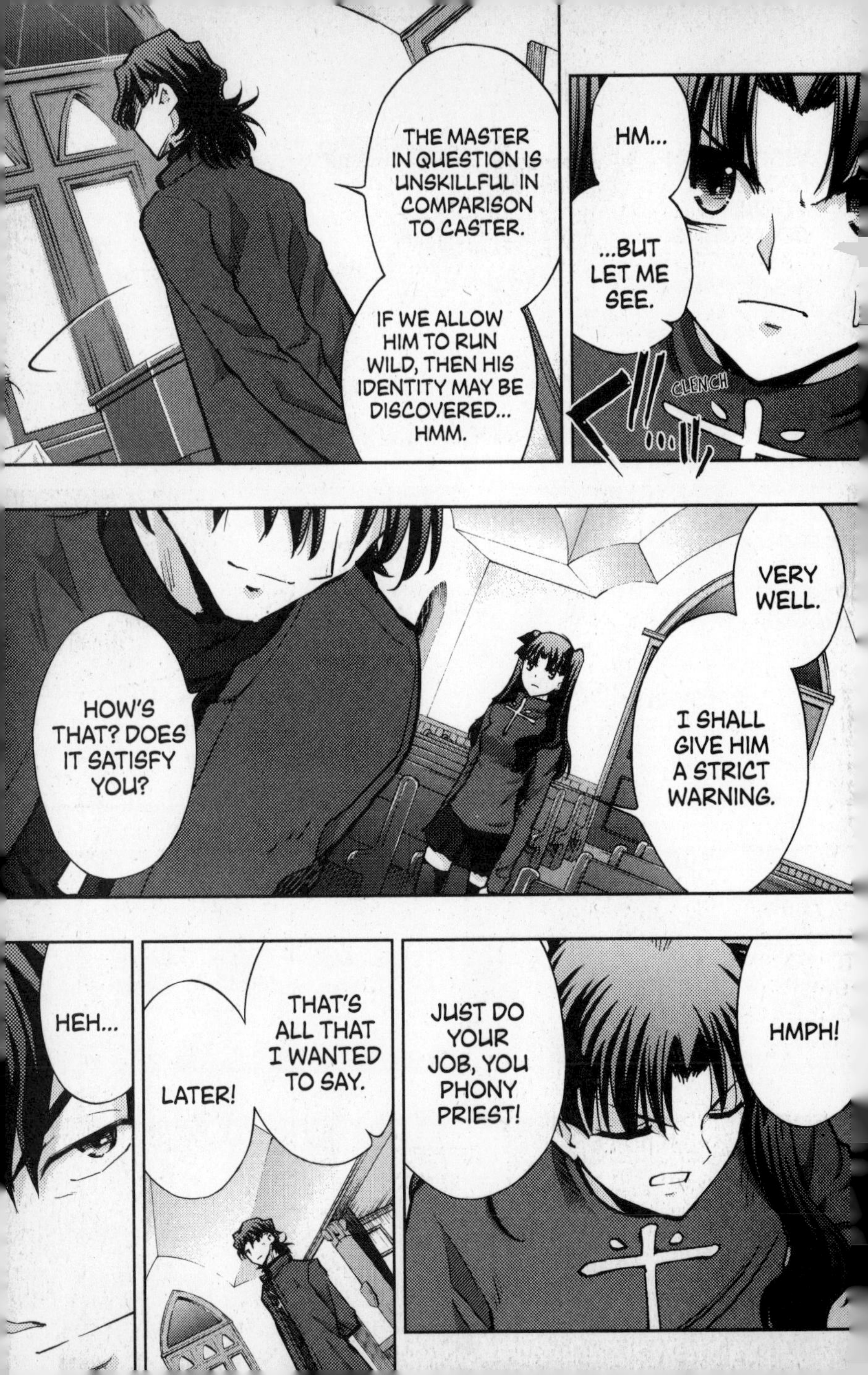
HM...
...BUT LET ME SEE.
CLENCH
THE MASTER IN QUESTION IS UNSKILLFUL IN COMPARISON TO CASTER.
IF WE ALLOW HIM TO RUN WILD, THEN HIS IDENTITY MAY BE DISCOVERED... HMM.
VERY WELL.
I SHALL GIVE HIM A STRICT WARNING.
HOW'S THAT? DOES IT SATISFY YOU?
HMPH!
JUST DO YOUR JOB, YOU PHONY PRIEST!
THAT'S ALL THAT I WANTED TO SAY.
LATER!
HEH...

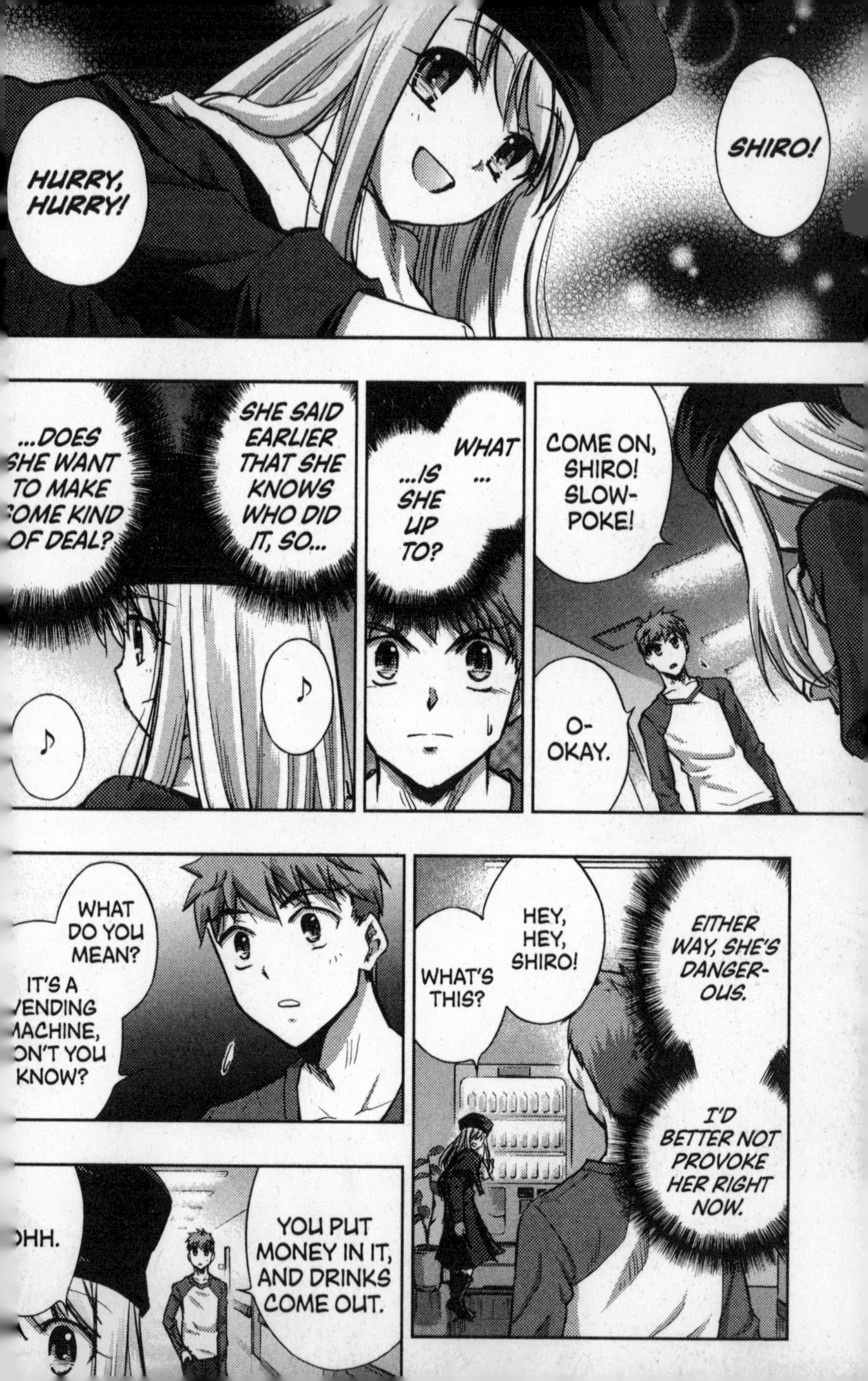
SHIRO!
HURRY, HURRY!
COME ON, SHIRO! SLOW-POKE!
O-OKAY.
WHAT ...
...IS SHE UP TO?
SHE SAID EARLIER THAT SHE KNOWS WHO DID IT, SO...
...DOES SHE WANT TO MAKE SOME KIND OF DEAL?
♪
♪
EITHER WAY, SHE'S DANGER-OUS.
HEY, HEY, SHIRO!
WHAT'S THIS?
I'D BETTER NOT PROVOKE HER RIGHT NOW.
WHAT DO YOU MEAN?
IT'S A ENDING ACHINE, ON'T YOU KNOW?
YOU PUT MONEY IN IT, AND DRINKS COME OUT.
HH.

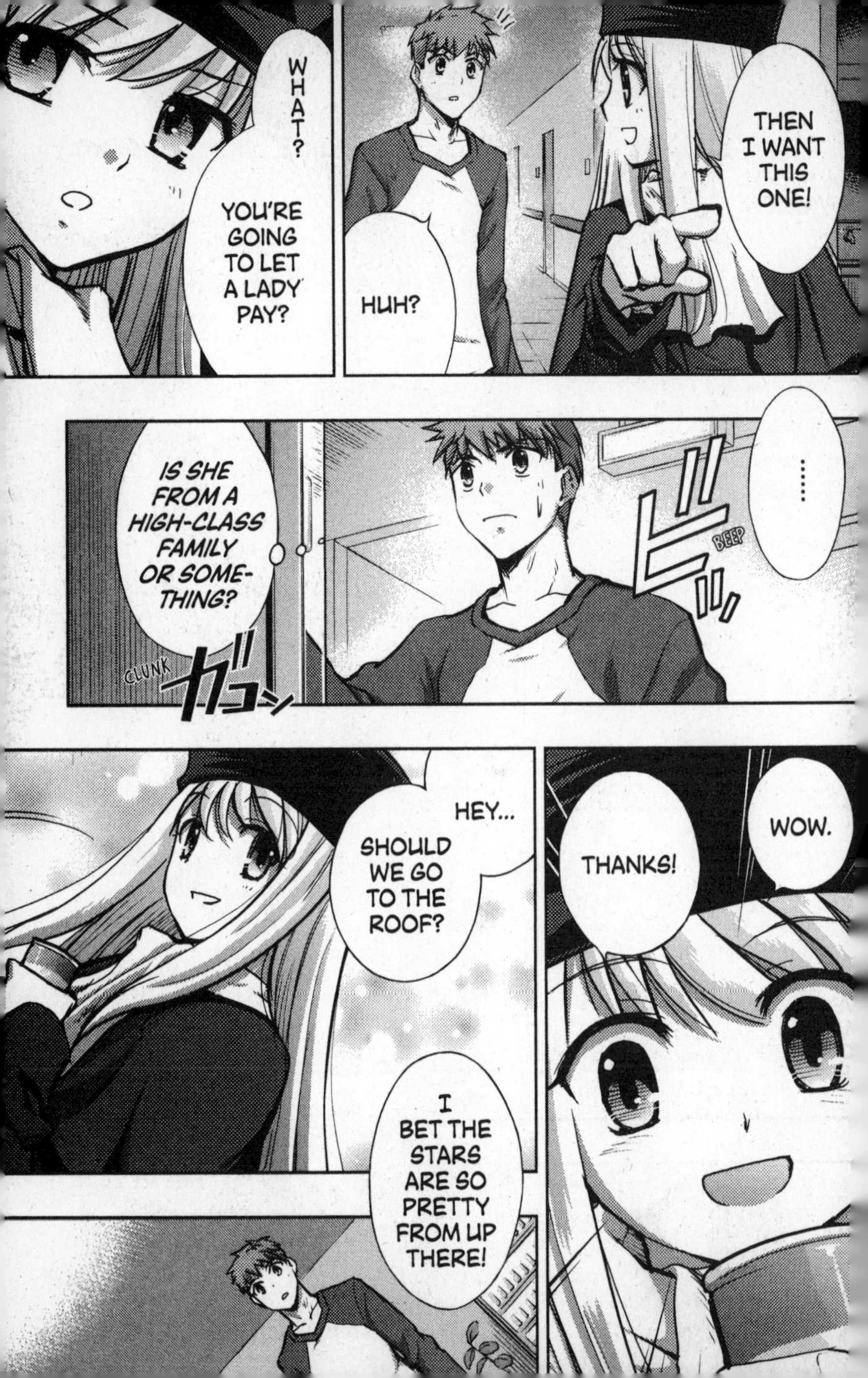
THEN I WANT THIS ONE!
HUH?
WHAT?
YOU'RE GOING TO LET A LADY PAY?
......
BEEP
IS SHE FROM A HIGH-CLASS FAMILY OR SOME-THING?
CLUNK
WOW.
THANKS!
HEY...
SHOULD WE GO TO THE ROOF?
I BET THE STARS ARE SO PRETTY FROM UP THERE!

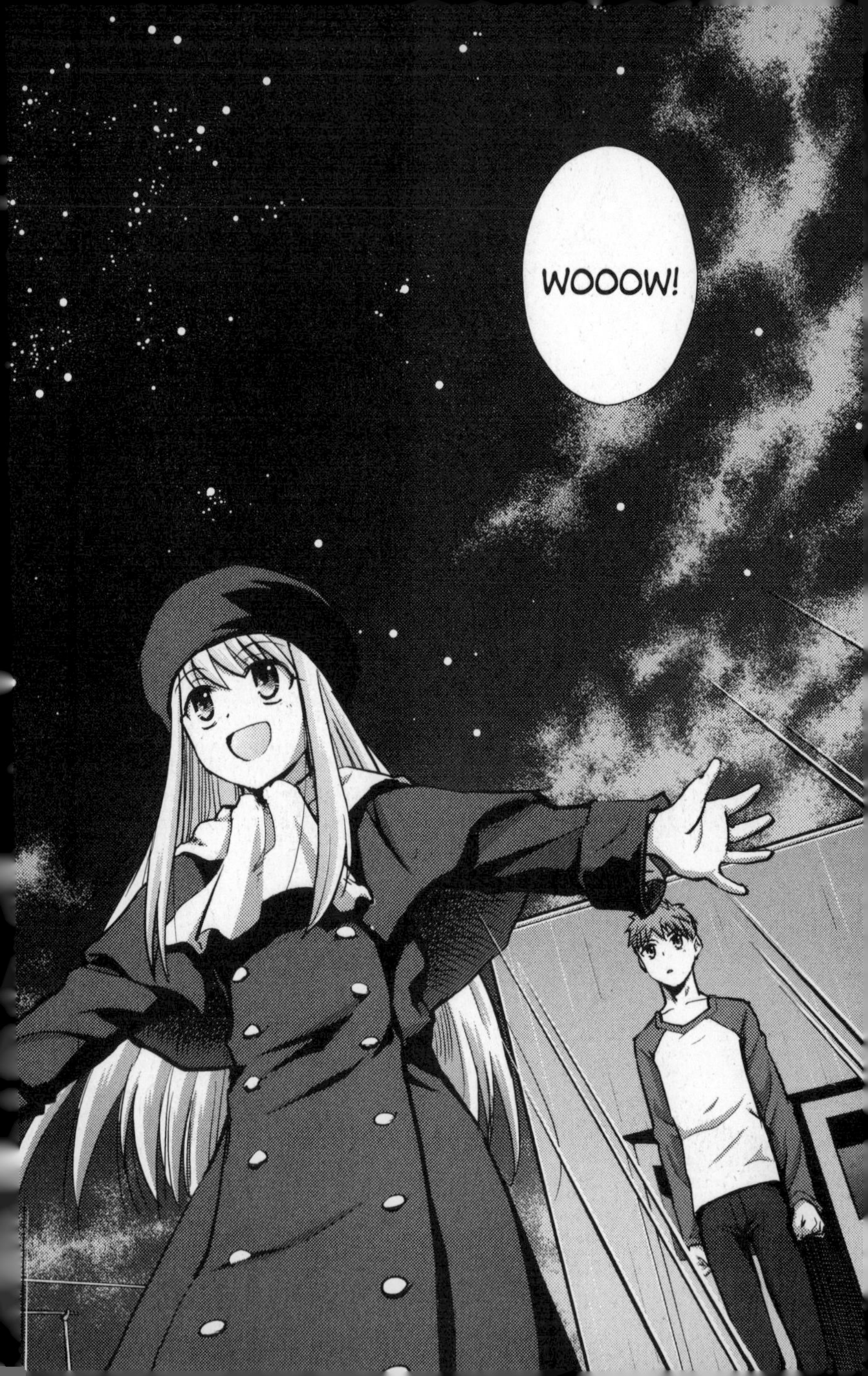
WOOOW!

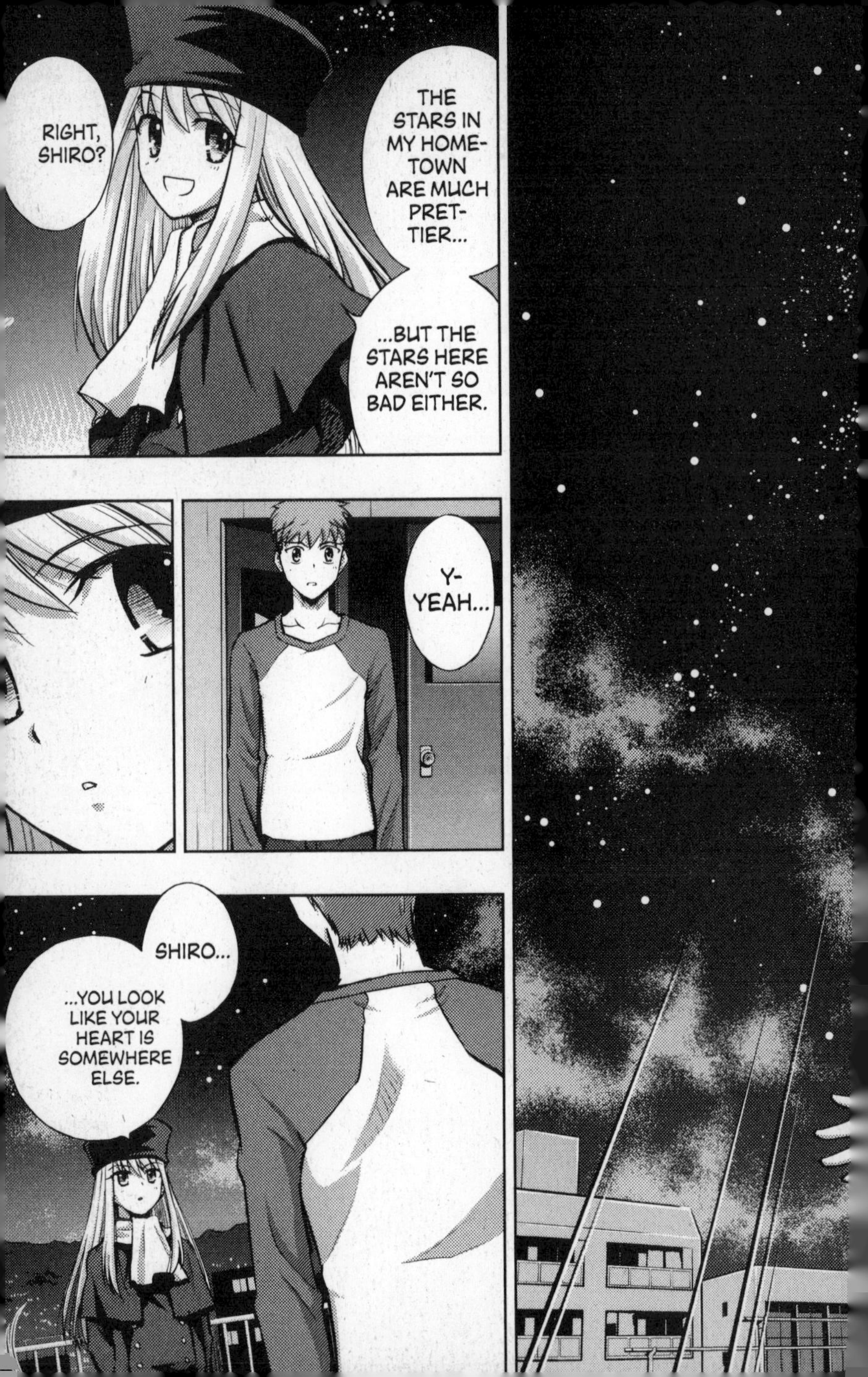
THE STARS IN MY HOME-TOWN ARE MUCH PRET-TIER...
...BUT THE STARS HERE AREN'T SO BAD EITHER.
RIGHT, SHIRO?
Y-YEAH...
SHIRO...
...YOU LOOK LIKE YOUR HEART IS SOMEWHERE ELSE.

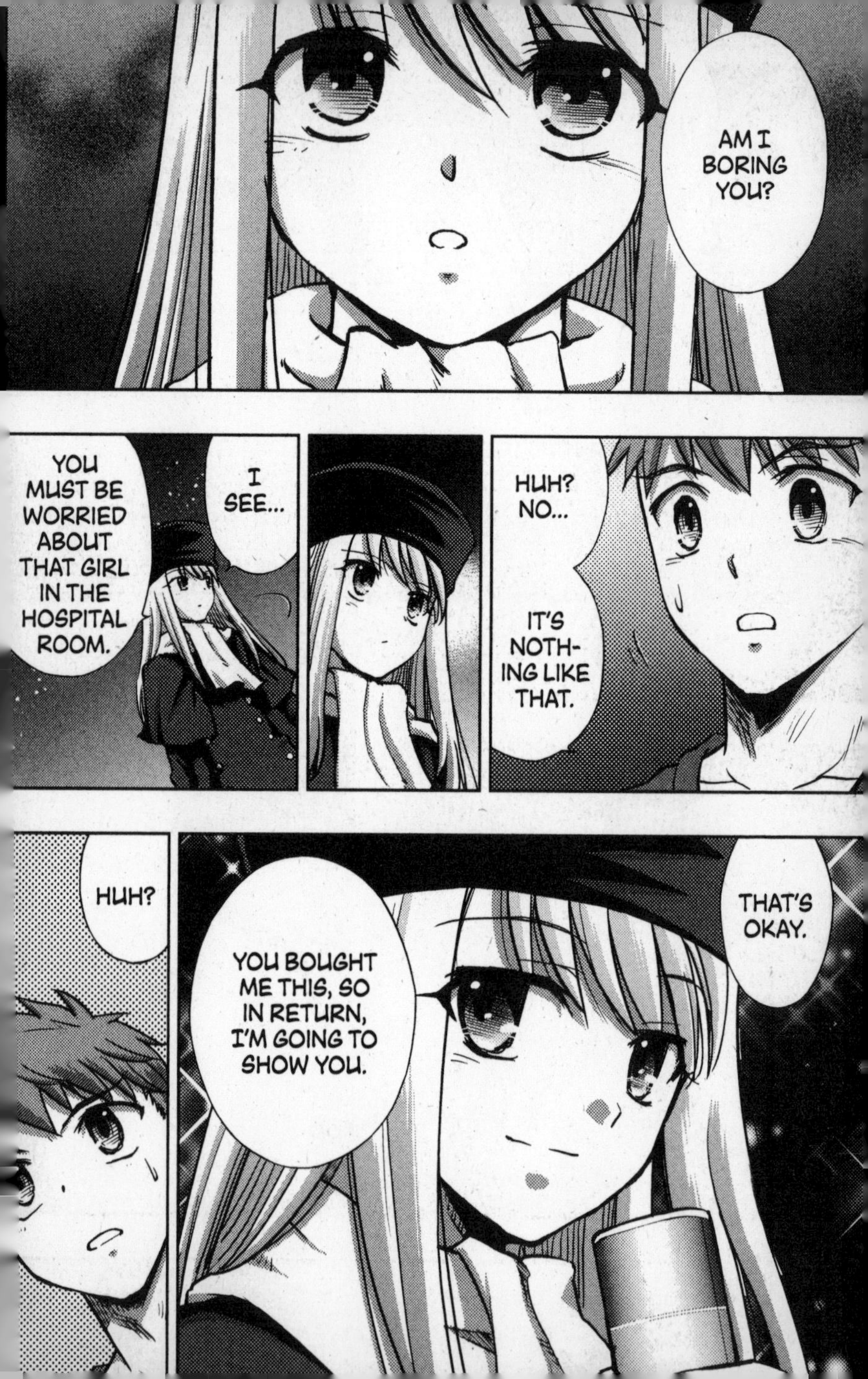
AM I BORING YOU?
HUH? NO...
IT'S NOTHING LIKE THAT.
I SEE...
YOU MUST BE WORRIED ABOUT THAT GIRL IN THE HOSPITAL ROOM.
THAT'S OKAY.
YOU BOUGHT ME THIS, SO IN RETURN, I'M GOING TO SHOW YOU.
HUH?

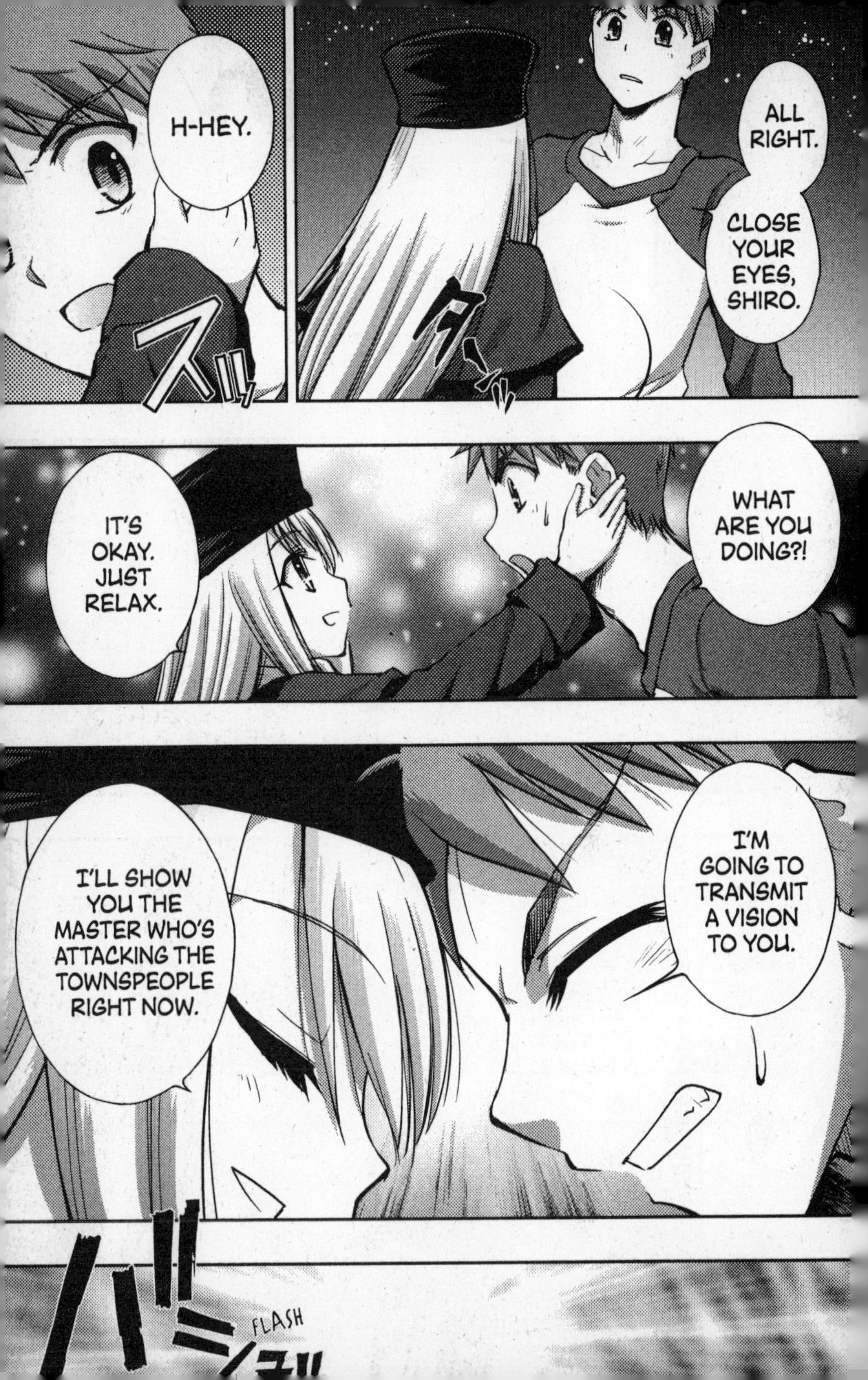
ALL RIGHT.
CLOSE YOUR EYES, SHIRO.
H-HEY.
WHAT ARE YOU DOING?!
IT'S OKAY. JUST RELAX.
I'M GOING TO TRANSMIT A VISION TO YOU.
I'LL SHOW YOU THE MASTER WHO'S ATTACKING THE TOWNSPEOPLE RIGHT NOW.
FLASH

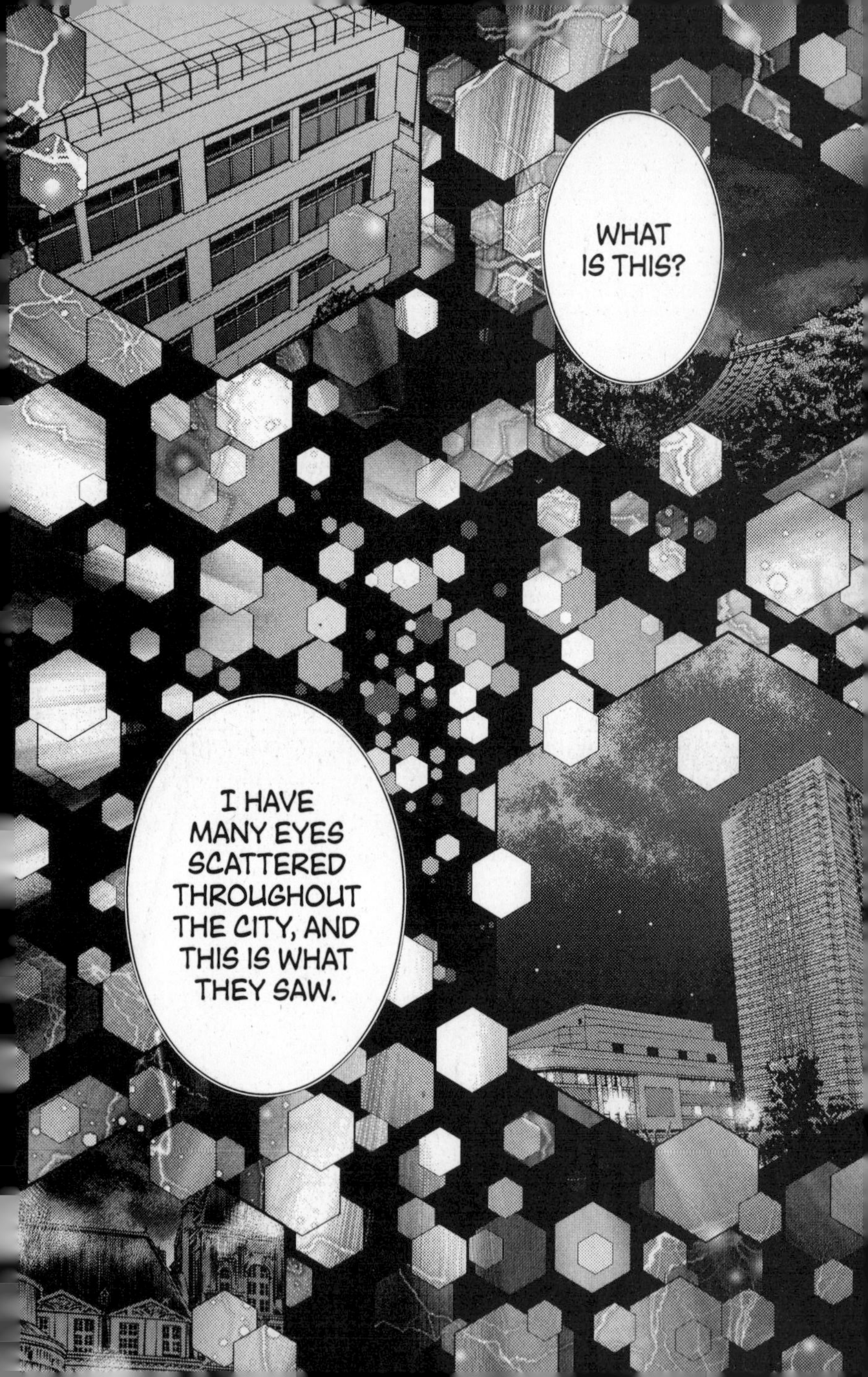
WHAT IS THIS?
I HAVE MANY EYES SCATTERED THROUGHOUT THE CITY, AND THIS IS WHAT THEY SAW.

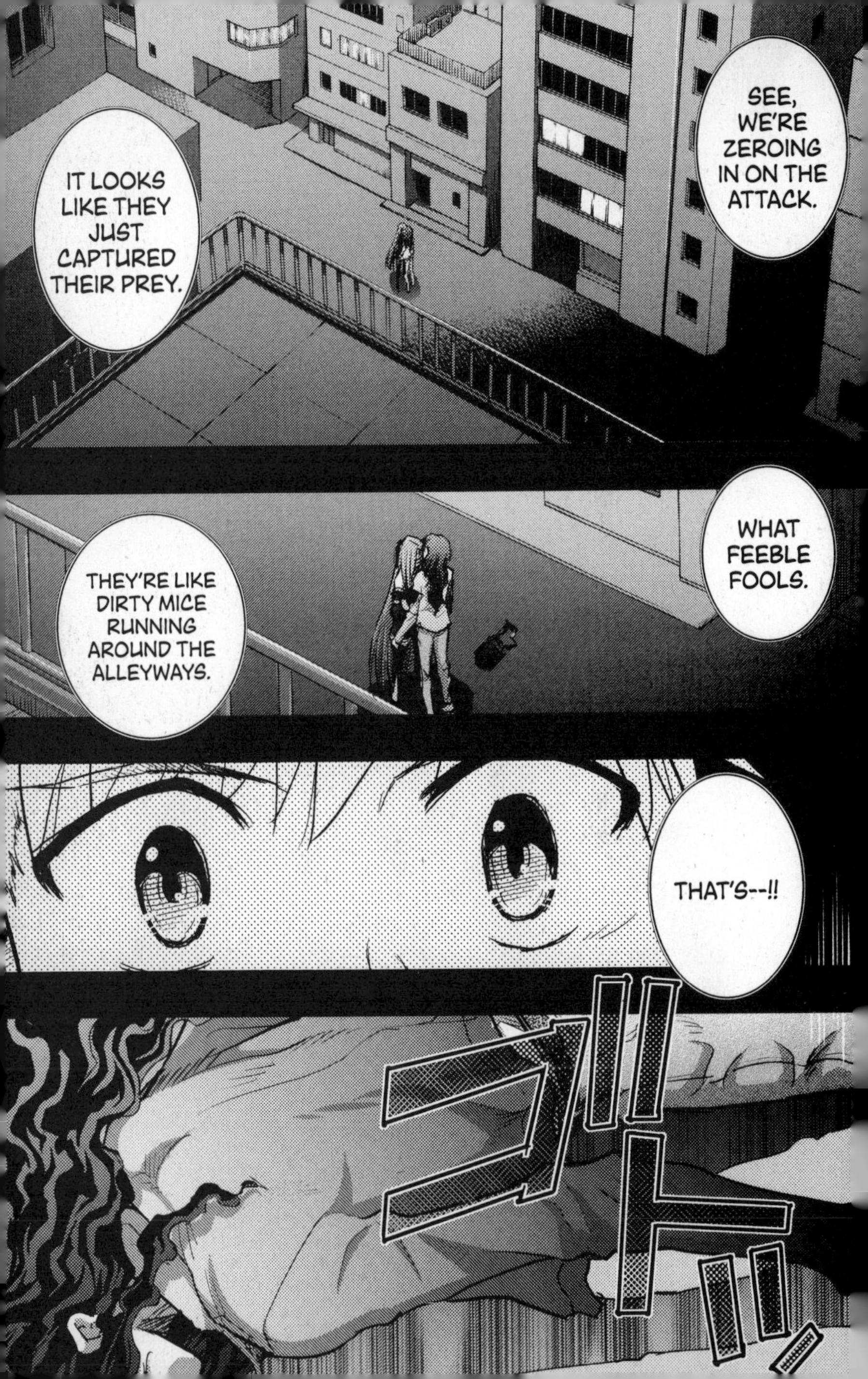
SEE, WE'RE ZEROING IN ON THE ATTACK.
IT LOOKS LIKE THEY JUST CAPTURED THEIR PREY.
WHAT FEEBLE FOOLS.
THEY'RE LIKE DIRTY MICE RUNNING AROUND THE ALLEYWAYS.
THAT'S--!!
ゴトッ

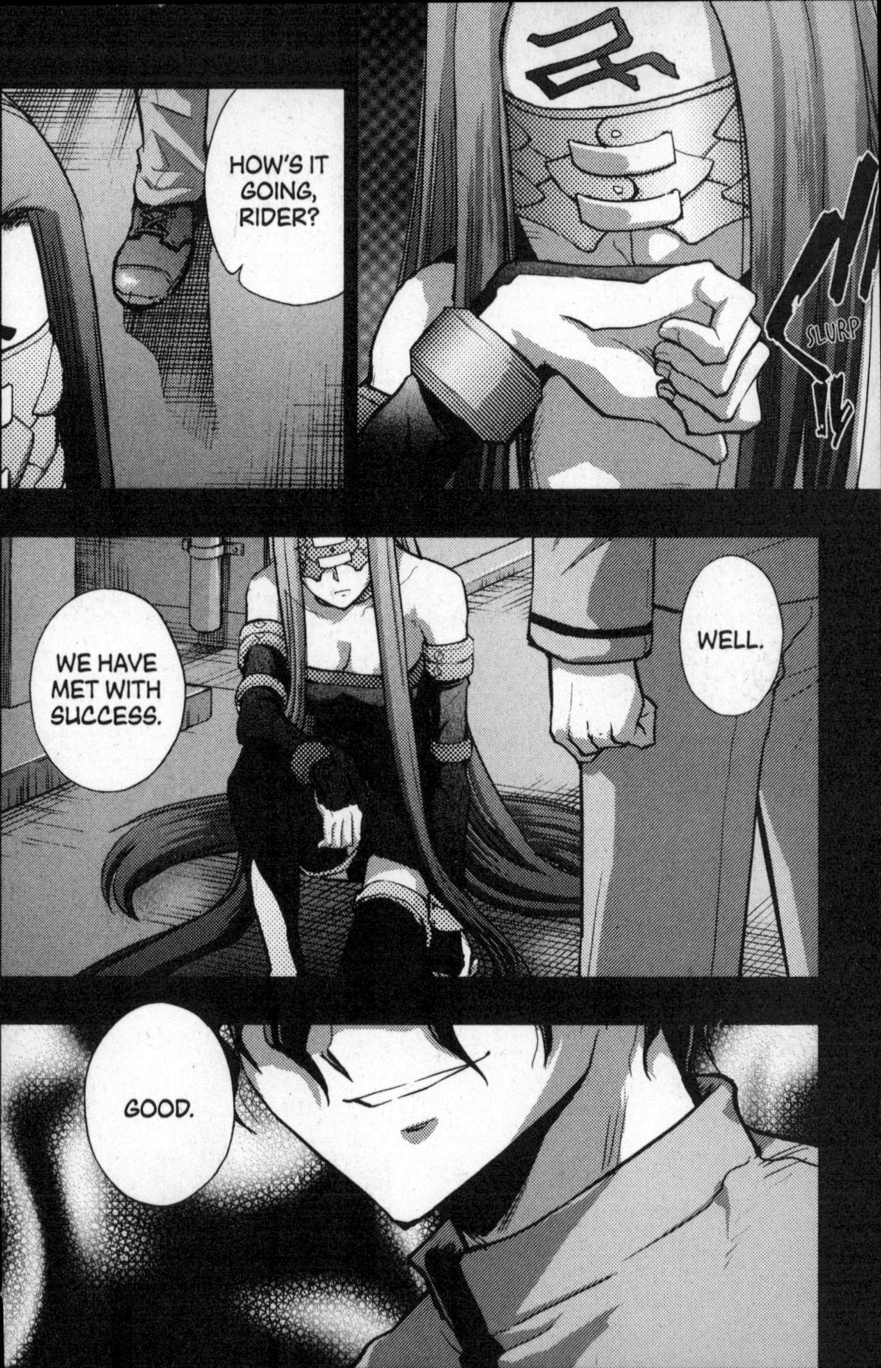
SLURP
HOW'S IT GOING, RIDER?
WELL.
WE HAVE MET WITH SUCCESS.
GOOD.

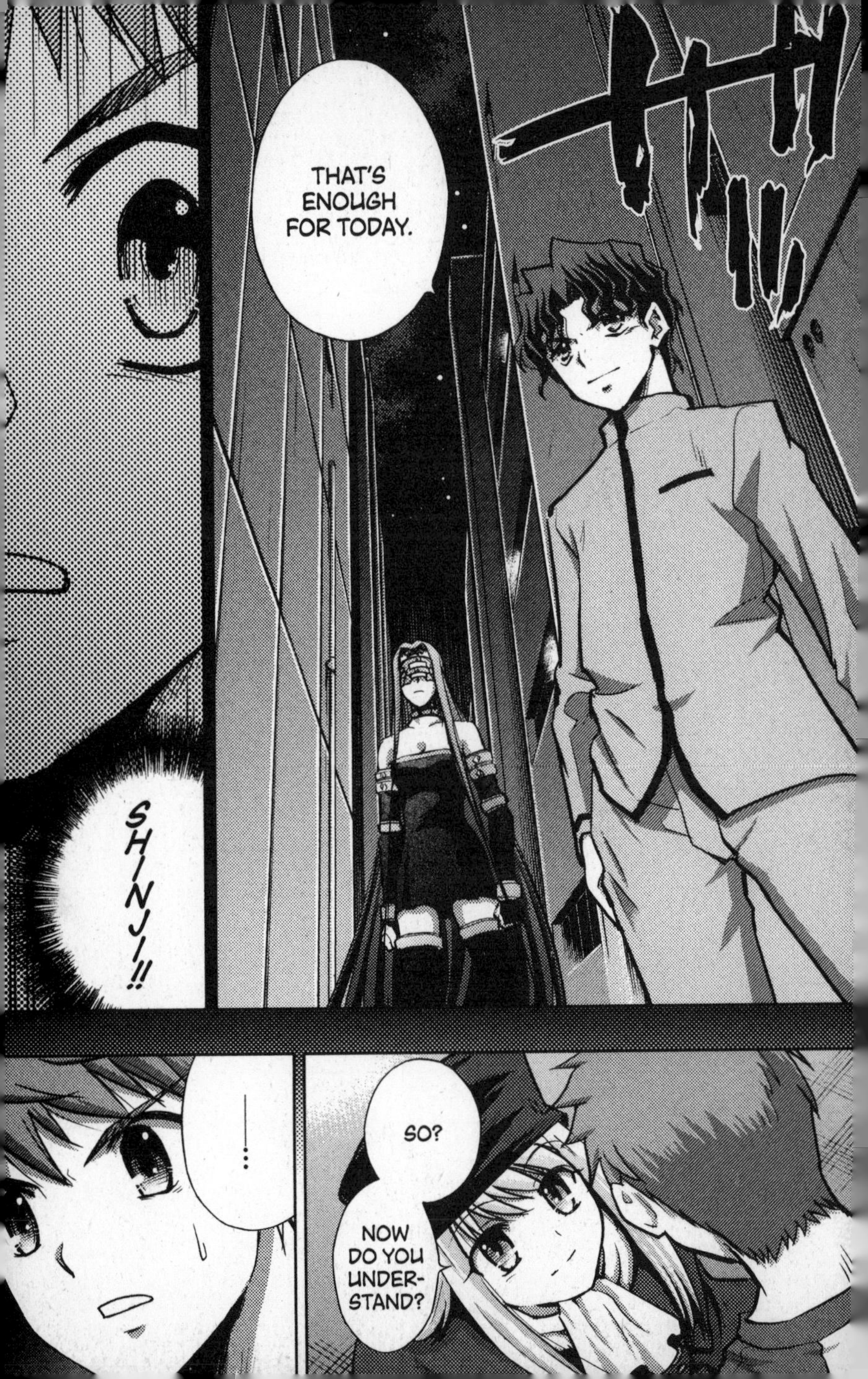
THAT'S ENOUGH FOR TODAY.
SHINJI!!
SO?
NOW DO YOU UNDER-STAND?
—...!

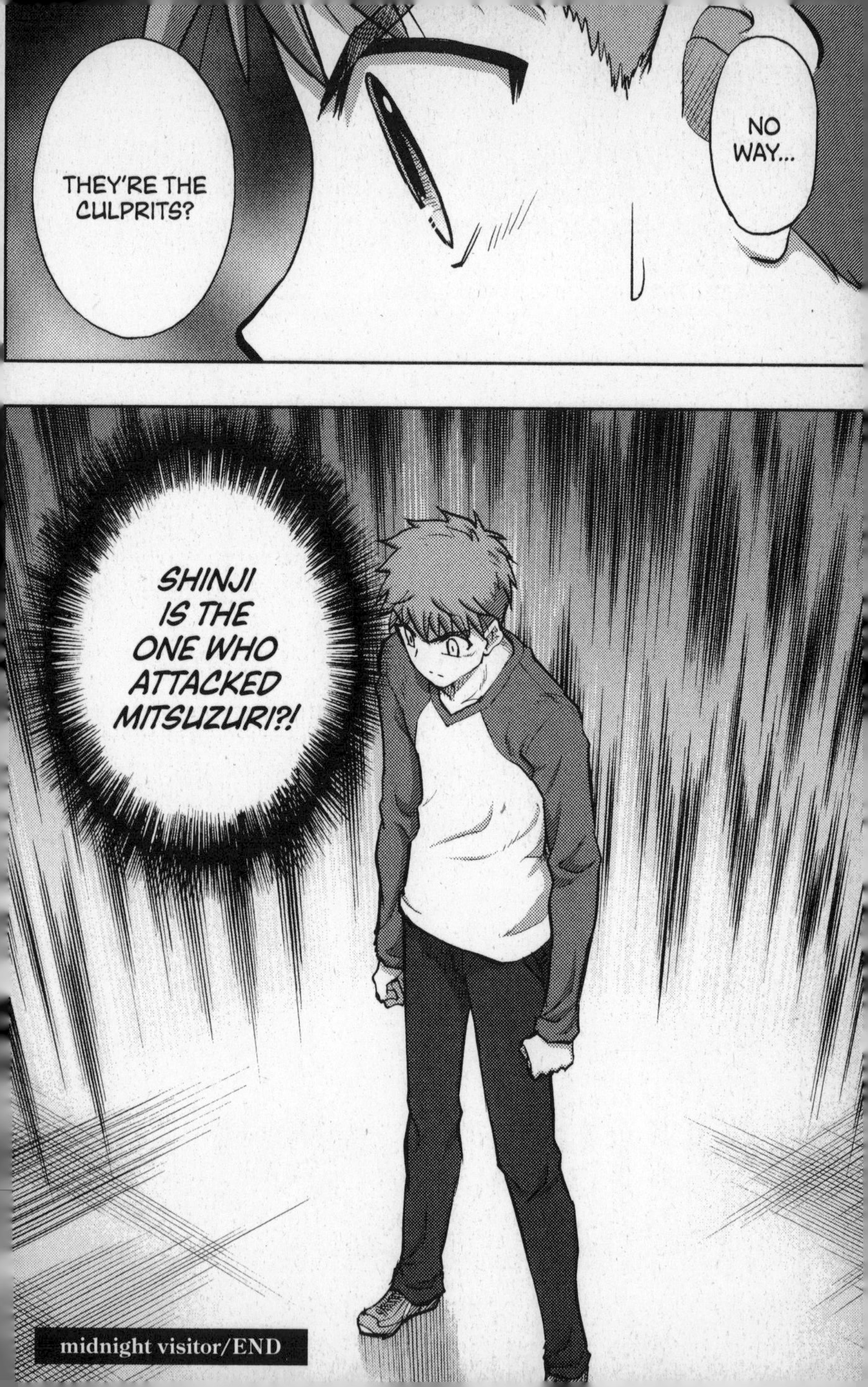
NO WAY...
THEY'RE THE CULPRITS?
SHINJI IS THE ONE WHO ATTACKED MITSUZURI?!
midnight visitor/END

Fate
stay night

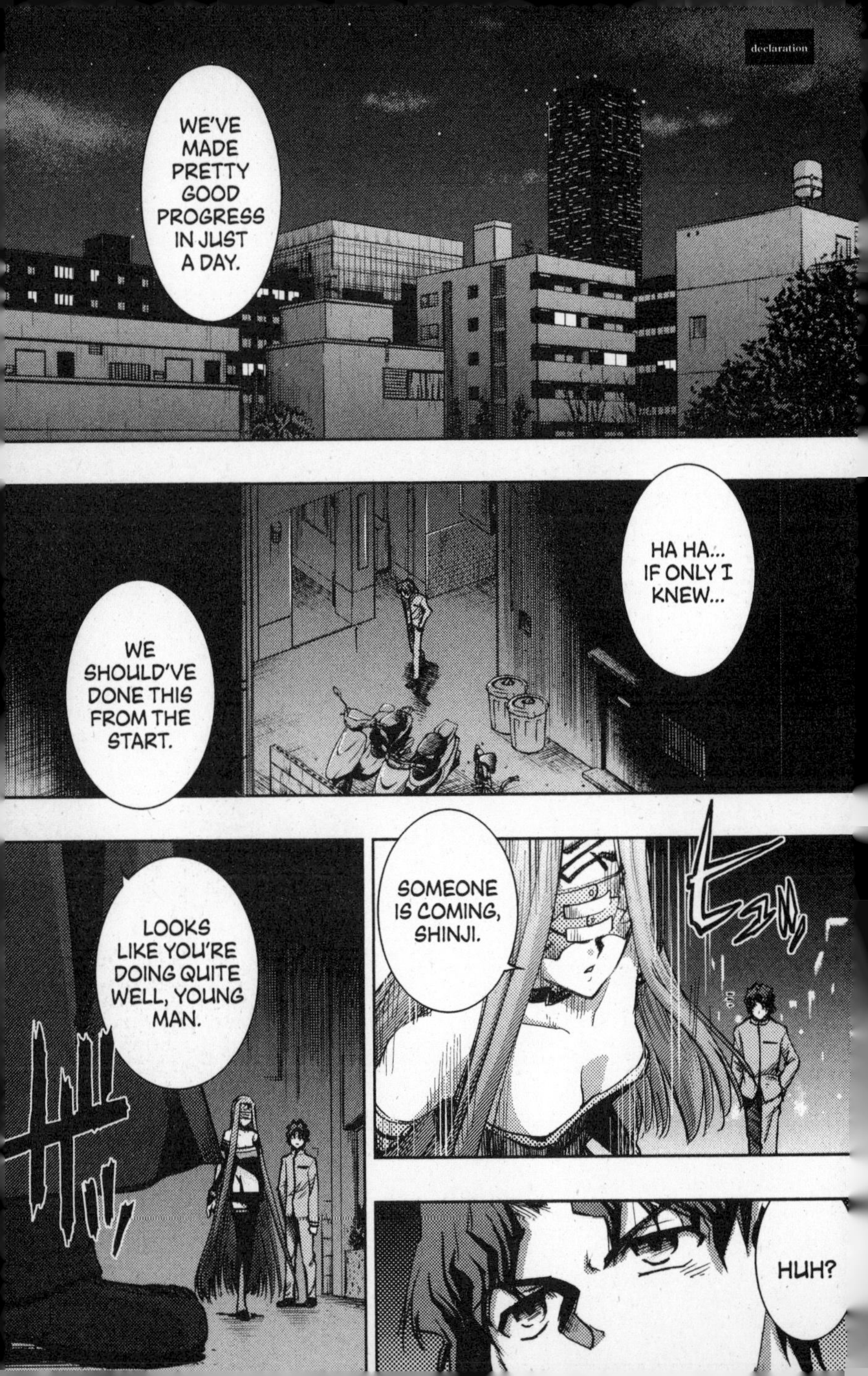
WE'VE MADE PRETTY GOOD PROGRESS IN JUST A DAY.
HA HA... IF ONLY I KNEW...
WE SHOULD'VE DONE THIS FROM THE START.
SOMEONE IS COMING, SHINJI.
HUH?
LOOKS LIKE YOU'RE DOING QUITE WELL, YOUNG MAN.

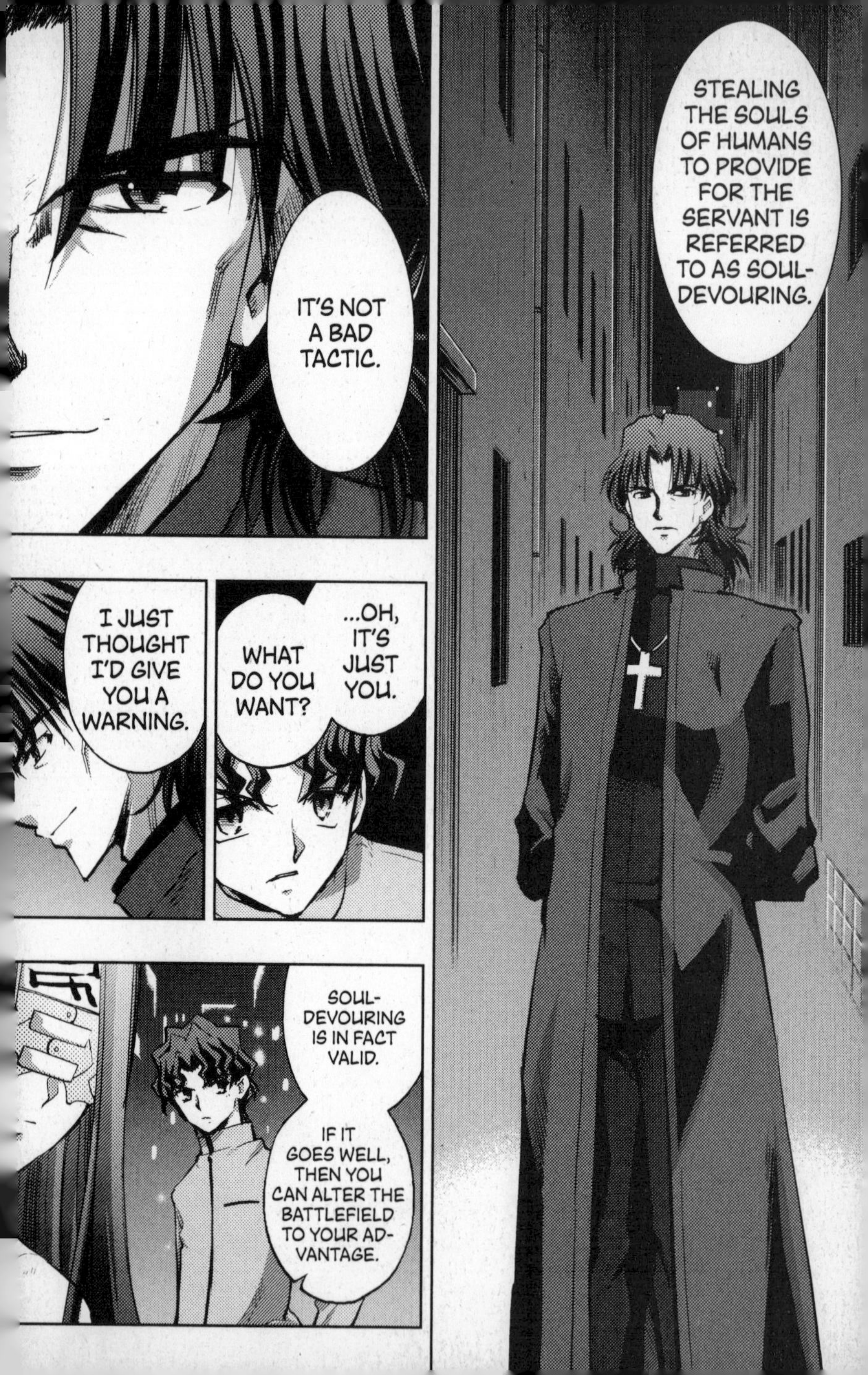
STEALING THE SOULS OF HUMANS TO PROVIDE FOR THE SERVANT IS REFERRED TO AS SOUL-DEVOURING.
IT'S NOT A BAD TACTIC.
...OH, IT'S JUST YOU.
WHAT DO YOU WANT?
I JUST THOUGHT I'D GIVE YOU A WARNING.
SOUL-DEVOURING IS IN FACT VALID.
IF IT GOES WELL, THEN YOU CAN ALTER THE BATTLEFIELD TO YOUR AD-VANTAGE.

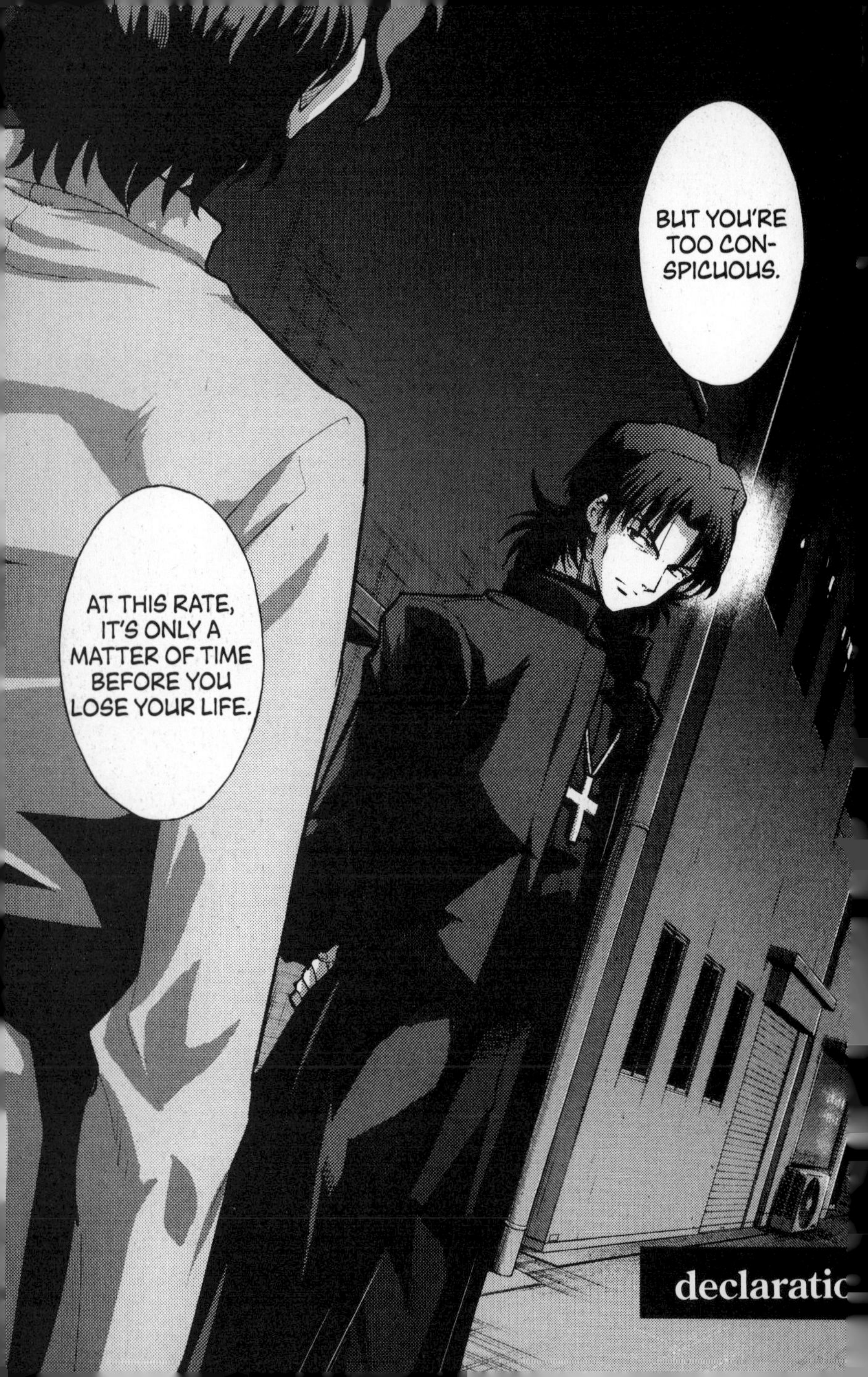
BUT YOU'RE TOO CON-SPICUOUS.
AT THIS RATE, IT'S ONLY A MATTER OF TIME BEFORE YOU LOSE YOUR LIFE.
declaratic

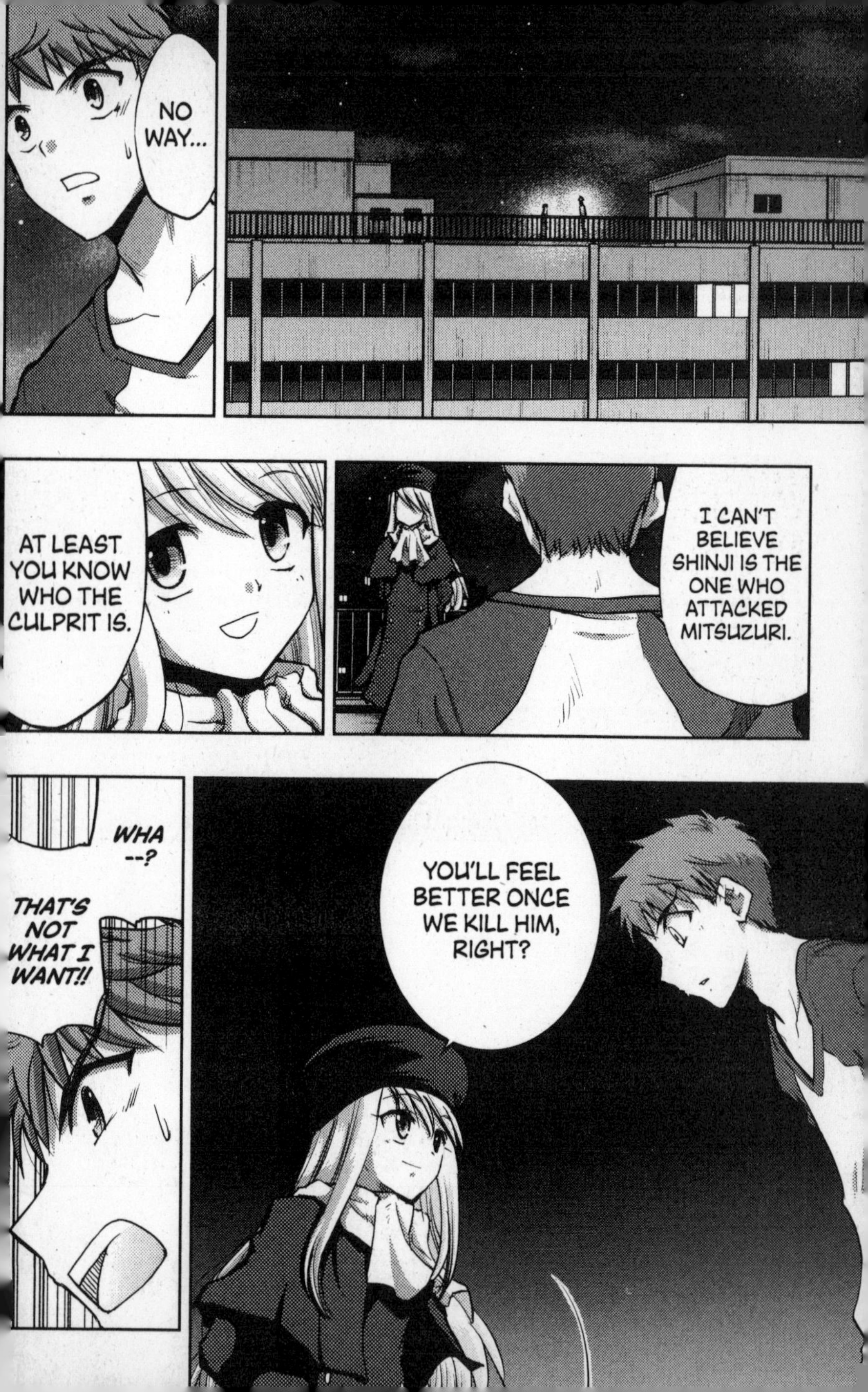
NO WAY...
I CAN'T BELIEVE SHINJI IS THE ONE WHO ATTACKED MITSUZURI.
AT LEAST YOU KNOW WHO THE CULPRIT IS.
YOU'LL FEEL BETTER ONCE WE KILL HIM, RIGHT?
WHA --?
THAT'S NOT WHAT I WANT!!

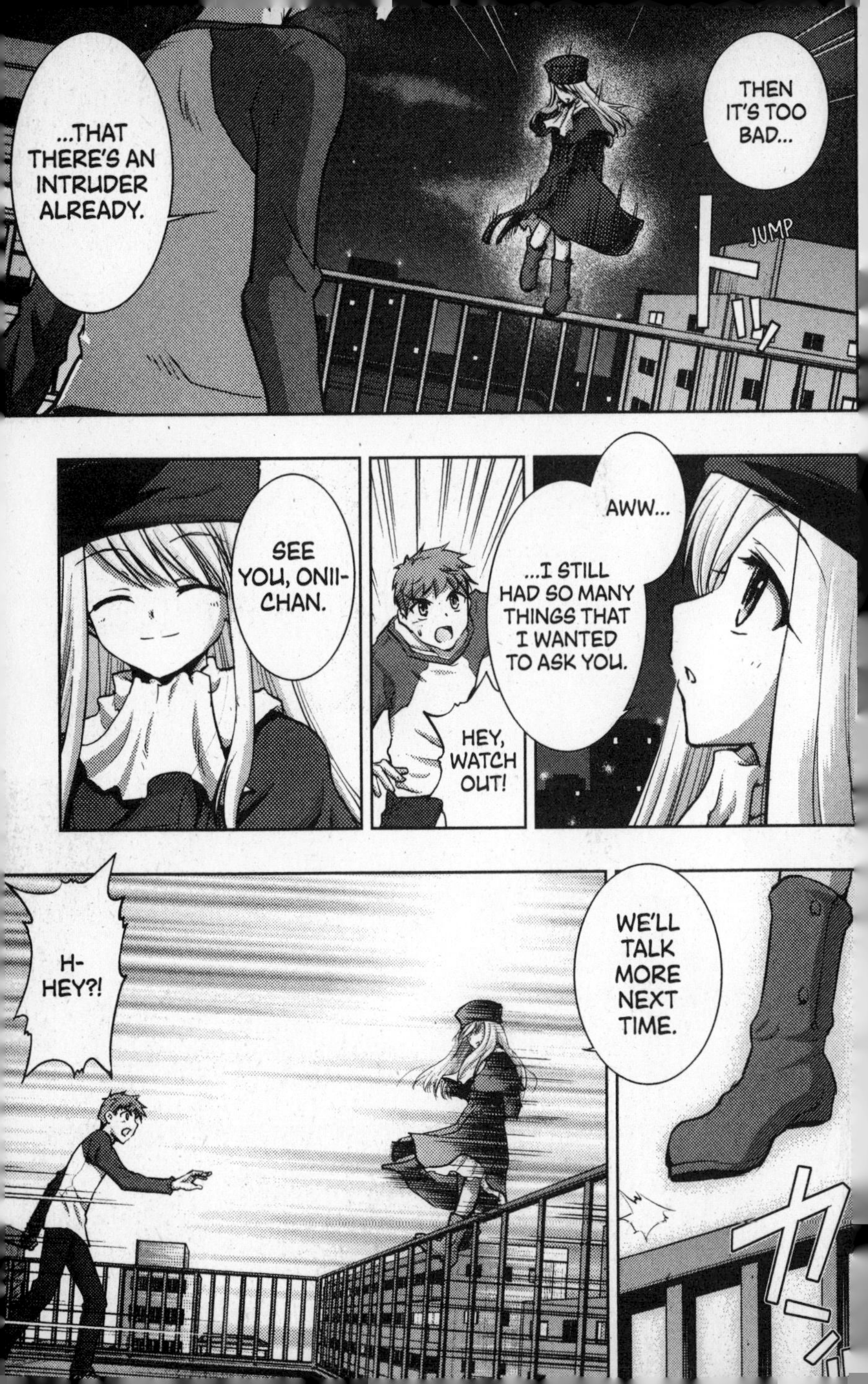
THEN IT'S TOO BAD...
JUMP
...THAT THERE'S AN INTRUDER ALREADY.
AWW...
...I STILL HAD SO MANY THINGS THAT I WANTED TO ASK YOU.
HEY, WATCH OUT!
SEE YOU, ONII-CHAN.
WE'LL TALK MORE NEXT TIME.
H- HEY?!

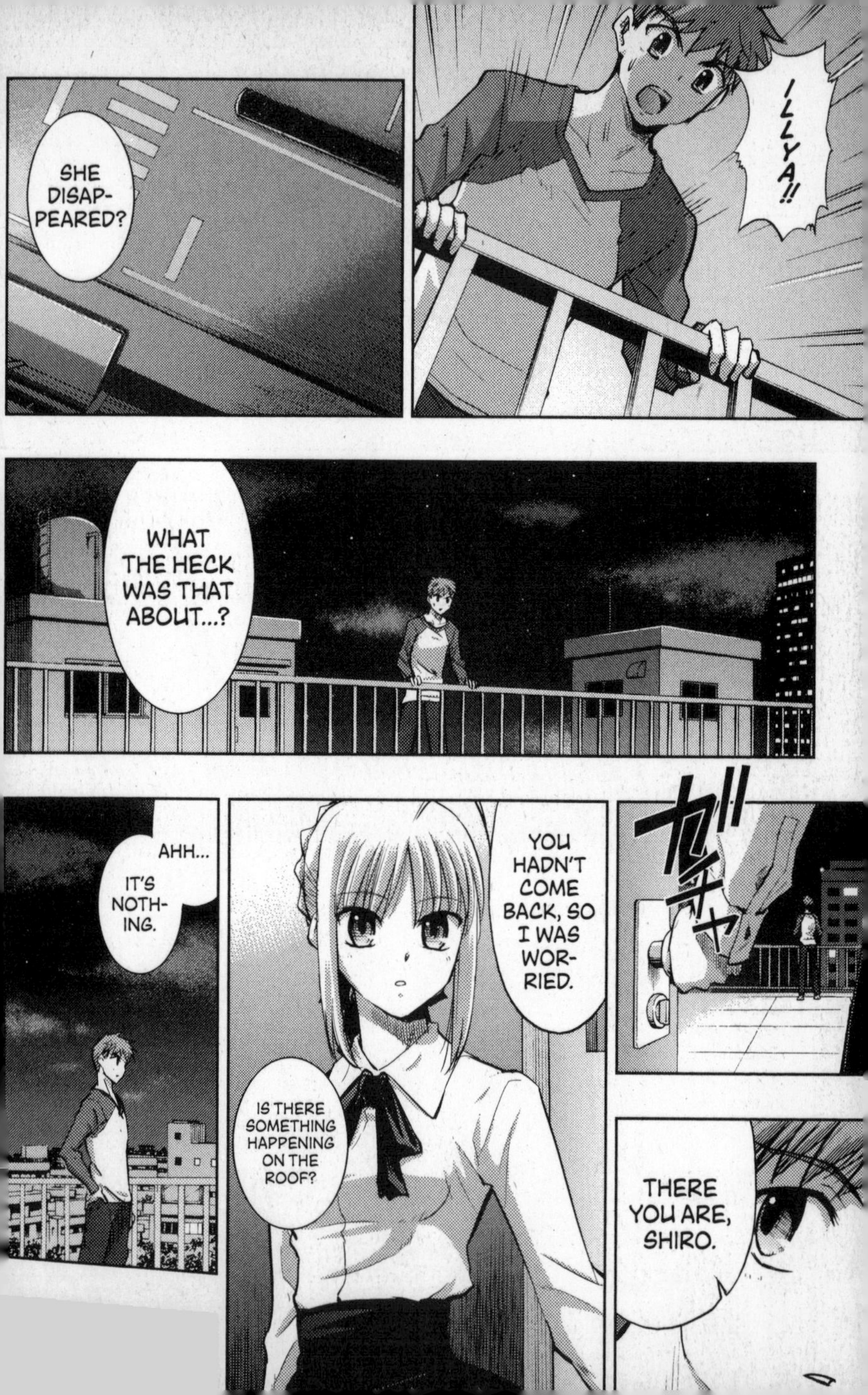
ILLYA!!
SHE DISAPPEARED?
WHAT THE HECK WAS THAT ABOUT...?
ガチャ
THERE YOU ARE, SHIRO.
YOU HADN'T COME BACK, SO I WAS WORRIED.
IS THERE SOMETHING HAPPENING ON THE ROOF?
AHH... IT'S NOTHING.

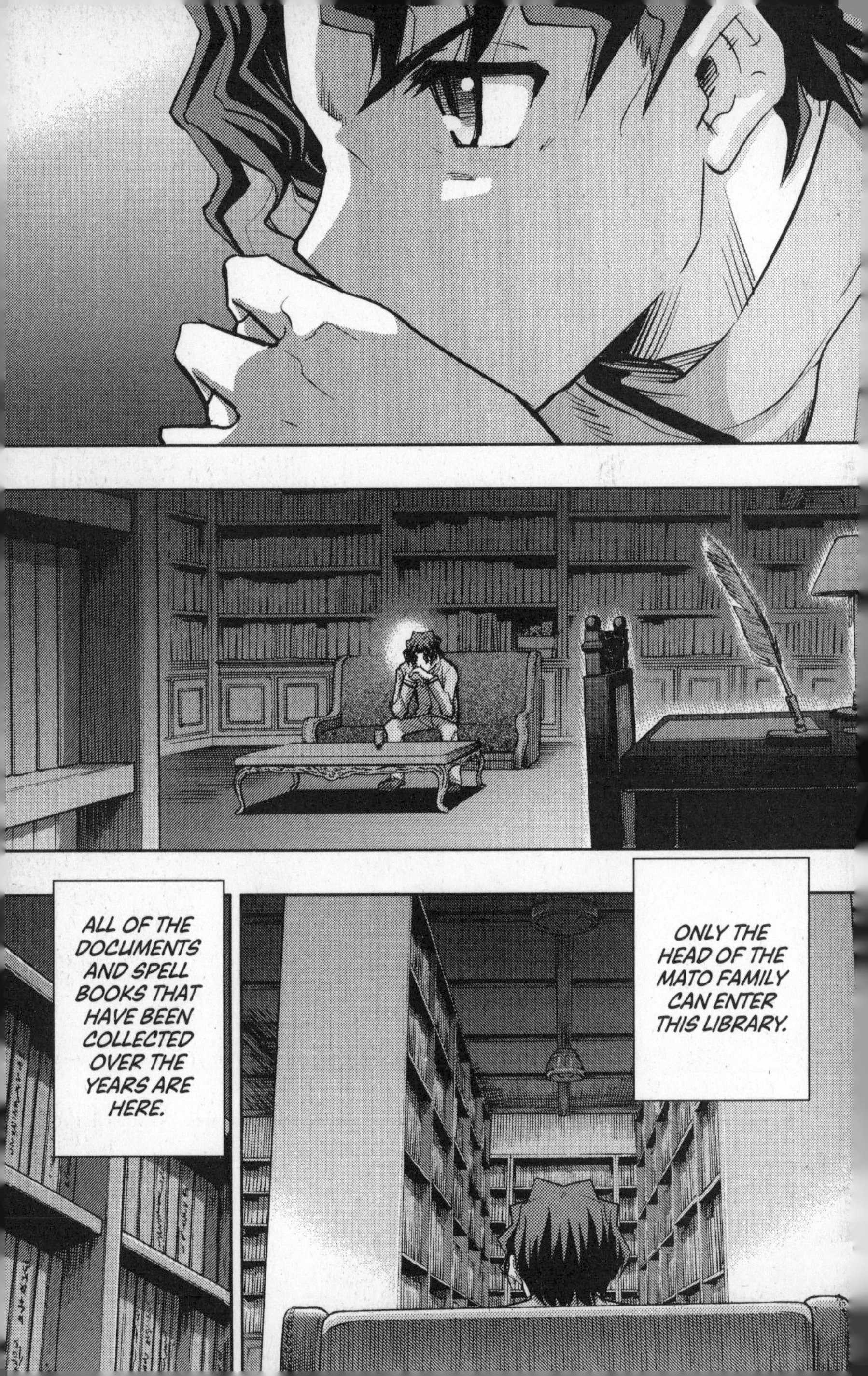
ONLY THE HEAD OF THE MATO FAMILY CAN ENTER THIS LIBRARY.
ALL OF THE DOCUMENTS AND SPELL BOOKS THAT HAVE BEEN COLLECTED OVER THE YEARS ARE HERE.

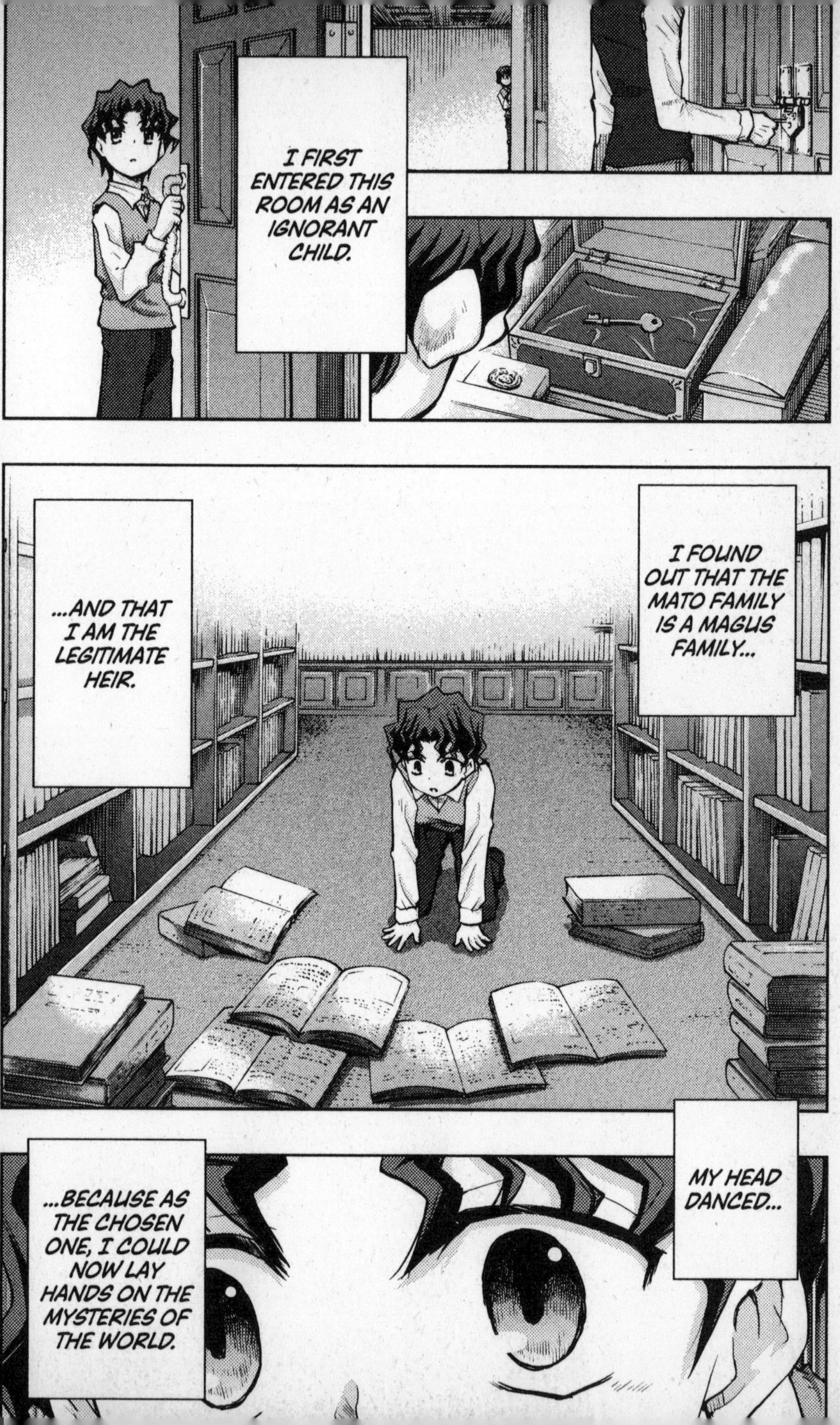
I FIRST ENTERED THIS ROOM AS AN IGNORANT CHILD.
I FOUND OUT THAT THE MATO FAMILY IS A MAGUS FAMILY...
...AND THAT I AM THE LEGITIMATE HEIR.
MY HEAD DANCED...
...BECAUSE AS THE CHOSEN ONE, I COULD NOW LAY HANDS ON THE MYSTERIES OF THE WORLD.

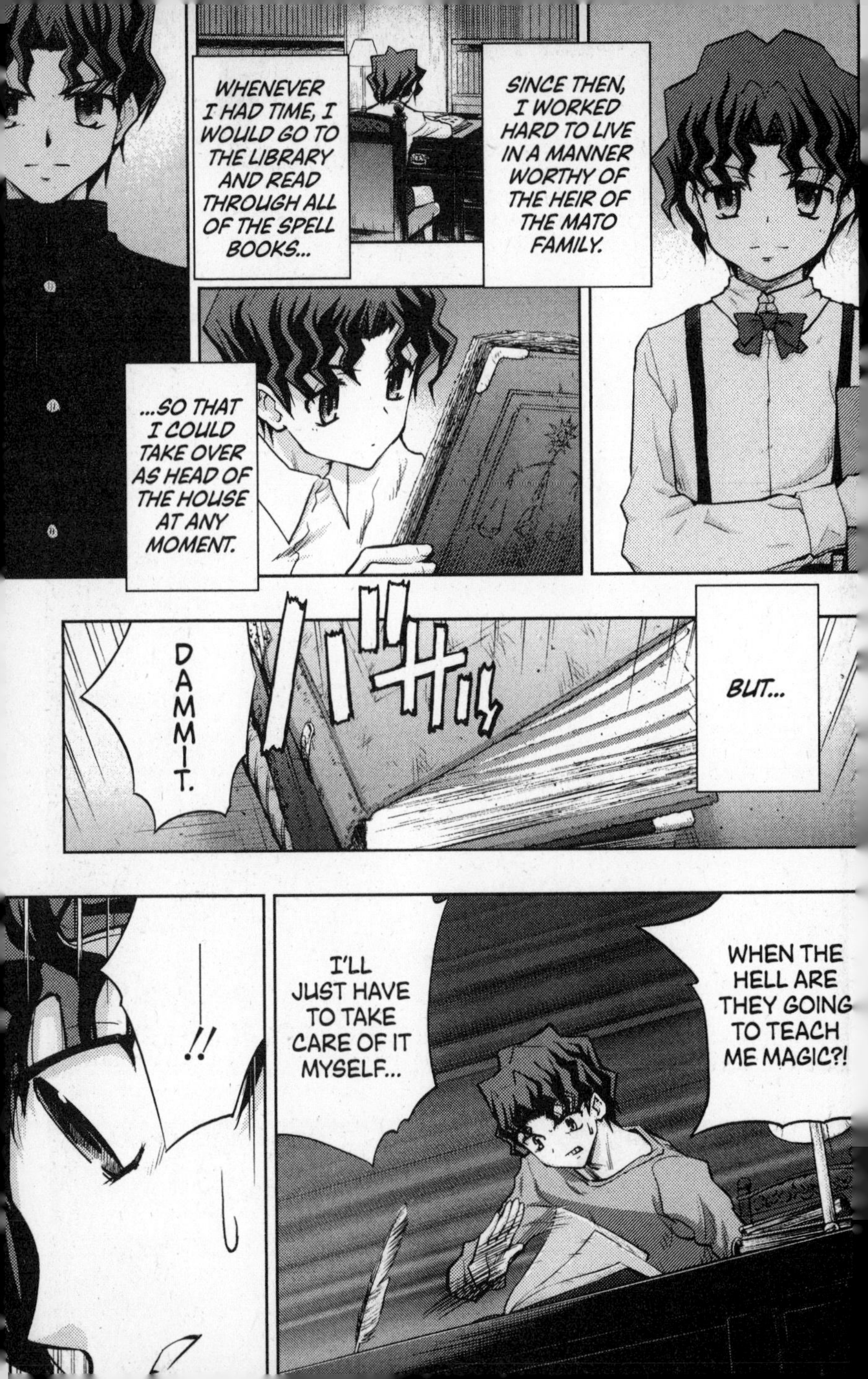
SINCE THEN, I WORKED HARD TO LIVE IN A MANNER WORTHY OF THE HEIR OF THE MATO FAMILY.
WHENEVER I HAD TIME, I WOULD GO TO THE LIBRARY AND READ THROUGH ALL OF THE SPELL BOOKS...
...SO THAT I COULD TAKE OVER AS HEAD OF THE HOUSE AT ANY MOMENT.
BUT...
DAMMIT.
WHEN THE HELL ARE THEY GOING TO TEACH ME MAGIC?!
I'LL JUST HAVE TO TAKE CARE OF IT MYSELF...
!!

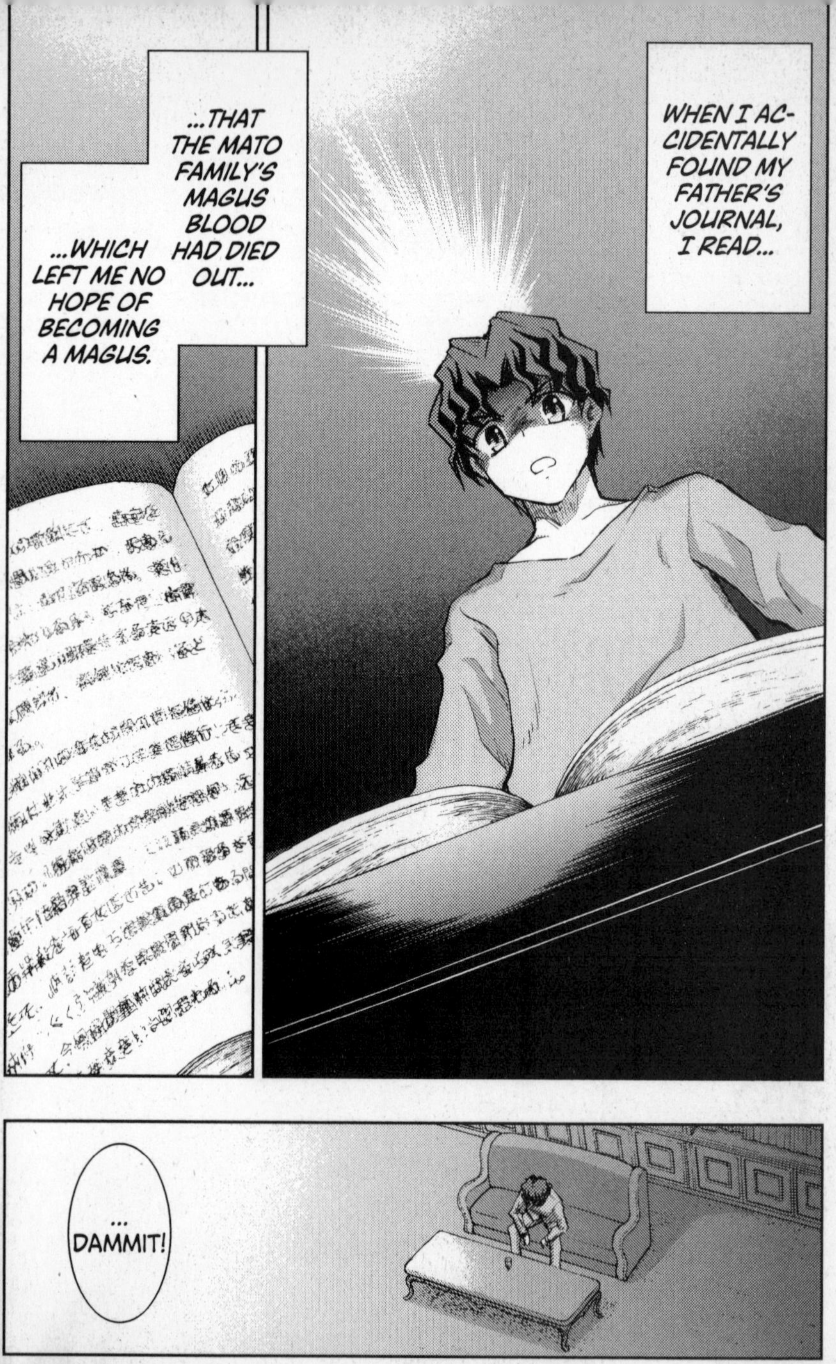
WHEN I ACCIDENTALLY FOUND MY FATHER'S JOURNAL, I READ...
...THAT THE MATO FAMILY'S MAGUS BLOOD HAD DIED OUT...
...WHICH LEFT ME NO HOPE OF BECOMING A MAGUS.
... DAMMIT!

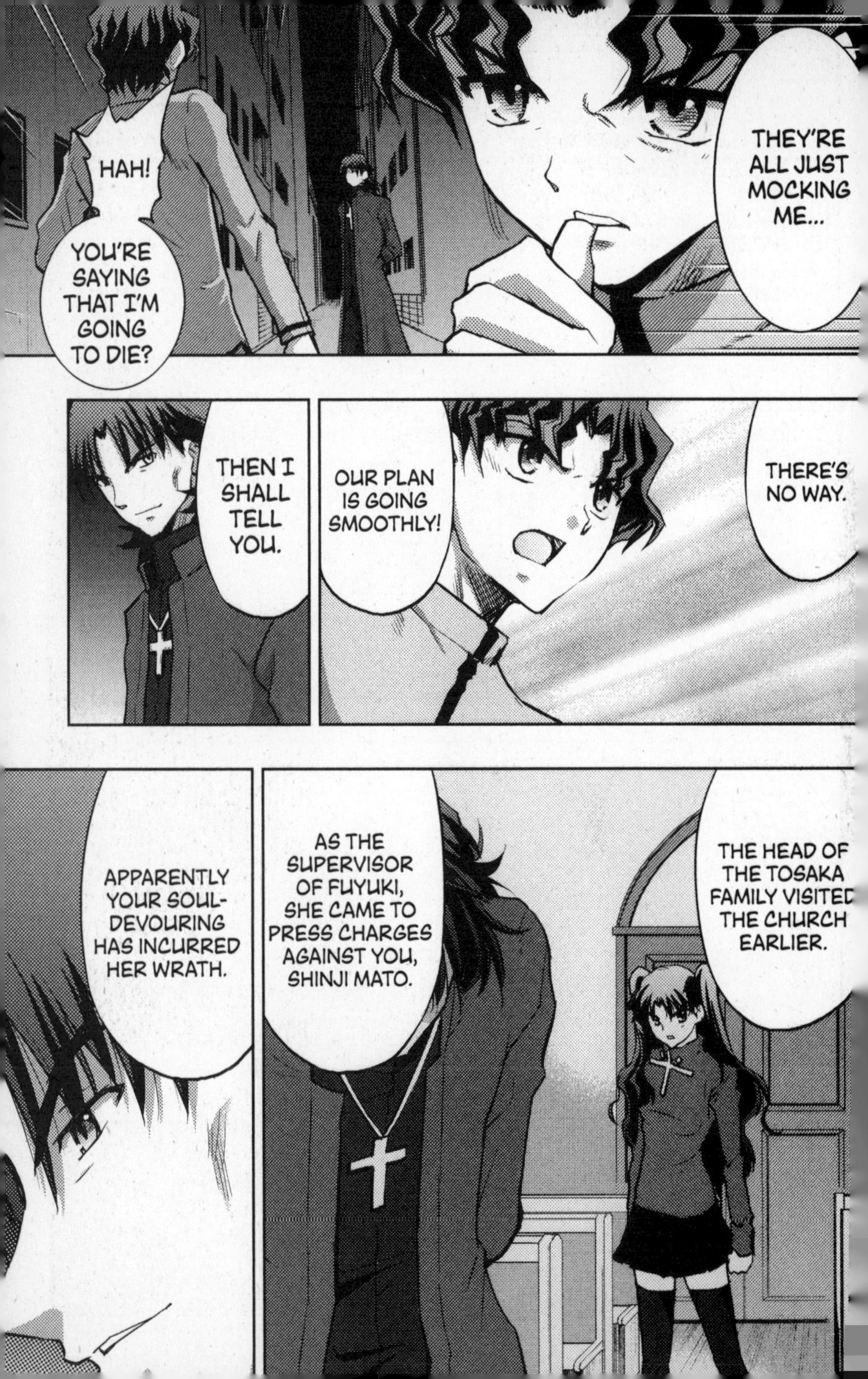
THEY'RE ALL JUST MOCKING ME...
HAH!
YOU'RE SAYING THAT I'M GOING TO DIE?
THERE'S NO WAY.
OUR PLAN IS GOING SMOOTHLY!
THEN I SHALL TELL YOU.
THE HEAD OF THE TOSAKA FAMILY VISITED THE CHURCH EARLIER.
AS THE SUPERVISOR OF FUYUKI, SHE CAME TO PRESS CHARGES AGAINST YOU, SHINJI MATO.
APPARENTLY YOUR SOUL-DEVOURING HAS INCURRED HER WRATH.

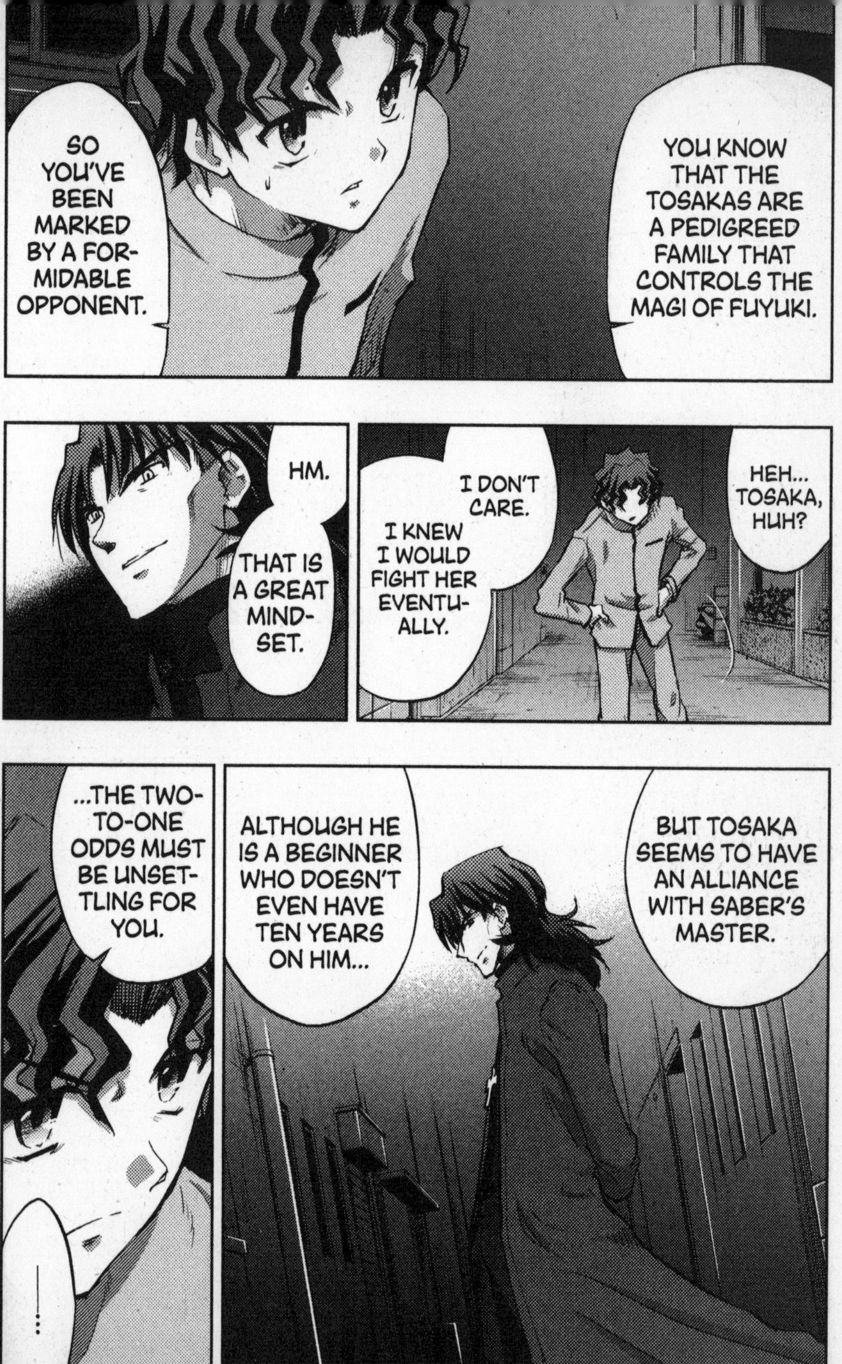
YOU KNOW THAT THE TOSAKAS ARE A PEDIGREED FAMILY THAT CONTROLS THE MAGI OF FUYUKI.
SO YOU'VE BEEN MARKED BY A FORMIDABLE OPPONENT.
HEH... TOSAKA, HUH?
I DON'T CARE.
I KNEW I WOULD FIGHT HER EVENTUALLY.
HM.
THAT IS A GREAT MINDSET.
BUT TOSAKA SEEMS TO HAVE AN ALLIANCE WITH SABER'S MASTER.
ALTHOUGH HE IS A BEGINNER WHO DOESN'T EVEN HAVE TEN YEARS ON HIM...
...THE TWO-TO-ONE ODDS MUST BE UNSETTLING FOR YOU.
......

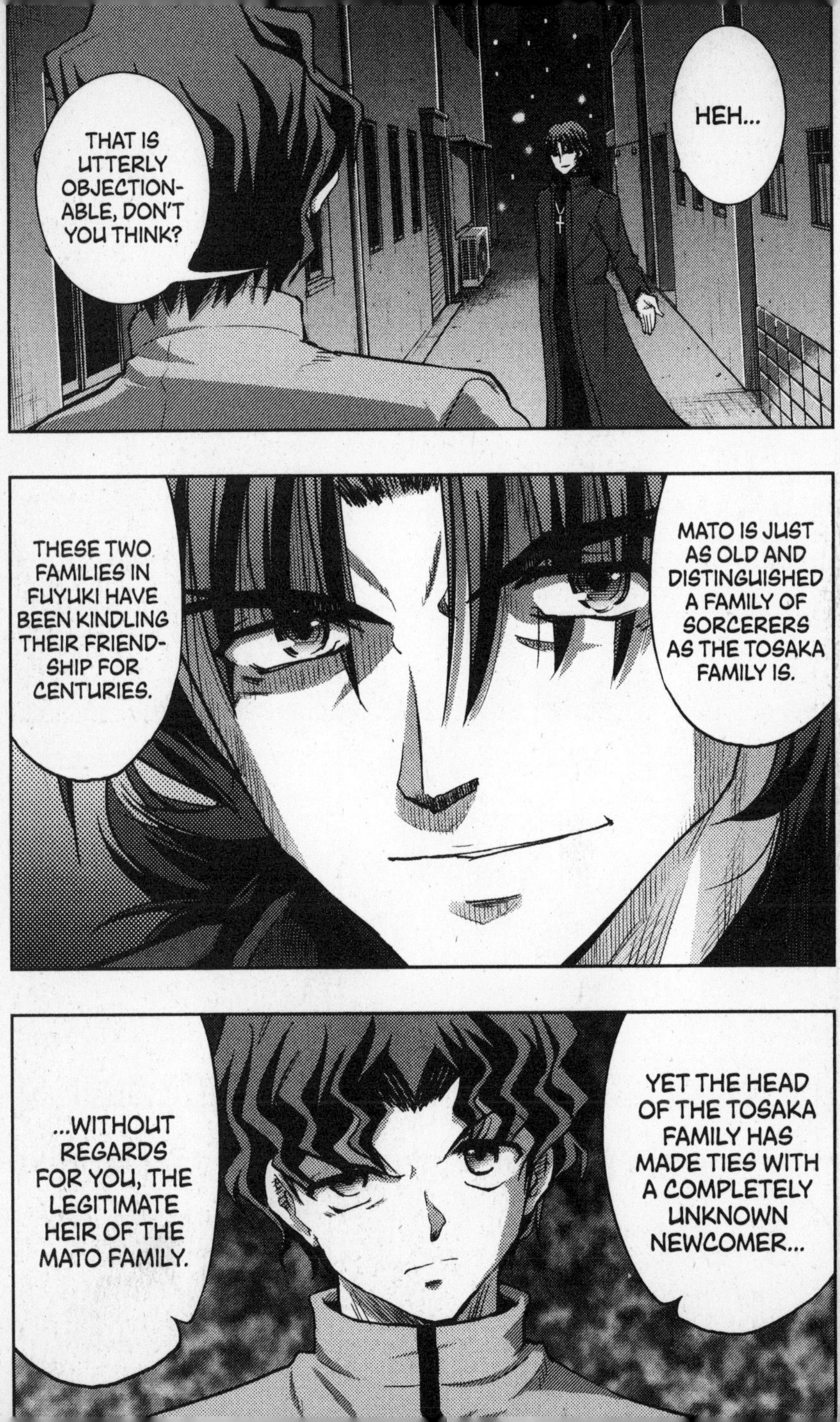
HEH...
THAT IS UTTERLY OBJECTION-ABLE, DON'T YOU THINK?
MATO IS JUST AS OLD AND DISTINGUISHED A FAMILY OF SORCERERS AS THE TOSAKA FAMILY IS.
THESE TWO FAMILIES IN FUYUKI HAVE BEEN KINDLING THEIR FRIEND-SHIP FOR CENTURIES.
YET THE HEAD OF THE TOSAKA FAMILY HAS MADE TIES WITH A COMPLETELY UNKNOWN NEWCOMER...
...WITHOUT REGARDS FOR YOU, THE LEGITIMATE HEIR OF THE MATO FAMILY.

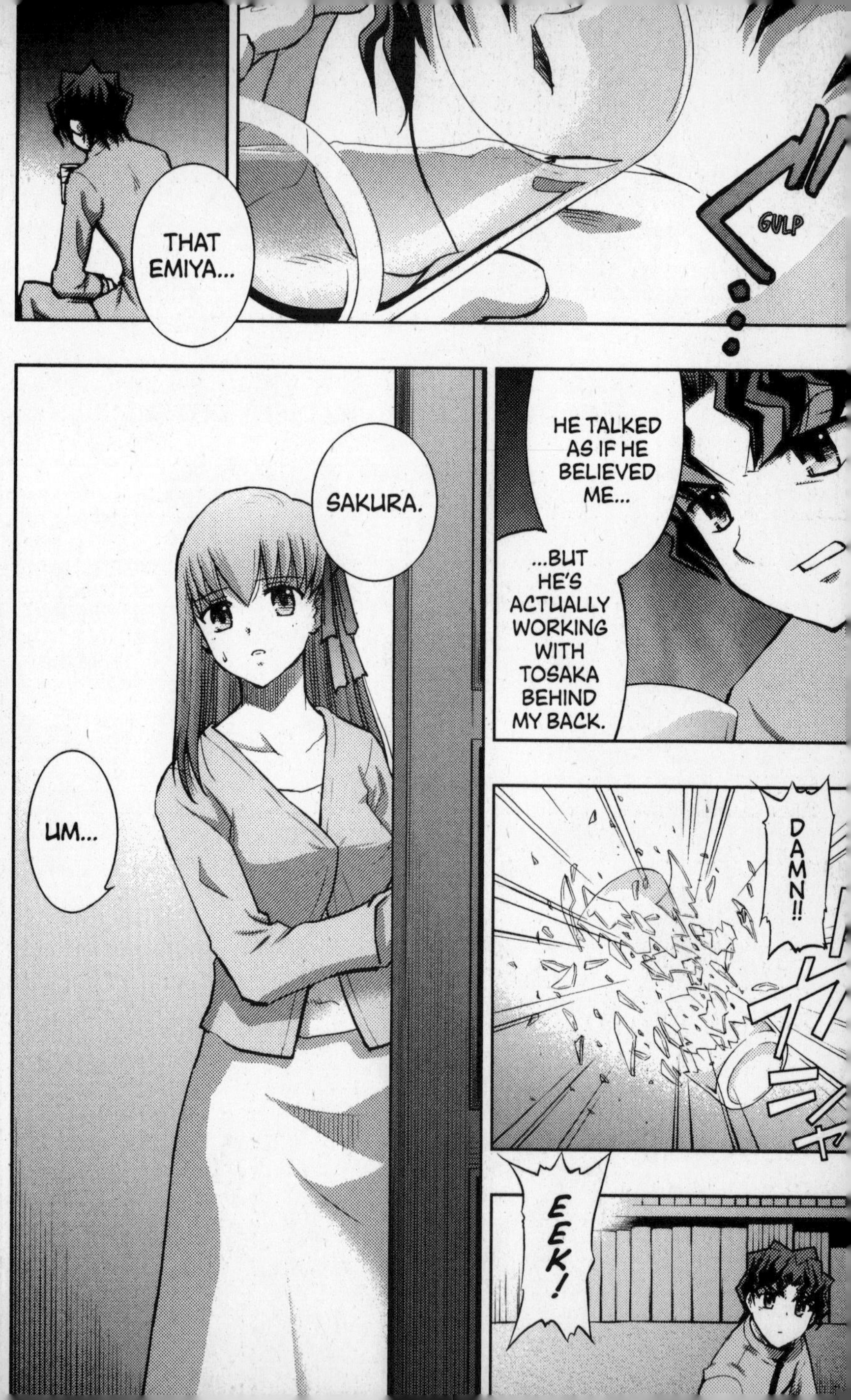
GULP
THAT EMIYA...
HE TALKED AS IF HE BELIEVED ME...
...BUT HE'S ACTUALLY WORKING WITH TOSAKA BEHIND MY BACK.
DAMN!!
EEK!
SAKURA.
UM...

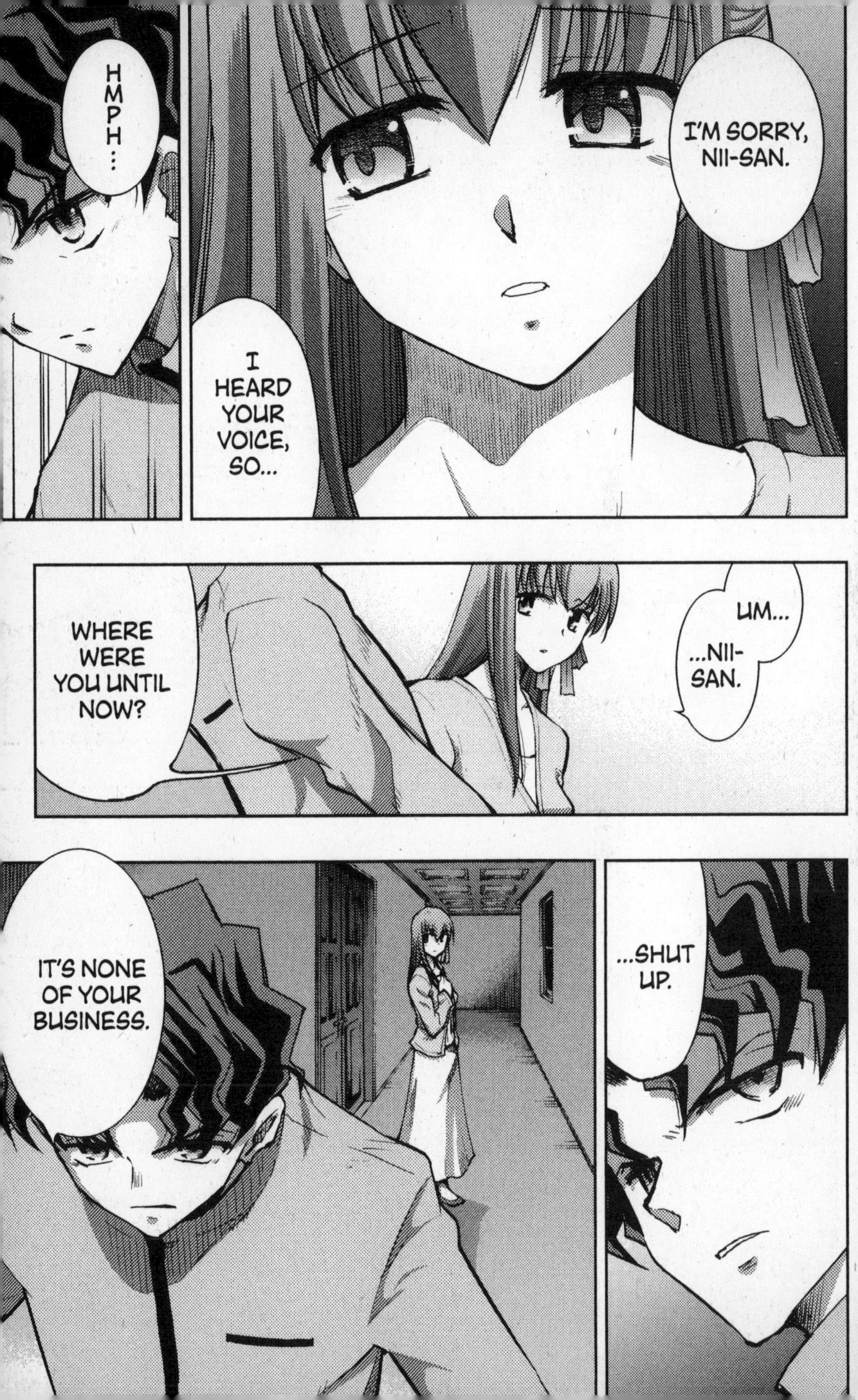
I'M SORRY, NII-SAN.
I HEARD YOUR VOICE, SO...
HMPH...
UM... ...NII-SAN.
WHERE WERE YOU UNTIL NOW?
...SHUT UP.
IT'S NONE OF YOUR BUSINESS.

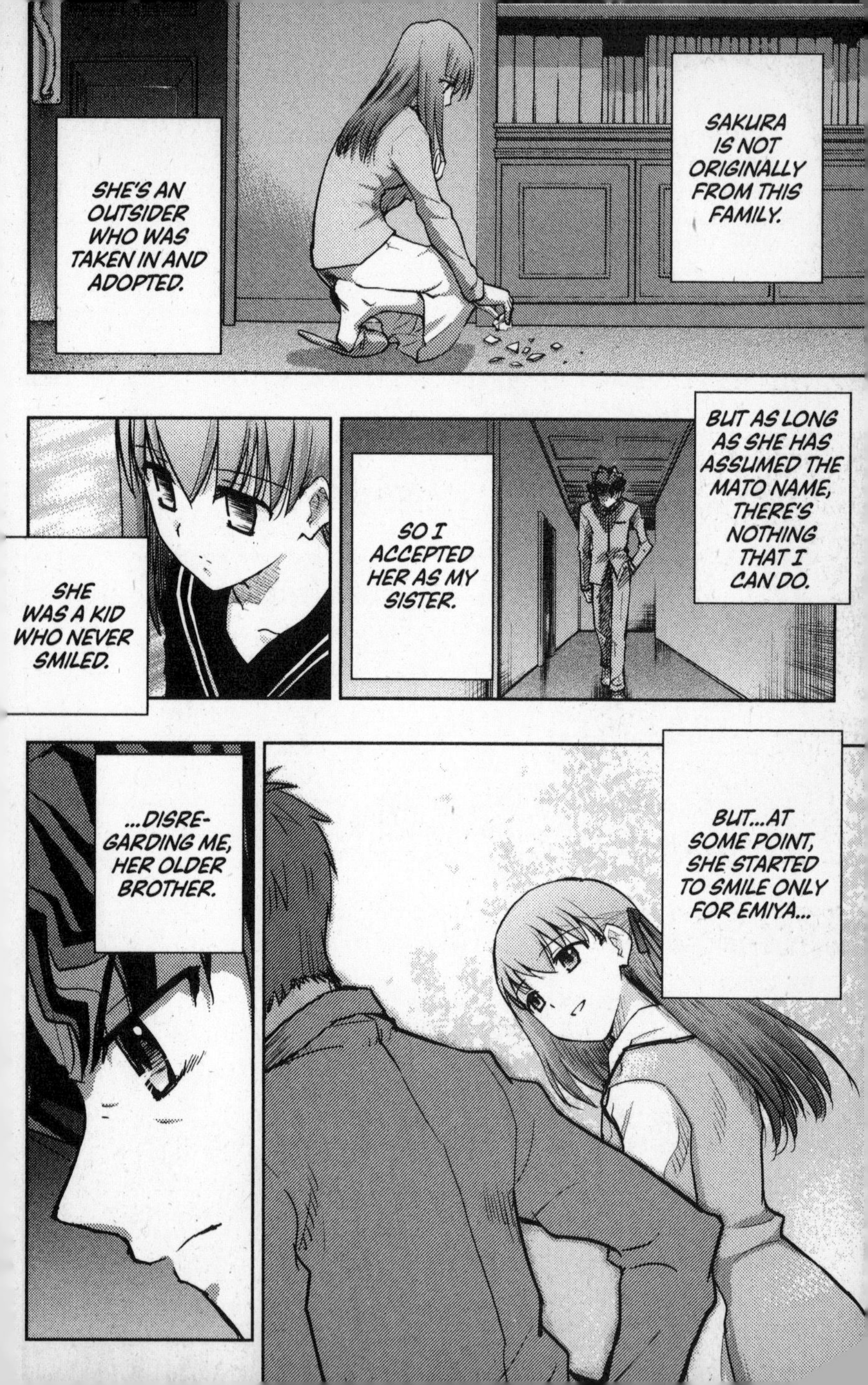
SAKURA IS NOT ORIGINALLY FROM THIS FAMILY.
SHE'S AN OUTSIDER WHO WAS TAKEN IN AND ADOPTED.
BUT AS LONG AS SHE HAS ASSUMED THE MATO NAME, THERE'S NOTHING THAT I CAN DO.
SO I ACCEPTED HER AS MY SISTER.
SHE WAS A KID WHO NEVER SMILED.
BUT...AT SOME POINT, SHE STARTED TO SMILE ONLY FOR EMIYA...
...DISRE-GARDING ME, HER OLDER BROTHER.

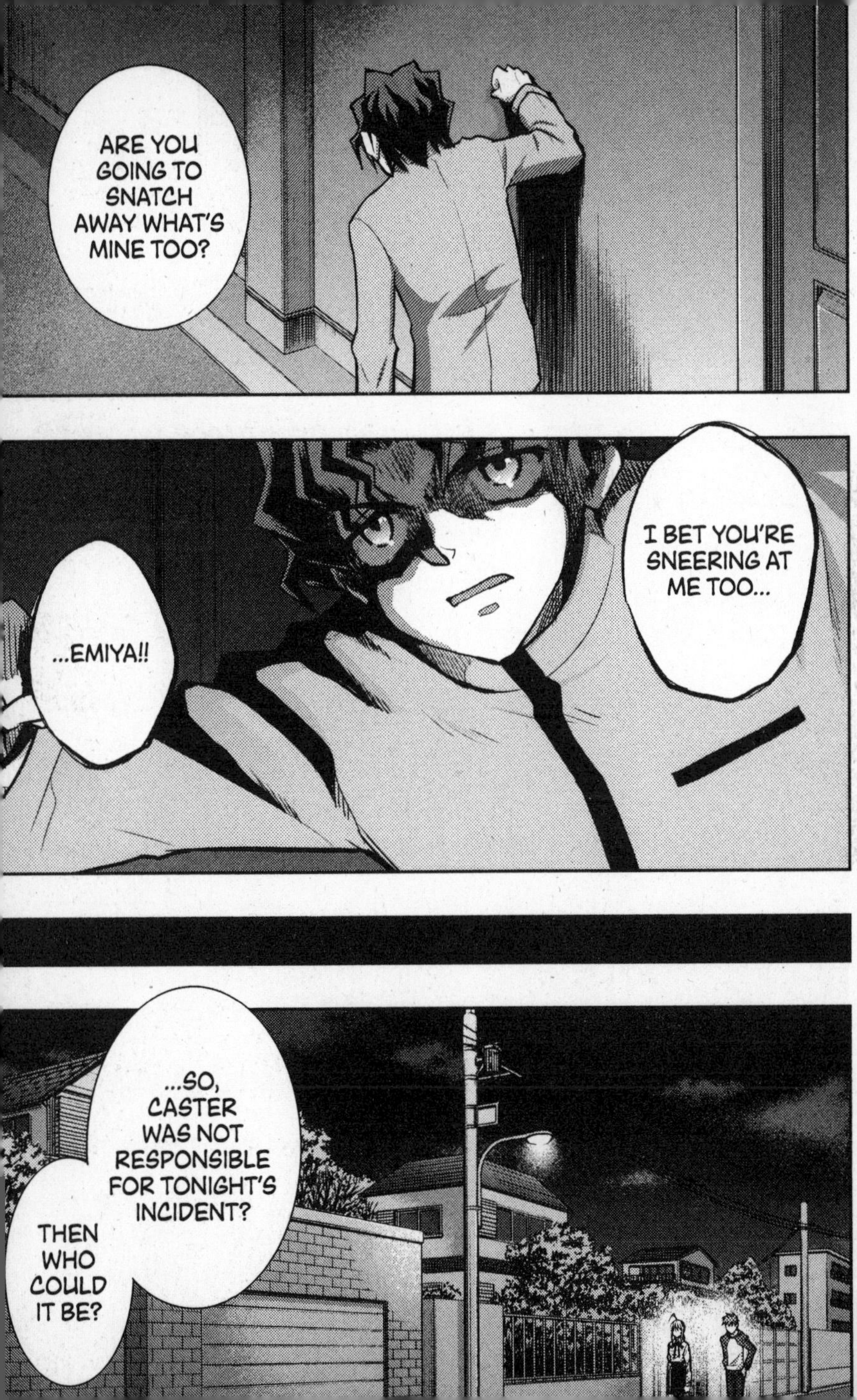
ARE YOU GOING TO SNATCH AWAY WHAT'S MINE TOO?
I BET YOU'RE SNEERING AT ME TOO...
...EMIYA!!
...SO, CASTER WAS NOT RESPONSIBLE FOR TONIGHT'S INCIDENT?
THEN WHO COULD IT BE?

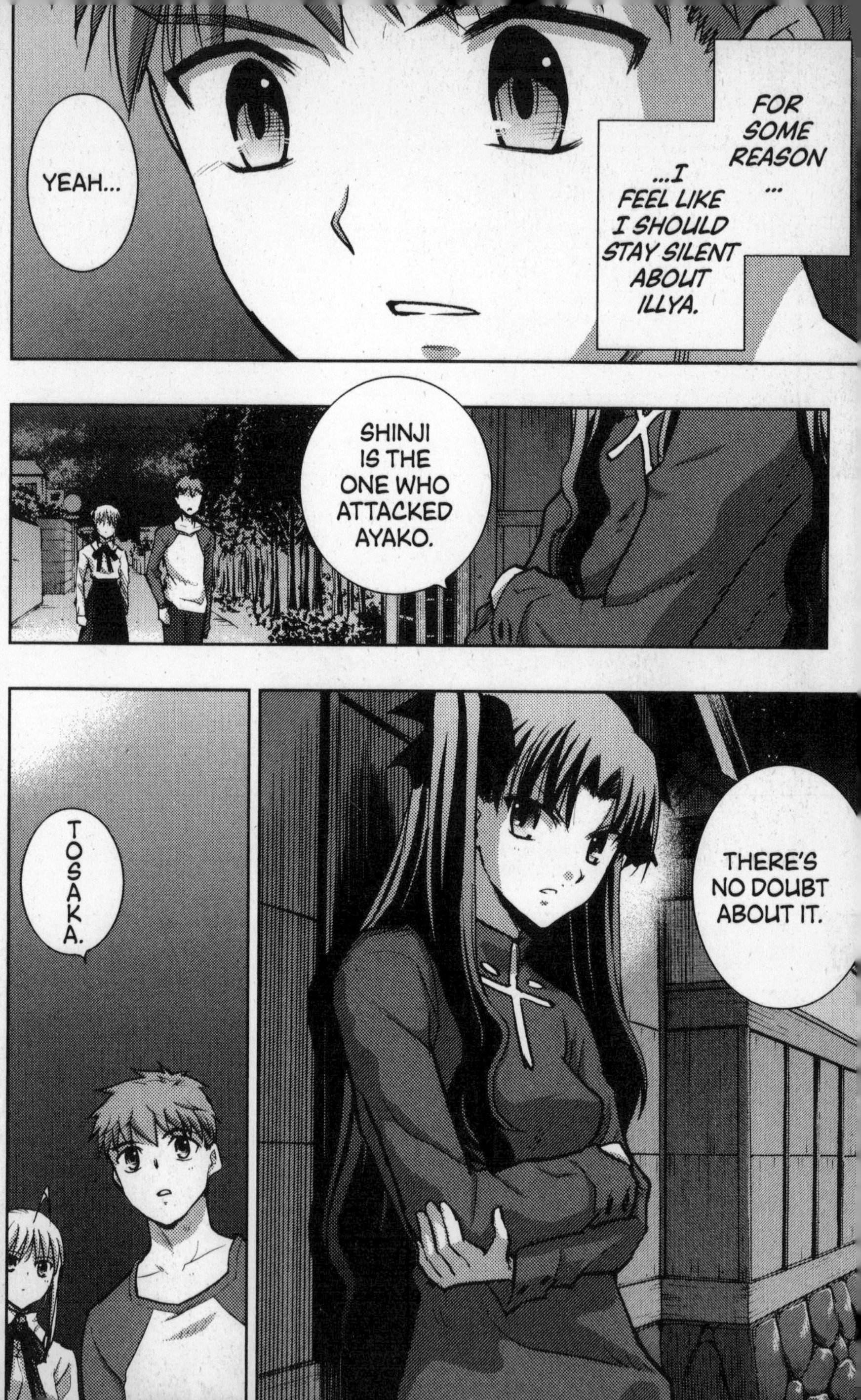
FOR SOME REASON ...
...I FEEL LIKE I SHOULD STAY SILENT ABOUT ILLYA.
YEAH...
SHINJI IS THE ONE WHO ATTACKED AYAKO.
THERE'S NO DOUBT ABOUT IT.
TOSAKA.

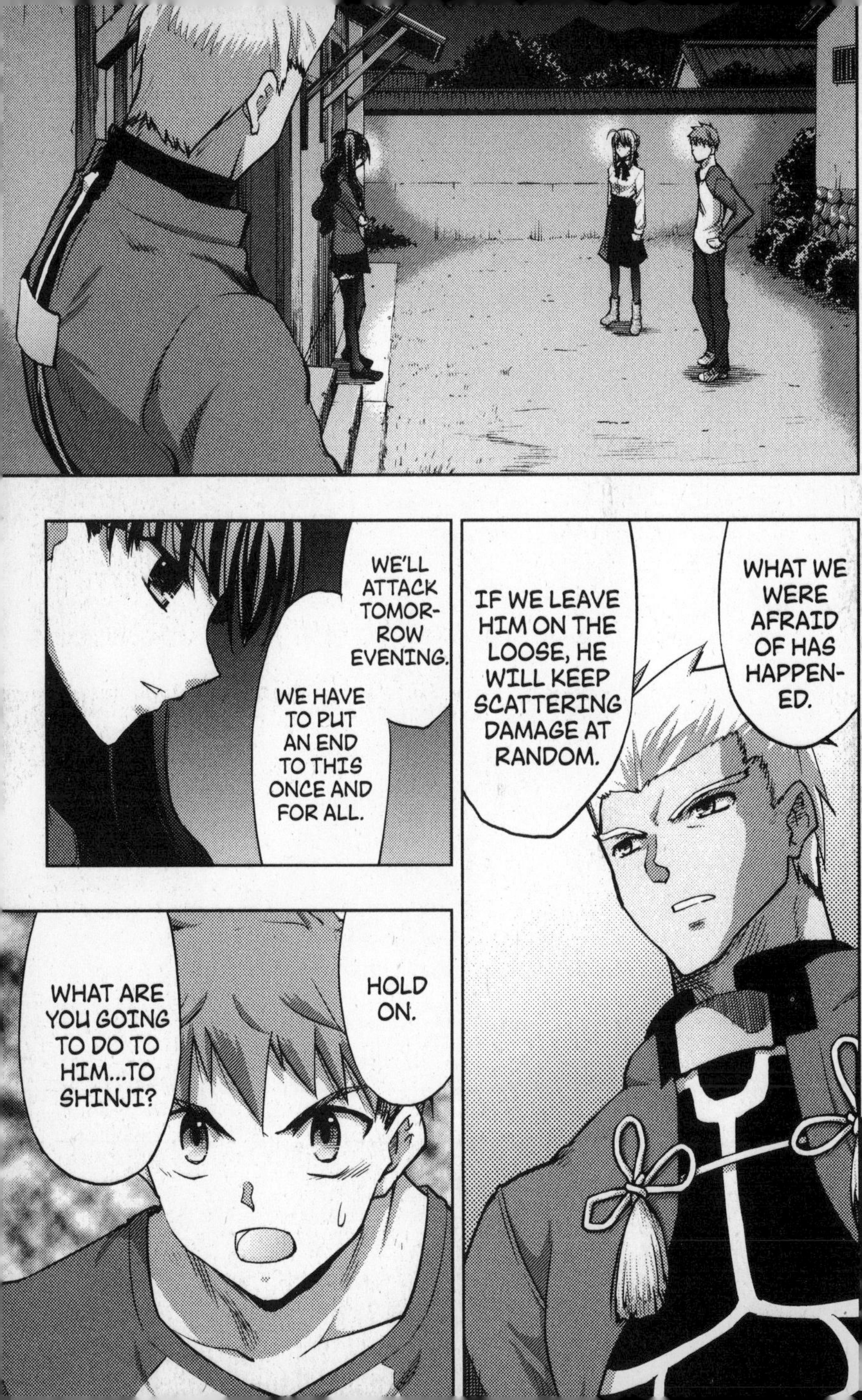
WHAT WE WERE AFRAID OF HAS HAPPEN-ED.
IF WE LEAVE HIM ON THE LOOSE, HE WILL KEEP SCATTERING DAMAGE AT RANDOM.
WE'LL ATTACK TOMOR-ROW EVENING.
WE HAVE TO PUT AN END TO THIS ONCE AND FOR ALL.
HOLD ON.
WHAT ARE YOU GOING TO DO TO HIM...TO SHINJI?

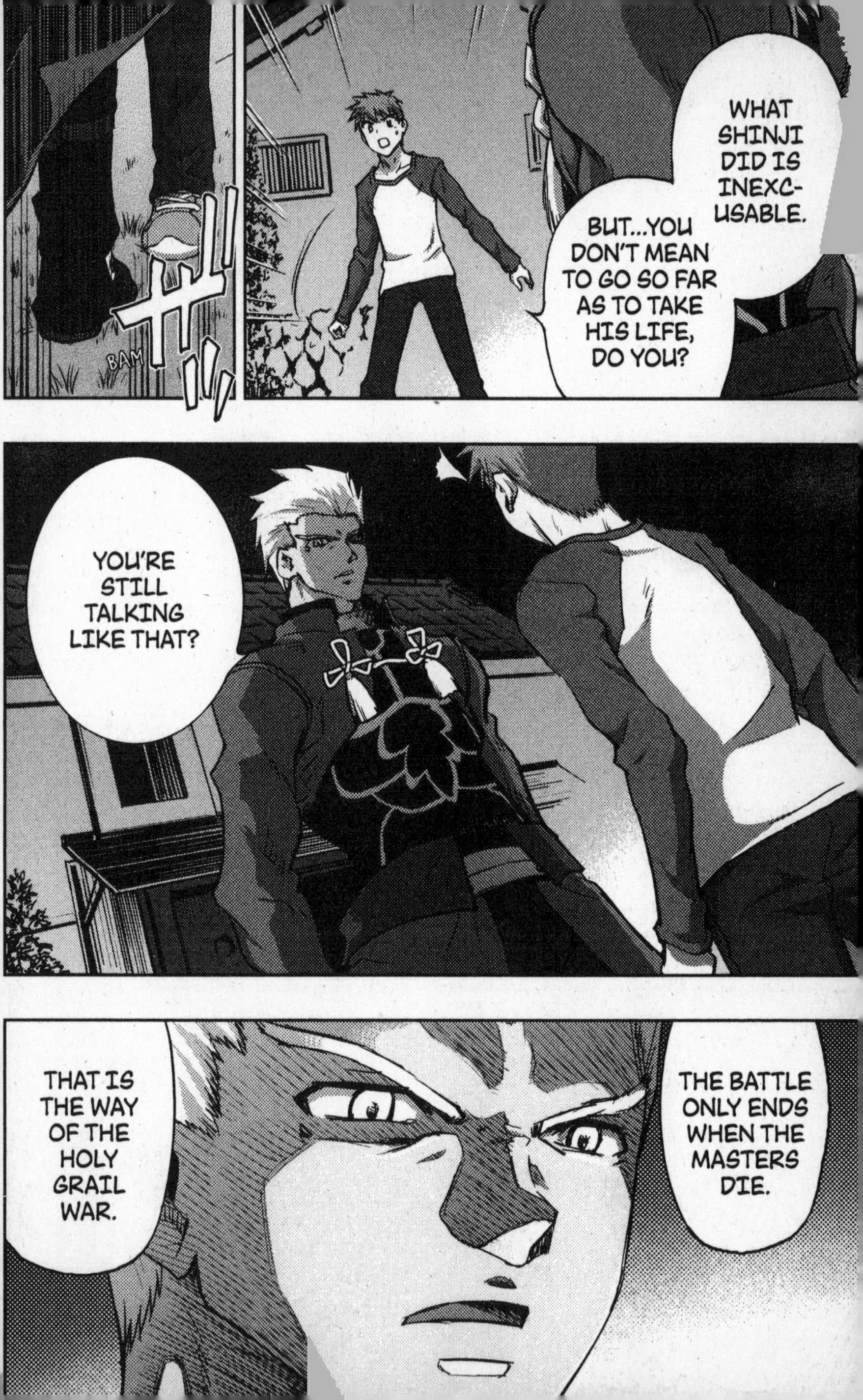
WHAT SHINJI DID IS INEXC-USABLE.
BUT...YOU DON'T MEAN TO GO SO FAR AS TO TAKE HIS LIFE, DO YOU?
BAM
YOU'RE STILL TALKING LIKE THAT?
THE BATTLE ONLY ENDS WHEN THE MASTERS DIE.
THAT IS THE WAY OF THE HOLY GRAIL WAR.

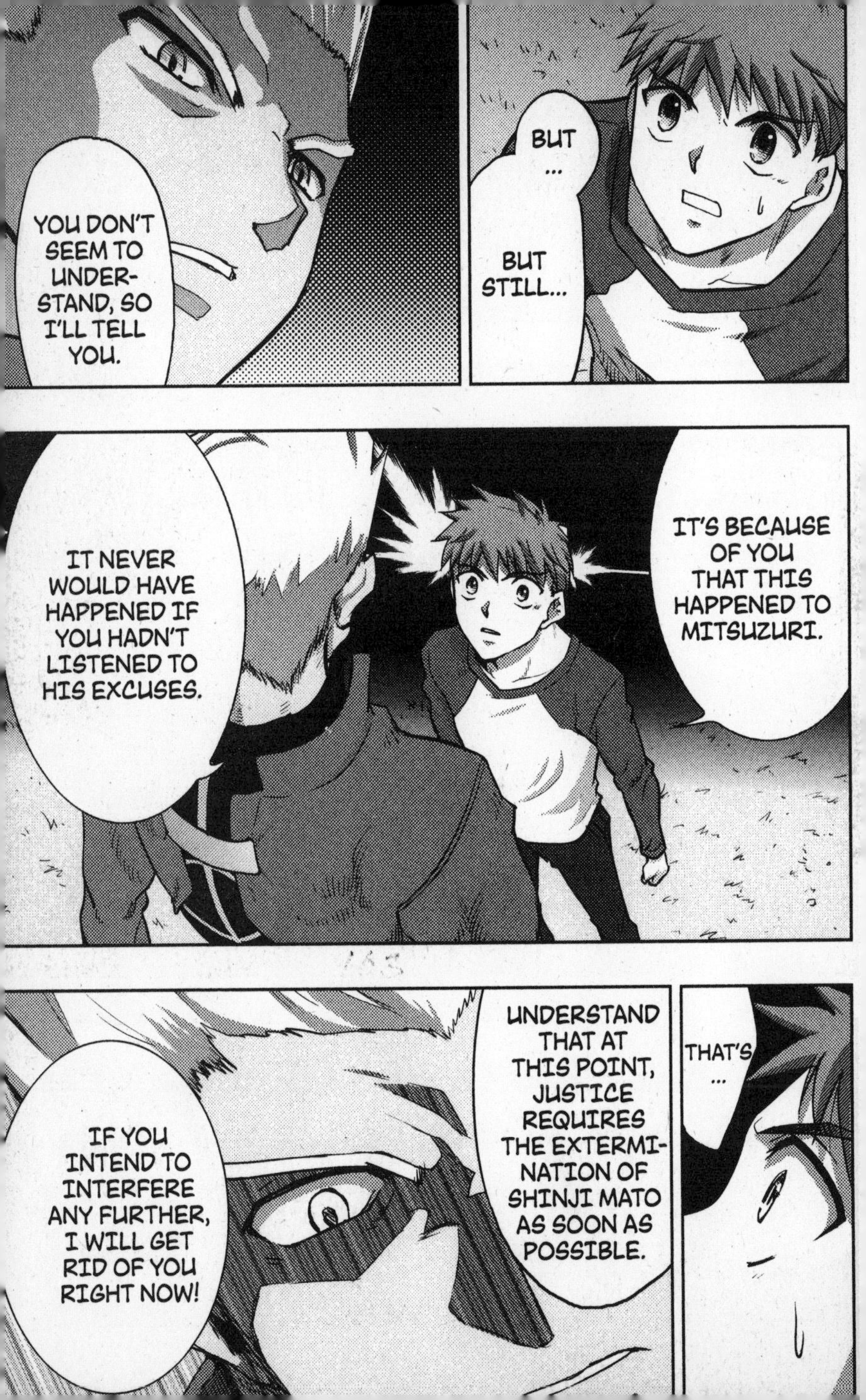
BUT ...
BUT STILL...
YOU DON'T SEEM TO UNDER-STAND, SO I'LL TELL YOU.
IT'S BECAUSE OF YOU THAT THIS HAPPENED TO MITSUZURI.
IT NEVER WOULD HAVE HAPPENED IF YOU HADN'T LISTENED TO HIS EXCUSES.
THAT'S ...
UNDERSTAND THAT AT THIS POINT, JUSTICE REQUIRES THE EXTERMI-NATION OF SHINJI MATO AS SOON AS POSSIBLE.
IF YOU INTEND TO INTERFERE ANY FURTHER, I WILL GET RID OF YOU RIGHT NOW!

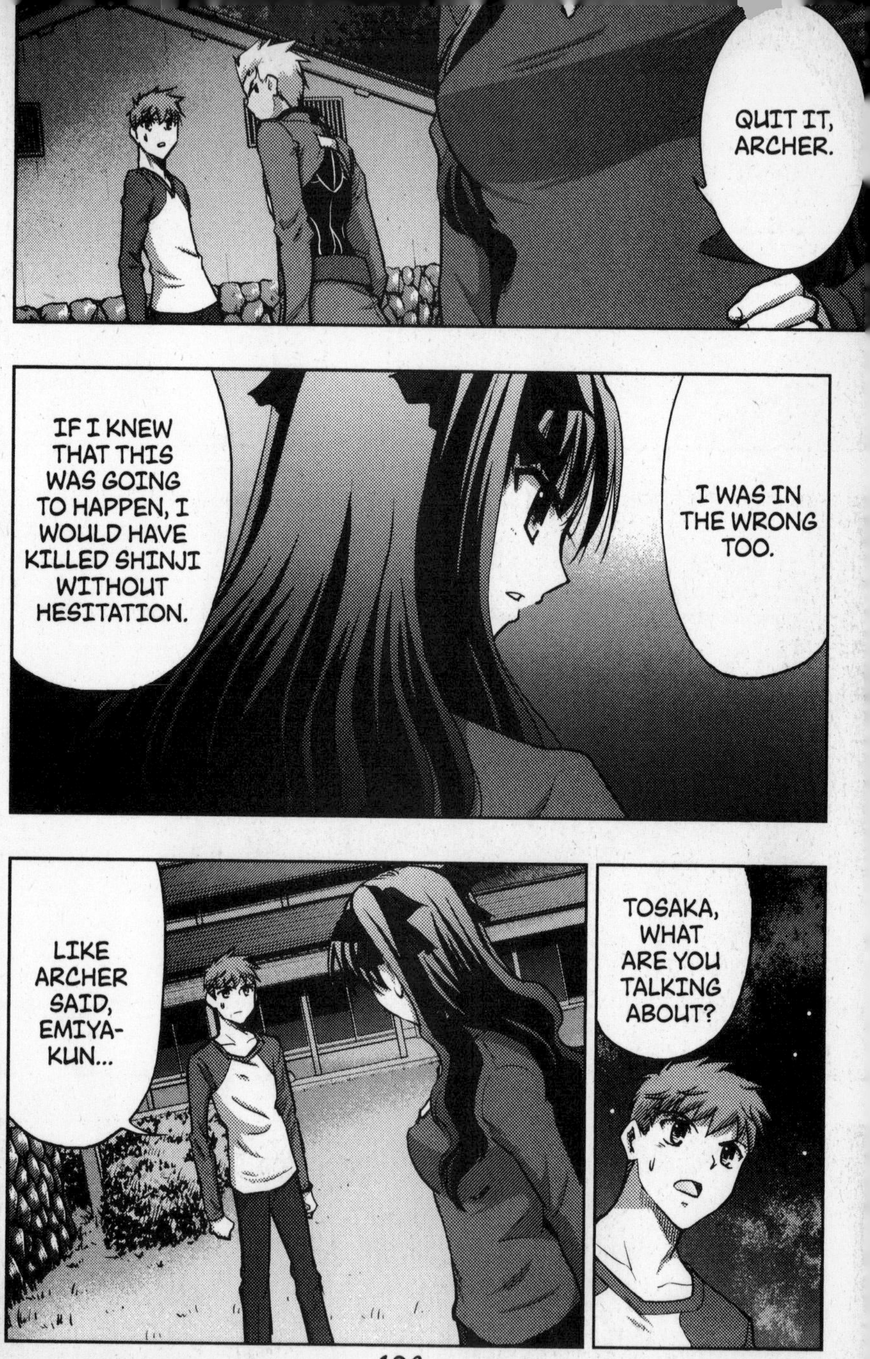
QUIT IT, ARCHER.
I WAS IN THE WRONG TOO.
IF I KNEW THAT THIS WAS GOING TO HAPPEN, I WOULD HAVE KILLED SHINJI WITHOUT HESITATION.
TOSAKA, WHAT ARE YOU TALKING ABOUT?
LIKE ARCHER SAID, EMIYA-KUN...

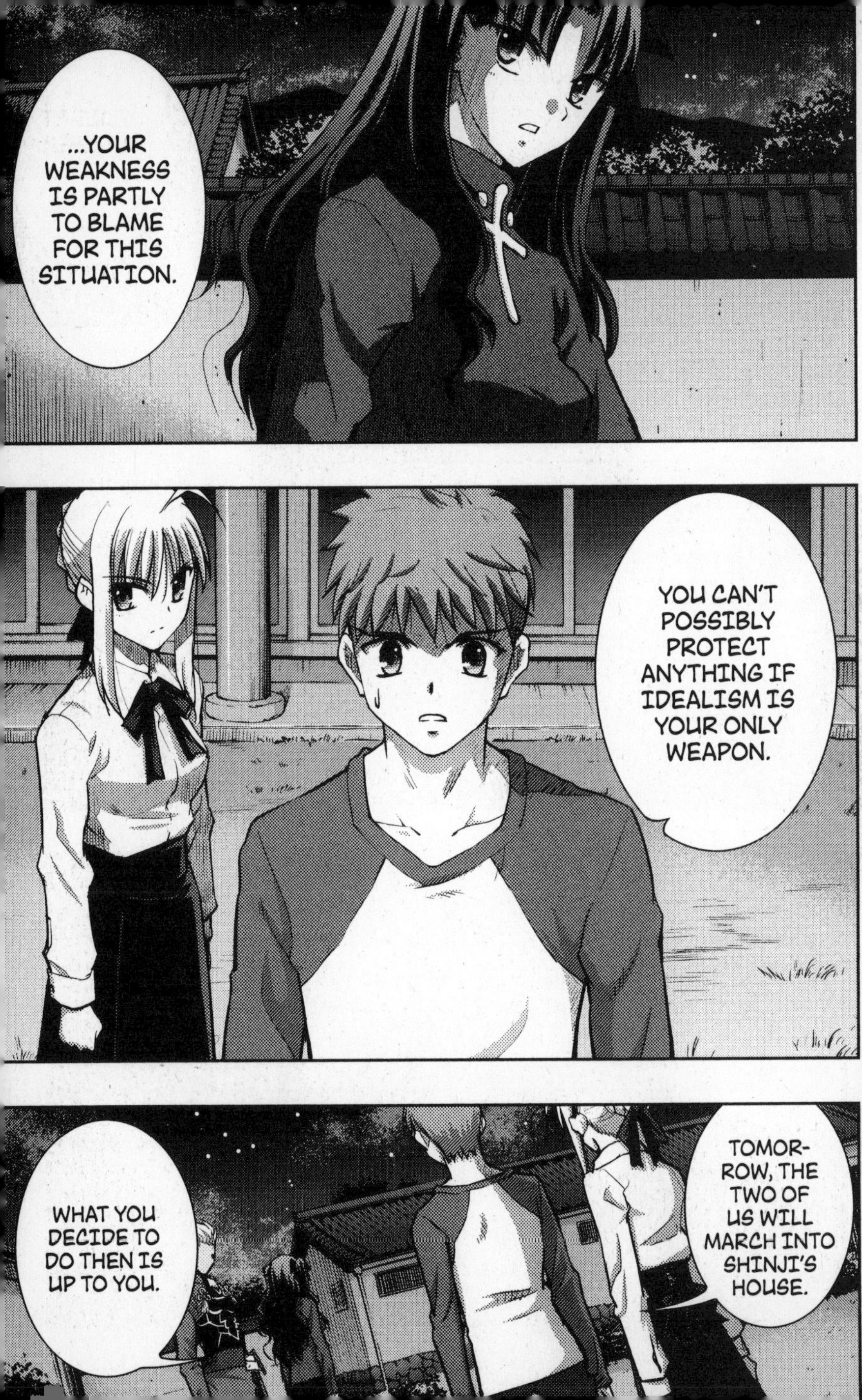
...YOUR WEAKNESS IS PARTLY TO BLAME FOR THIS SITUATION.
YOU CAN'T POSSIBLY PROTECT ANYTHING IF IDEALISM IS YOUR ONLY WEAPON.
TOMOR-ROW, THE TWO OF US WILL MARCH INTO SHINJI'S HOUSE.
WHAT YOU DECIDE TO DO THEN IS UP TO YOU.

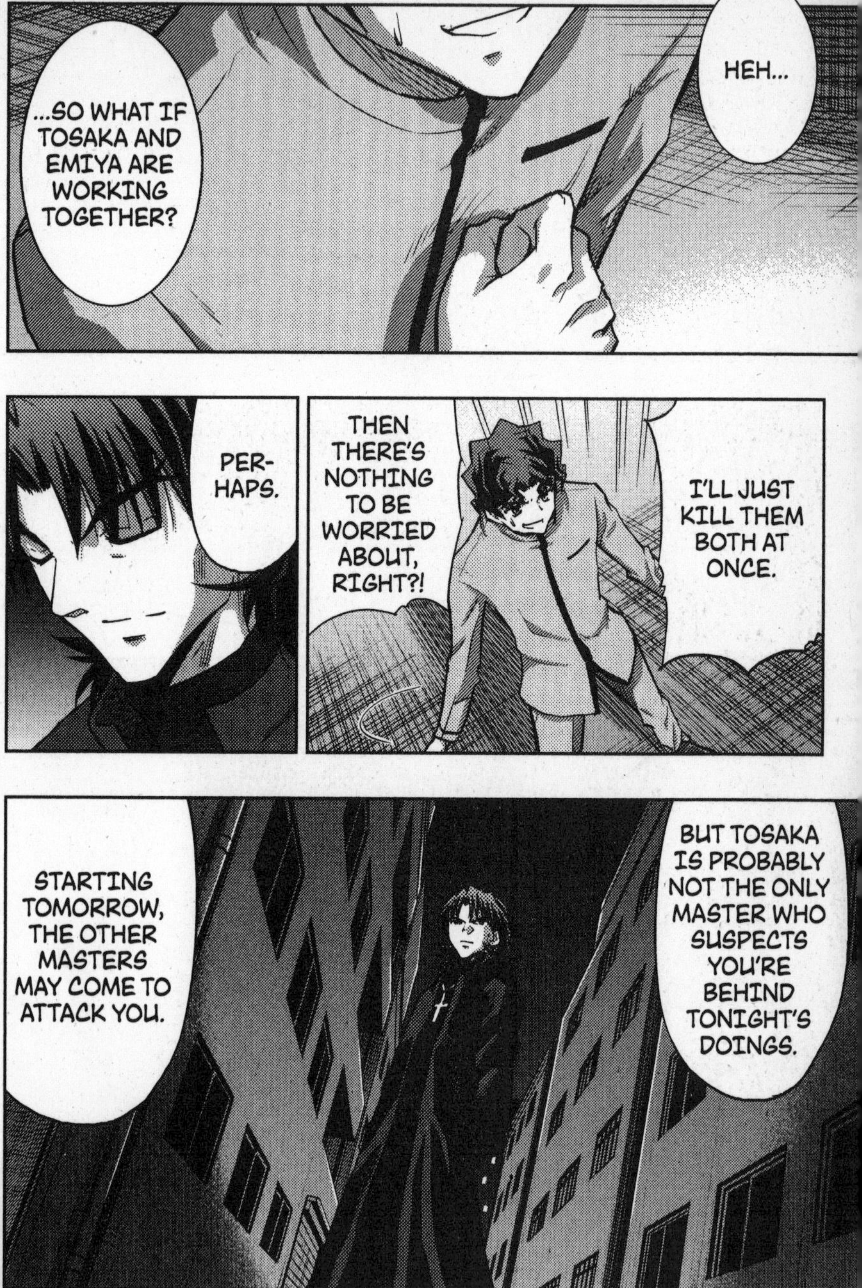
HEH...
...SO WHAT IF TOSAKA AND EMIYA ARE WORKING TOGETHER?
THEN THERE'S NOTHING TO BE WORRIED ABOUT, RIGHT?!
I'LL JUST KILL THEM BOTH AT ONCE.
PER-HAPS.
BUT TOSAKA IS PROBABLY NOT THE ONLY MASTER WHO SUSPECTS YOU'RE BEHIND TONIGHT'S DOINGS.
STARTING TOMORROW, THE OTHER MASTERS MAY COME TO ATTACK YOU.

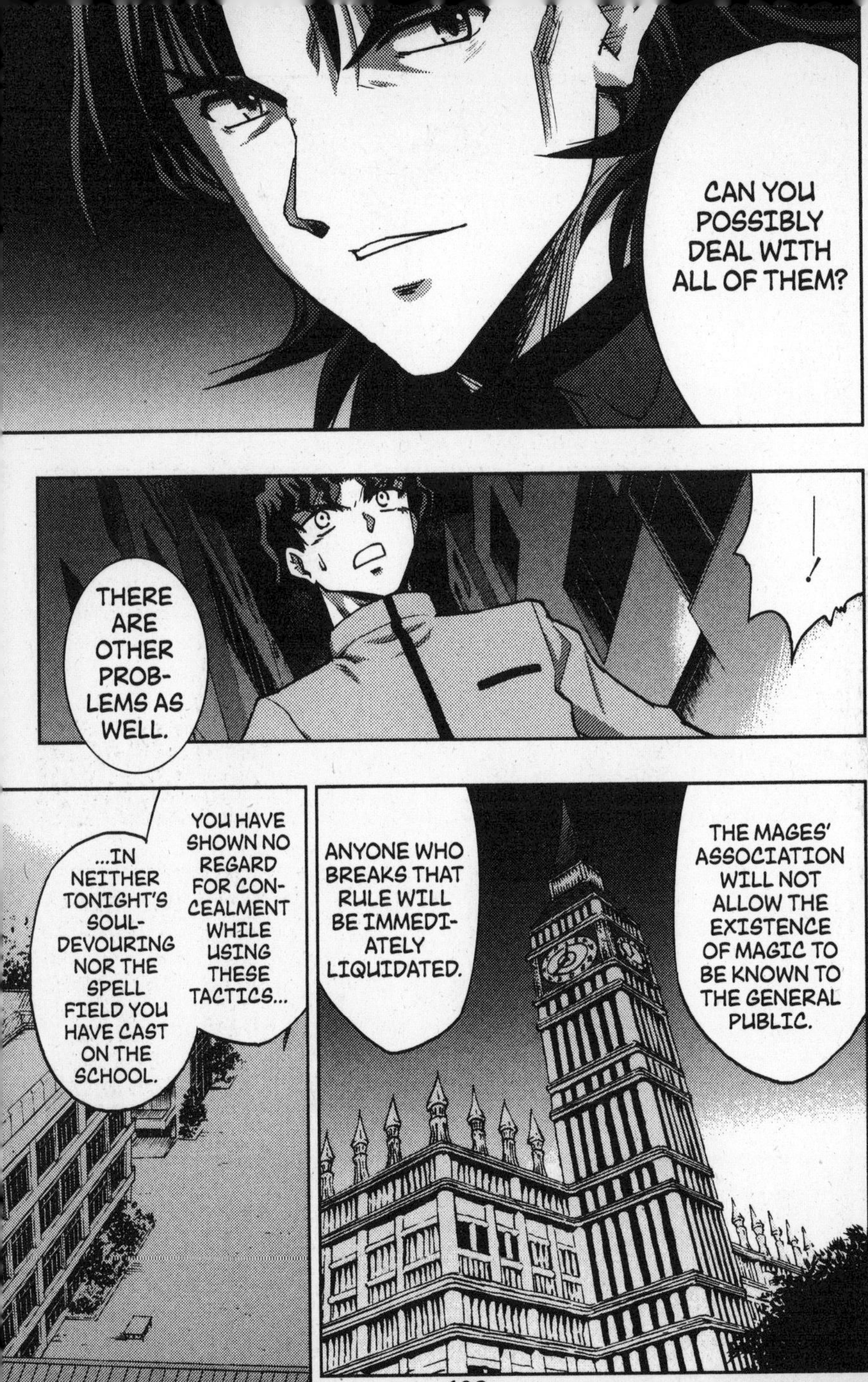
CAN YOU POSSIBLY DEAL WITH ALL OF THEM?
!
THERE ARE OTHER PROBLEMS AS WELL.
THE MAGES' ASSOCIATION WILL NOT ALLOW THE EXISTENCE OF MAGIC TO BE KNOWN TO THE GENERAL PUBLIC.
ANYONE WHO BREAKS THAT RULE WILL BE IMMEDIATELY LIQUIDATED.
YOU HAVE SHOWN NO REGARD FOR CONCEALMENT WHILE USING THESE TACTICS...
...IN NEITHER TONIGHT'S SOUL-DEVOURING NOR THE SPELL FIELD YOU HAVE CAST ON THE SCHOOL.

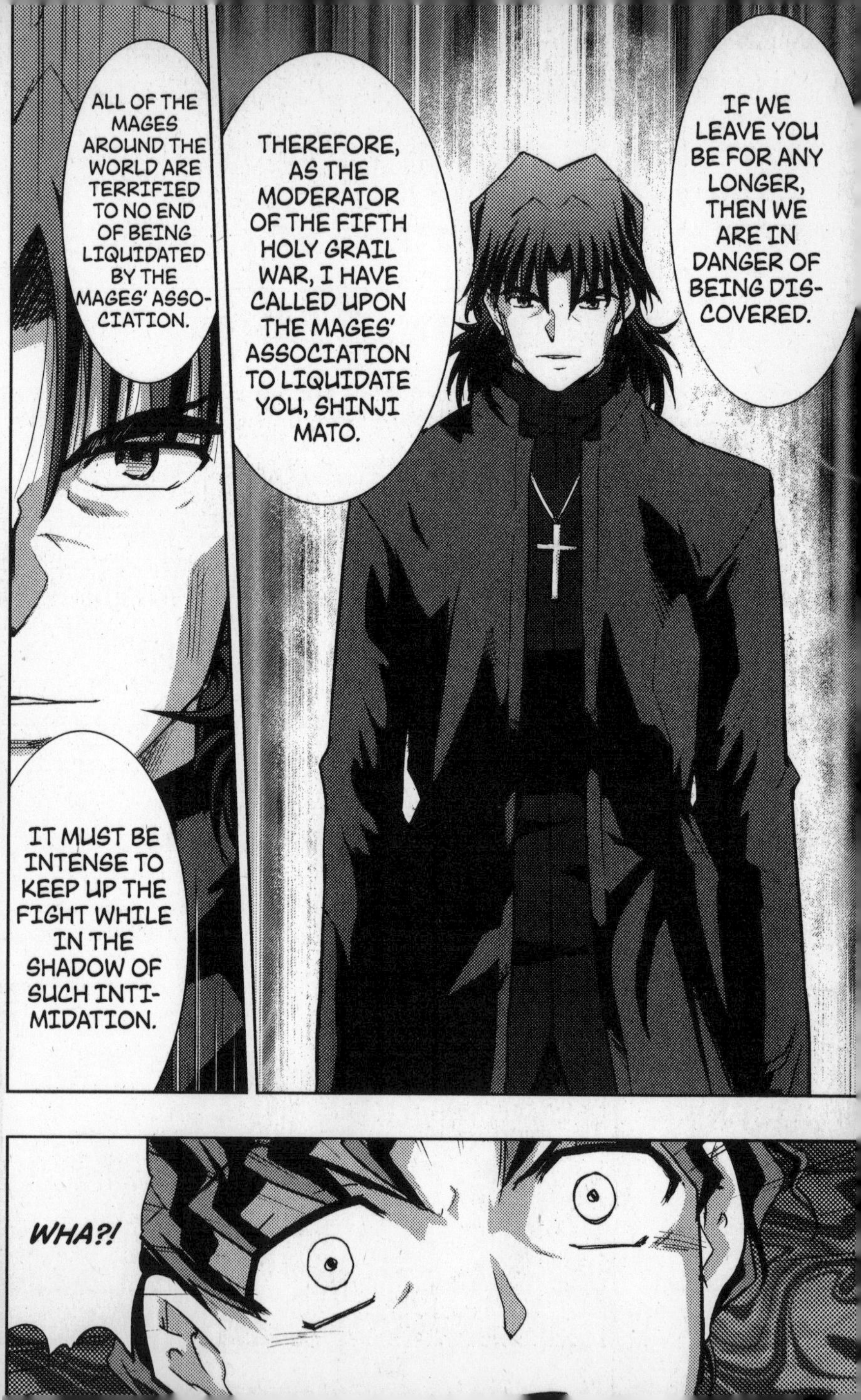
IF WE LEAVE YOU BE FOR ANY LONGER, THEN WE ARE IN DANGER OF BEING DISCOVERED.
THEREFORE, AS THE MODERATOR OF THE FIFTH HOLY GRAIL WAR, I HAVE CALLED UPON THE MAGES' ASSOCIATION TO LIQUIDATE YOU, SHINJI MATO.
ALL OF THE MAGES AROUND THE WORLD ARE TERRIFIED TO NO END OF BEING LIQUIDATED BY THE MAGES' ASSOCIATION.
IT MUST BE INTENSE TO KEEP UP THE FIGHT WHILE IN THE SHADOW OF SUCH INTIMIDATION.
WHA?!

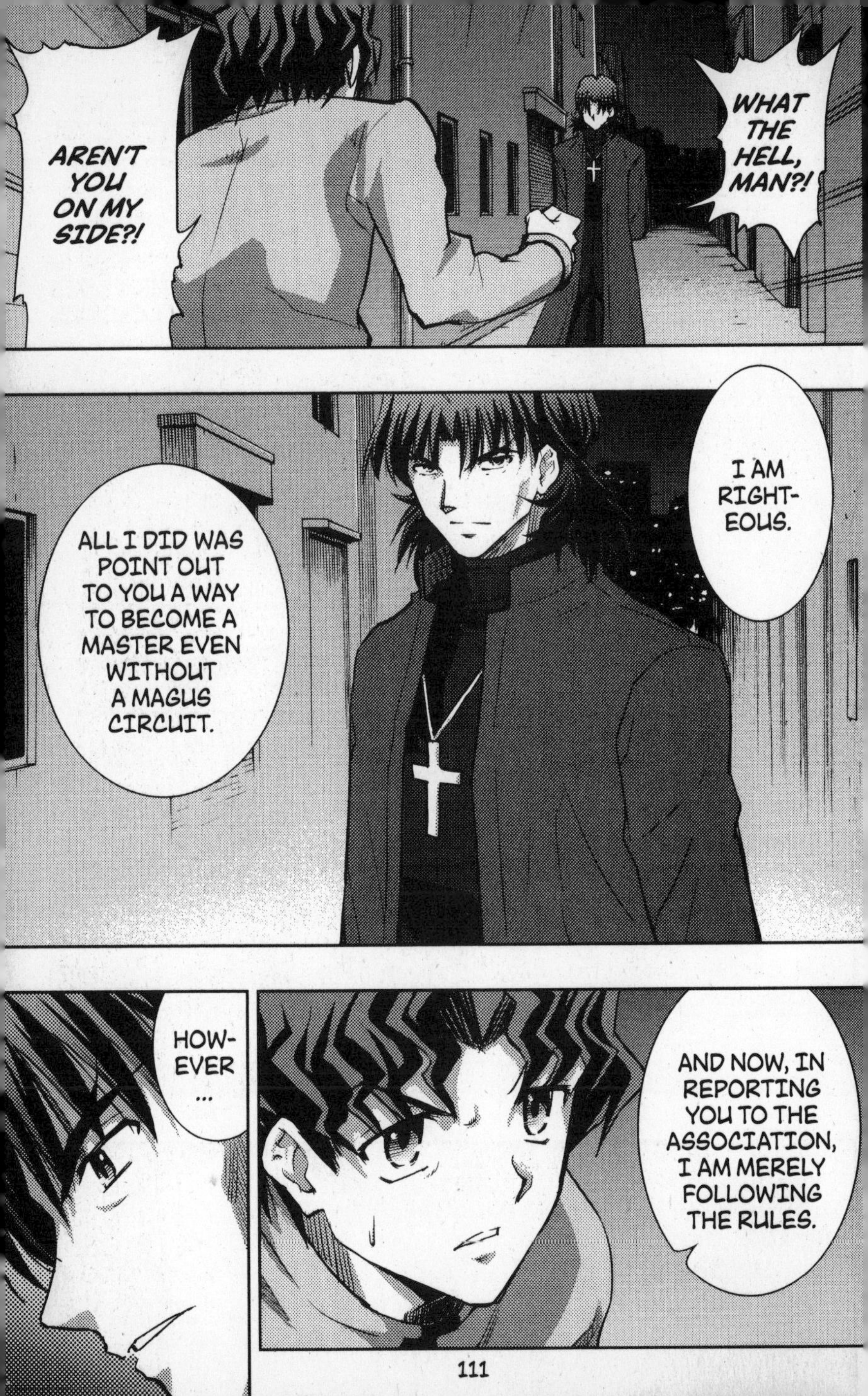
WHAT THE HELL, MAN?!
AREN'T YOU ON MY SIDE?!
I AM RIGHTEOUS.
ALL I DID WAS POINT OUT TO YOU A WAY TO BECOME A MASTER EVEN WITHOUT A MAGUS CIRCUIT.
AND NOW, IN REPORTING YOU TO THE ASSOCIATION, I AM MERELY FOLLOWING THE RULES.
HOWEVER ...

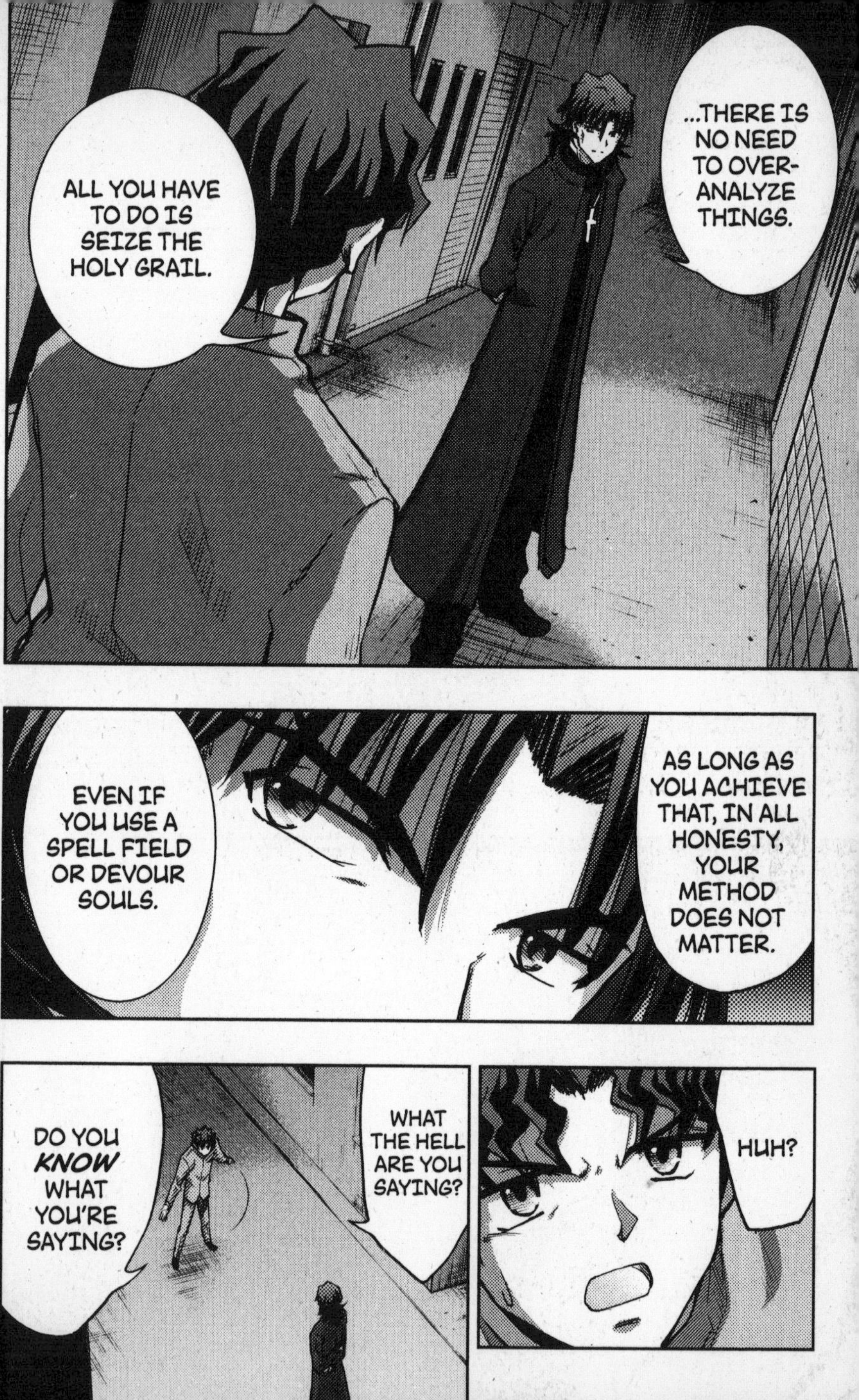
...THERE IS NO NEED TO OVER-ANALYZE THINGS.
ALL YOU HAVE TO DO IS SEIZE THE HOLY GRAIL.
AS LONG AS YOU ACHIEVE THAT, IN ALL HONESTY, YOUR METHOD DOES NOT MATTER.
EVEN IF YOU USE A SPELL FIELD OR DEVOUR SOULS.
HUH?
WHAT THE HELL ARE YOU SAYING?
DO YOU *KNOW* WHAT YOU'RE SAYING?

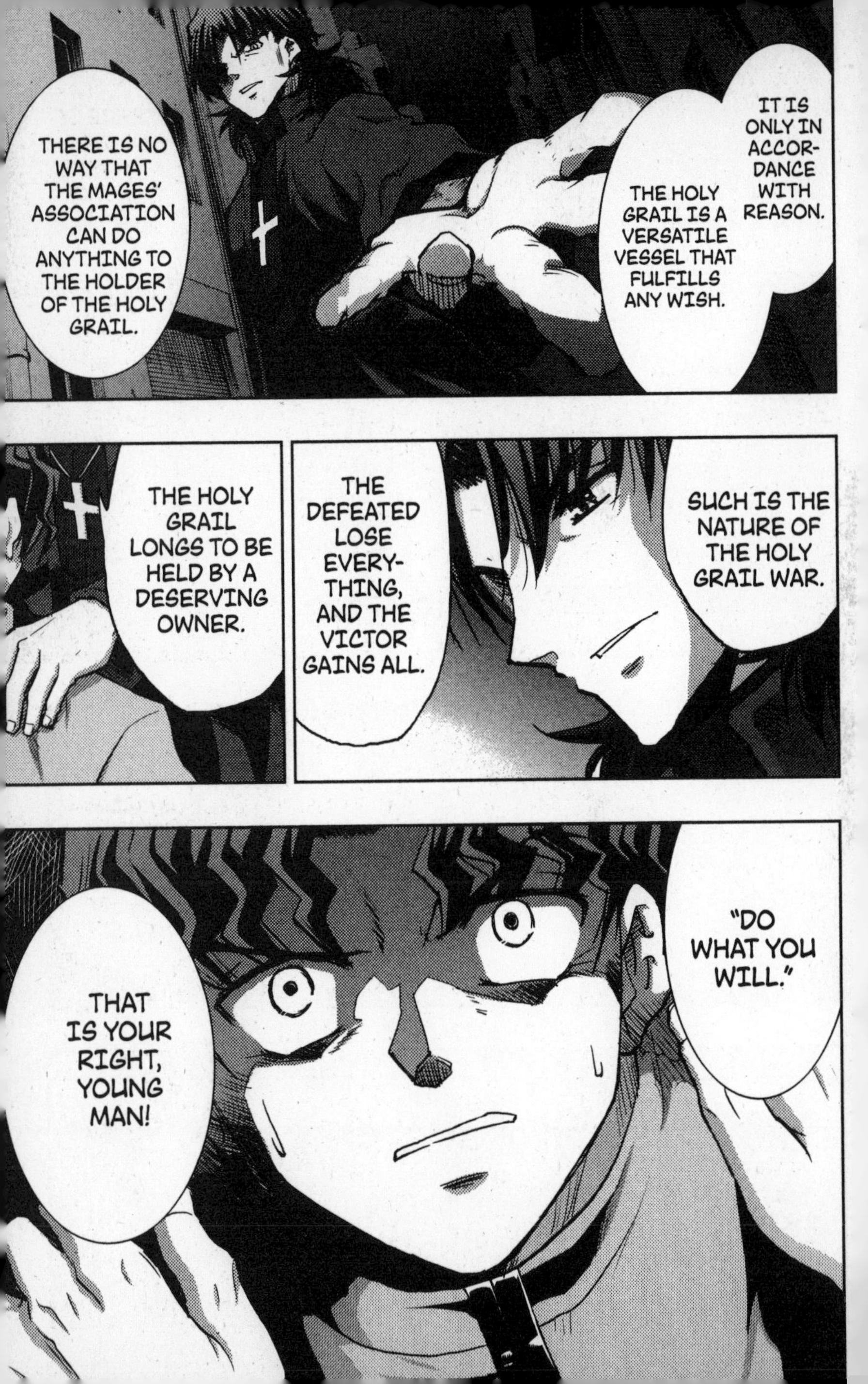
IT IS ONLY IN ACCORDANCE WITH REASON.
THE HOLY GRAIL IS A VERSATILE VESSEL THAT FULFILLS ANY WISH.
THERE IS NO WAY THAT THE MAGES' ASSOCIATION CAN DO ANYTHING TO THE HOLDER OF THE HOLY GRAIL.
SUCH IS THE NATURE OF THE HOLY GRAIL WAR.
THE DEFEATED LOSE EVERYTHING, AND THE VICTOR GAINS ALL.
THE HOLY GRAIL LONGS TO BE HELD BY A DESERVING OWNER.
"DO WHAT YOU WILL."
THAT IS YOUR RIGHT, YOUNG MAN!

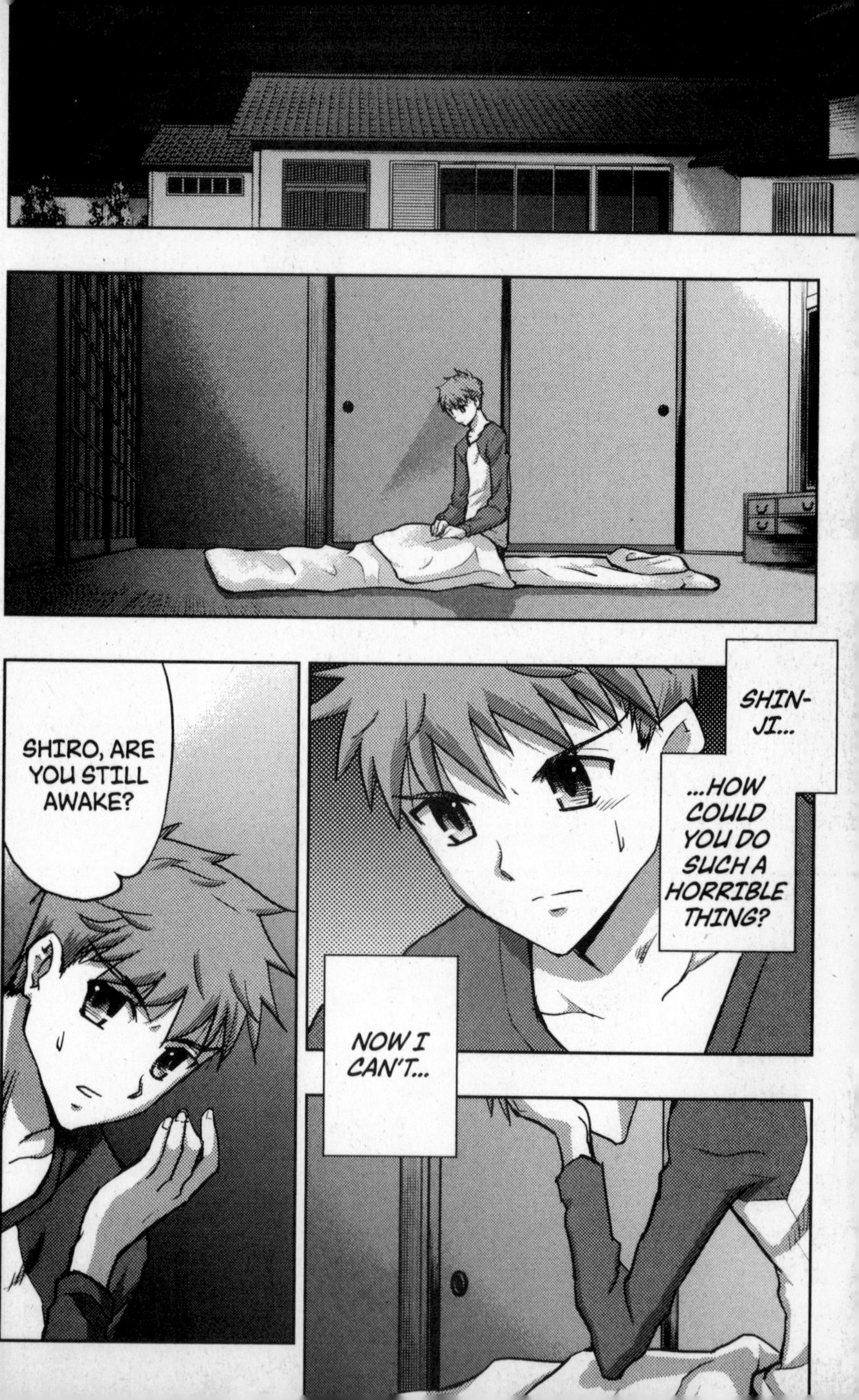
SHIN-JI...
...HOW COULD YOU DO SUCH A HORRIBLE THING?
NOW I CAN'T...
SHIRO, ARE YOU STILL AWAKE?

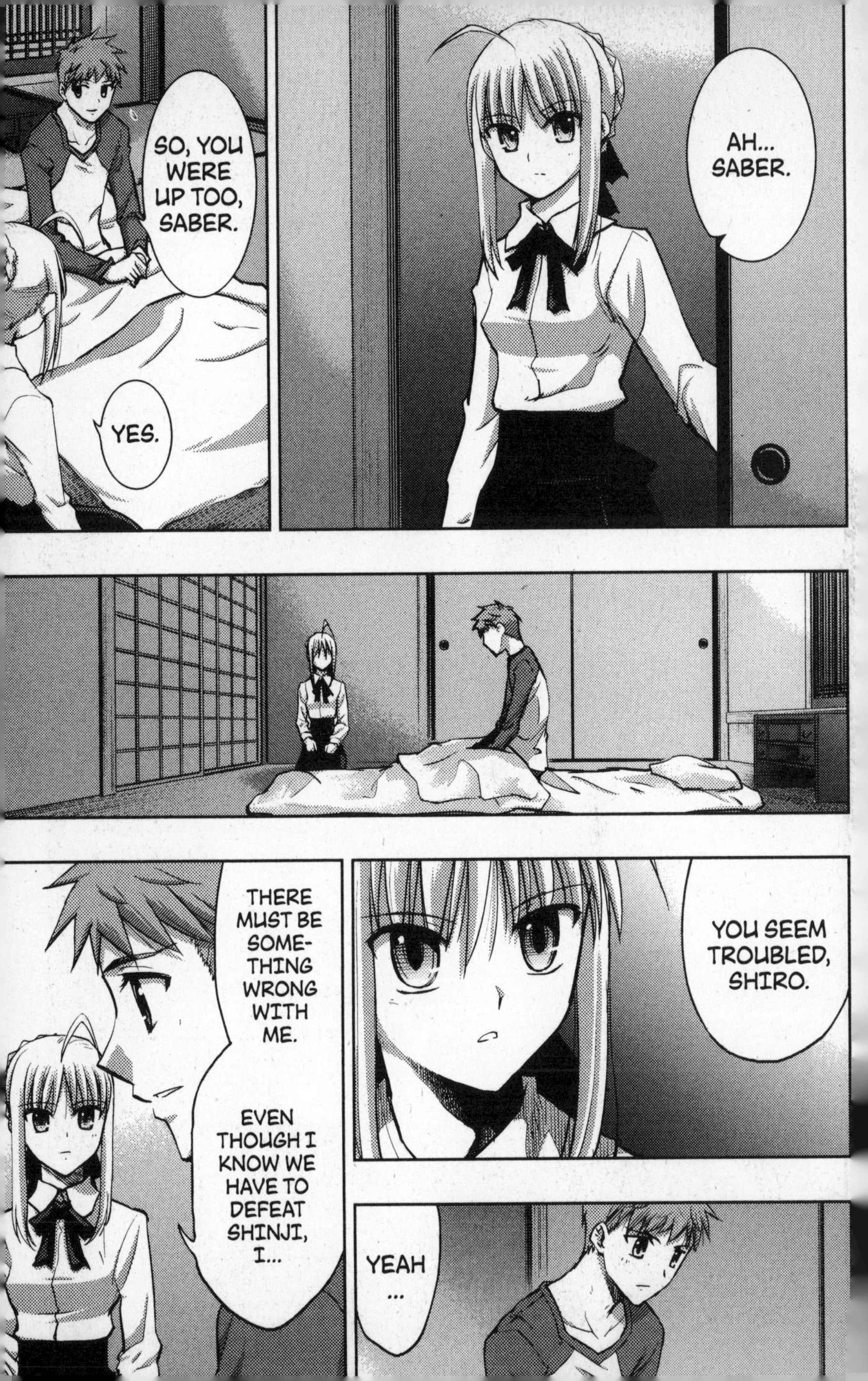
AH... SABER.
SO, YOU WERE UP TOO, SABER.
YES.
YOU SEEM TROUBLED, SHIRO.
YEAH ...
THERE MUST BE SOME-THING WRONG WITH ME.
EVEN THOUGH I KNOW WE HAVE TO DEFEAT SHINJI, I...

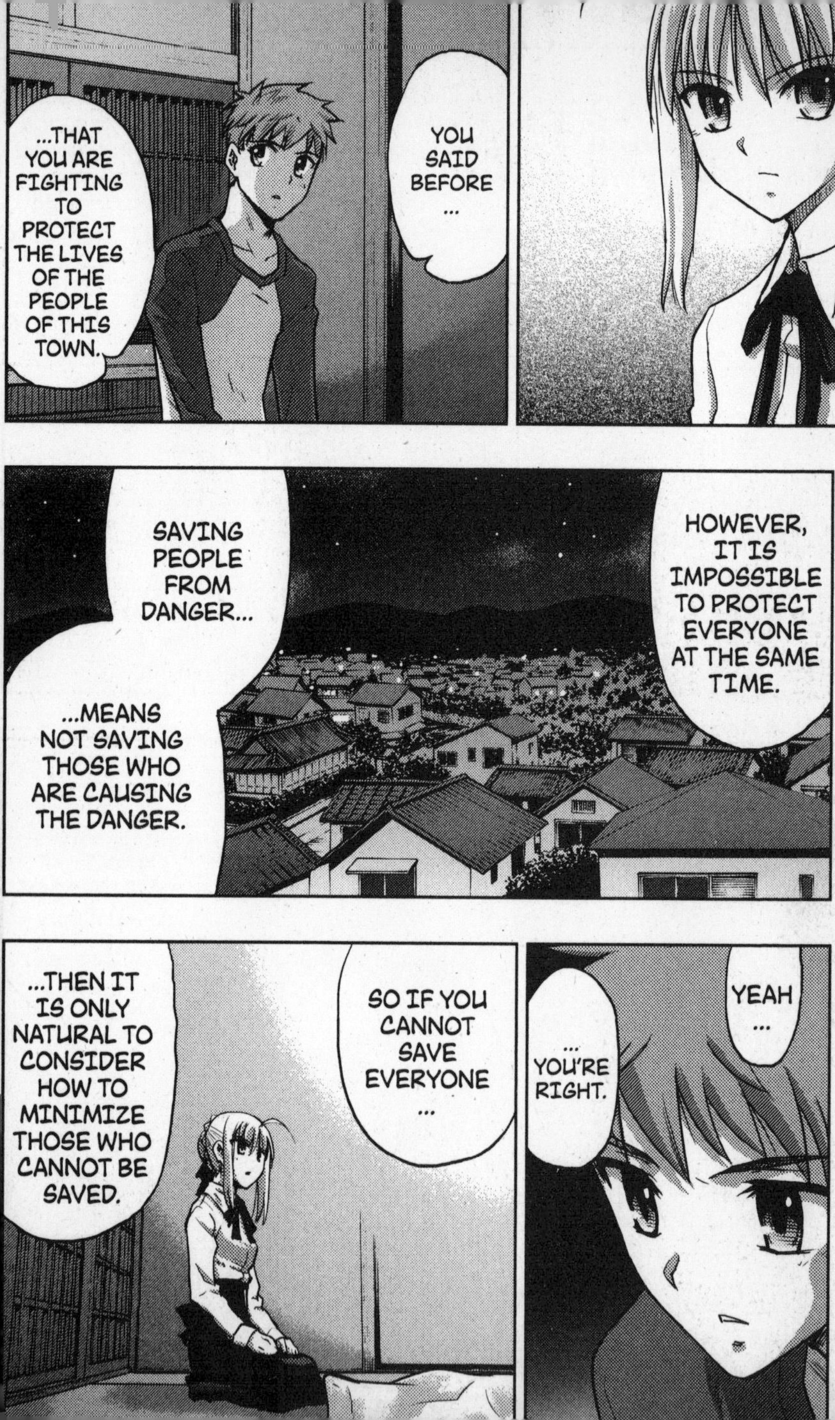
YOU SAID BEFORE ...
...THAT YOU ARE FIGHTING TO PROTECT THE LIVES OF THE PEOPLE OF THIS TOWN.
HOWEVER, IT IS IMPOSSIBLE TO PROTECT EVERYONE AT THE SAME TIME.
SAVING PEOPLE FROM DANGER...
...MEANS NOT SAVING THOSE WHO ARE CAUSING THE DANGER.
YEAH ...
... YOU'RE RIGHT.
SO IF YOU CANNOT SAVE EVERYONE ...
...THEN IT IS ONLY NATURAL TO CONSIDER HOW TO MINIMIZE THOSE WHO CANNOT BE SAVED.

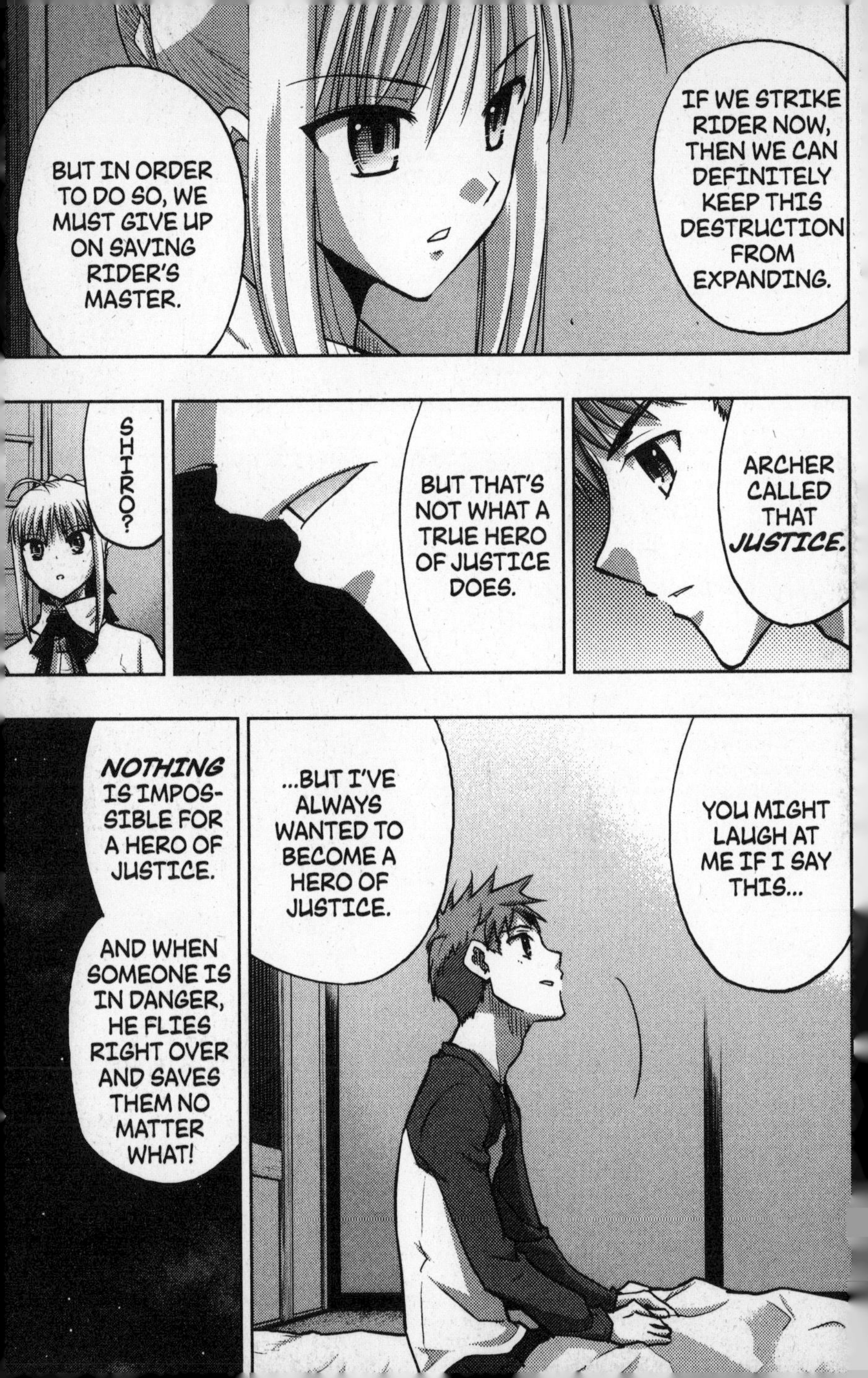
IF WE STRIKE RIDER NOW, THEN WE CAN DEFINITELY KEEP THIS DESTRUCTION FROM EXPANDING.
BUT IN ORDER TO DO SO, WE MUST GIVE UP ON SAVING RIDER'S MASTER.
ARCHER CALLED THAT *JUSTICE.*
BUT THAT'S NOT WHAT A TRUE HERO OF JUSTICE DOES.
SHIRO?
YOU MIGHT LAUGH AT ME IF I SAY THIS...
...BUT I'VE ALWAYS WANTED TO BECOME A HERO OF JUSTICE.
NOTHING IS IMPOSSIBLE FOR A HERO OF JUSTICE.
AND WHEN SOMEONE IS IN DANGER, HE FLIES RIGHT OVER AND SAVES THEM NO MATTER WHAT!

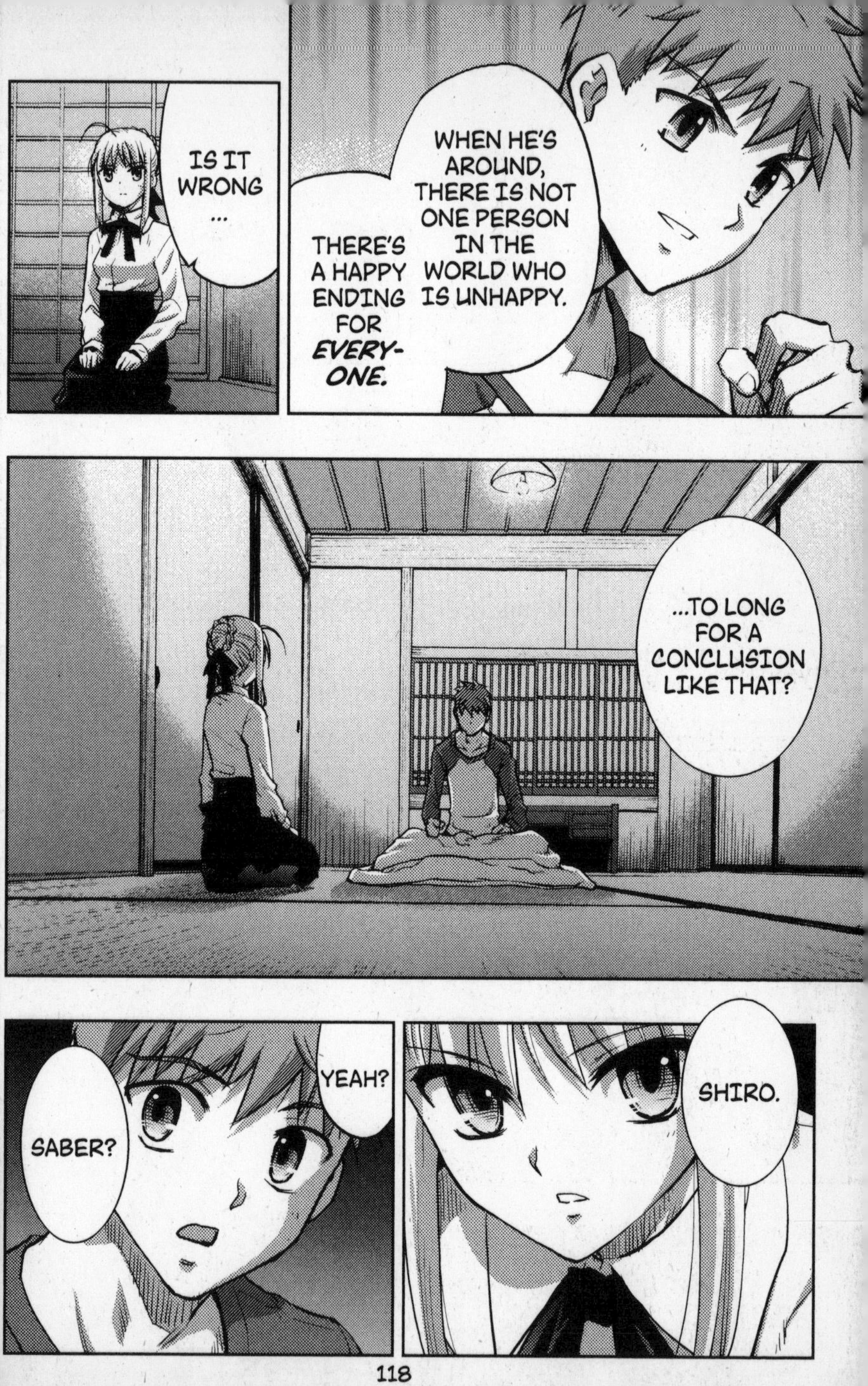
WHEN HE'S AROUND, THERE IS NOT ONE PERSON IN THE WORLD WHO IS UNHAPPY.
THERE'S A HAPPY ENDING FOR *EVERYONE.*
IS IT WRONG ...
...TO LONG FOR A CONCLUSION LIKE THAT?
SHIRO.
YEAH?
SABER?

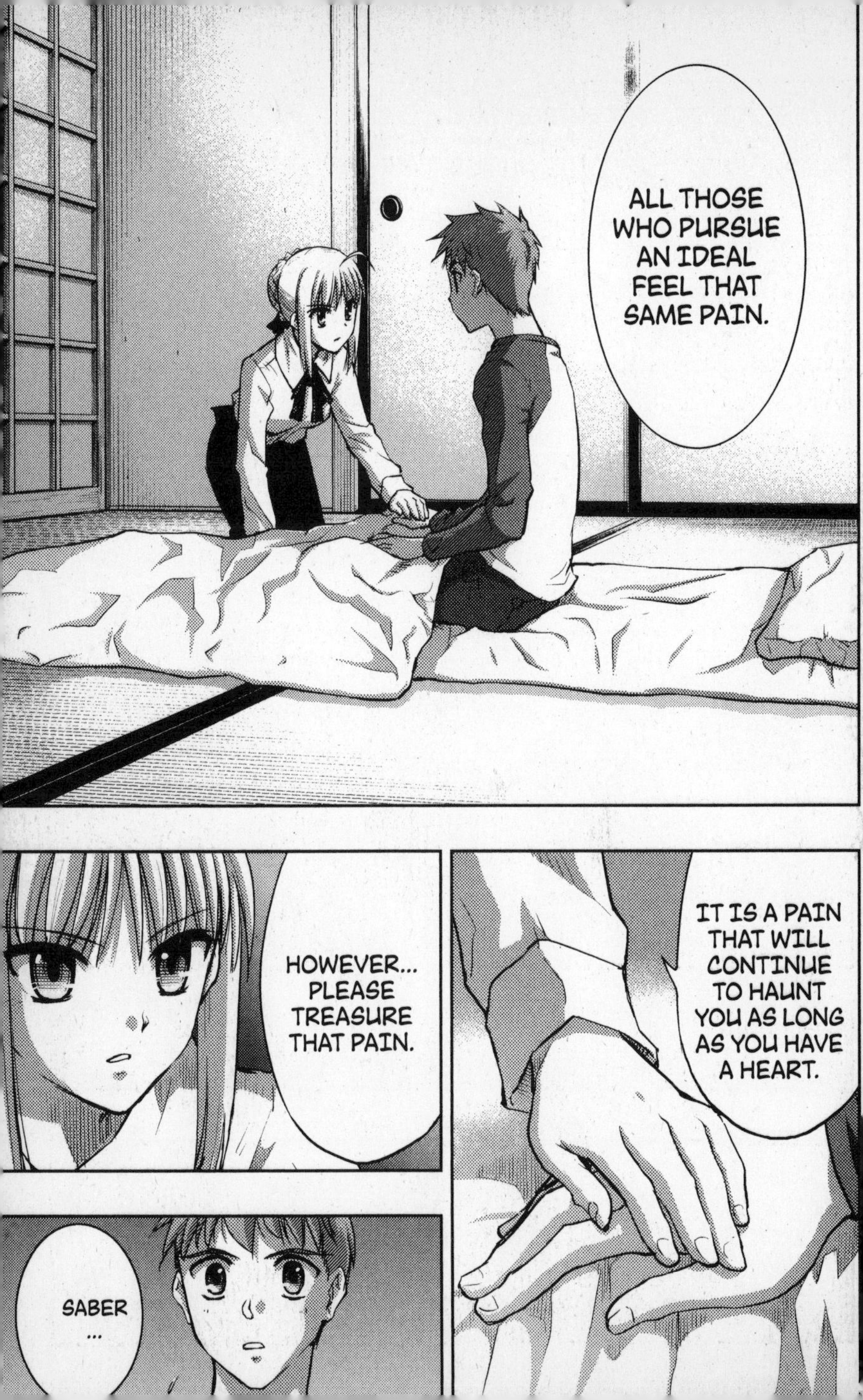
ALL THOSE WHO PURSUE AN IDEAL FEEL THAT SAME PAIN.
IT IS A PAIN THAT WILL CONTINUE TO HAUNT YOU AS LONG AS YOU HAVE A HEART.
HOWEVER... PLEASE TREASURE THAT PAIN.
SABER ...

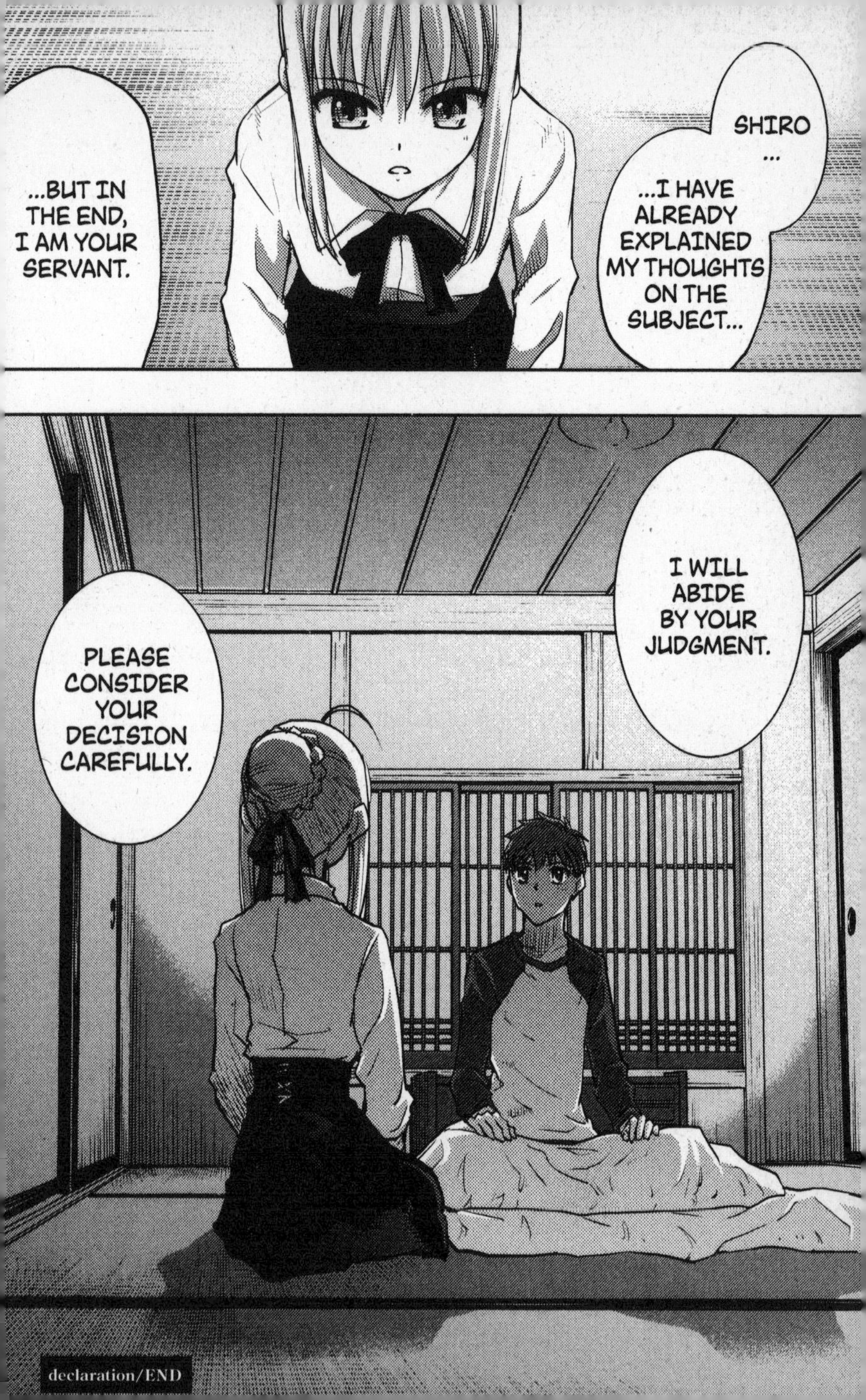
SHIRO ...
...I HAVE ALREADY EXPLAINED MY THOUGHTS ON THE SUBJECT...
...BUT IN THE END, I AM YOUR SERVANT.
I WILL ABIDE BY YOUR JUDGMENT.
PLEASE CONSIDER YOUR DECISION CAREFULLY.
declaration/END

Fate
stay night

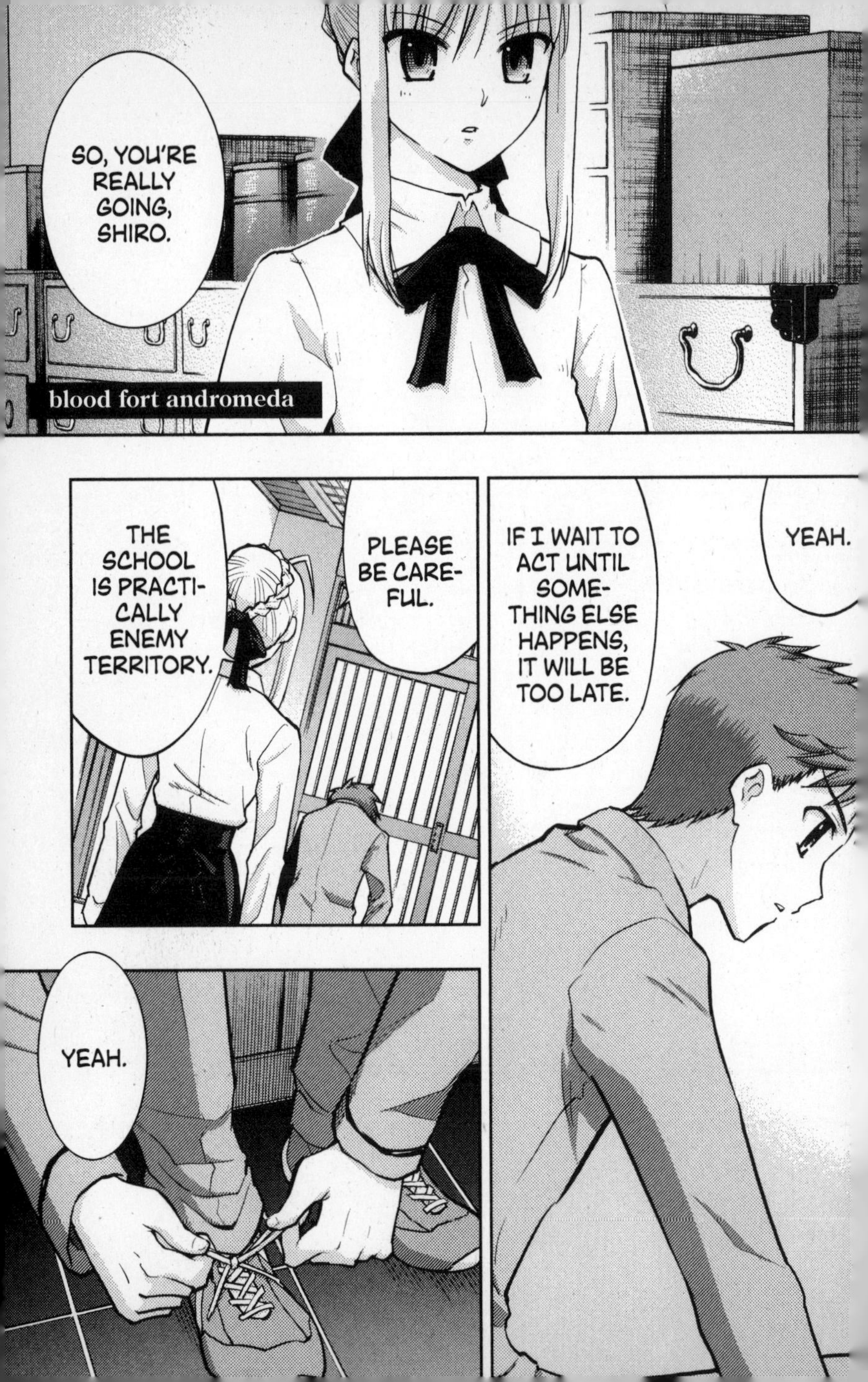
SO, YOU'RE REALLY GOING, SHIRO.
blood fort andromeda
YEAH.
IF I WAIT TO ACT UNTIL SOME-THING ELSE HAPPENS, IT WILL BE TOO LATE.
PLEASE BE CARE-FUL.
THE SCHOOL IS PRACTI-CALLY ENEMY TERRITORY.
YEAH.

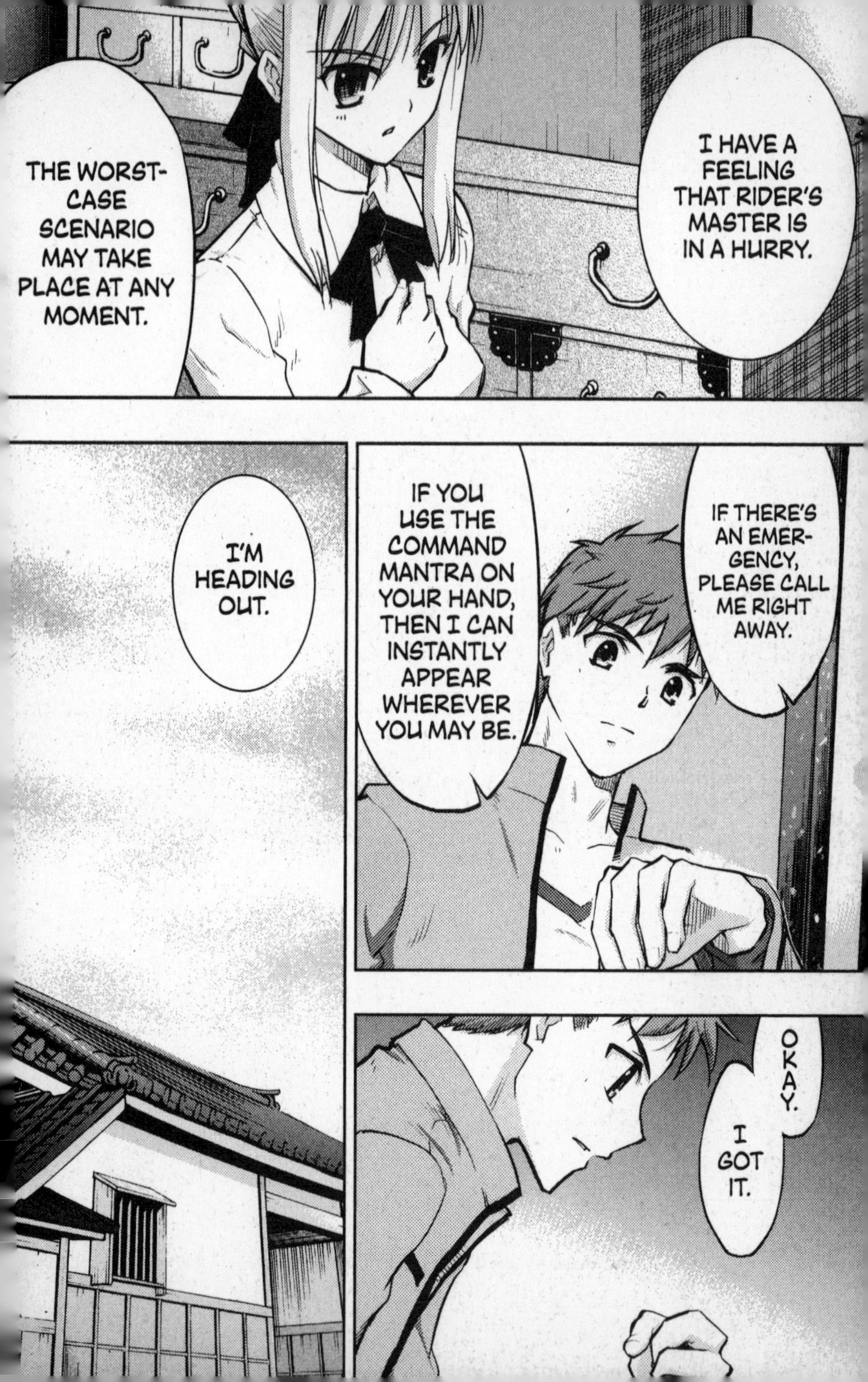
I HAVE A FEELING THAT RIDER'S MASTER IS IN A HURRY.
THE WORST-CASE SCENARIO MAY TAKE PLACE AT ANY MOMENT.
IF THERE'S AN EMERGENCY, PLEASE CALL ME RIGHT AWAY.
IF YOU USE THE COMMAND MANTRA ON YOUR HAND, THEN I CAN INSTANTLY APPEAR WHEREVER YOU MAY BE.
OKAY.
I GOT IT.
I'M HEADING OUT.

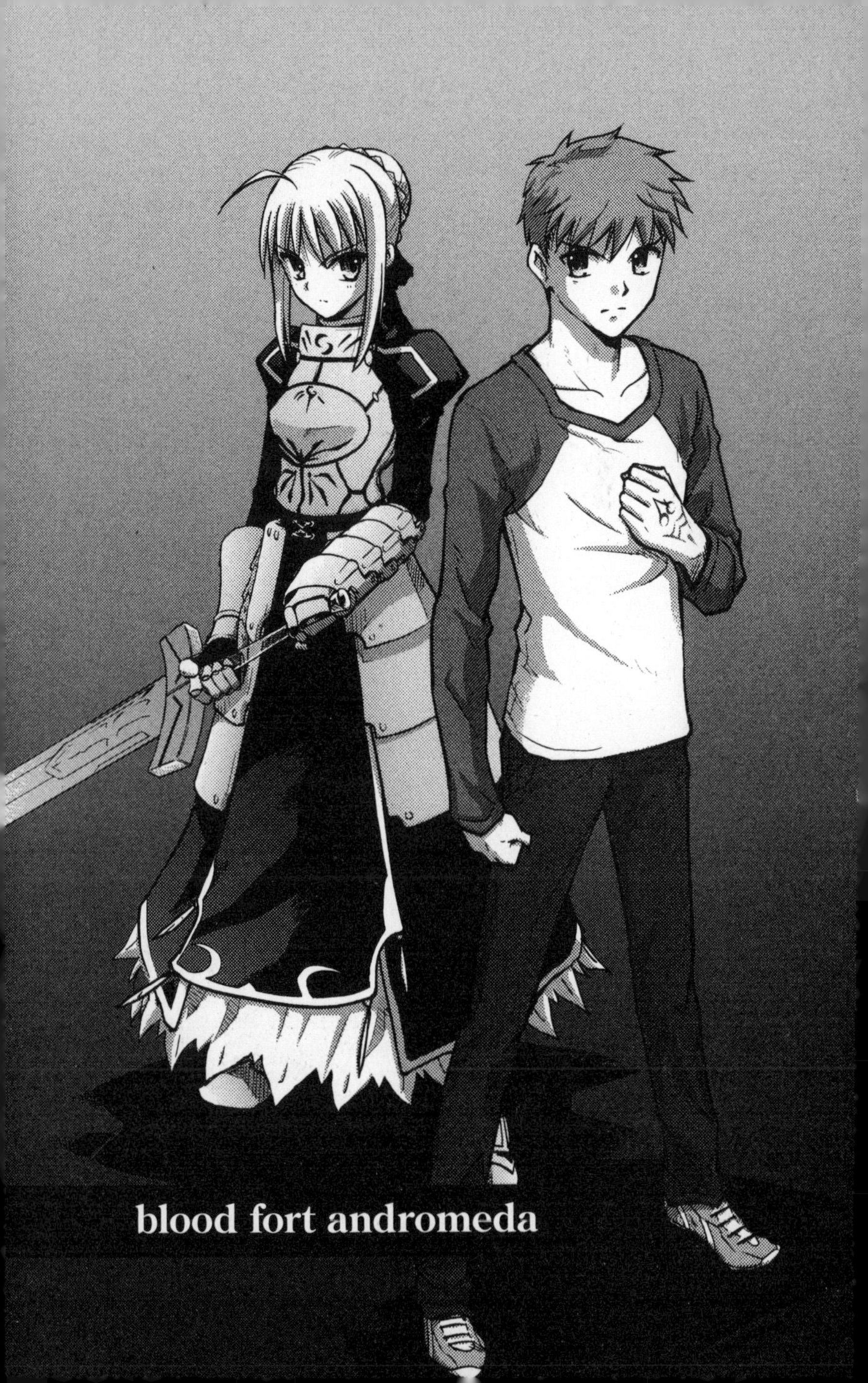
blood fort andromeda

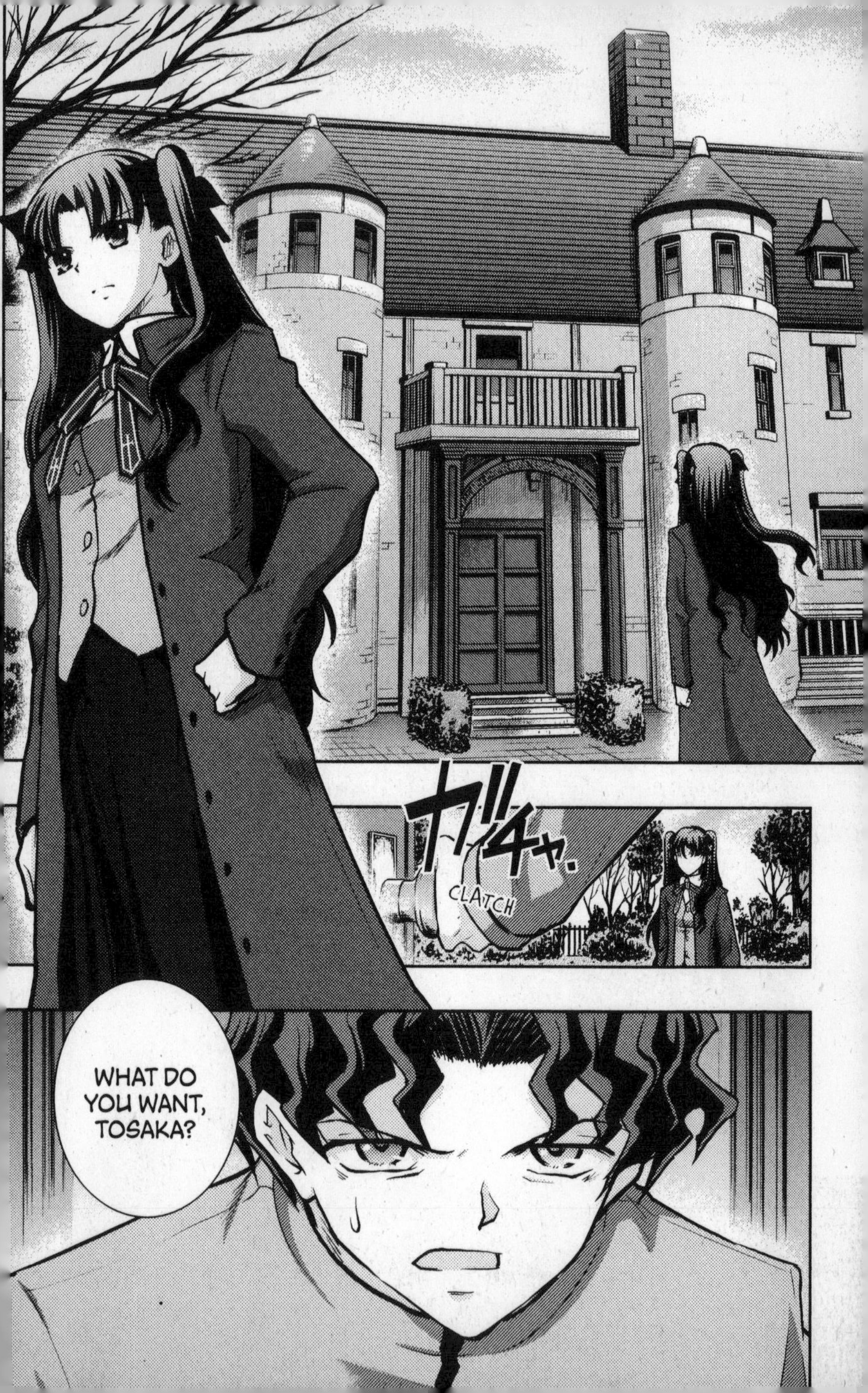
ガチャ.
CLATCH
WHAT DO YOU WANT, TOSAKA?

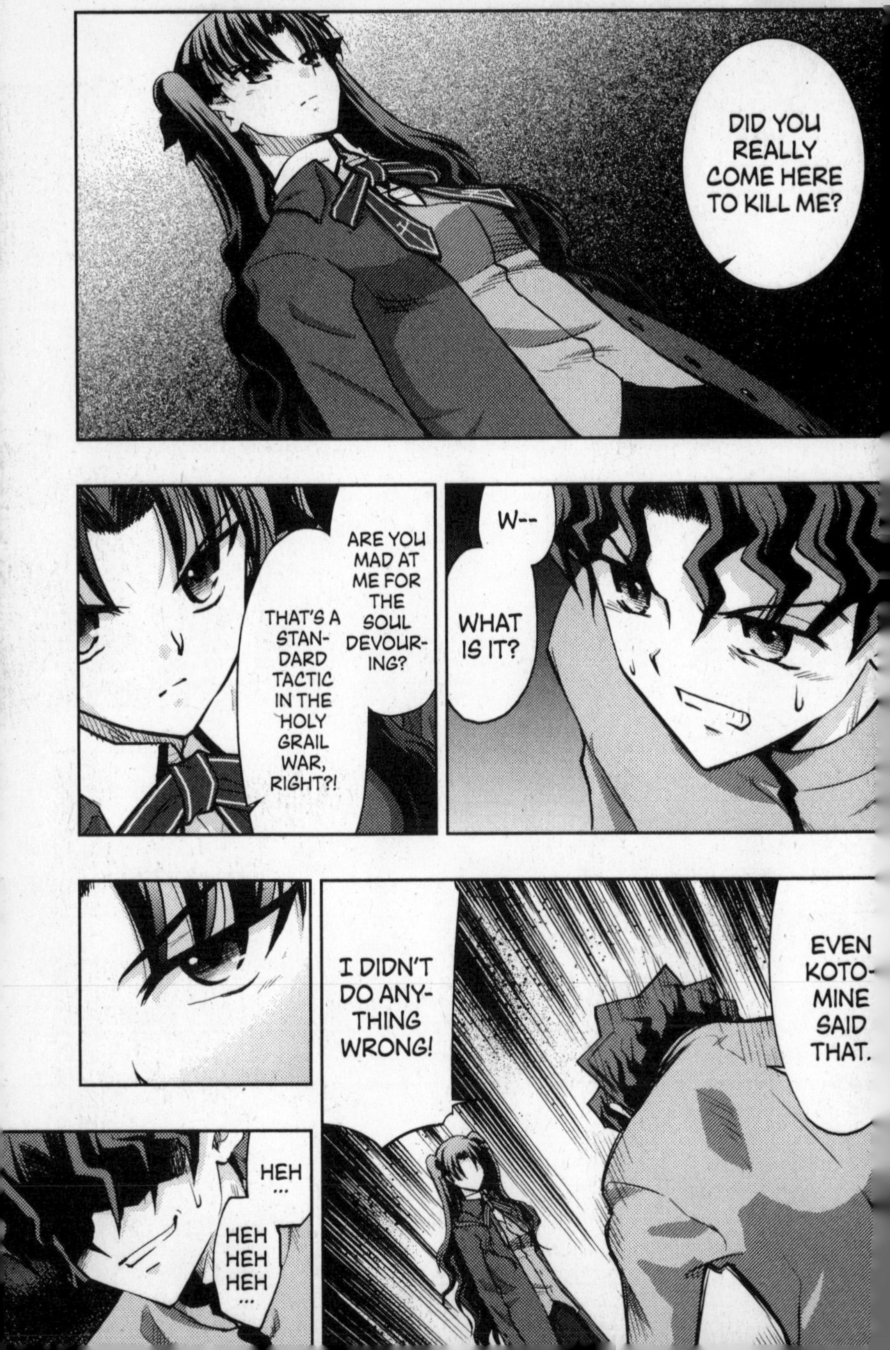
DID YOU REALLY COME HERE TO KILL ME?
W--
WHAT IS IT?
ARE YOU MAD AT ME FOR THE SOUL DEVOURING?
THAT'S A STANDARD TACTIC IN THE HOLY GRAIL WAR, RIGHT?!
EVEN KOTOMINE SAID THAT.
I DIDN'T DO ANYTHING WRONG!
HEH...
HEH HEH HEH...

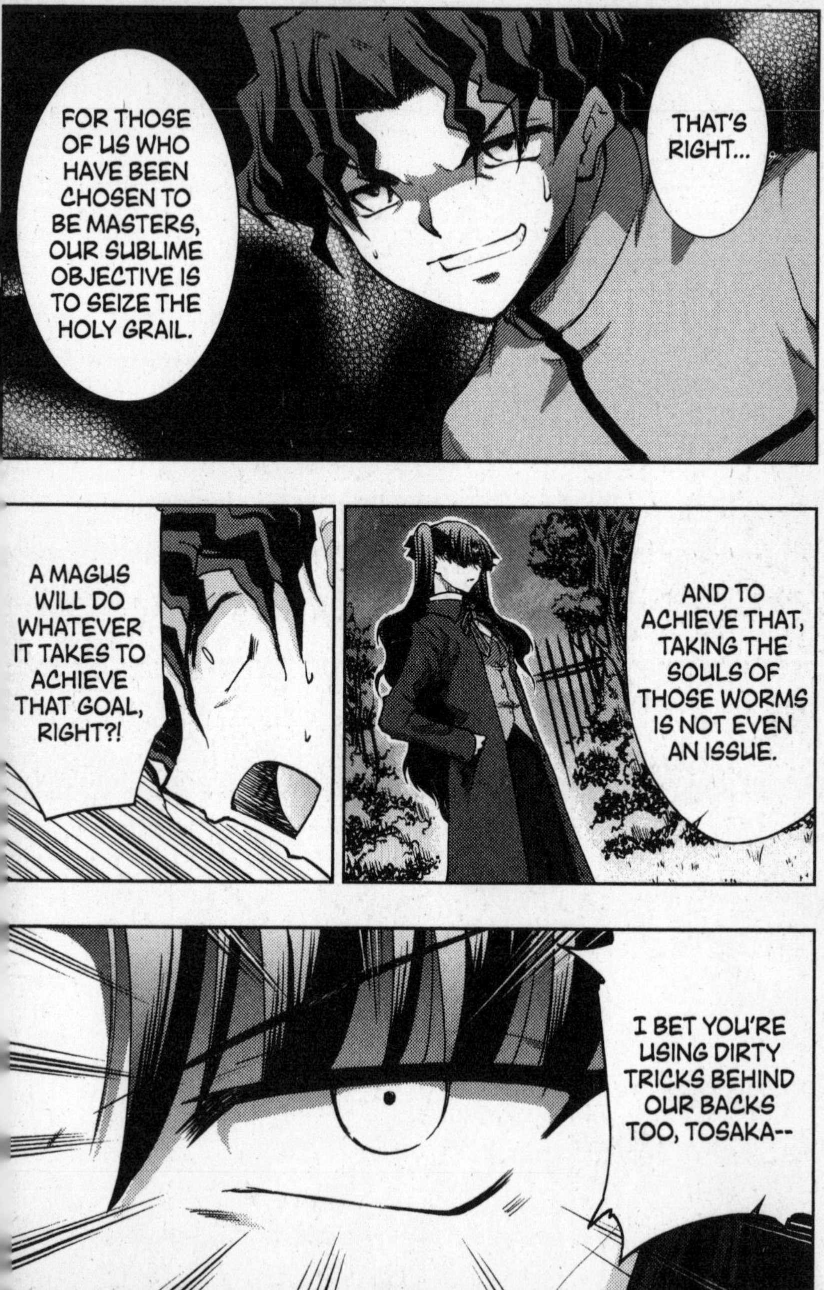
THAT'S RIGHT...
FOR THOSE OF US WHO HAVE BEEN CHOSEN TO BE MASTERS, OUR SUBLIME OBJECTIVE IS TO SEIZE THE HOLY GRAIL.
AND TO ACHIEVE THAT, TAKING THE SOULS OF THOSE WORMS IS NOT EVEN AN ISSUE.
A MAGUS WILL DO WHATEVER IT TAKES TO ACHIEVE THAT GOAL, RIGHT?!
I BET YOU'RE USING DIRTY TRICKS BEHIND OUR BACKS TOO, TOSAKA--

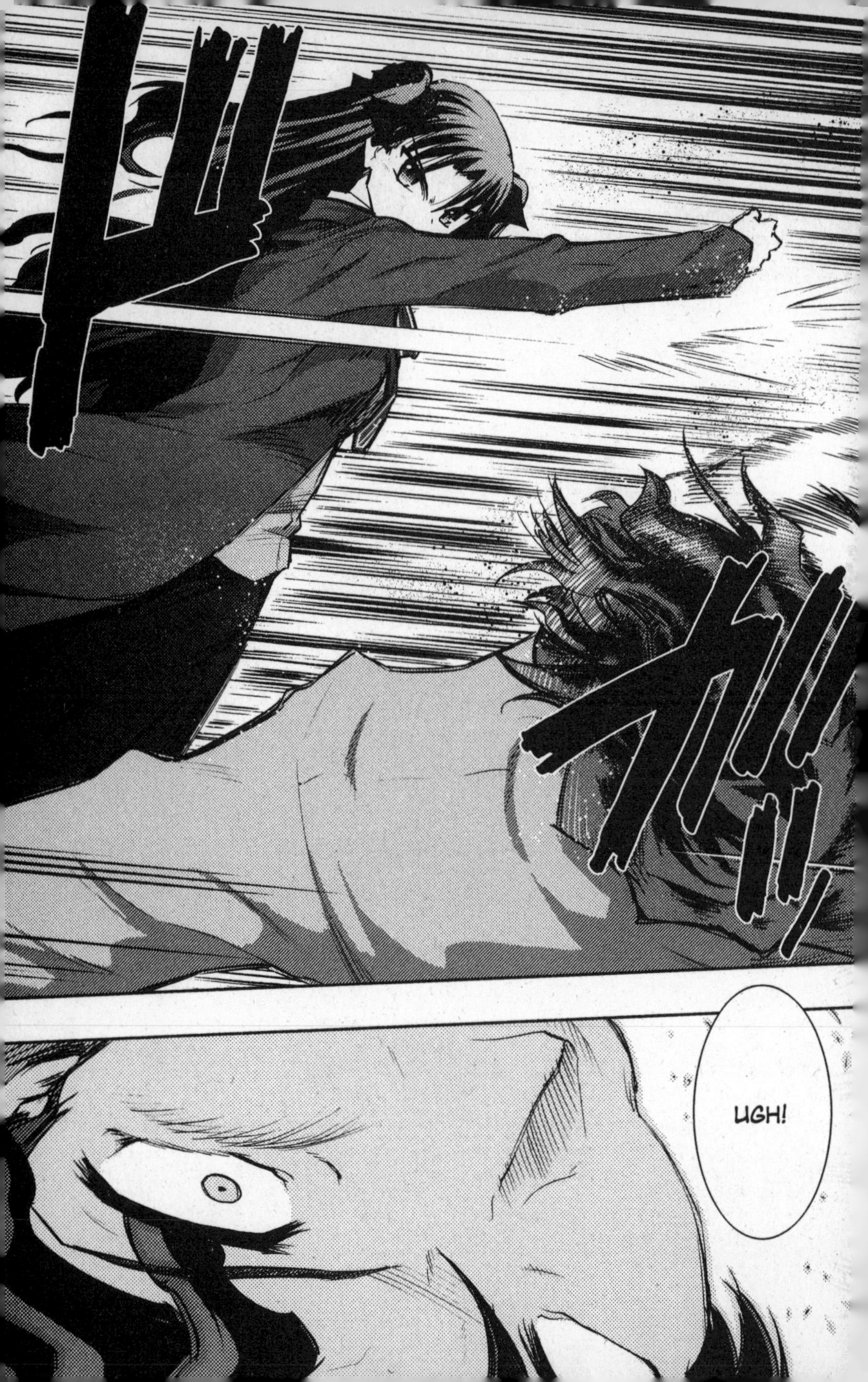
UGH!

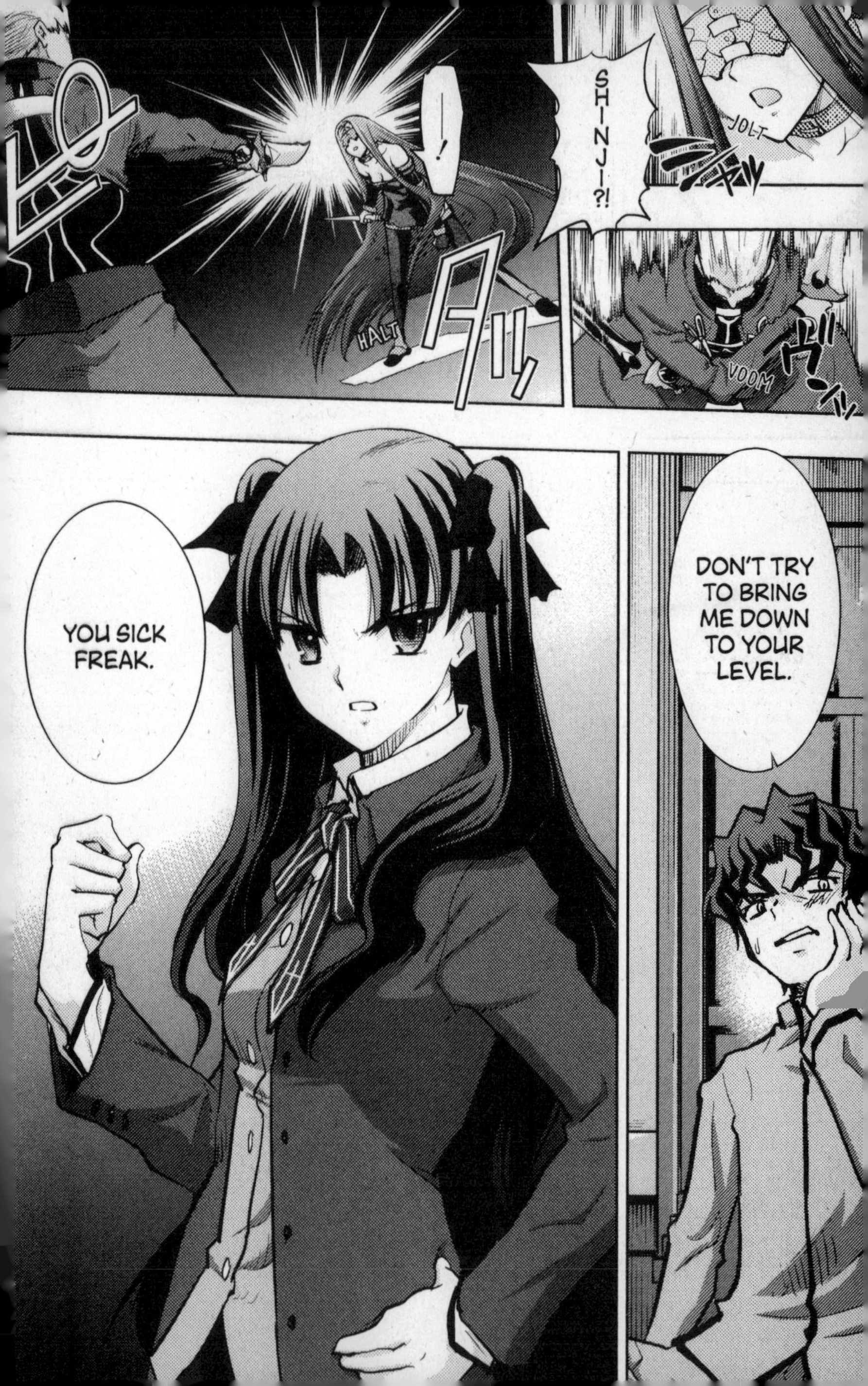
SHINJI?!
JOLT
VOOM
!
HALT
DON'T TRY TO BRING ME DOWN TO YOUR LEVEL.
YOU SICK FREAK.

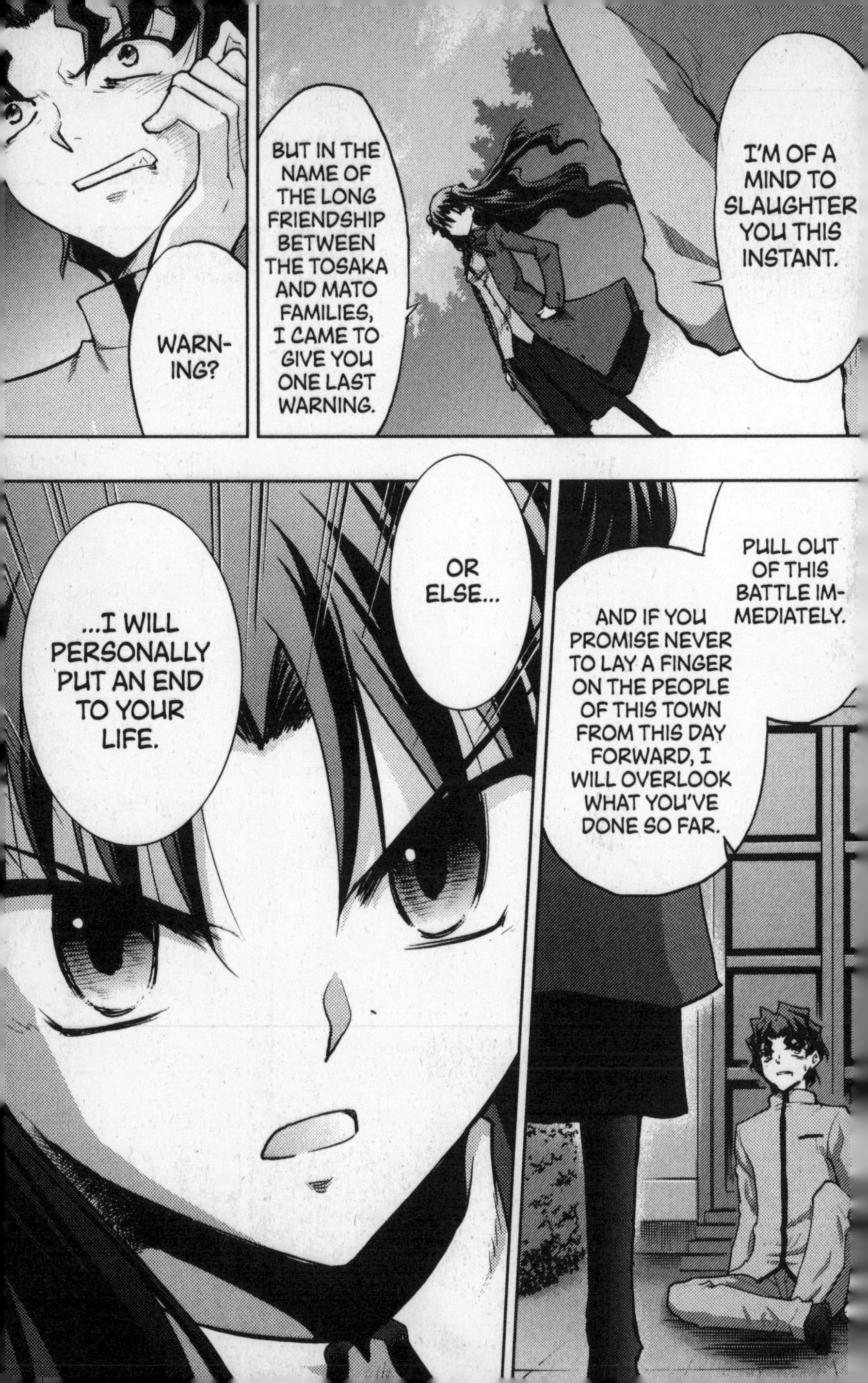
I'M OF A MIND TO SLAUGHTER YOU THIS INSTANT.
BUT IN THE NAME OF THE LONG FRIENDSHIP BETWEEN THE TOSAKA AND MATO FAMILIES, I CAME TO GIVE YOU ONE LAST WARNING.
WARN-ING?
PULL OUT OF THIS BATTLE IM-MEDIATELY.
AND IF YOU PROMISE NEVER TO LAY A FINGER ON THE PEOPLE OF THIS TOWN FROM THIS DAY FORWARD, I WILL OVERLOOK WHAT YOU'VE DONE SO FAR.
OR ELSE...
...I WILL PERSONALLY PUT AN END TO YOUR LIFE.

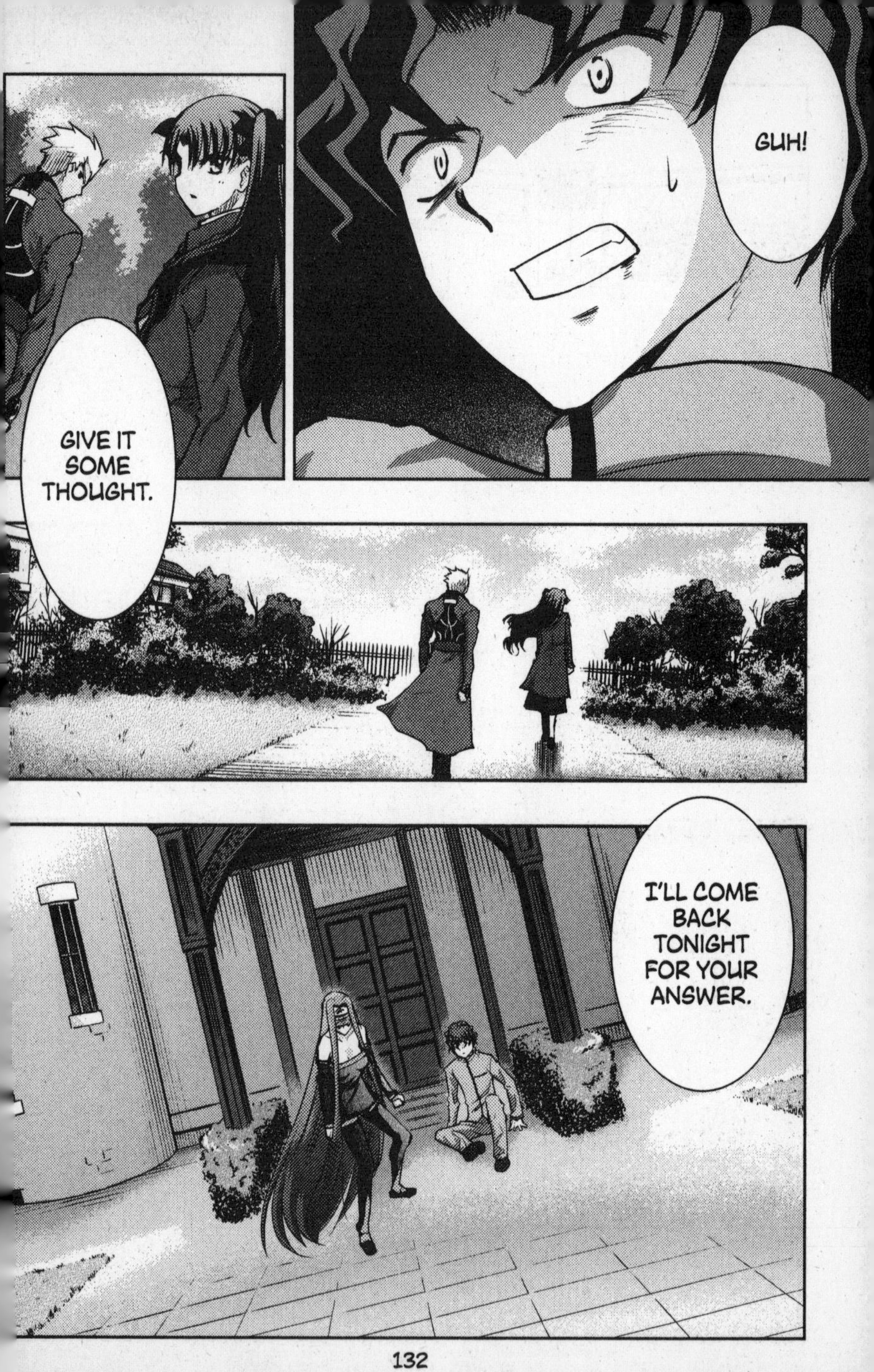
GUH!
GIVE IT SOME THOUGHT.
I'LL COME BACK TONIGHT FOR YOUR ANSWER.

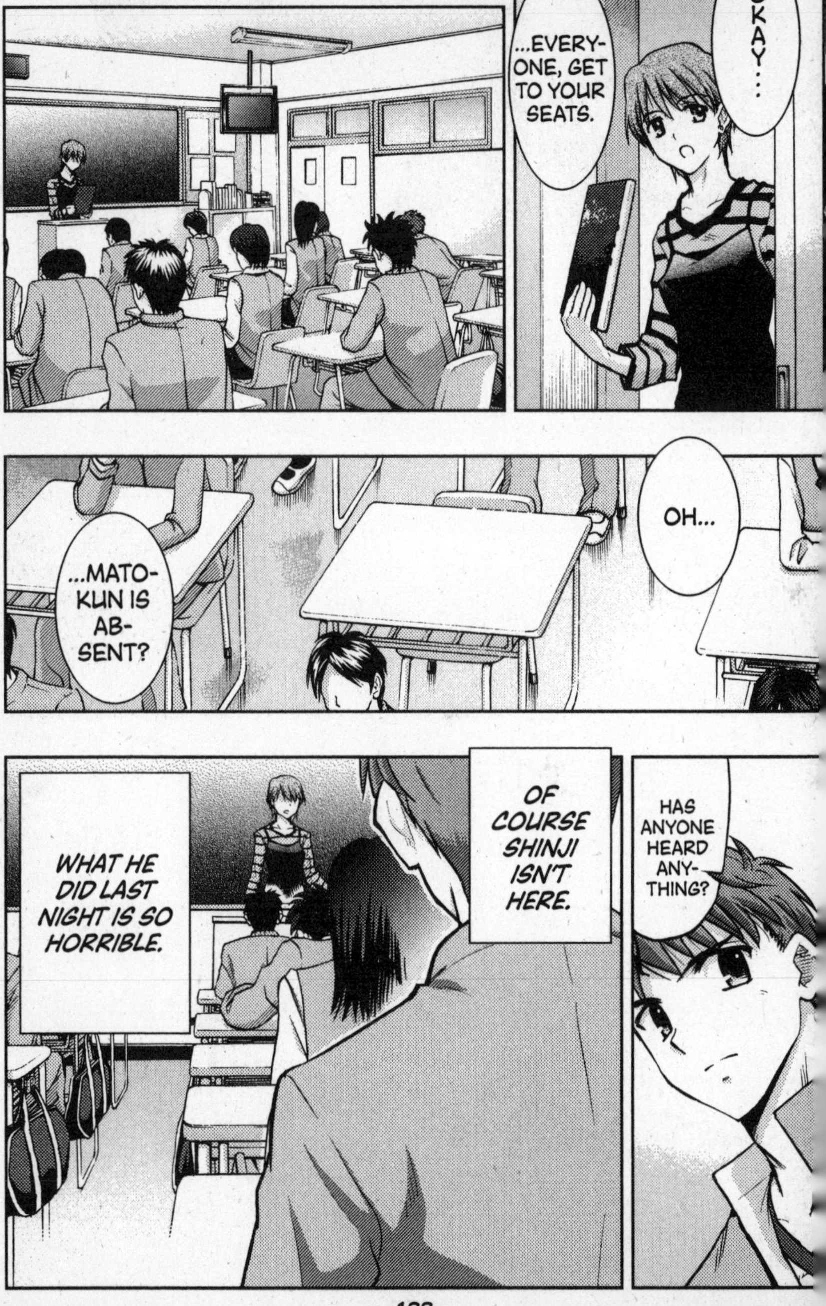
OKAY...
...EVERY-ONE, GET TO YOUR SEATS.
OH...
...MATO-KUN IS AB-SENT?
HAS ANYONE HEARD ANY-THING?
OF COURSE SHINJI ISN'T HERE.
WHAT HE DID LAST NIGHT IS SO HORRIBLE.

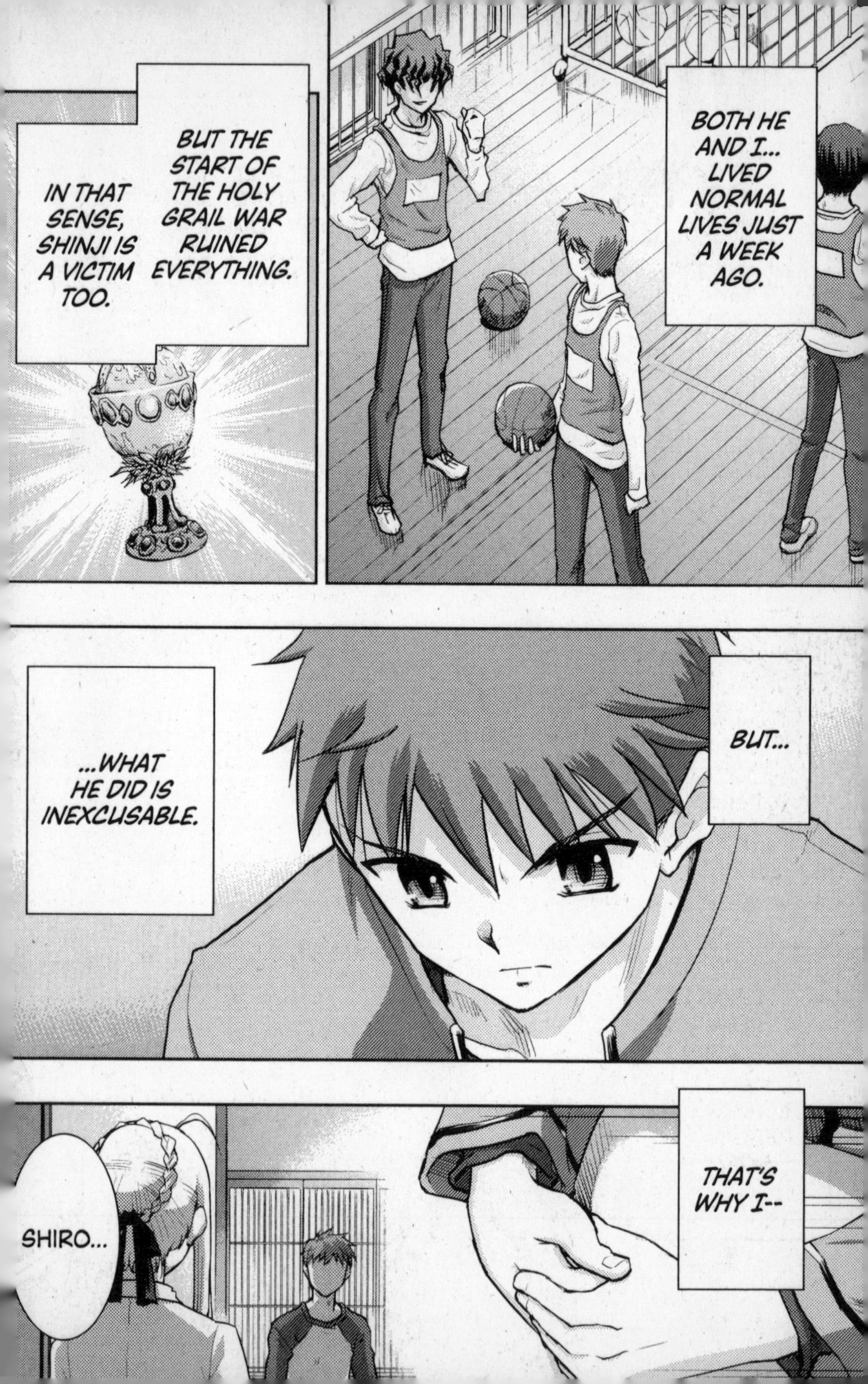
BOTH HE AND I... LIVED NORMAL LIVES JUST A WEEK AGO.
IN THAT SENSE, SHINJI IS A VICTIM TOO.
BUT THE START OF THE HOLY GRAIL WAR RUINED EVERYTHING.
BUT...
...WHAT HE DID IS INEXCUSABLE.
THAT'S WHY I--
SHIRO...

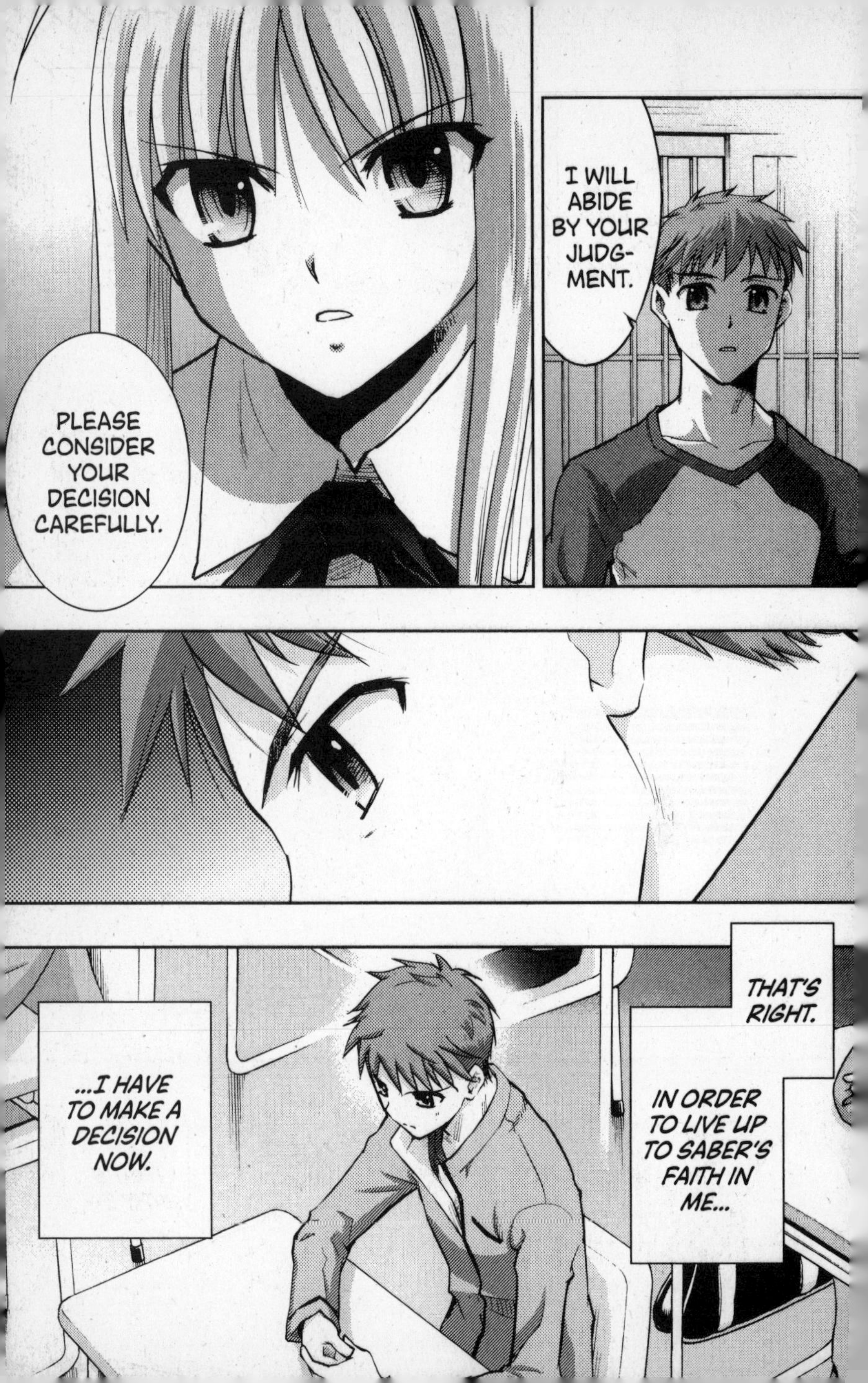
I WILL ABIDE BY YOUR JUDG-MENT.
PLEASE CONSIDER YOUR DECISION CAREFULLY.
THAT'S RIGHT.
IN ORDER TO LIVE UP TO SABER'S FAITH IN ME...
...I HAVE TO MAKE A DECISION NOW.

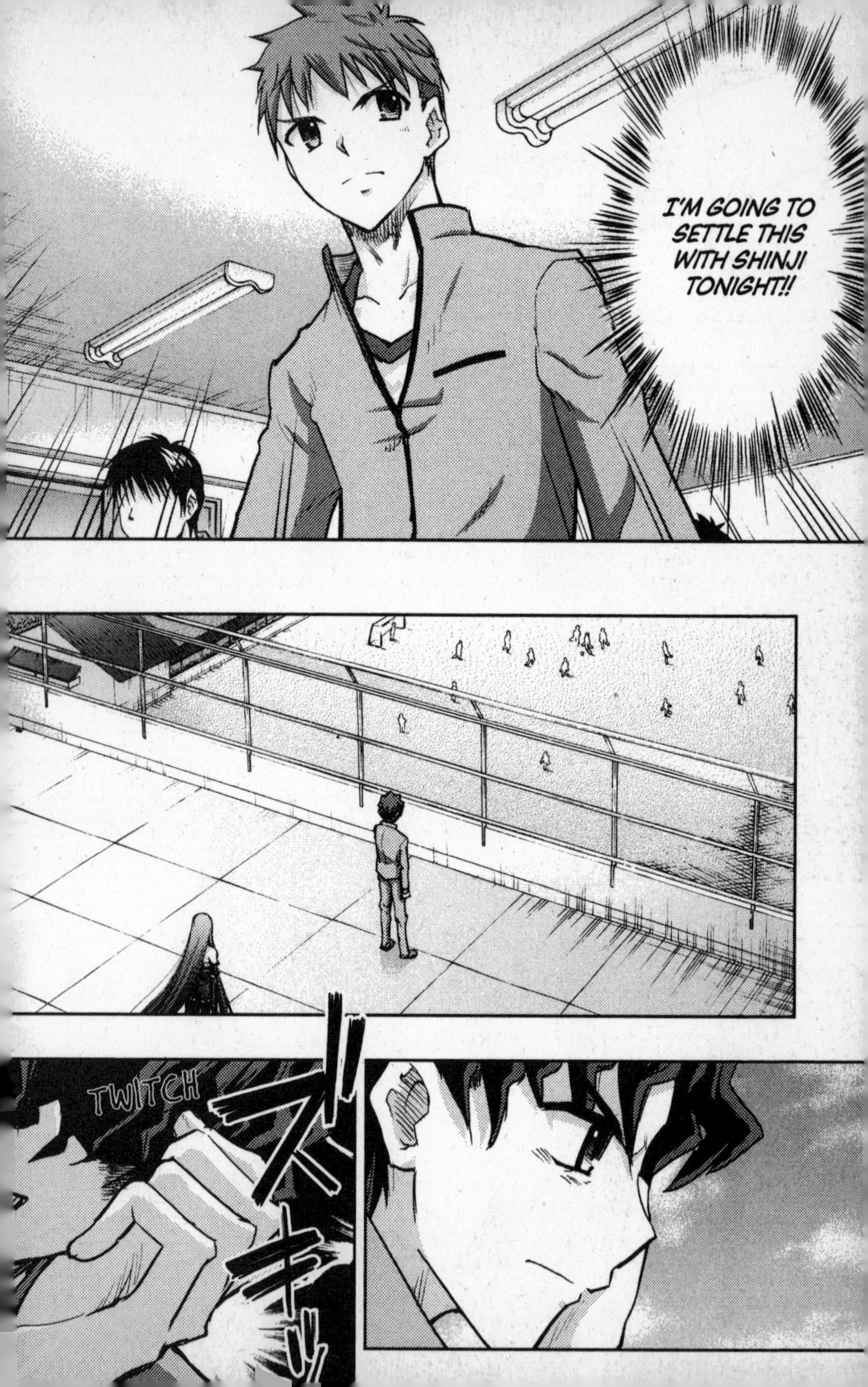
I'M GOING TO SETTLE THIS WITH SHINJI TONIGHT!!
TWITCH

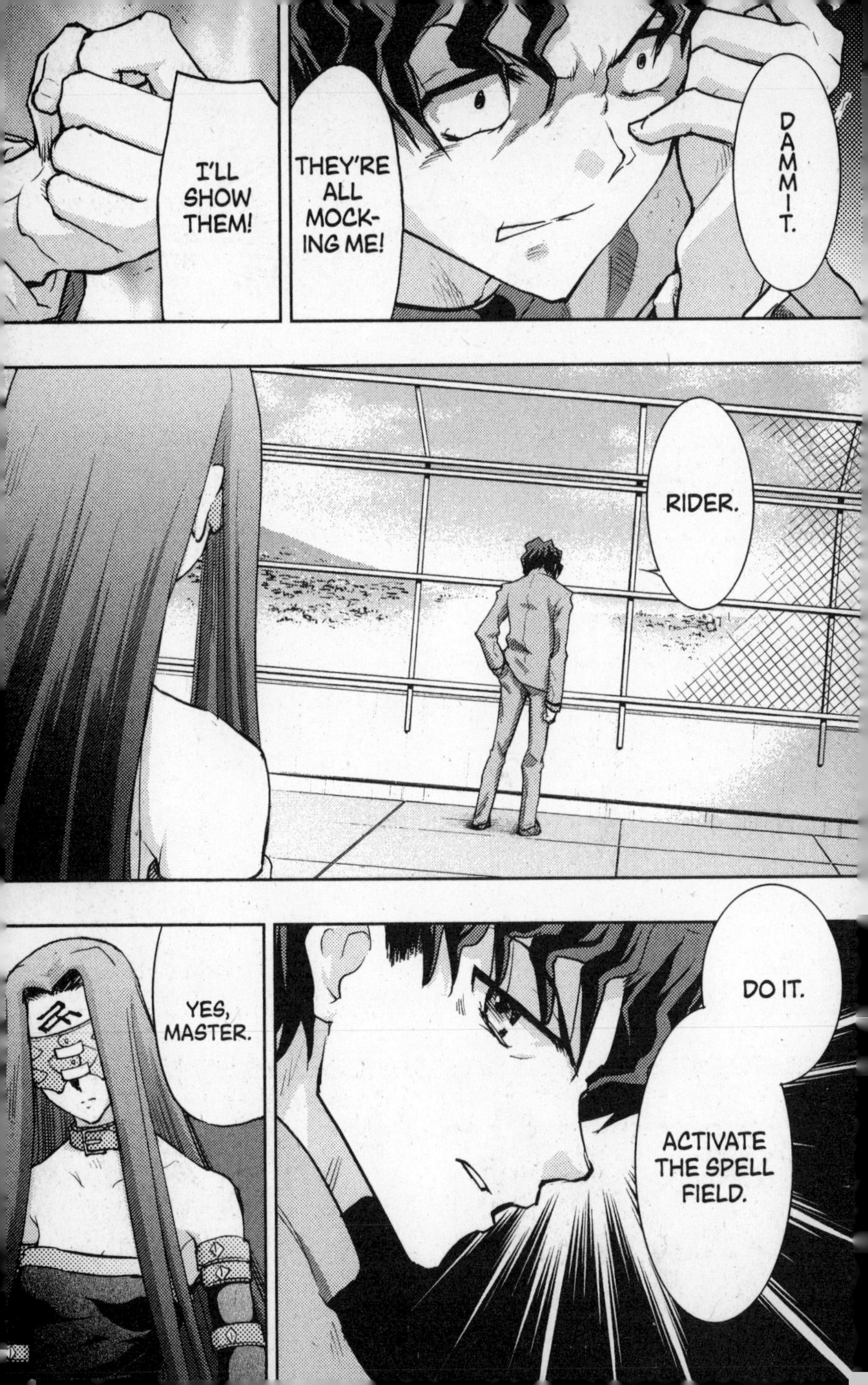
DAMMIT.
THEY'RE ALL MOCKING ME!
I'LL SHOW THEM!
RIDER.
DO IT.
ACTIVATE THE SPELL FIELD.
YES, MASTER.

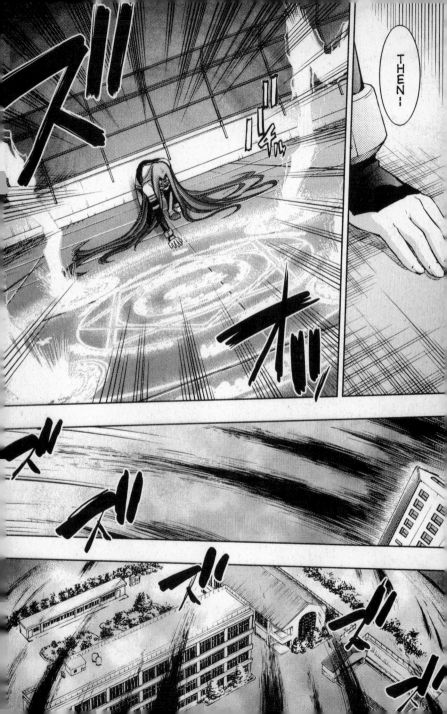

THEN!!

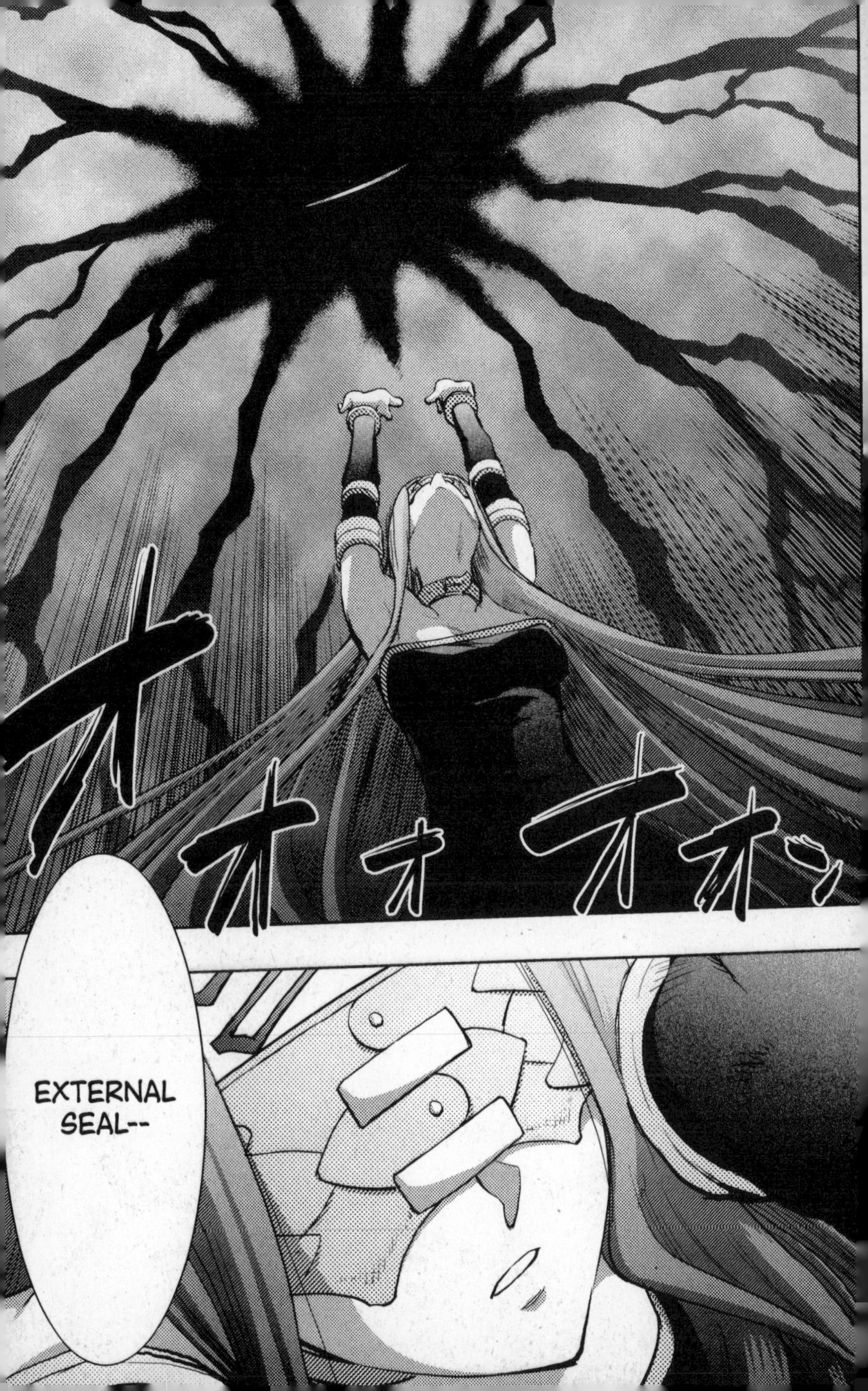
オオォオオ〜ッ
EXTERNAL SEAL--

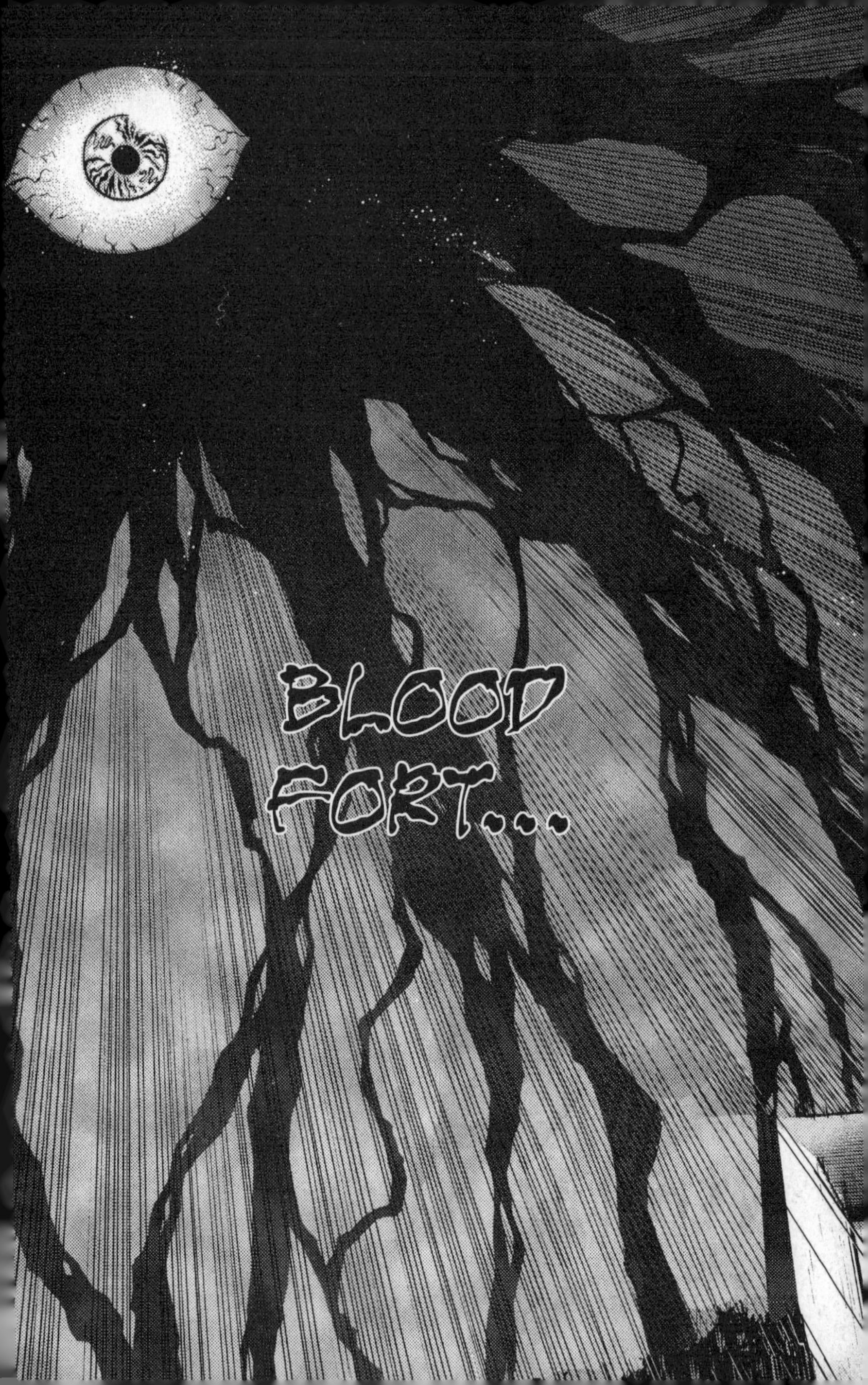
BLOOD FORT...

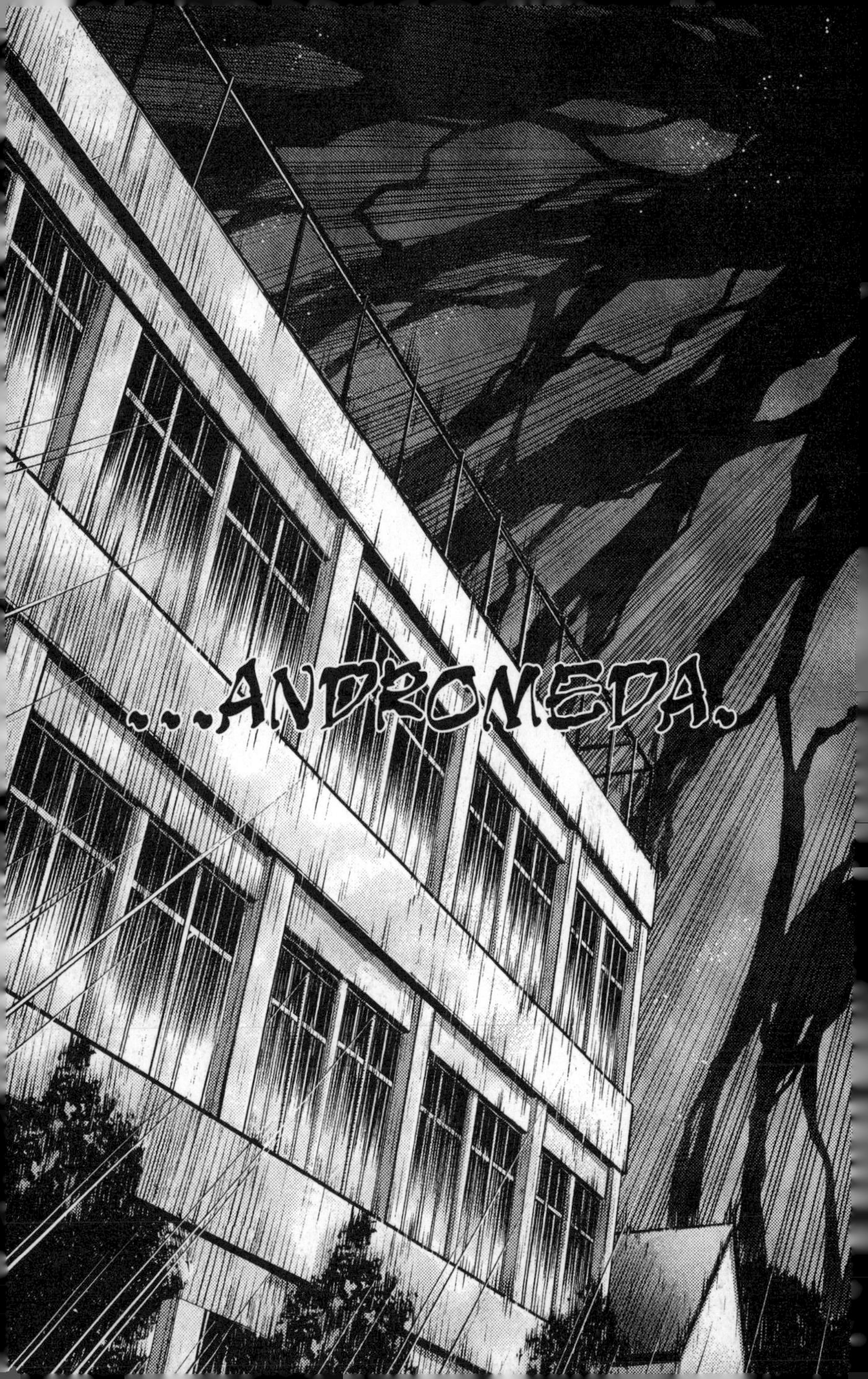
...ANDROMEDA.

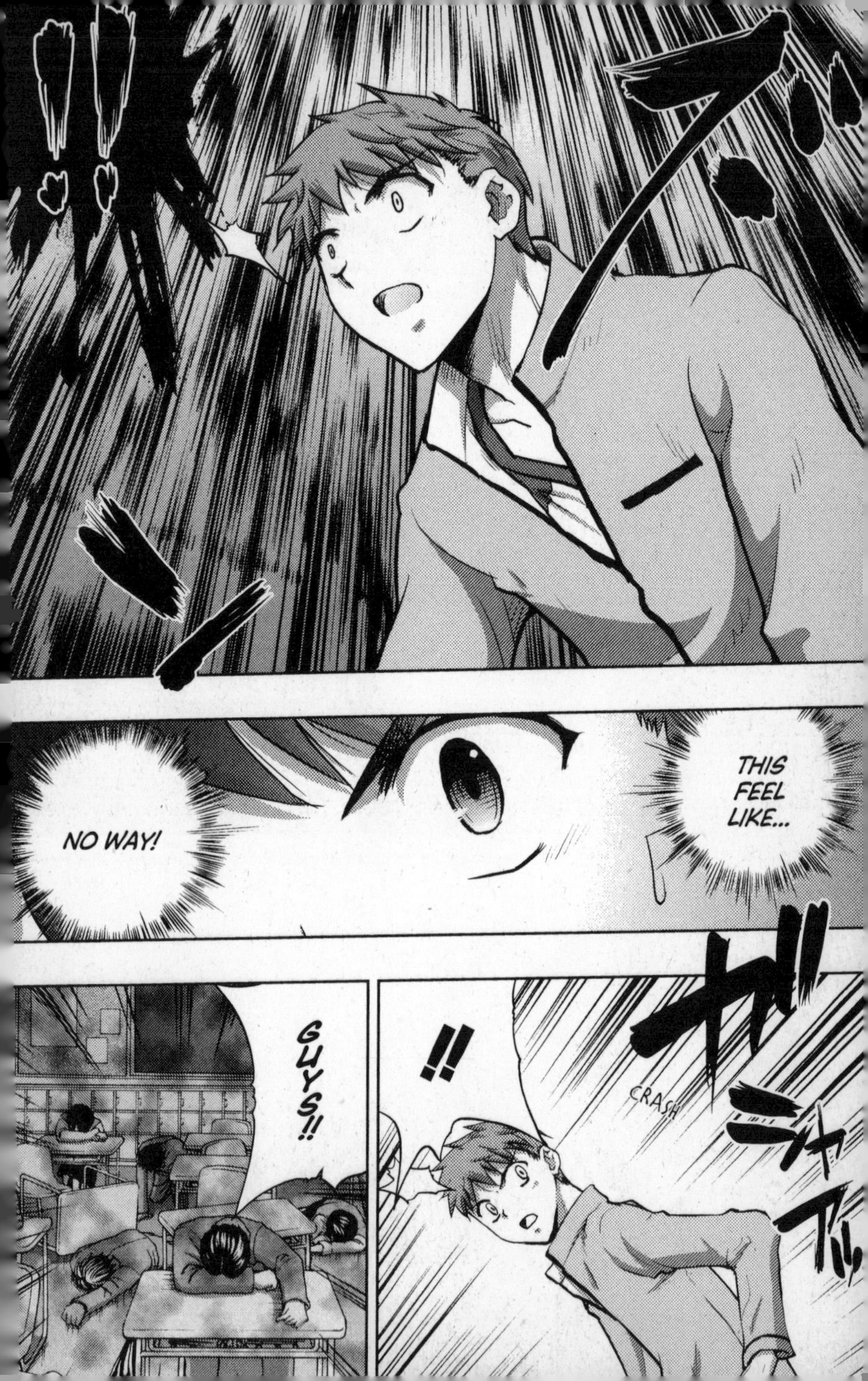
THIS FEEL LIKE...
NO WAY!
!!
CRASH
GUYS!!

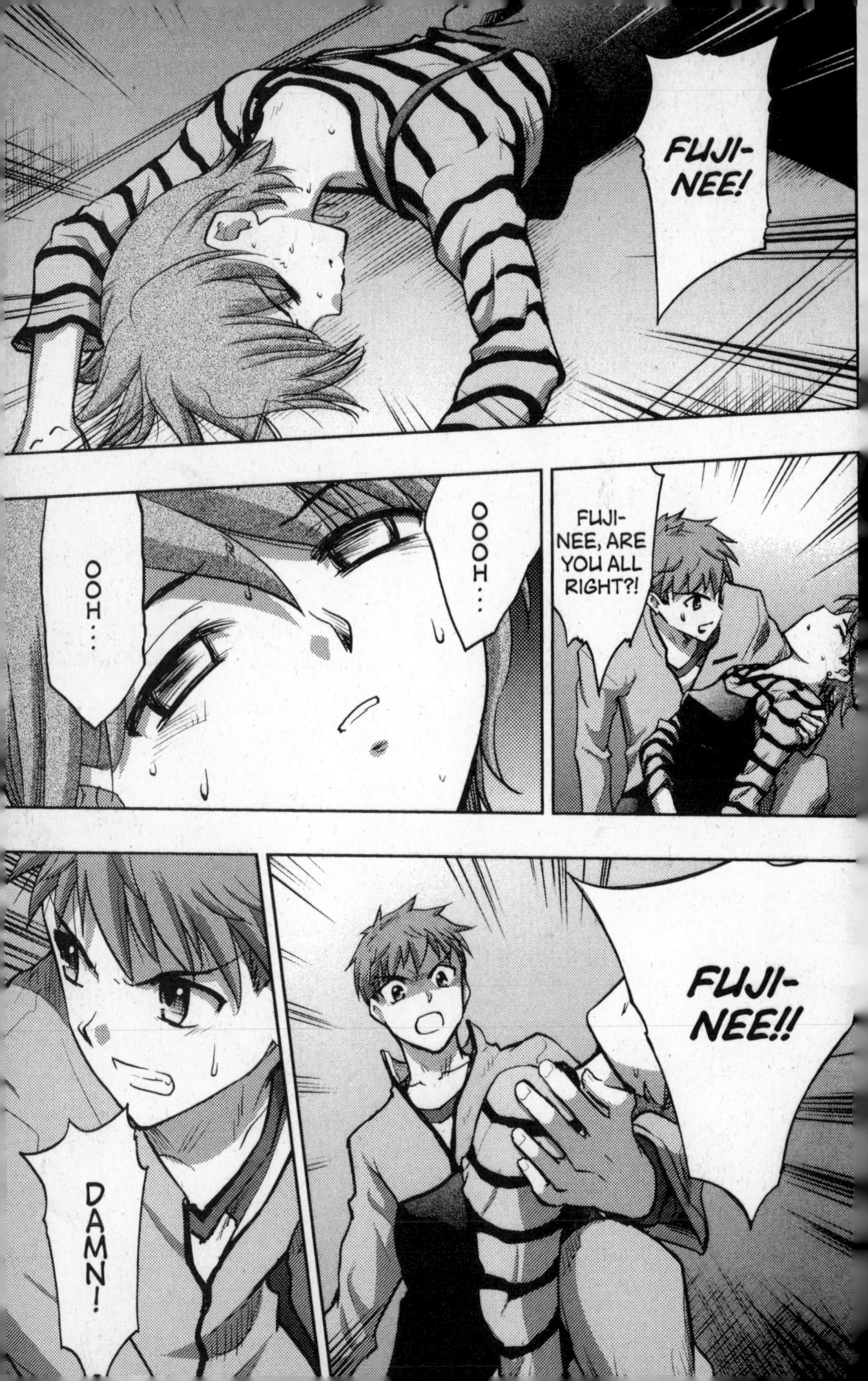
FUJI-NEE!
FUJI-NEE, ARE YOU ALL RIGHT?!
OOOH...
OOH...
FUJI-NEE!!
DAMN!

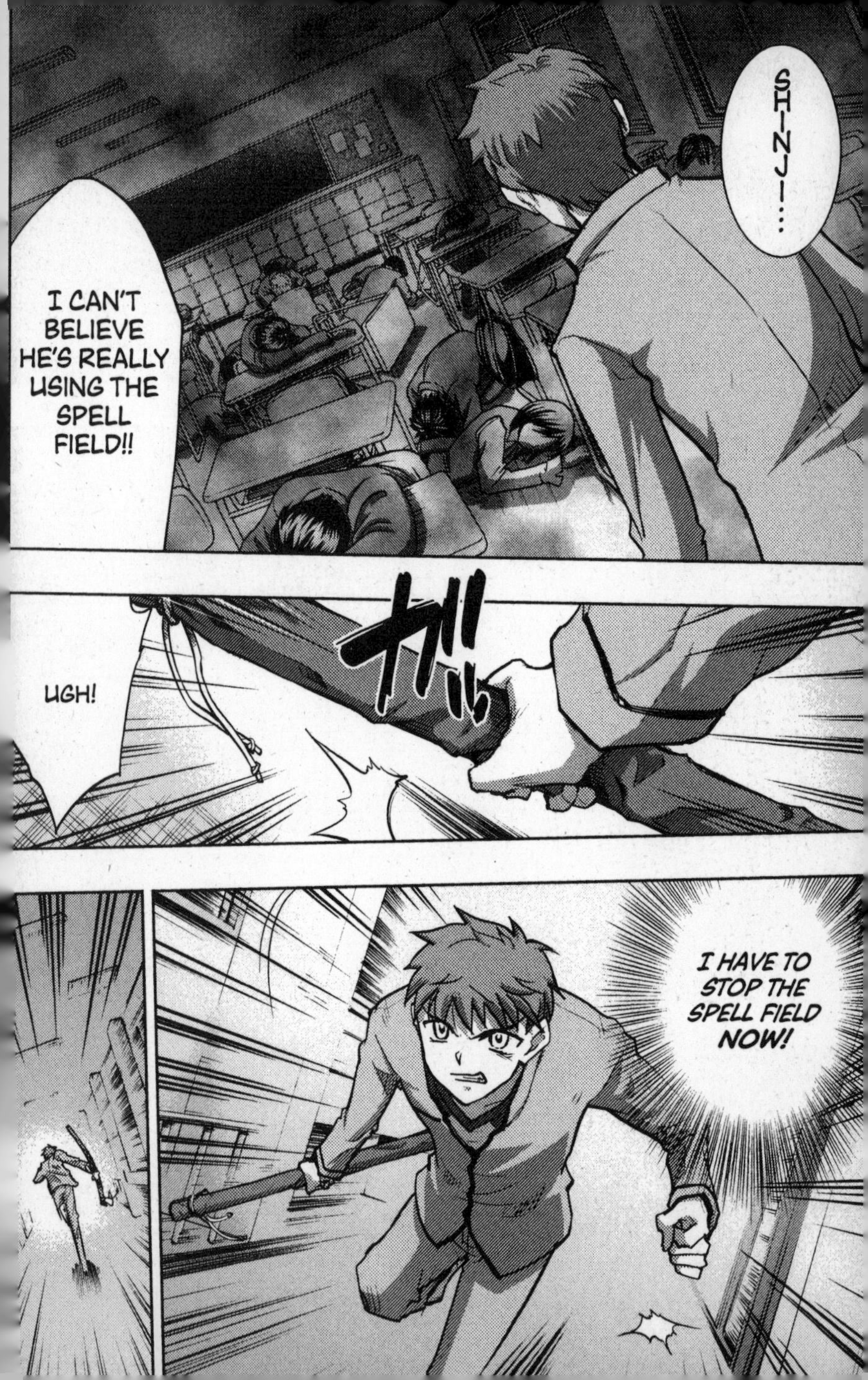
SHINJI...
I CAN'T BELIEVE HE'S REALLY USING THE SPELL FIELD!!
ガッ
UGH!
I HAVE TO STOP THE SPELL FIELD NOW!

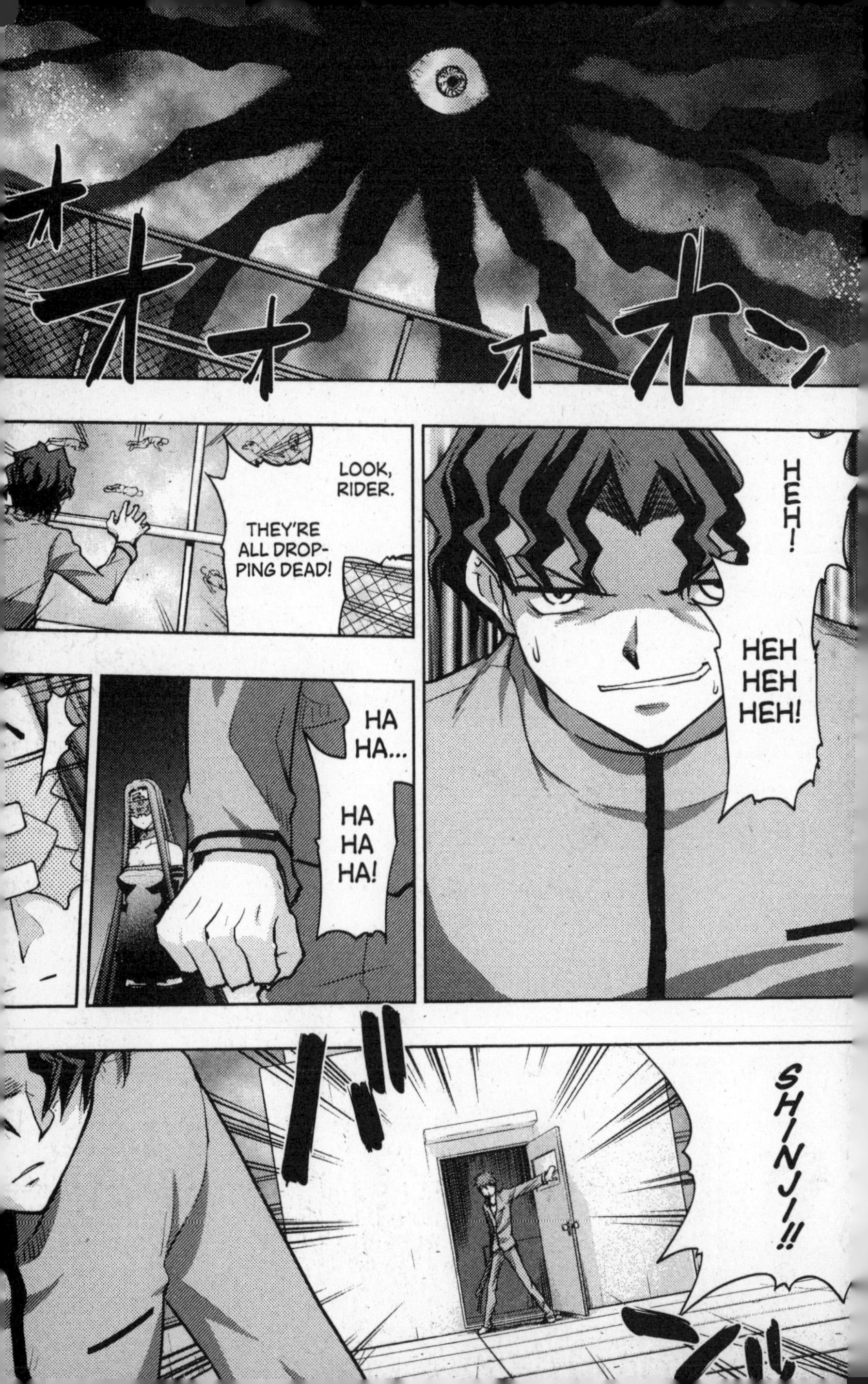

HEH!
HEH HEH HEH!
LOOK, RIDER.
THEY'RE ALL DROP-PING DEAD!
HA HA...
HA HA HA!
SHINJI!!

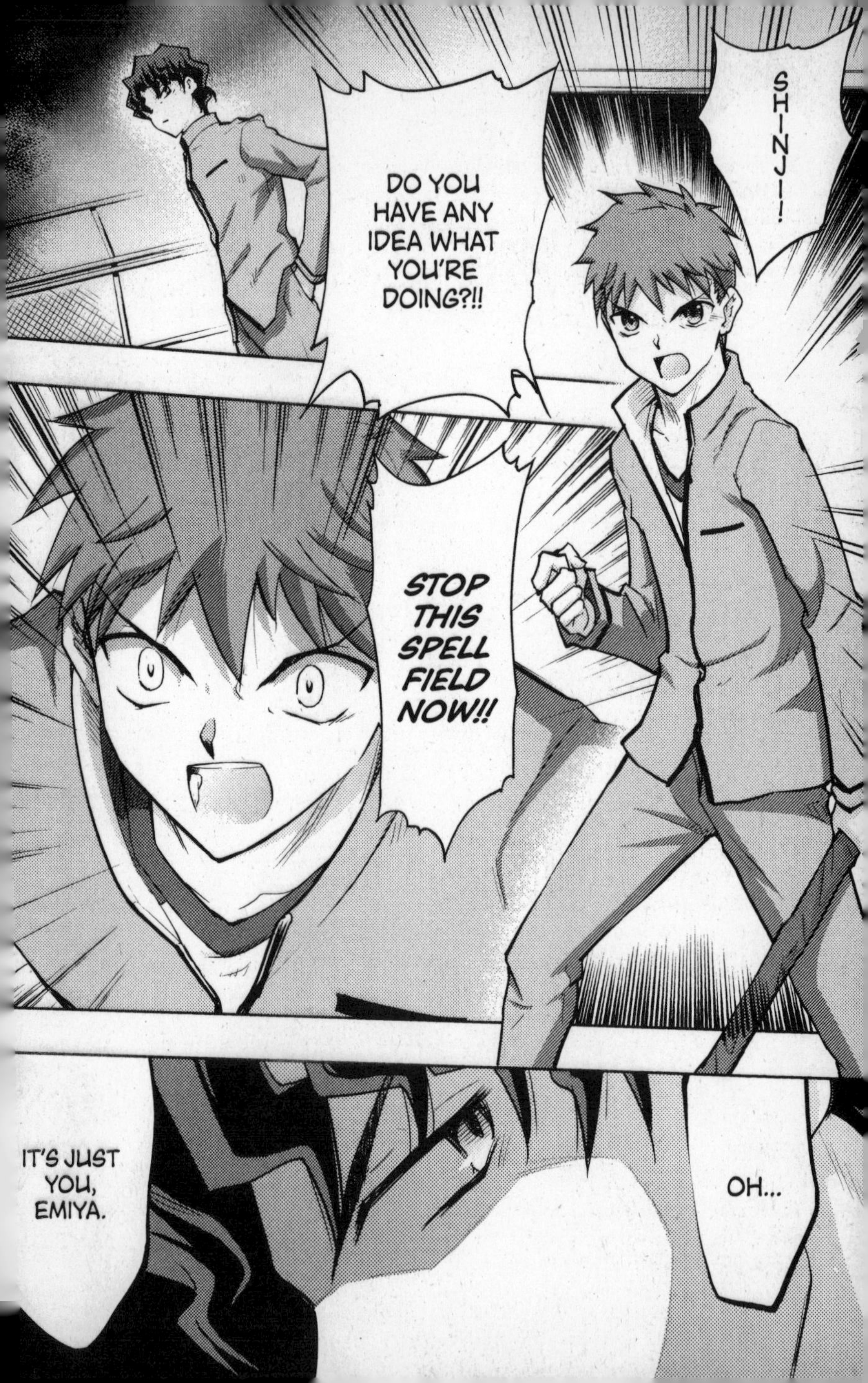
SHINJI!!
DO YOU HAVE ANY IDEA WHAT YOU'RE DOING?!!
STOP THIS SPELL FIELD NOW!!
OH...
IT'S JUST YOU, EMIYA.

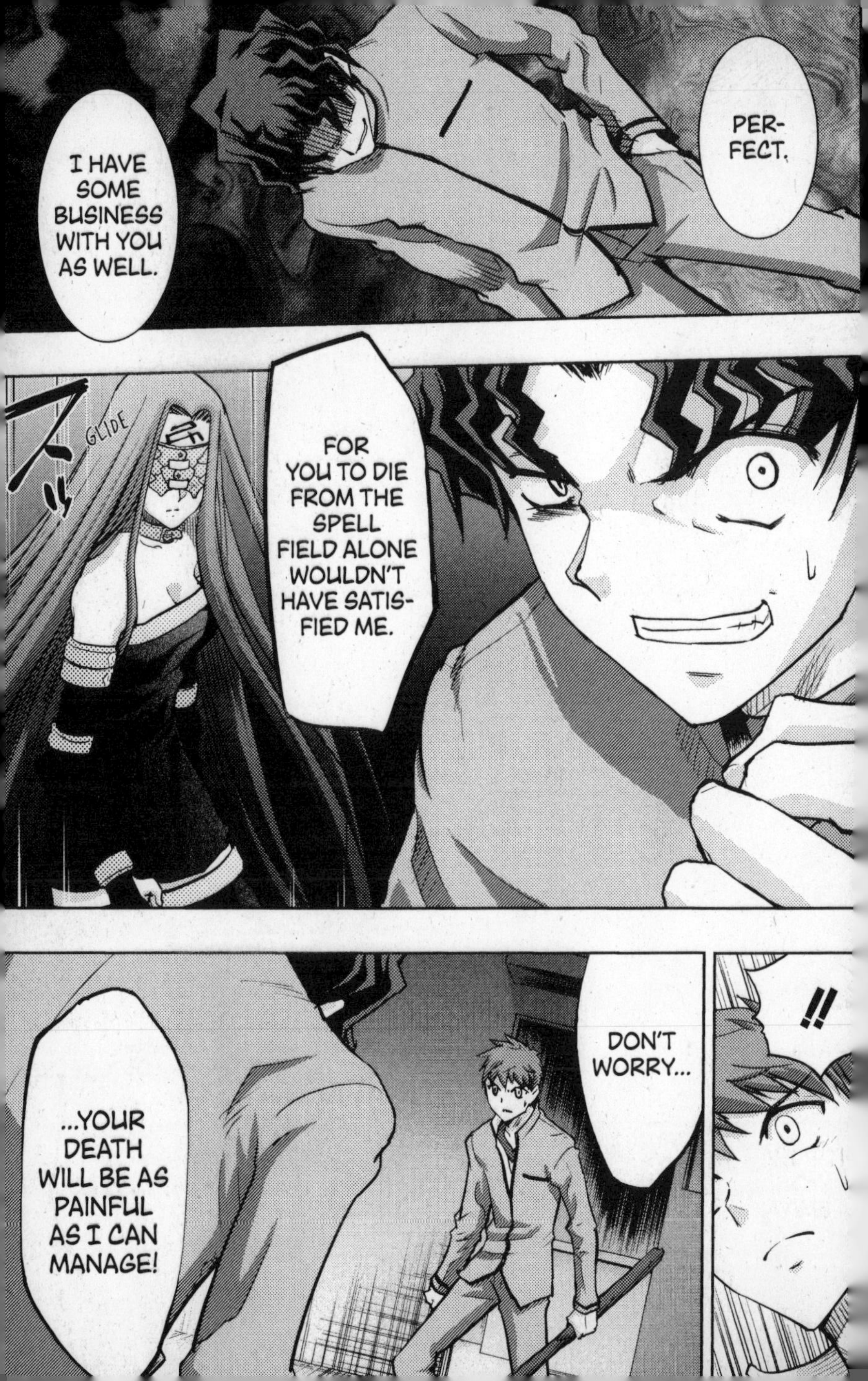
PER-FECT.
I HAVE SOME BUSINESS WITH YOU AS WELL.
FOR YOU TO DIE FROM THE SPELL FIELD ALONE WOULDN'T HAVE SATIS-FIED ME.
GLIDE
!!
DON'T WORRY...
...YOUR DEATH WILL BE AS PAINFUL AS I CAN MANAGE!

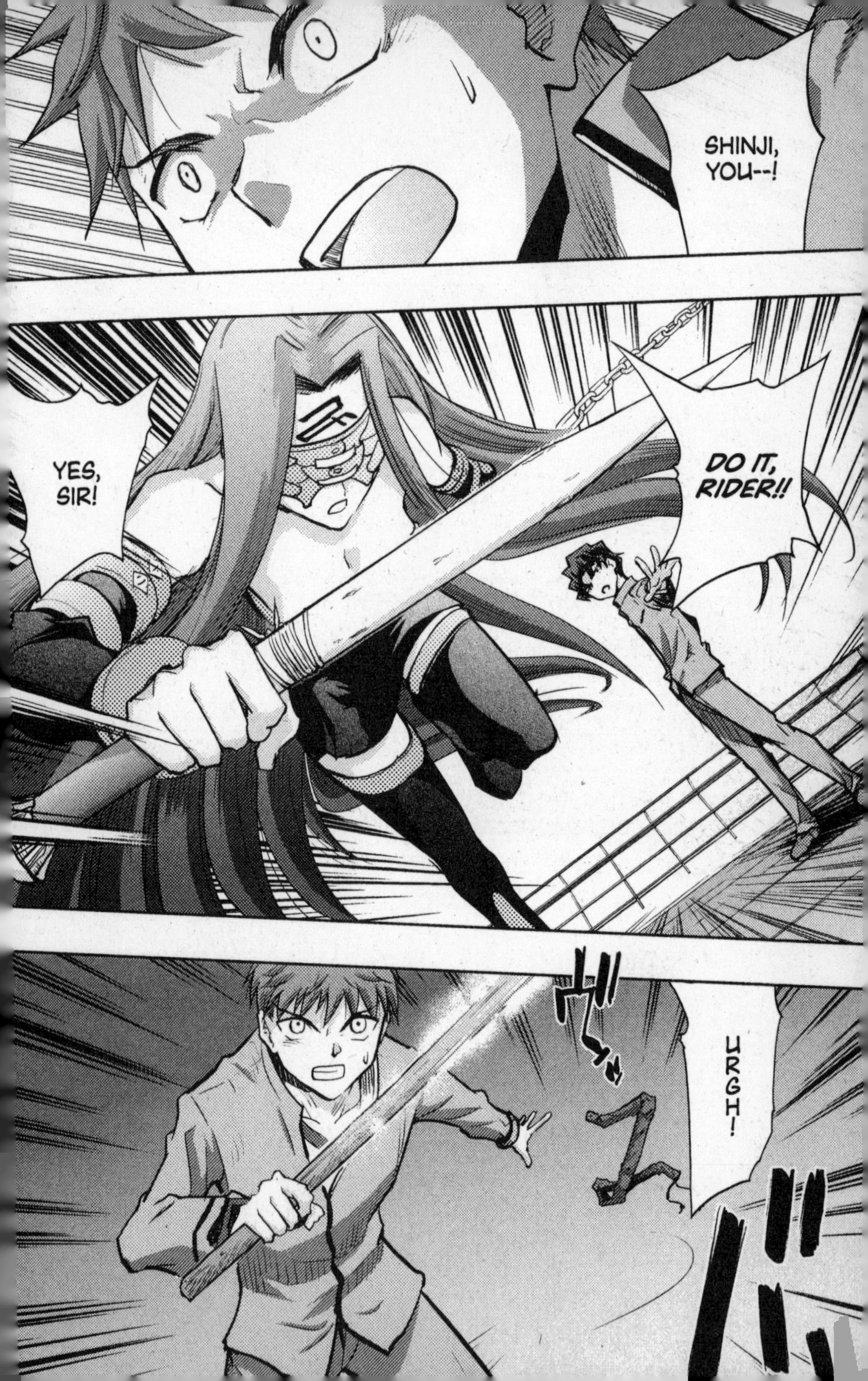
SHINJI, YOU--!
DO IT, RIDER!!
YES, SIR!
URGH!

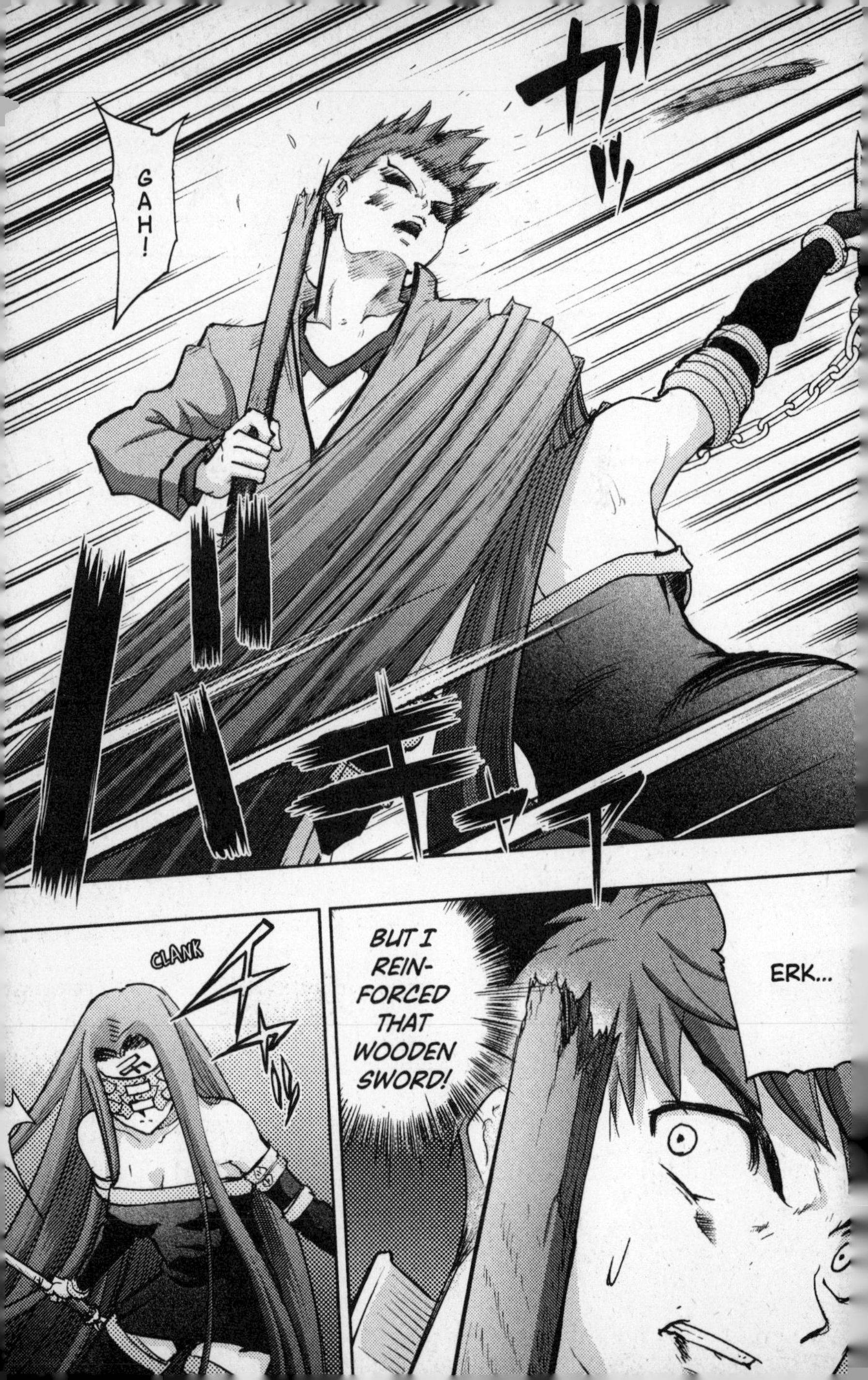
GAH!
ERK...
BUT I REIN-FORCED THAT WOODEN SWORD!
CLANK

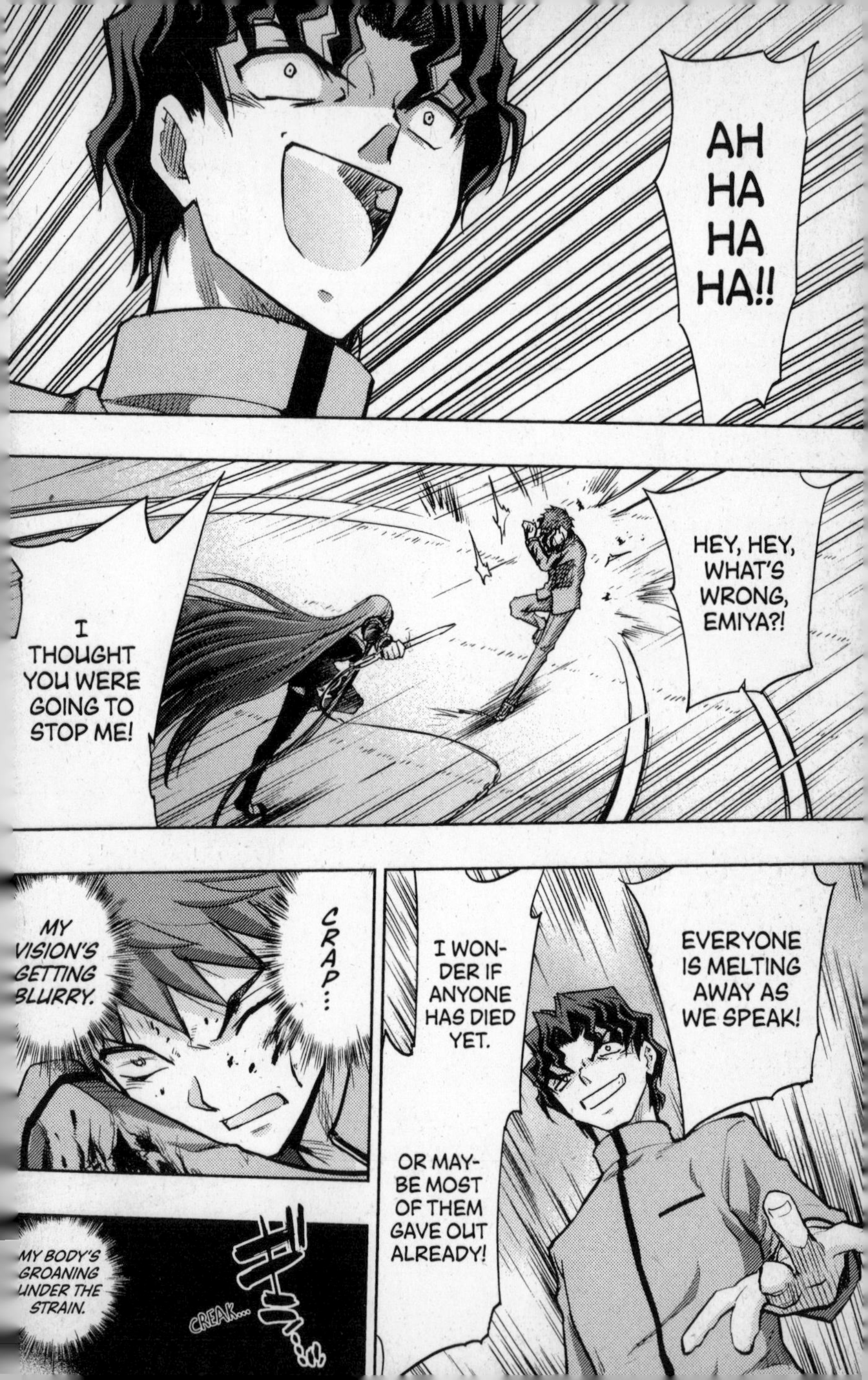
AH HA HA HA!!
HEY, HEY, WHAT'S WRONG, EMIYA?!
I THOUGHT YOU WERE GOING TO STOP ME!
EVERYONE IS MELTING AWAY AS WE SPEAK!
I WONDER IF ANYONE HAS DIED YET.
OR MAYBE MOST OF THEM GAVE OUT ALREADY!
CRAP...
MY VISION'S GETTING BLURRY.
MY BODY'S GROANING UNDER THE STRAIN.
CREAK...

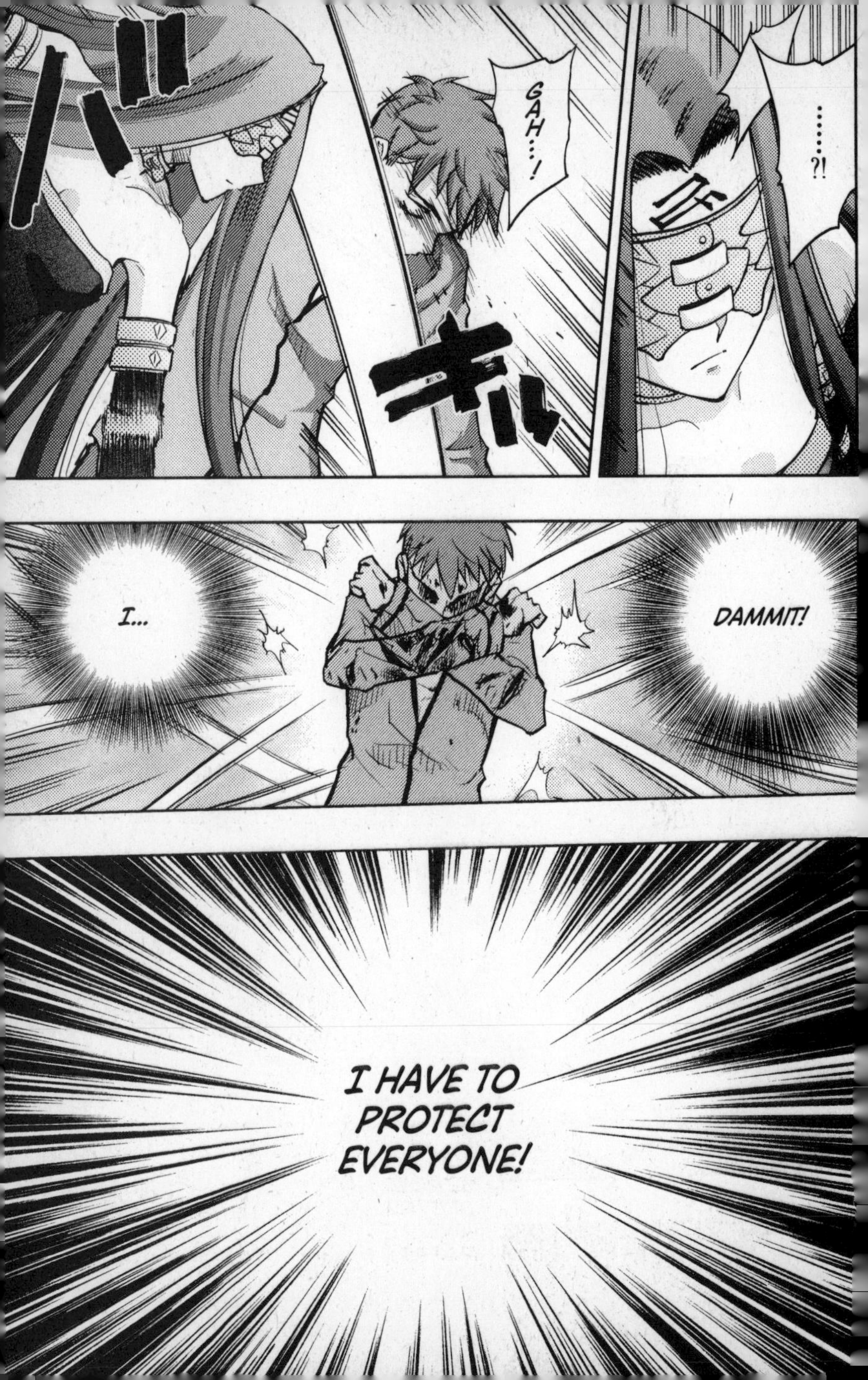
......?!
GAH...!
DAMMIT!
I...
I HAVE TO PROTECT EVERYONE!

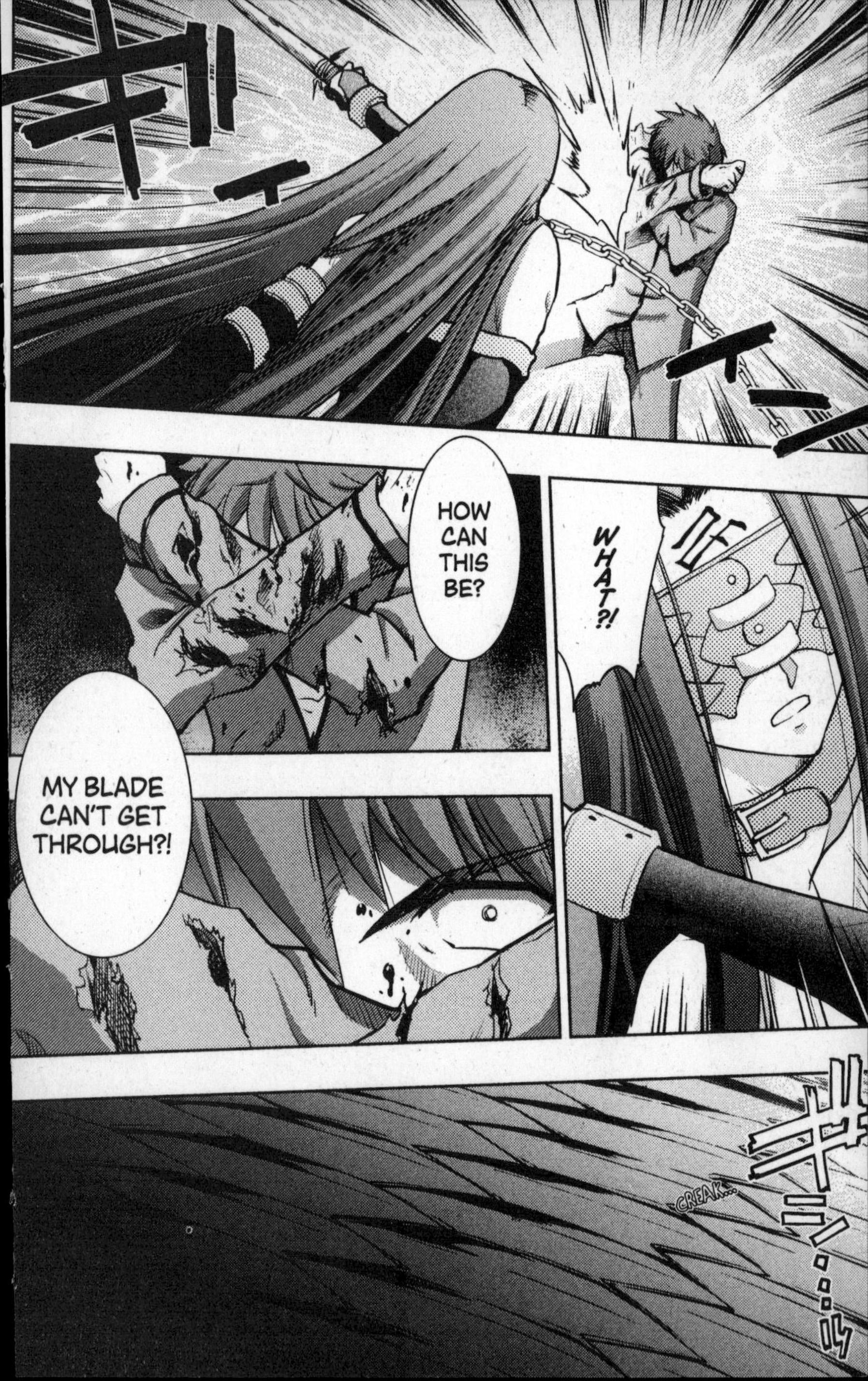
WHAT?!
HOW CAN THIS BE?
MY BLADE CAN'T GET THROUGH?!
CREAK...

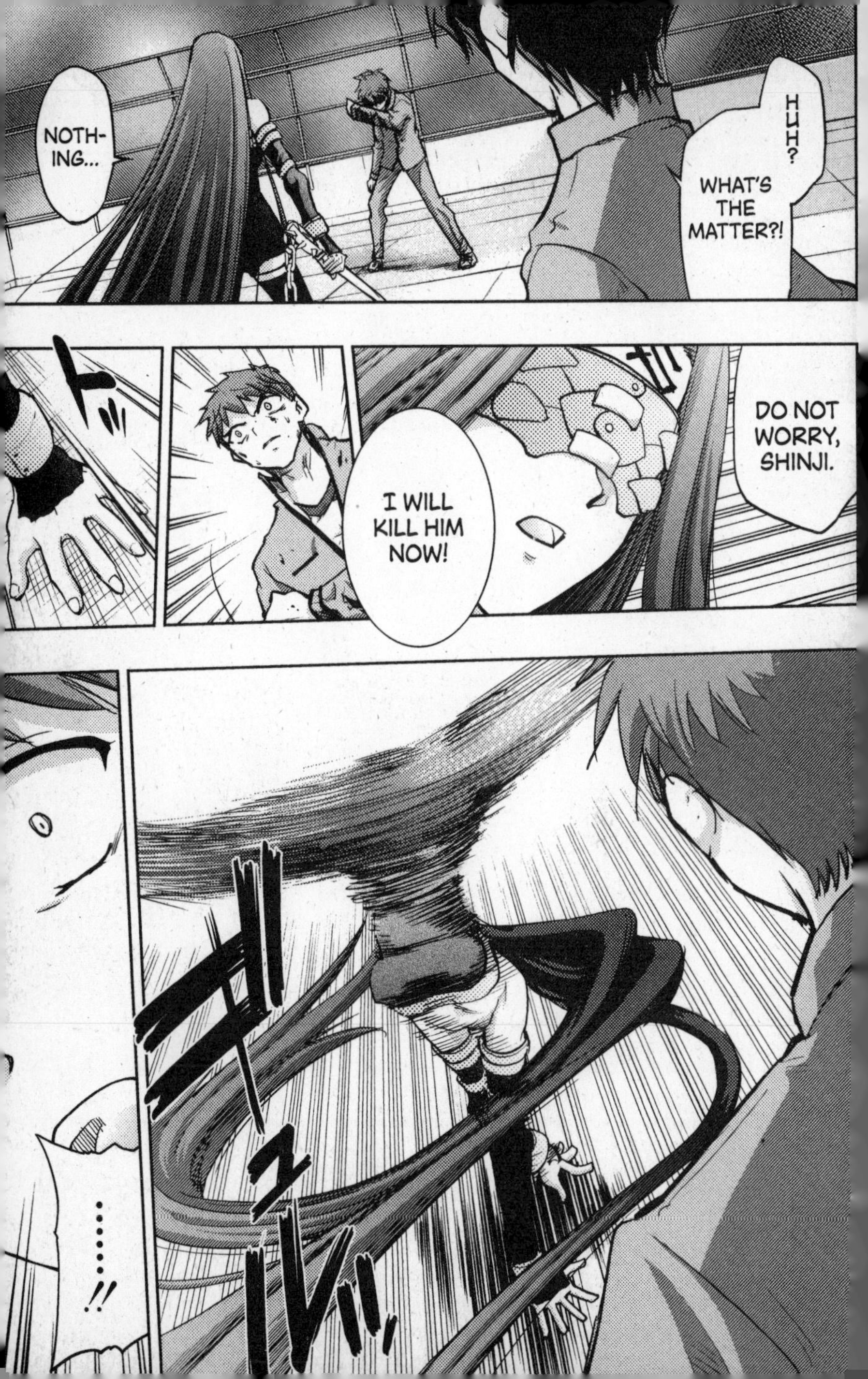
HUH?
WHAT'S THE MATTER?!
NOTH-ING...
DO NOT WORRY, SHINJI.
I WILL KILL HIM NOW!
......!!

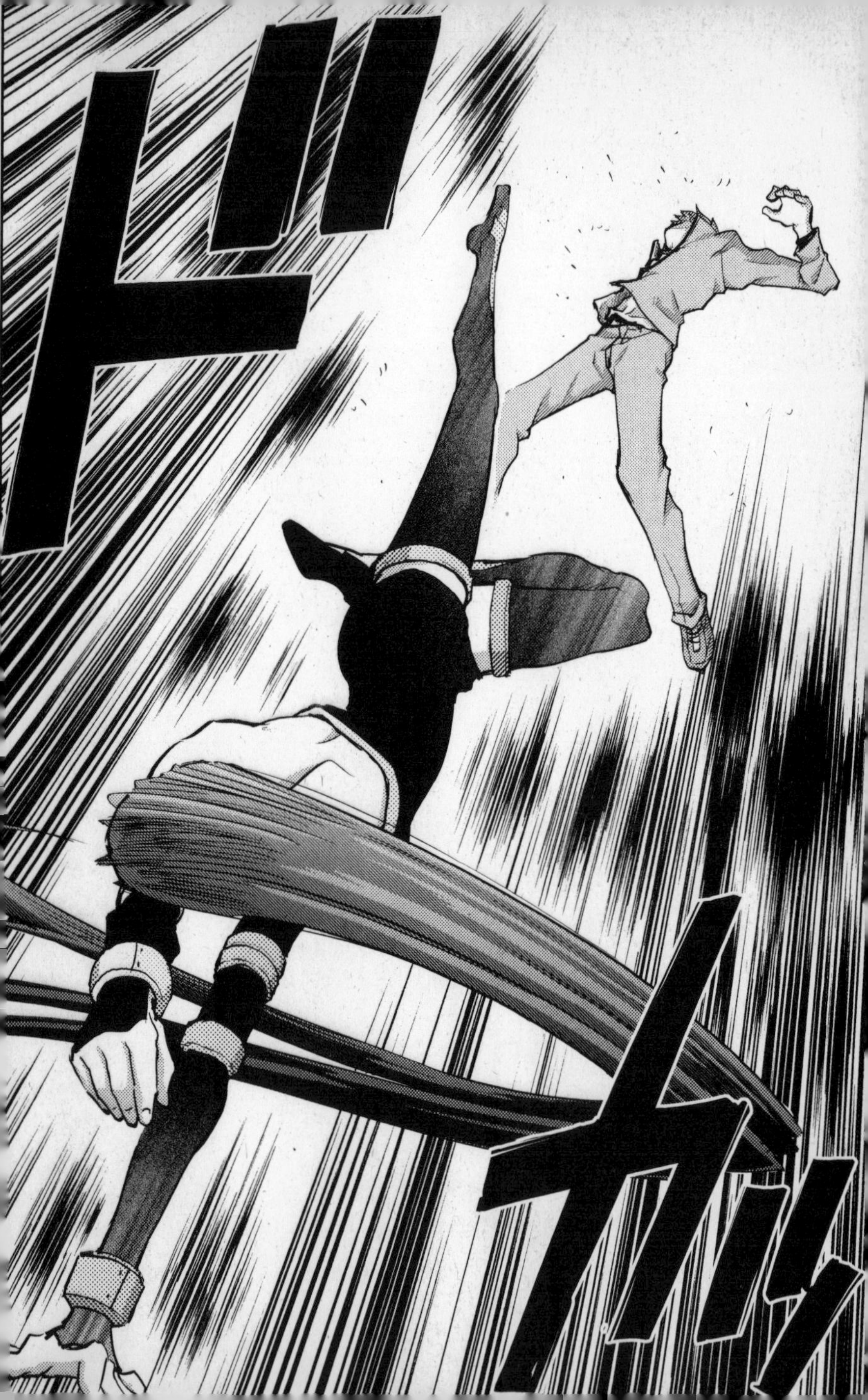
ド

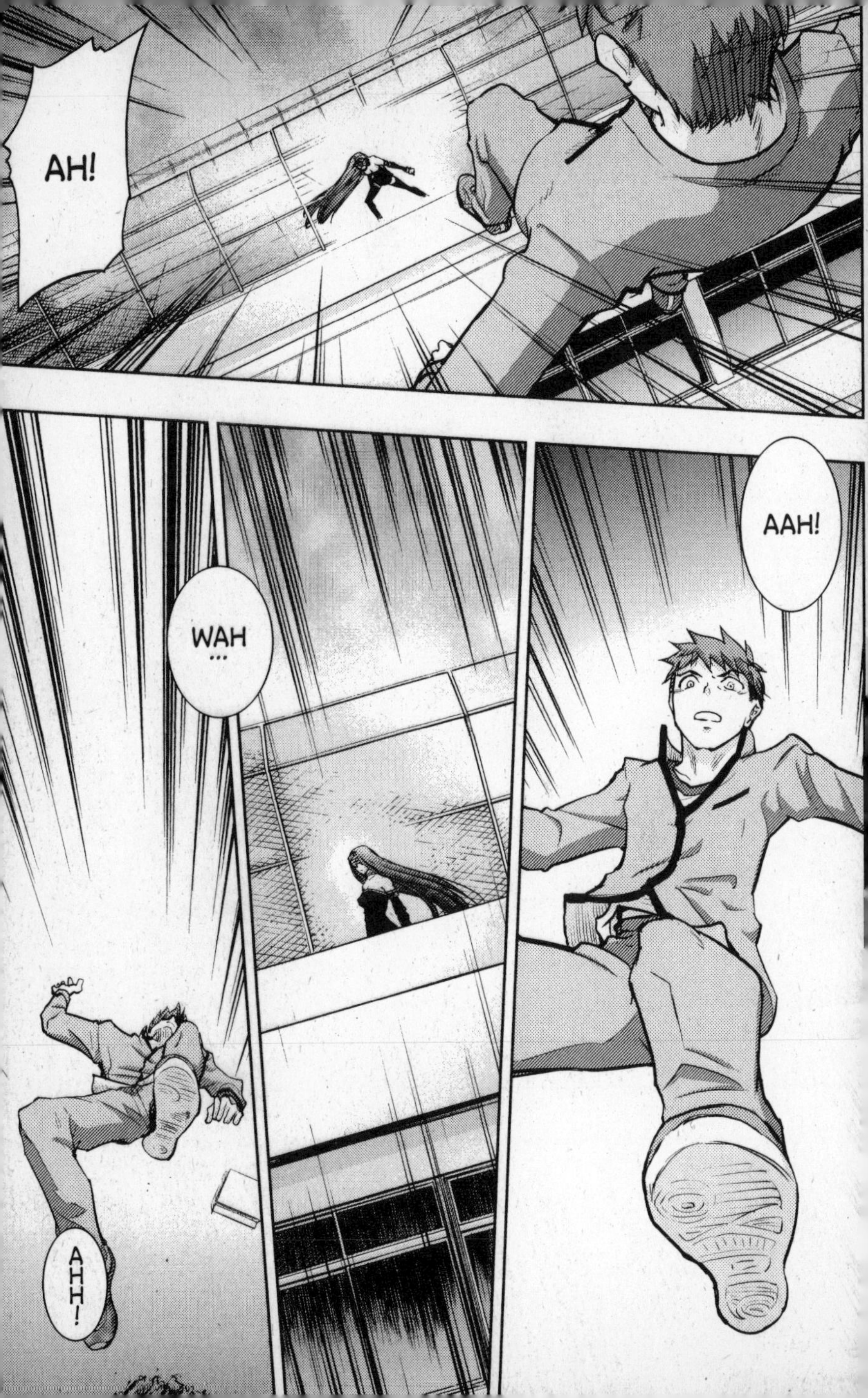
AH!
AAH!
WAH ...
AHH!

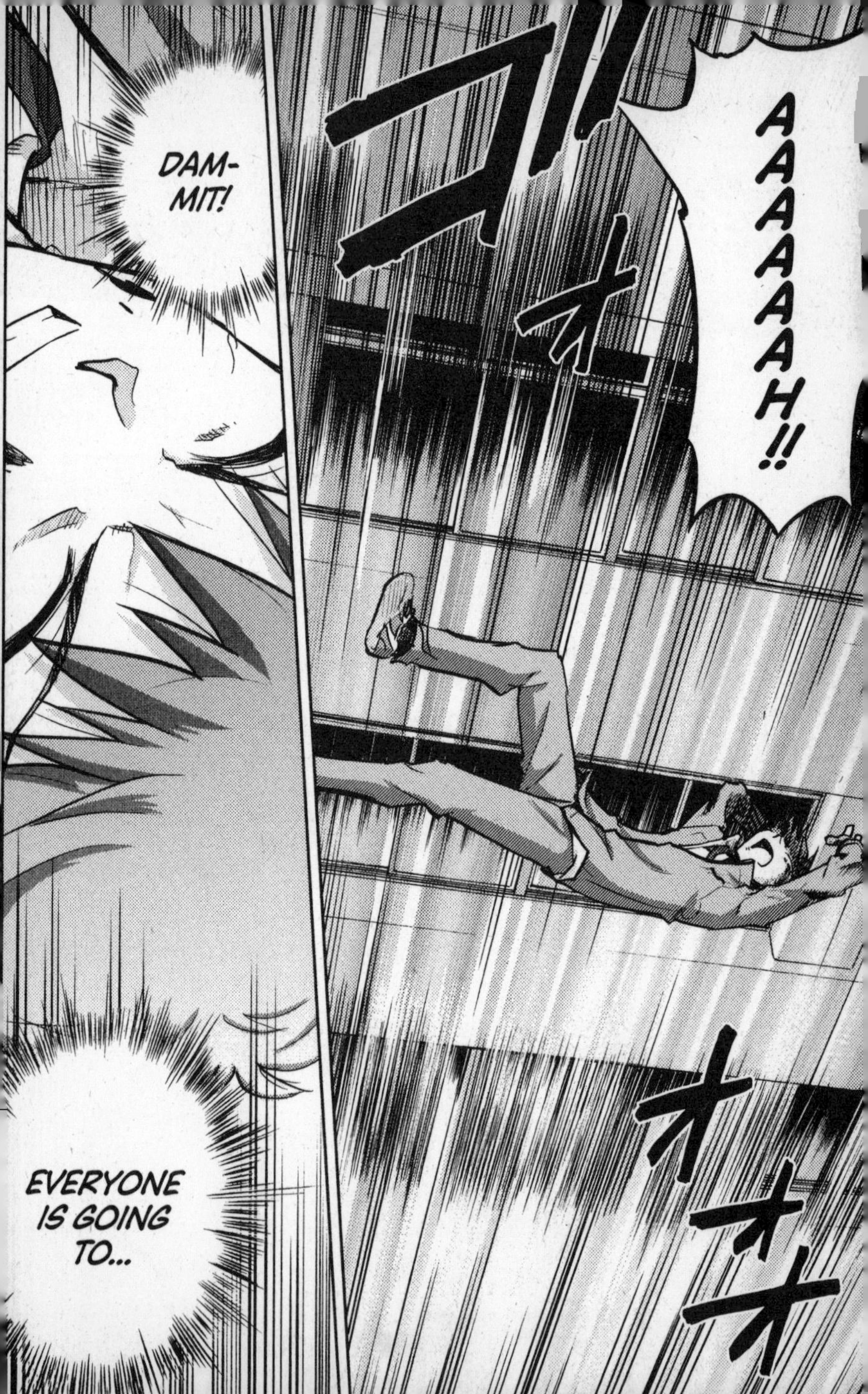
AAAAAAAH!!
ゴォ
オオオ
DAM-MIT!
EVERYONE IS GOING TO...

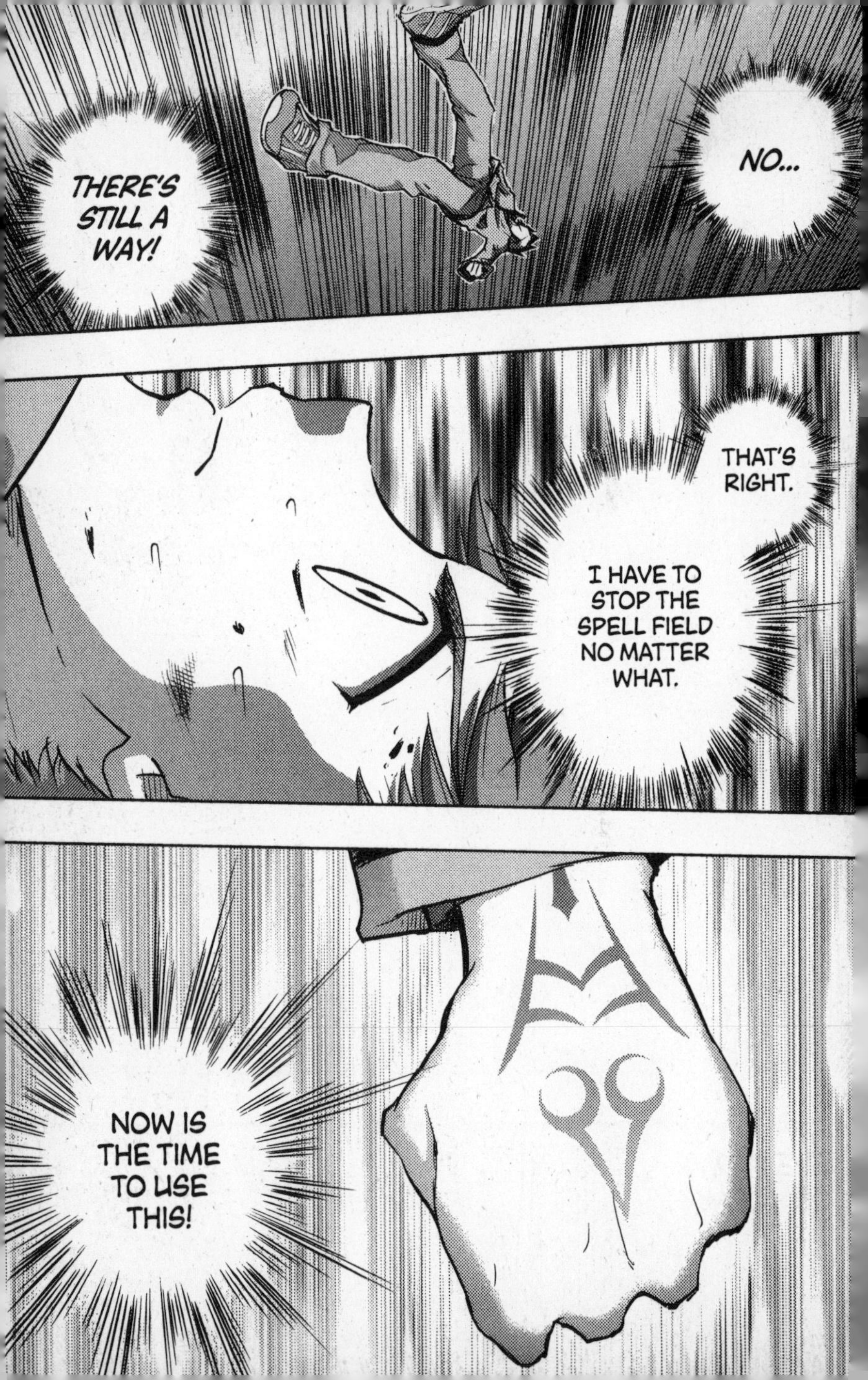
NO...
THERE'S STILL A WAY!
THAT'S RIGHT.
I HAVE TO STOP THE SPELL FIELD NO MATTER WHAT.
NOW IS THE TIME TO USE THIS!

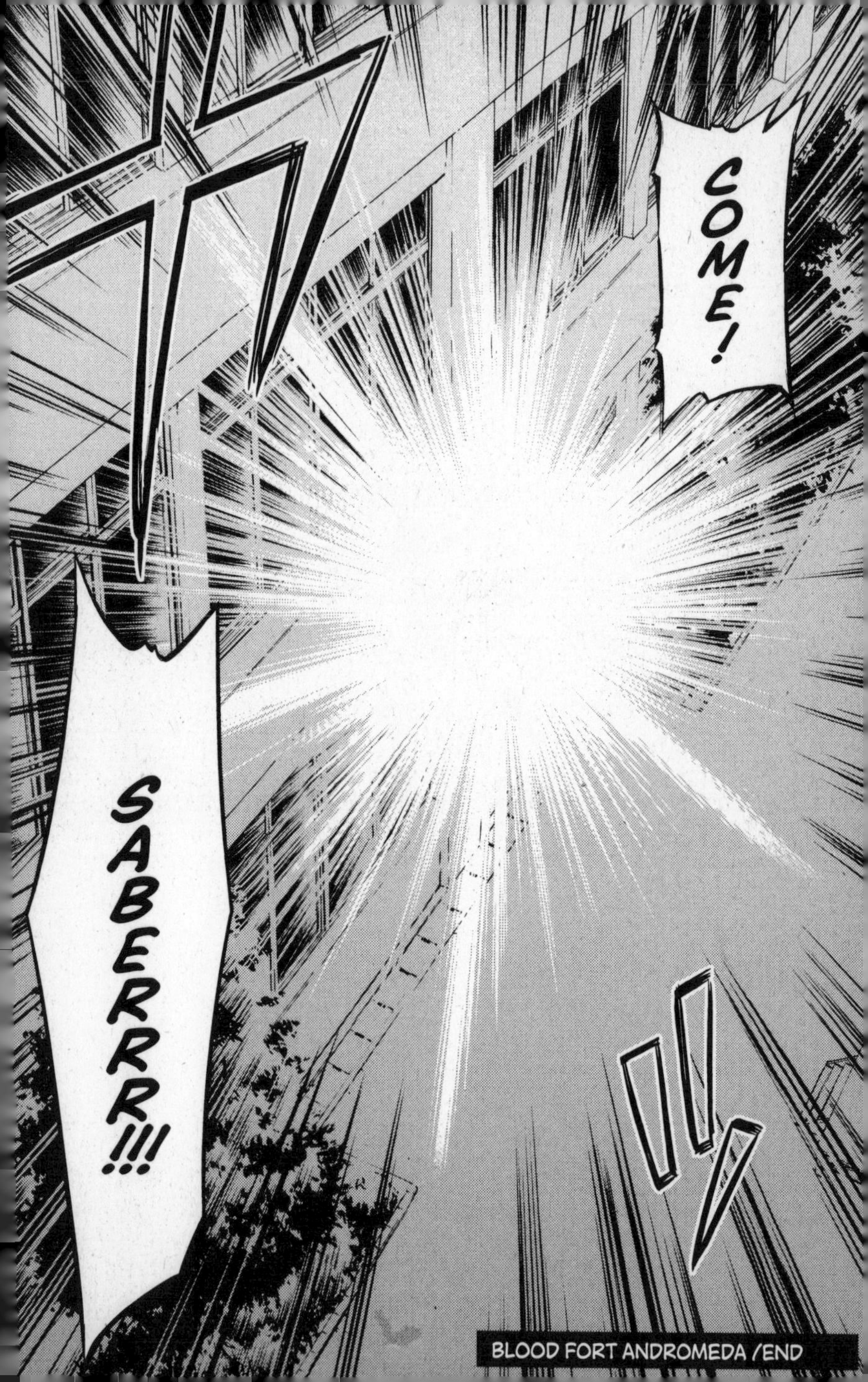
COME!
SABERRR!!!
BLOOD FORT ANDROMEDA /END

To Be Continued...

bonus II: recollection

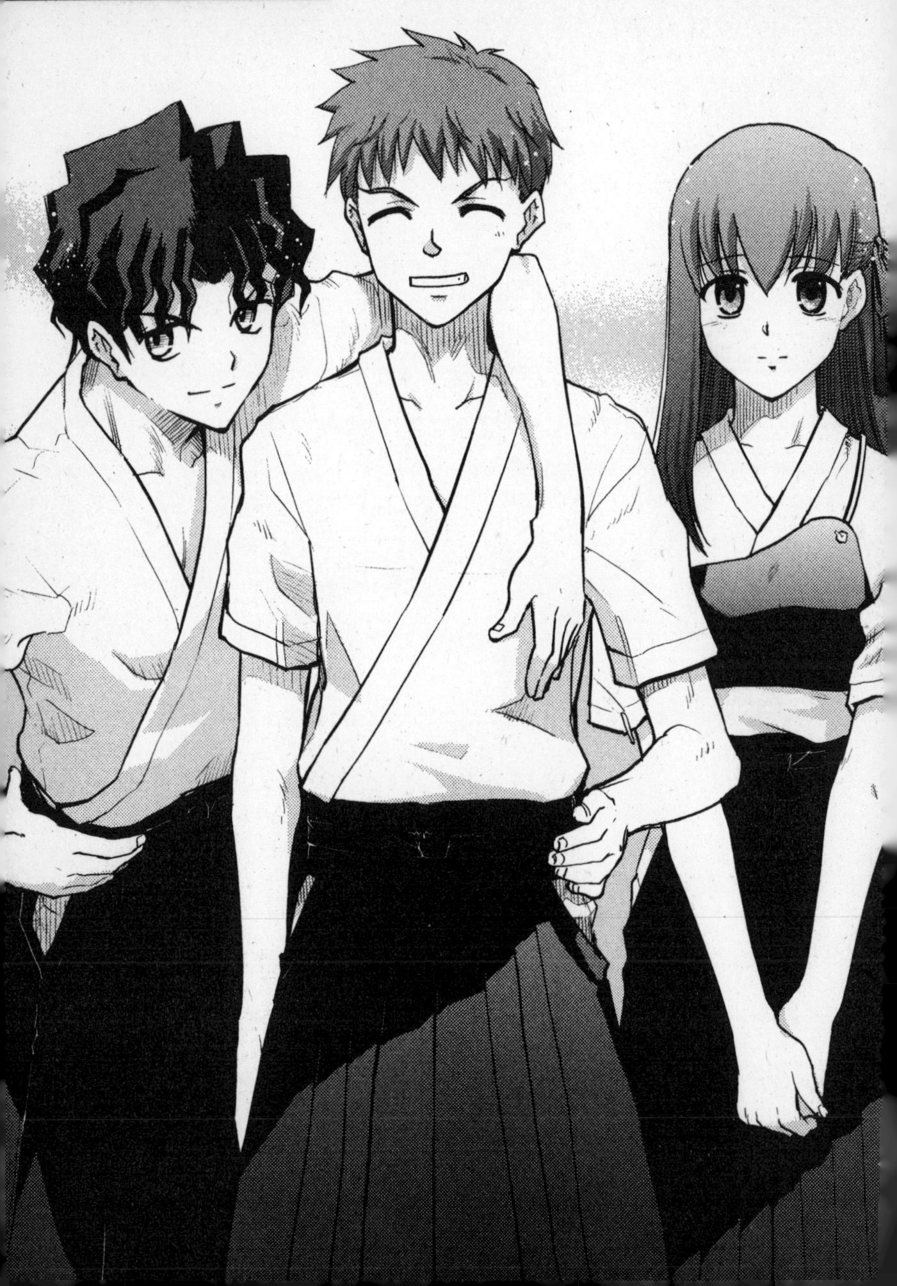

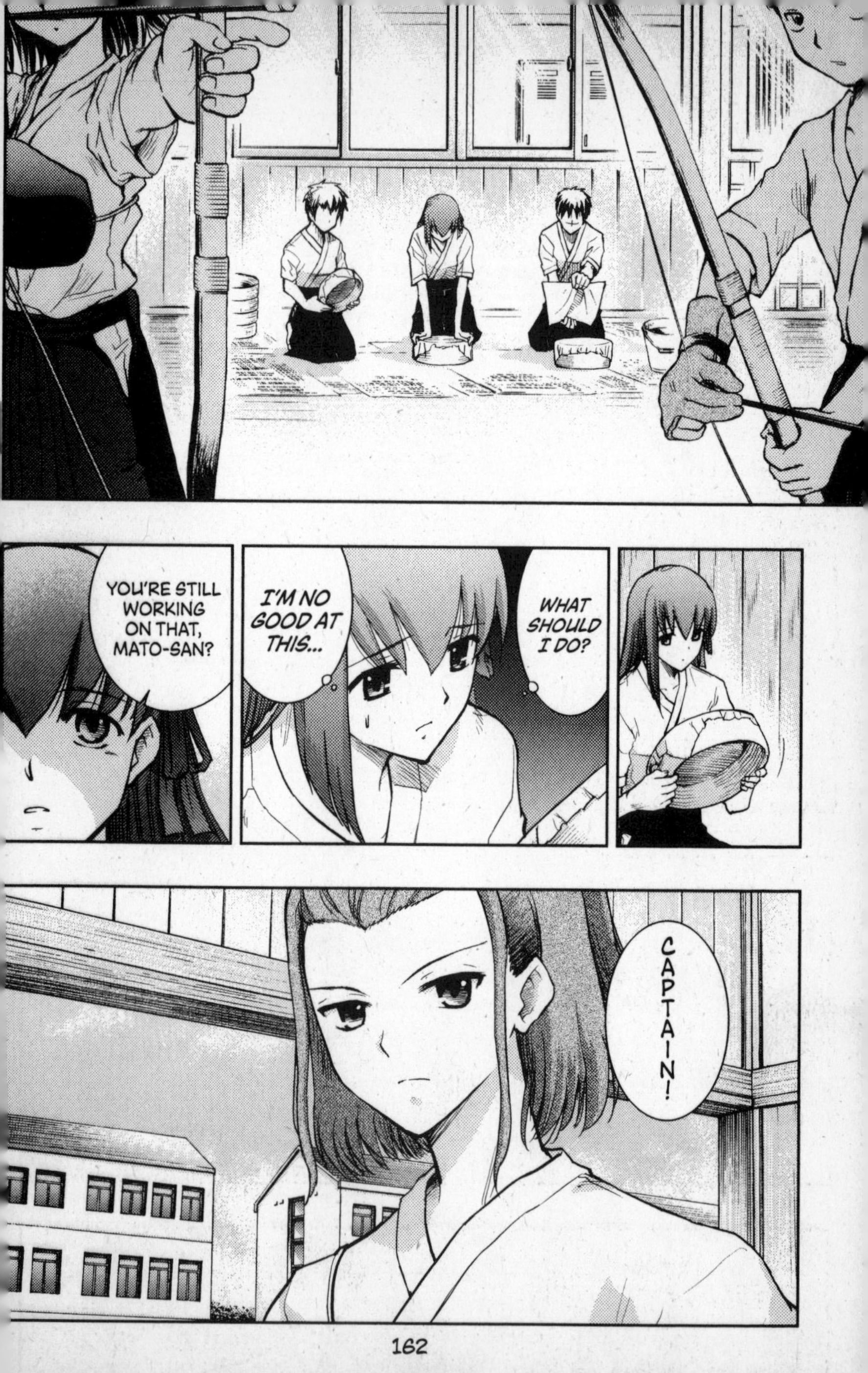
WHAT SHOULD I DO?
I'M NO GOOD AT THIS...
YOU'RE STILL WORKING ON THAT, MATO-SAN?
CAPTAIN!

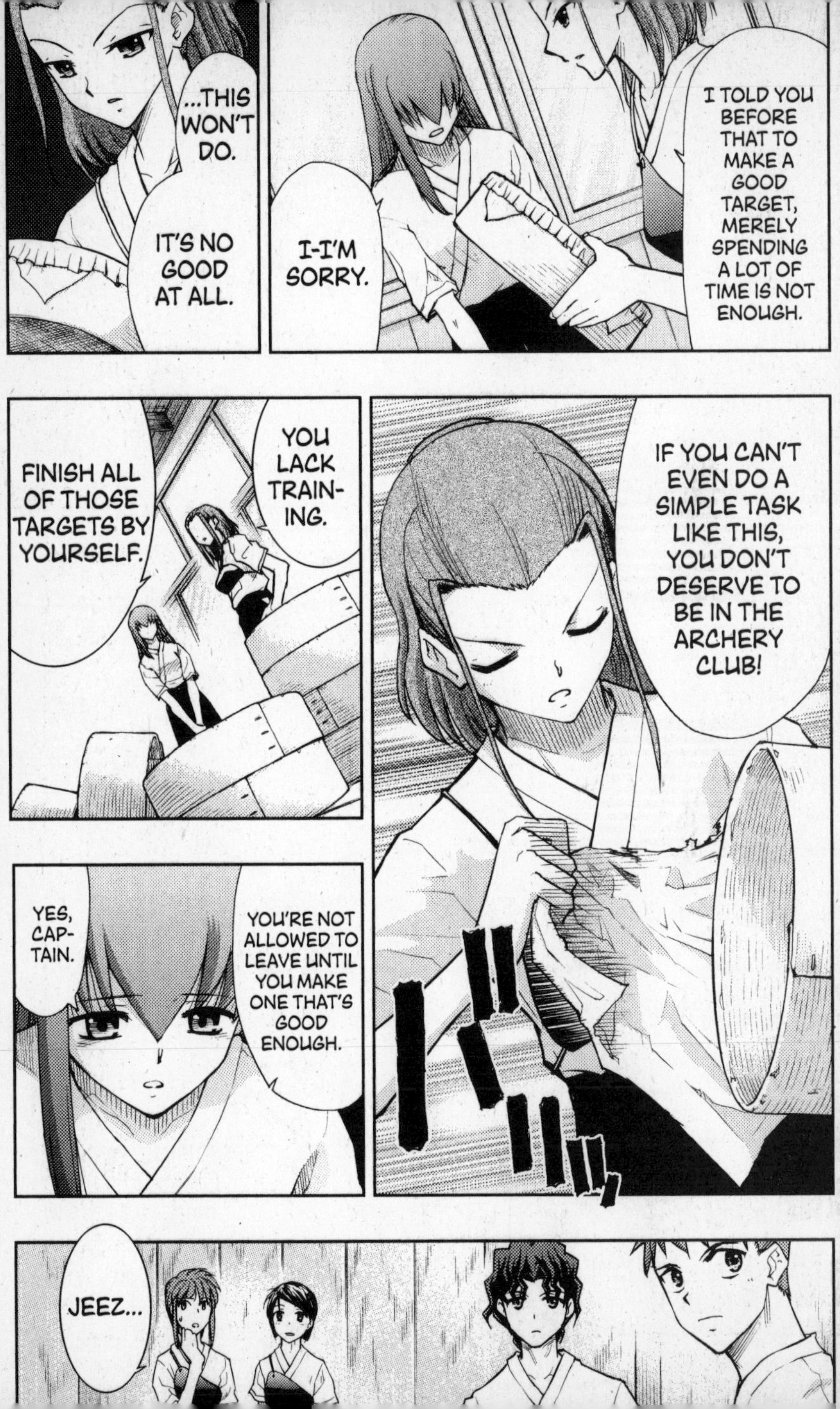
I TOLD YOU BEFORE THAT TO MAKE A GOOD TARGET, MERELY SPENDING A LOT OF TIME IS NOT ENOUGH.
I-I'M SORRY.
...THIS WON'T DO.
IT'S NO GOOD AT ALL.
IF YOU CAN'T EVEN DO A SIMPLE TASK LIKE THIS, YOU DON'T DESERVE TO BE IN THE ARCHERY CLUB!
YOU LACK TRAIN-ING.
FINISH ALL OF THOSE TARGETS BY YOURSELF.
YOU'RE NOT ALLOWED TO LEAVE UNTIL YOU MAKE ONE THAT'S GOOD ENOUGH.
YES, CAP-TAIN.
JEEZ...

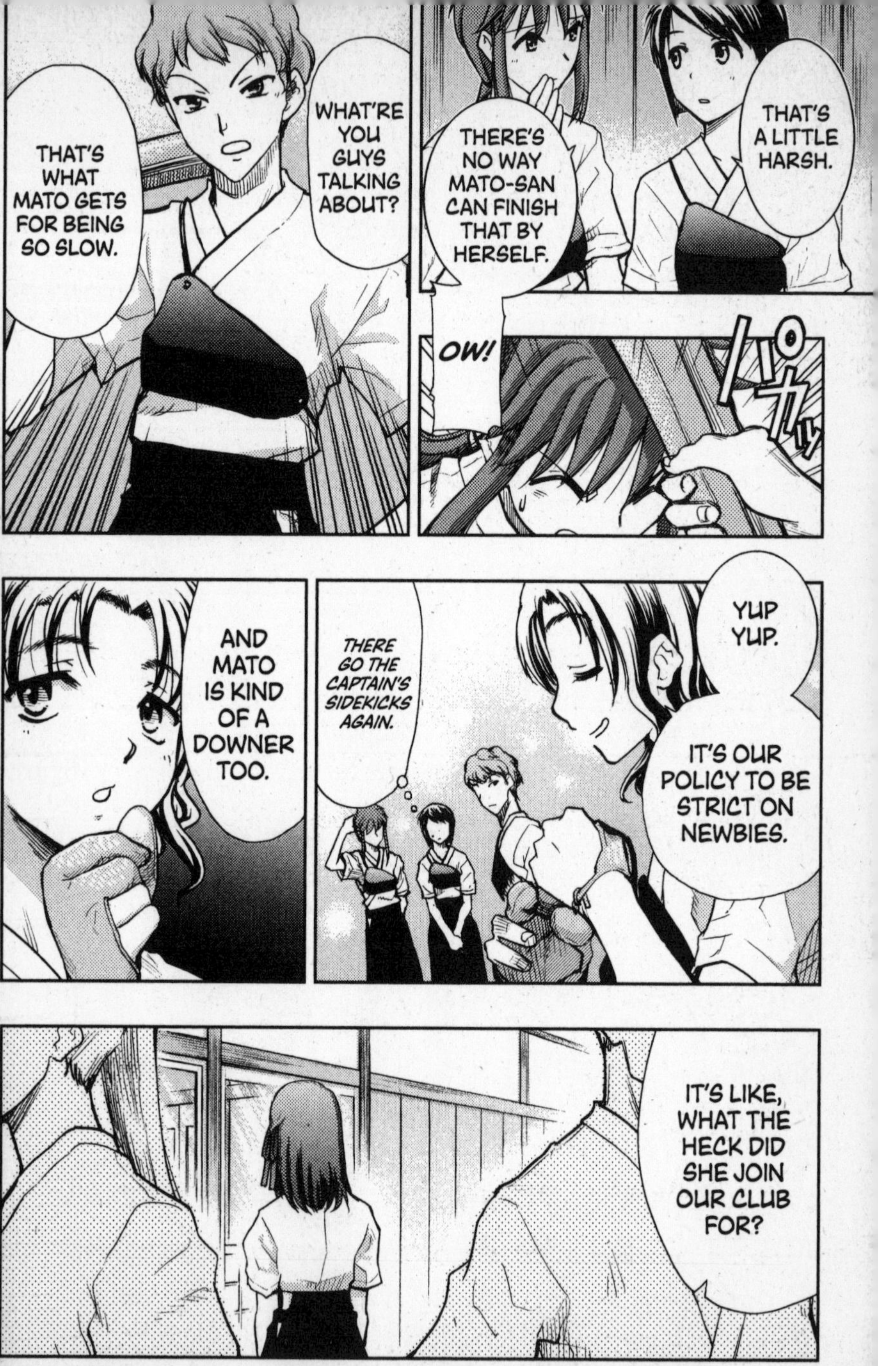
THAT'S A LITTLE HARSH.
THERE'S NO WAY MATO-SAN CAN FINISH THAT BY HERSELF.
パカッ
OW!
WHAT'RE YOU GUYS TALKING ABOUT?
THAT'S WHAT MATO GETS FOR BEING SO SLOW.
YUP YUP.
IT'S OUR POLICY TO BE STRICT ON NEWBIES.
THERE GO THE CAPTAIN'S SIDEKICKS AGAIN.
AND MATO IS KIND OF A DOWNER TOO.
IT'S LIKE, WHAT THE HECK DID SHE JOIN OUR CLUB FOR?

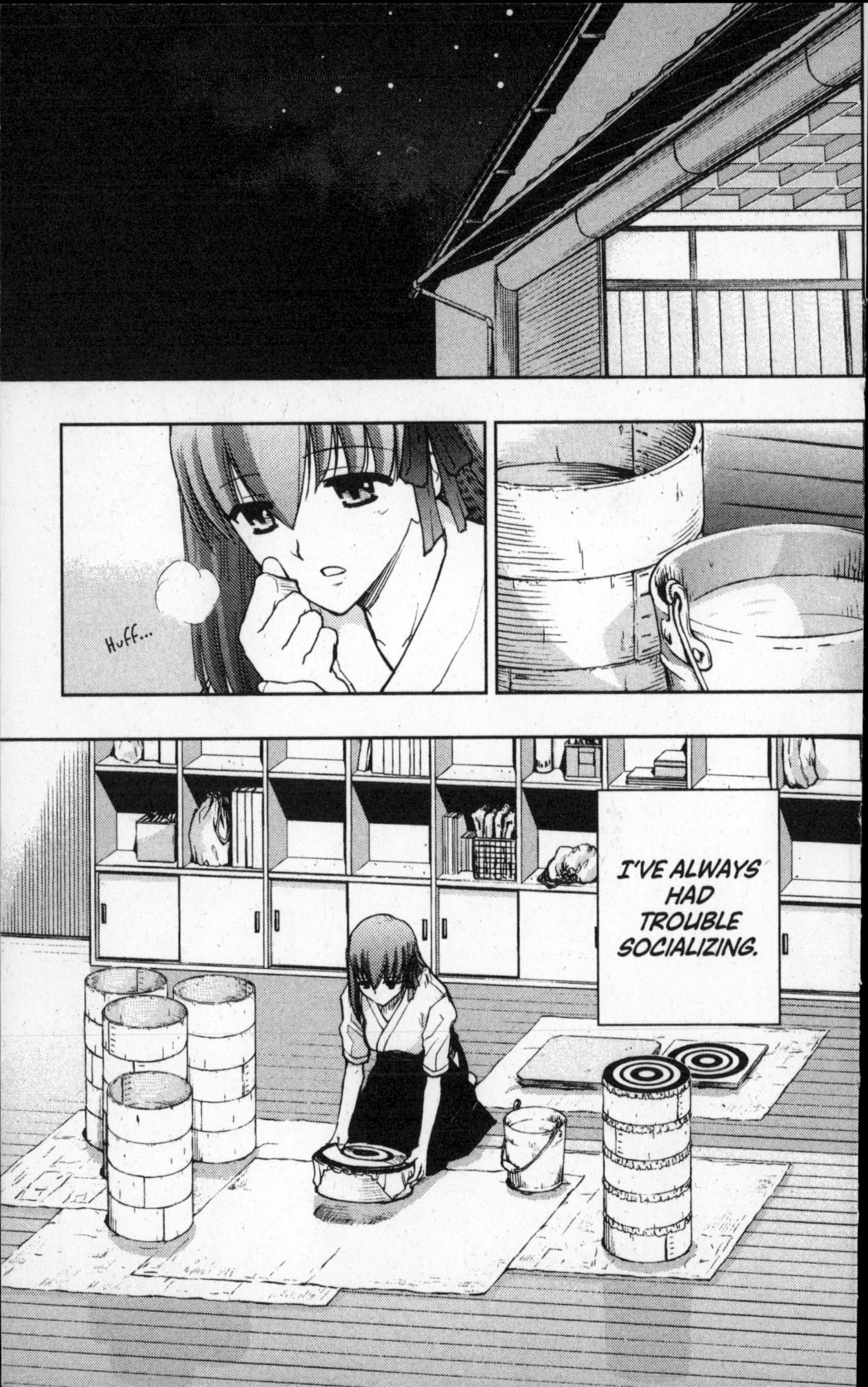
Huff...
I'VE ALWAYS HAD TROUBLE SOCIALIZING.

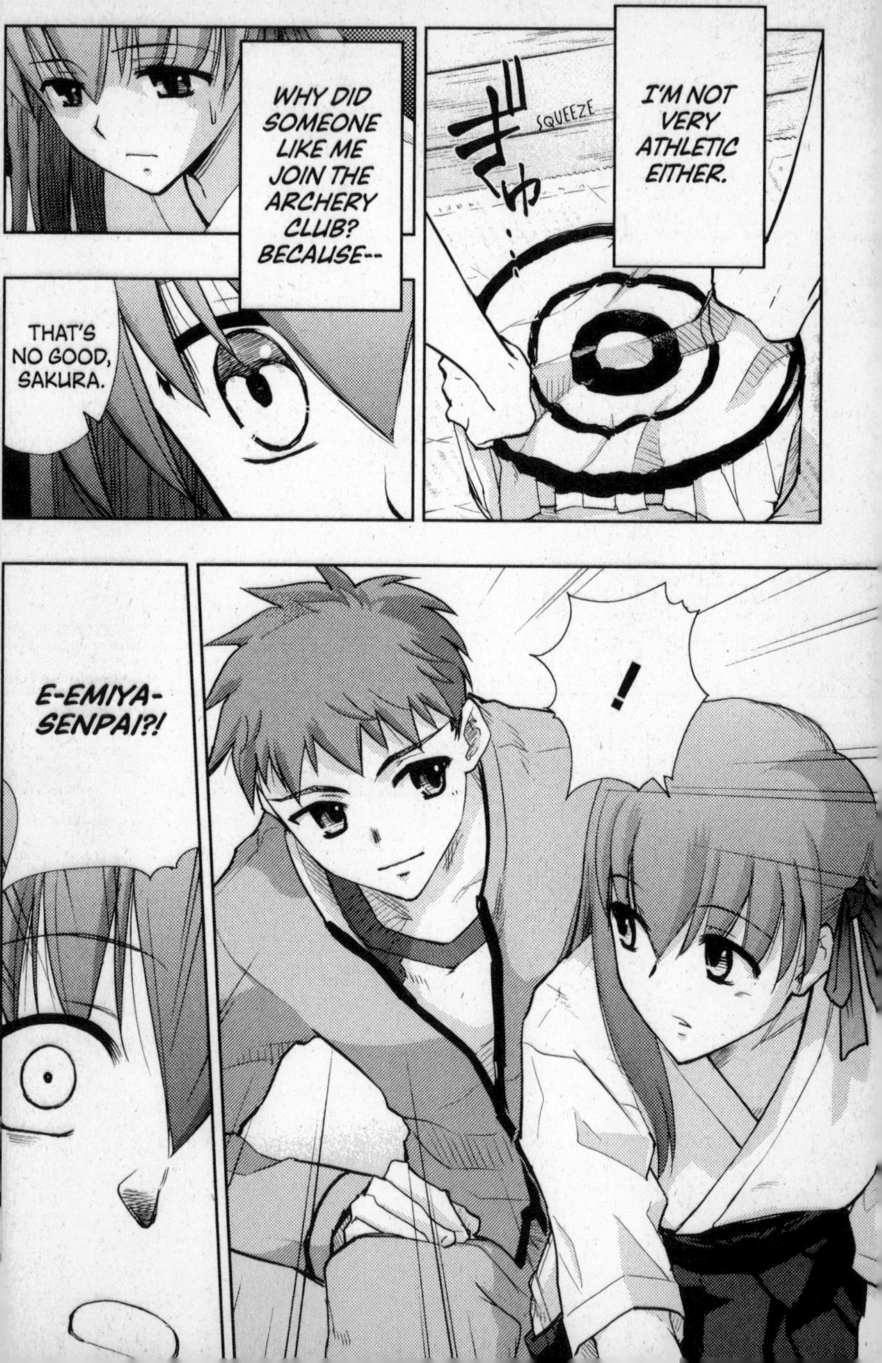
I'M NOT VERY ATHLETIC EITHER.
SQUEEZE
ぎゅ…
WHY DID SOMEONE LIKE ME JOIN THE ARCHERY CLUB? BECAUSE--
THAT'S NO GOOD, SAKURA.
!
E-EMIYA-SENPAI?!

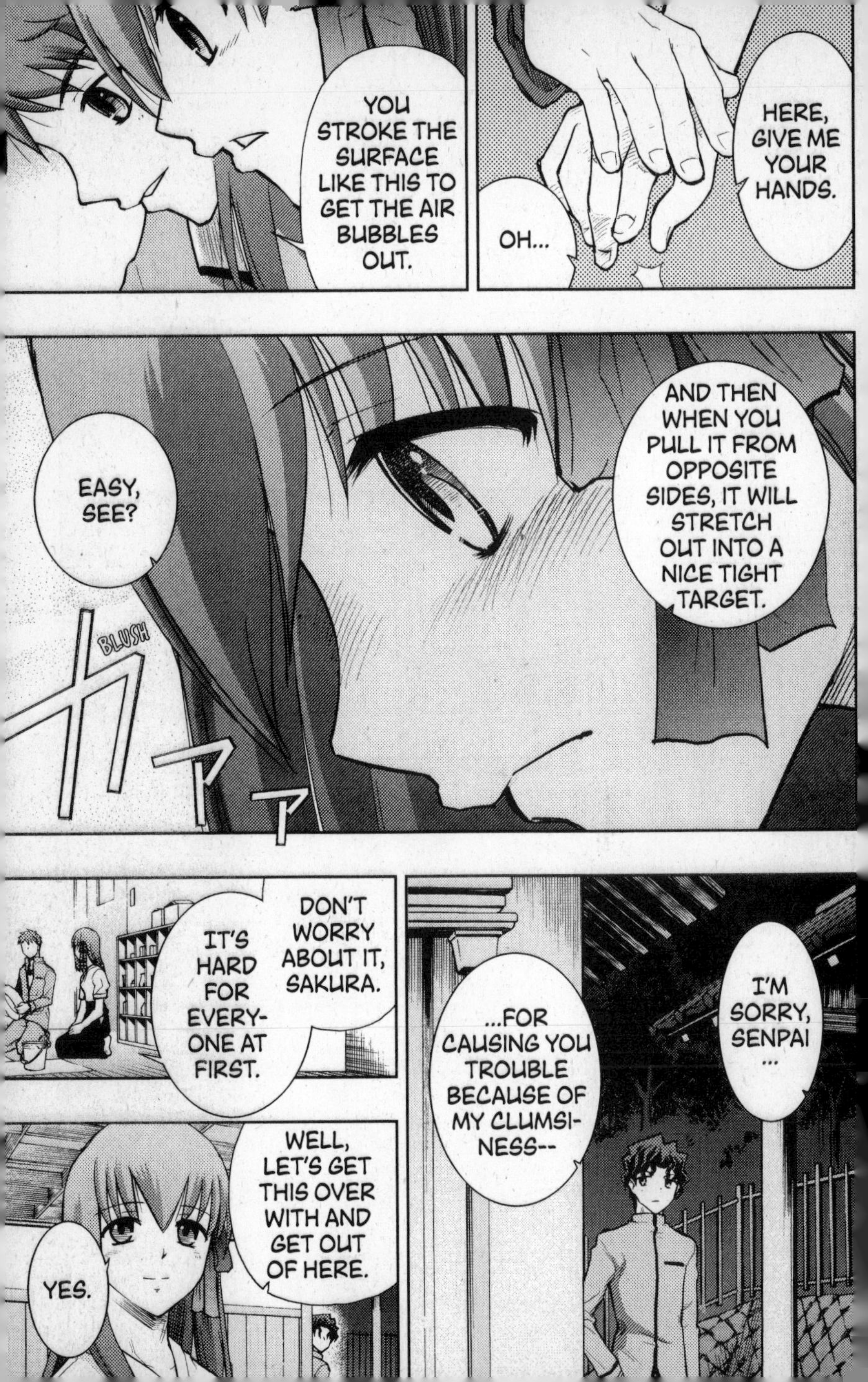
HERE, GIVE ME YOUR HANDS.
OH...
YOU STROKE THE SURFACE LIKE THIS TO GET THE AIR BUBBLES OUT.
AND THEN WHEN YOU PULL IT FROM OPPOSITE SIDES, IT WILL STRETCH OUT INTO A NICE TIGHT TARGET.
EASY, SEE?
BLUSH
I'M SORRY, SENPAI...
...FOR CAUSING YOU TROUBLE BECAUSE OF MY CLUMSI-NESS--
DON'T WORRY ABOUT IT, SAKURA.
IT'S HARD FOR EVERY-ONE AT FIRST.
WELL, LET'S GET THIS OVER WITH AND GET OUT OF HERE.
YES.

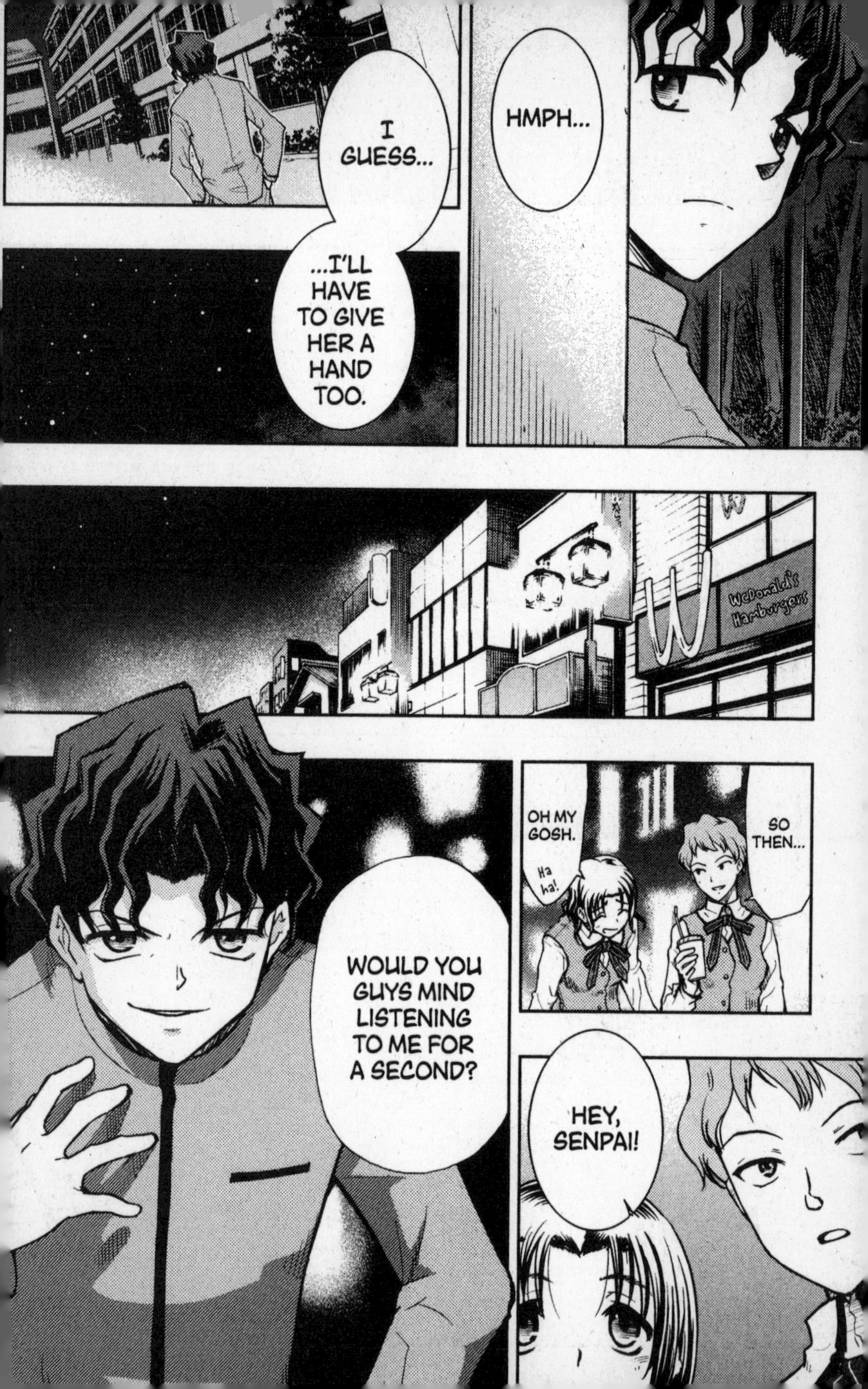
HMPH...
I GUESS...
...I'LL HAVE TO GIVE HER A HAND TOO.
WcDonald's Hamburgers
SO THEN...
OH MY GOSH.
Ha ha!
HEY, SENPAI!
WOULD YOU GUYS MIND LISTENING TO ME FOR A SECOND?

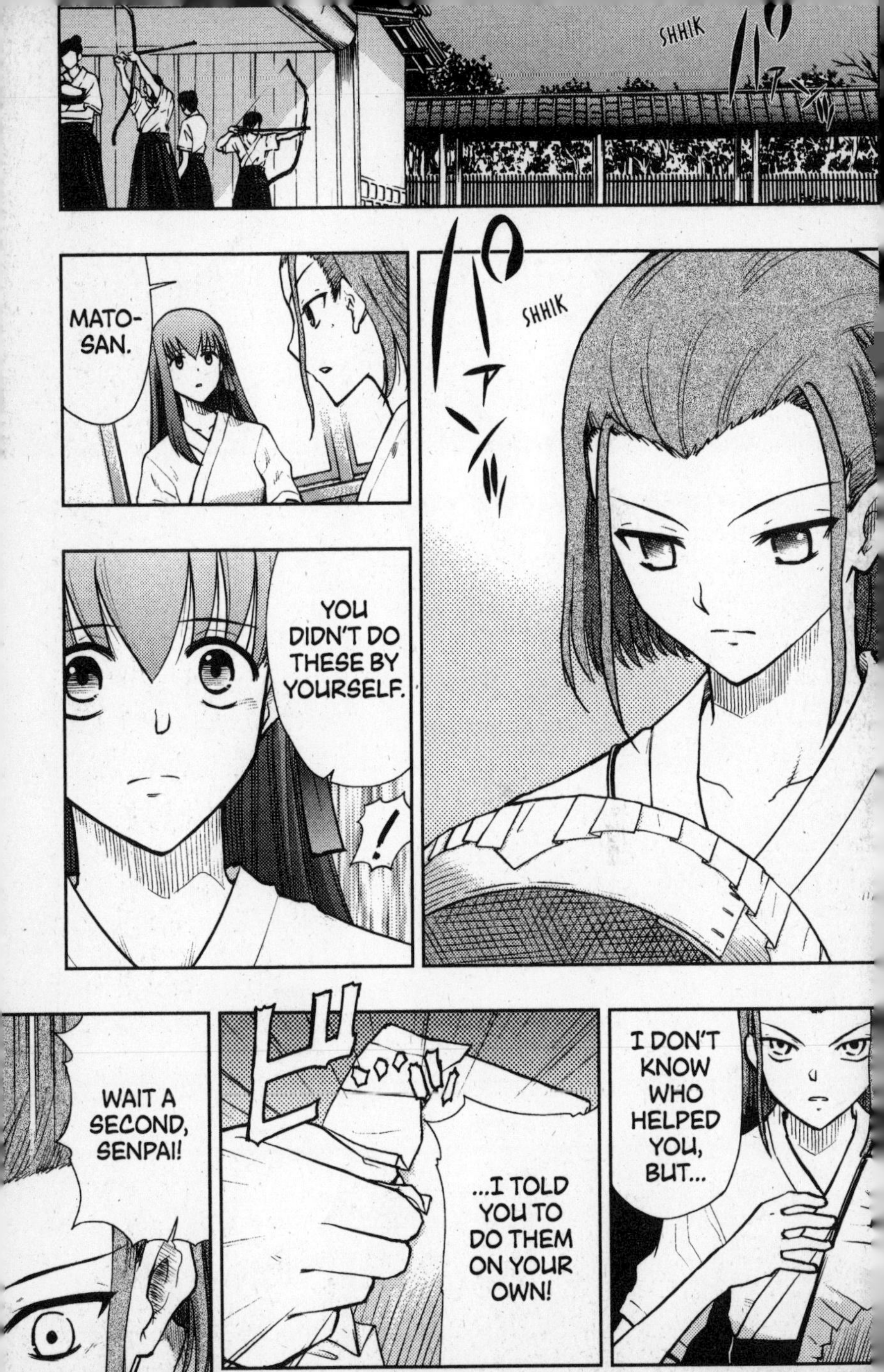
SHHIK
SHHIK
MATO-SAN.
YOU DIDN'T DO THESE BY YOURSELF.
!
I DON'T KNOW WHO HELPED YOU, BUT...
...I TOLD YOU TO DO THEM ON YOUR OWN!
WAIT A SECOND, SENPAI!

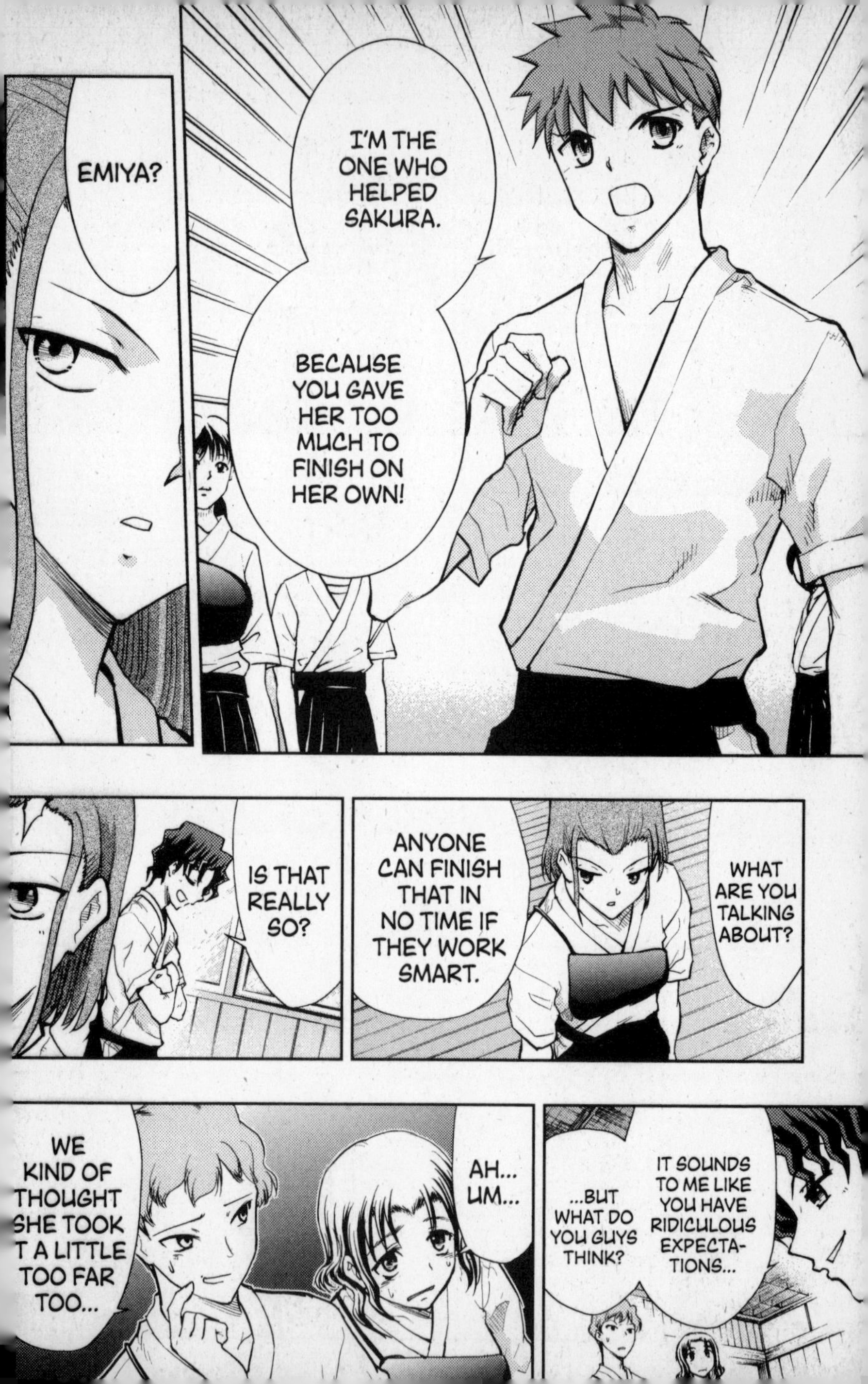
I'M THE ONE WHO HELPED SAKURA.
BECAUSE YOU GAVE HER TOO MUCH TO FINISH ON HER OWN!
EMIYA?
WHAT ARE YOU TALKING ABOUT?
ANYONE CAN FINISH THAT IN NO TIME IF THEY WORK SMART.
IS THAT REALLY SO?
IT SOUNDS TO ME LIKE YOU HAVE RIDICULOUS EXPECTATIONS...
...BUT WHAT DO YOU GUYS THINK?
AH... UM...
WE KIND OF THOUGHT SHE TOOK T A LITTLE TOO FAR TOO...

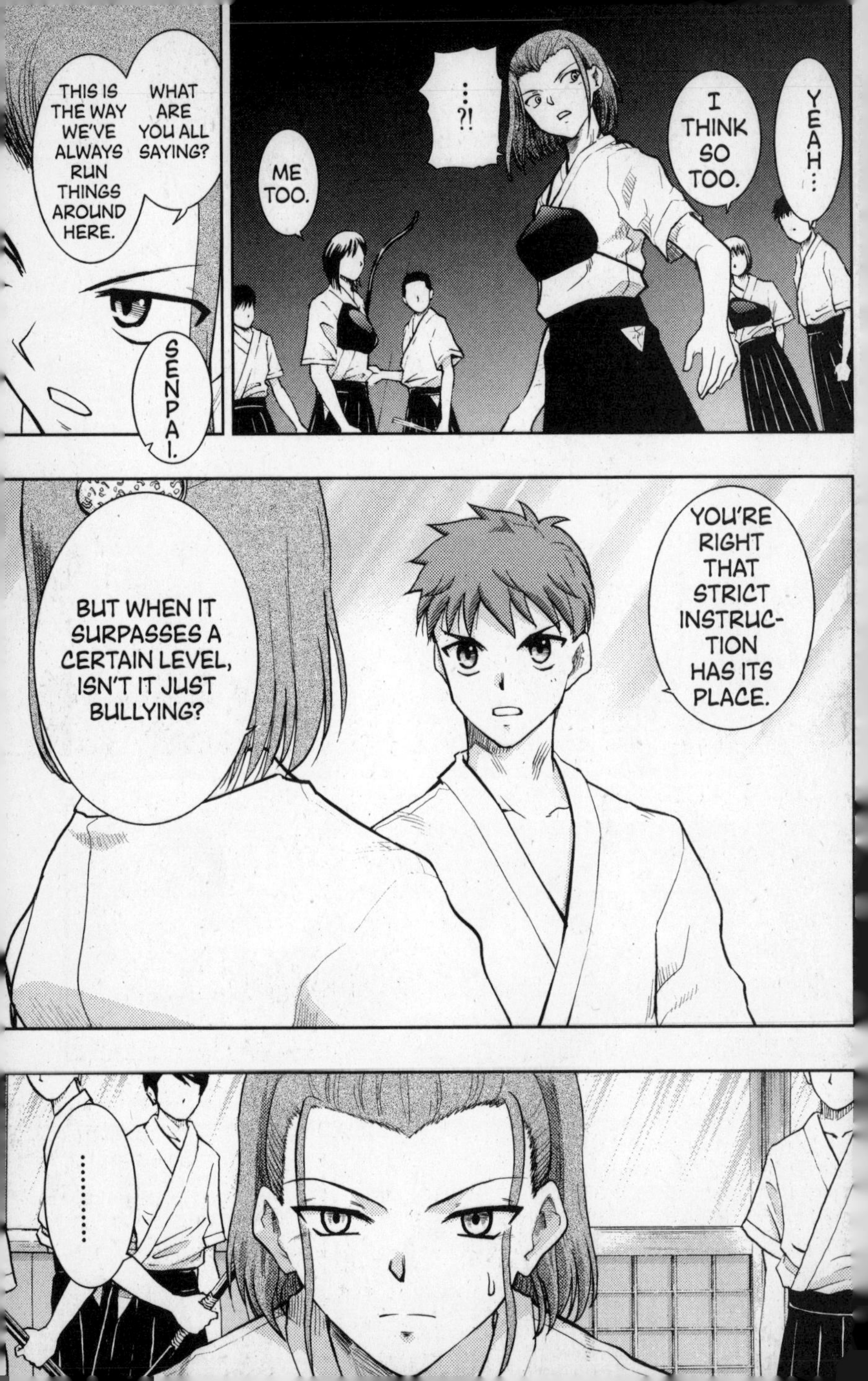
YEAH…
I THINK SO TOO.
…?!
ME TOO.
WHAT ARE YOU ALL SAYING?
THIS IS THE WAY WE'VE ALWAYS RUN THINGS AROUND HERE.
SENPAI.
YOU'RE RIGHT THAT STRICT INSTRUC-TION HAS ITS PLACE.
BUT WHEN IT SURPASSES A CERTAIN LEVEL, ISN'T IT JUST BULLYING?
………

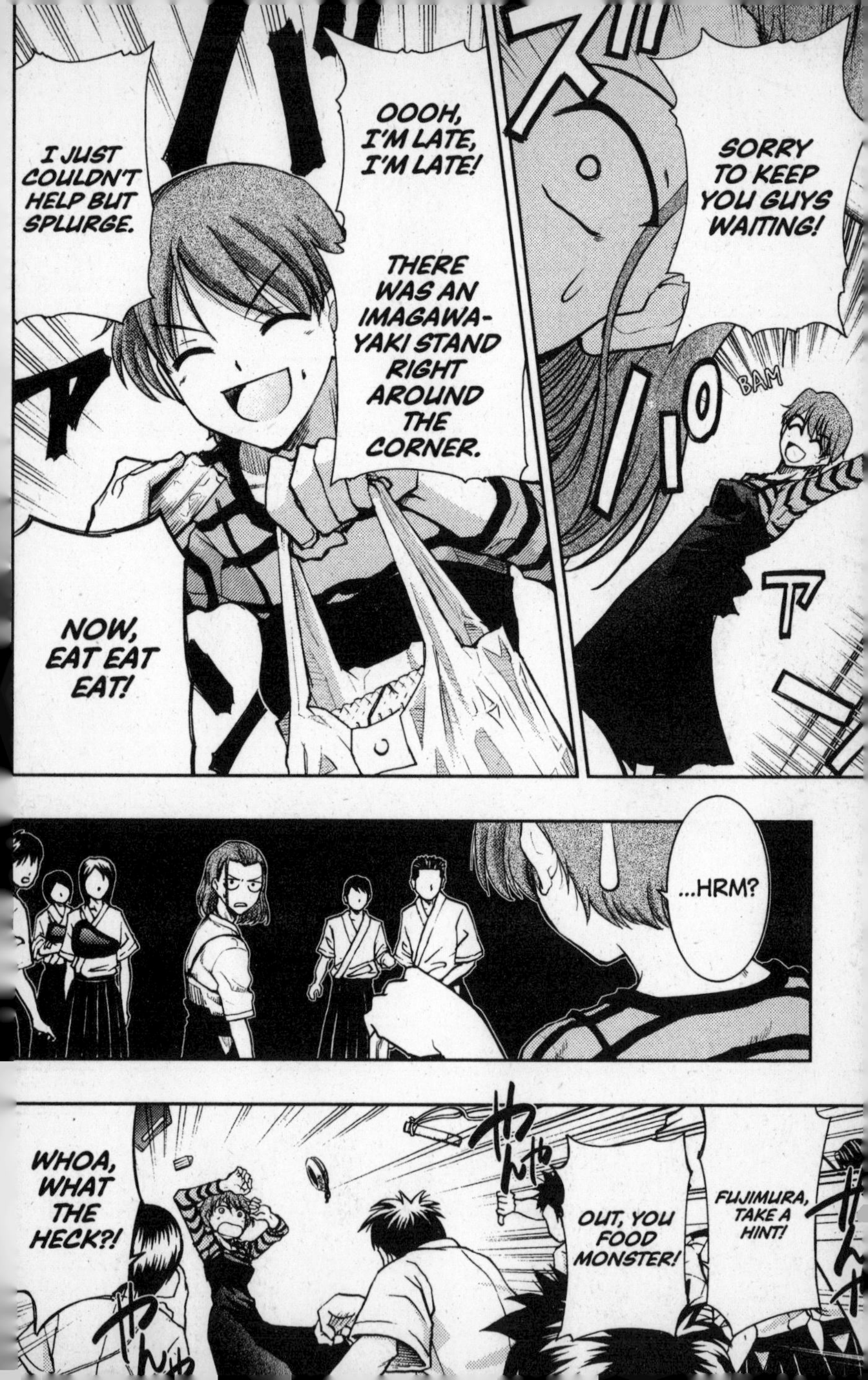
SORRY TO KEEP YOU GUYS WAITING!
BAM
OOOH, I'M LATE, I'M LATE!
THERE WAS AN IMAGAWA-YAKI STAND RIGHT AROUND THE CORNER.
I JUST COULDN'T HELP BUT SPLURGE.
NOW, EAT EAT EAT!
...HRM?
FUJIMURA, TAKE A HINT!
OUT, YOU FOOD MONSTER!
WHOA, WHAT THE HECK?!

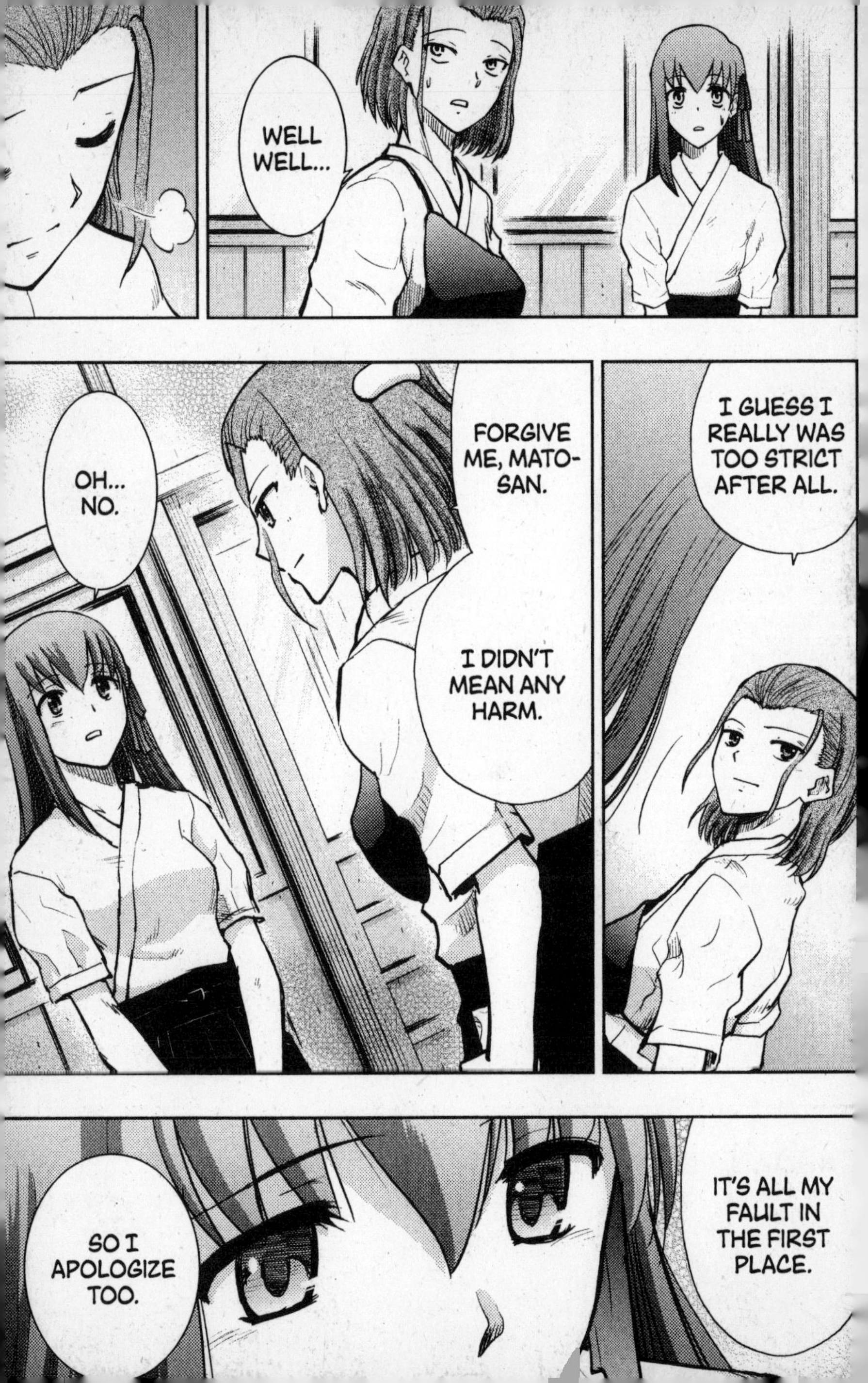
WELL WELL...
I GUESS I REALLY WAS TOO STRICT AFTER ALL.
FORGIVE ME, MATO-SAN.
I DIDN'T MEAN ANY HARM.
OH... NO.
IT'S ALL MY FAULT IN THE FIRST PLACE.
SO I APOLOGIZE TOO.

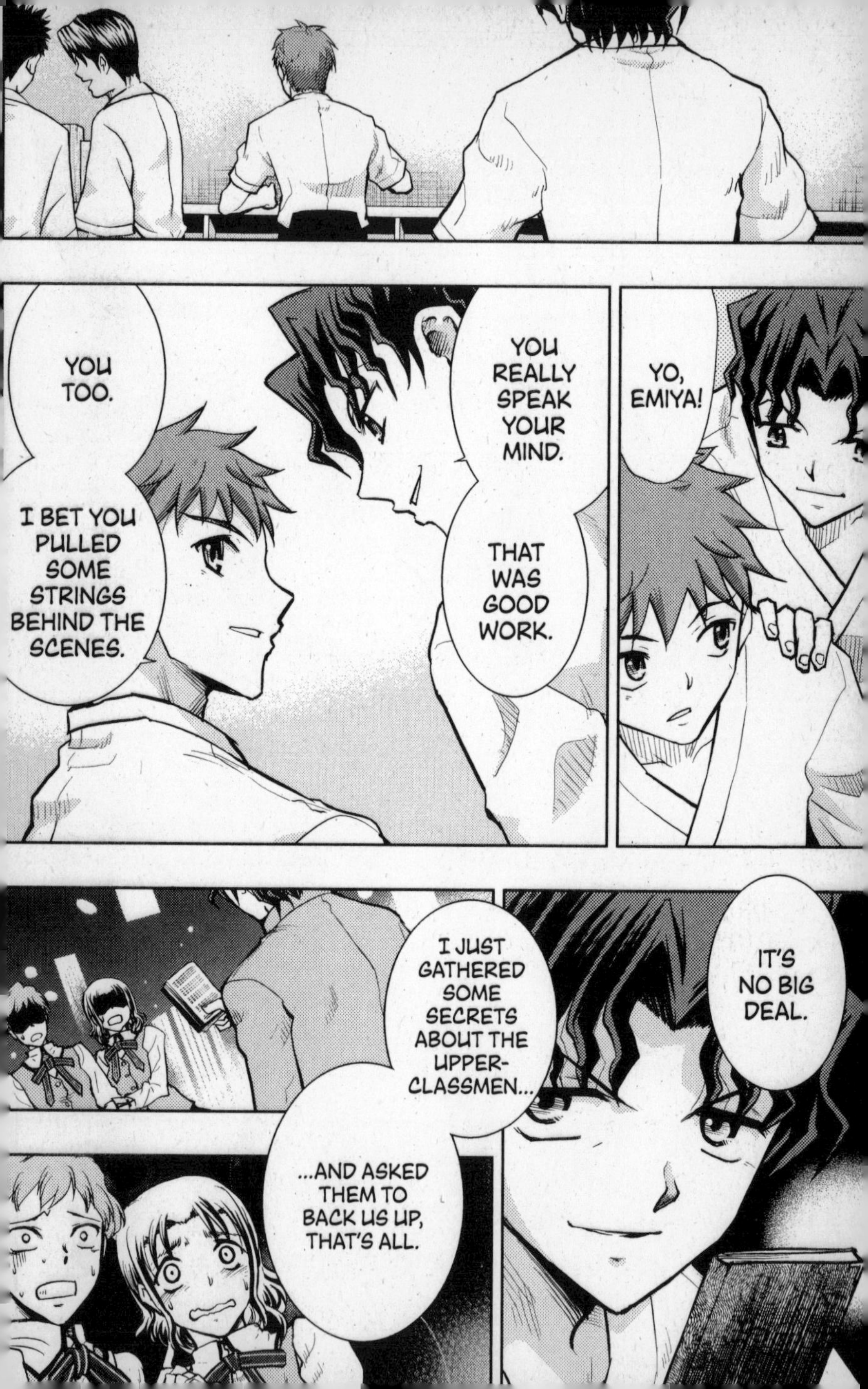
YO, EMIYA!
YOU REALLY SPEAK YOUR MIND.
THAT WAS GOOD WORK.
YOU TOO.
I BET YOU PULLED SOME STRINGS BEHIND THE SCENES.
IT'S NO BIG DEAL.
I JUST GATHERED SOME SECRETS ABOUT THE UPPER-CLASSMEN...
...AND ASKED THEM TO BACK US UP, THAT'S ALL.

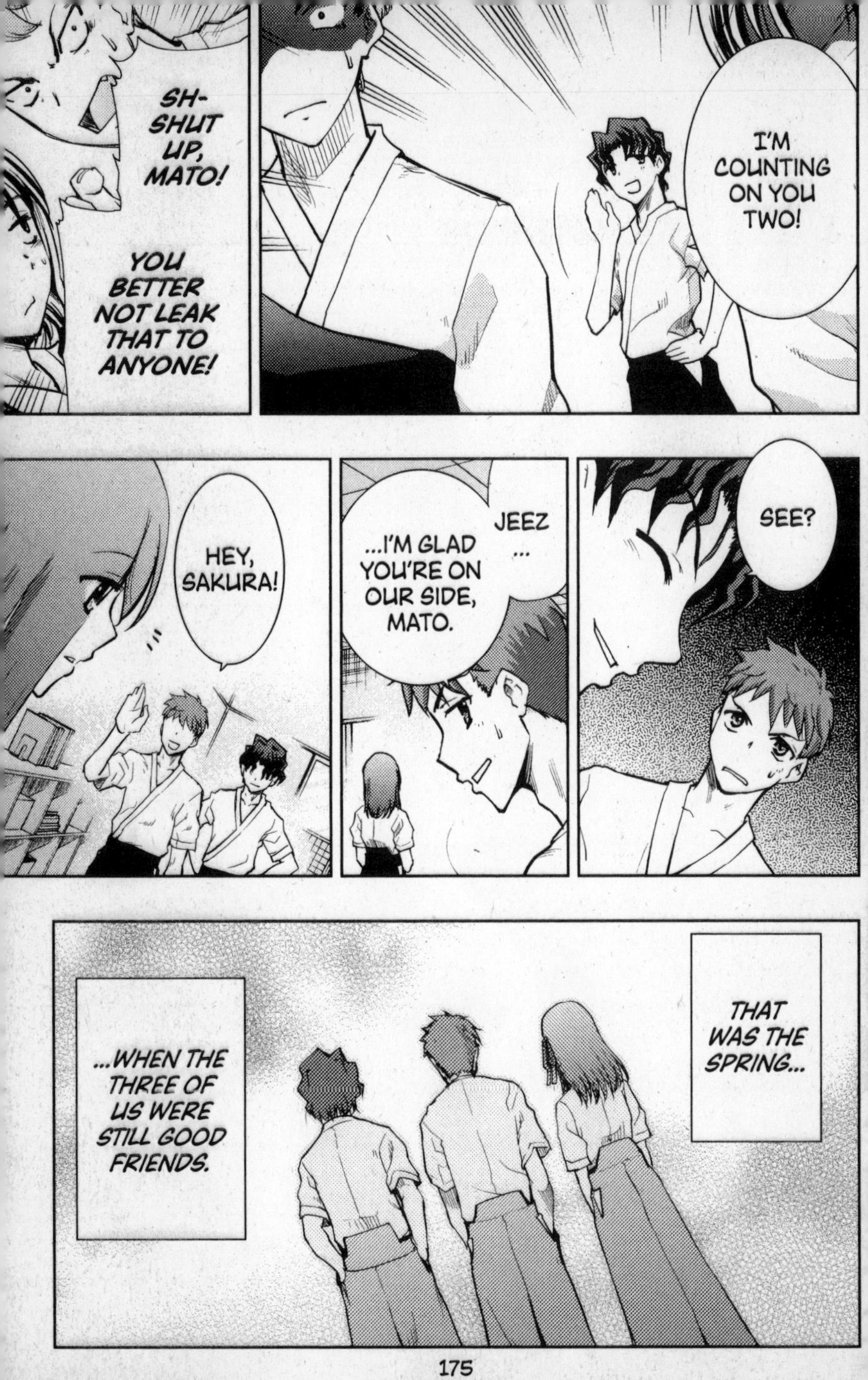
I'M COUNTING ON YOU TWO!
SH-SHUT UP, MATO!
YOU BETTER NOT LEAK THAT TO ANYONE!
SEE?
JEEZ ...
...I'M GLAD YOU'RE ON OUR SIDE, MATO.
HEY, SAKURA!
THAT WAS THE SPRING...
...WHEN THE THREE OF US WERE STILL GOOD FRIENDS.

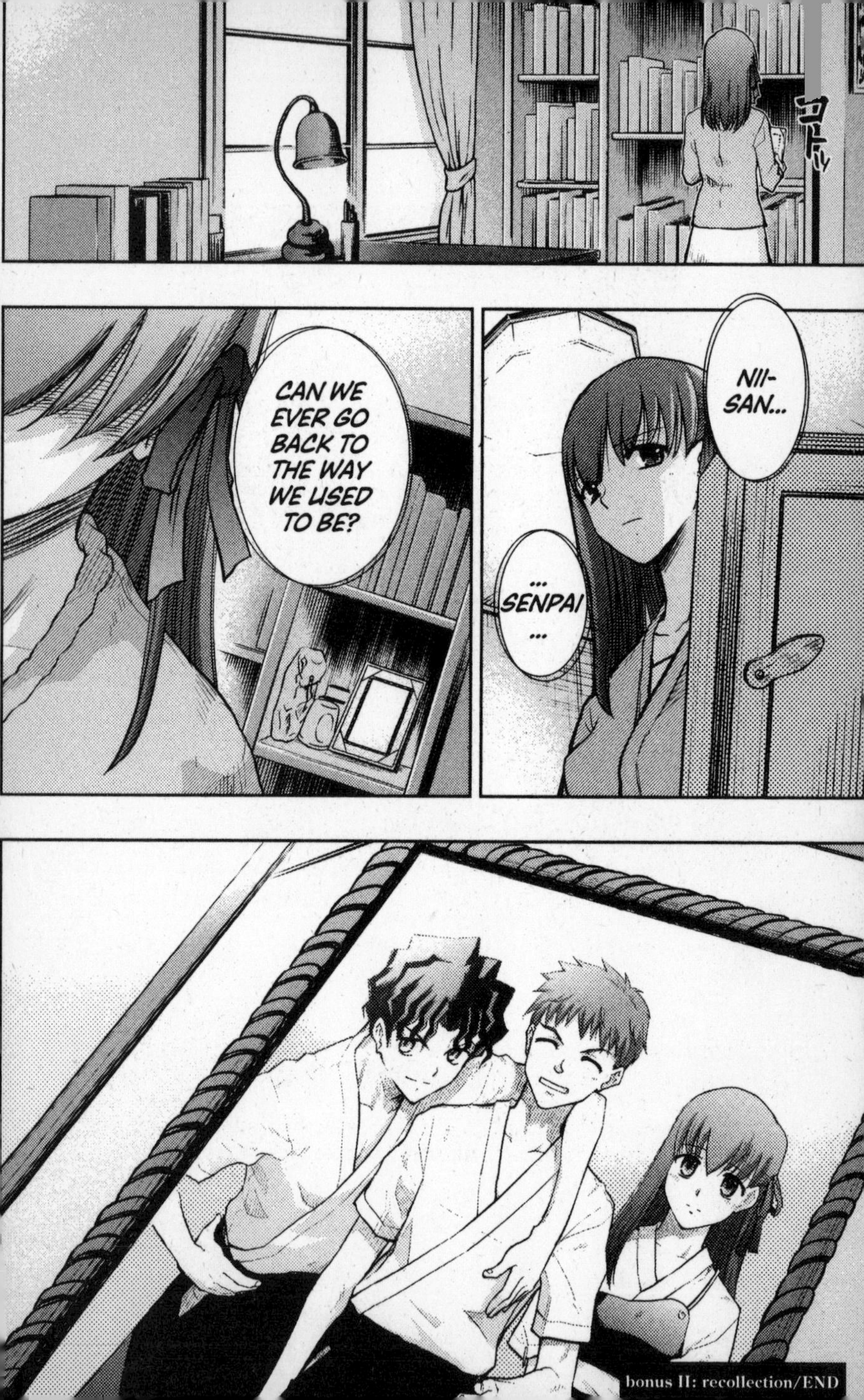
コトッ
NII-SAN...
...SENPAI...
CAN WE EVER GO BACK TO THE WAY WE USED TO BE?
bonus II: recollection/END

Next Time In...

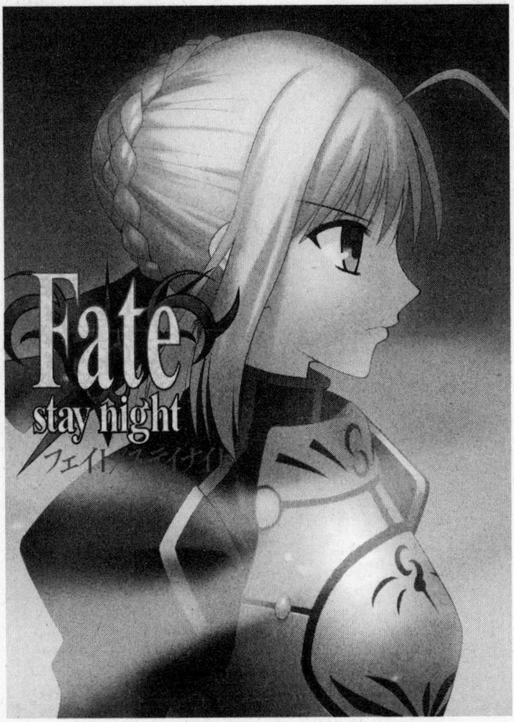
Fate
stay night

With the Blood Fort Andromeda spell field finally released, Shinji is well on his way to taking the lead in the Holy Grail War. But while Tosaka is willing to do anything to stop him, Shiro still refuses to give up on his friend. Unfortunately, Rider still has some tricks up her sleeve, and in the end Shiro's kindness may well be his undoing...

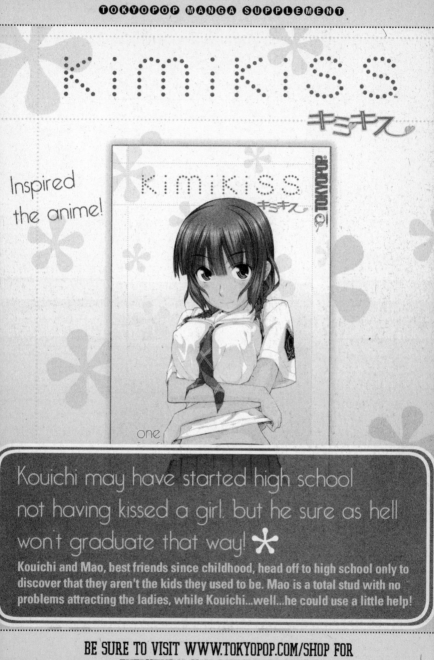

KARAKURI ODETTE

カラクリ オデット

SHE'S A HOT ROBOT IN HIGH SCHOOL

WHAT'S THE WORST THAT COULD HAPPEN?

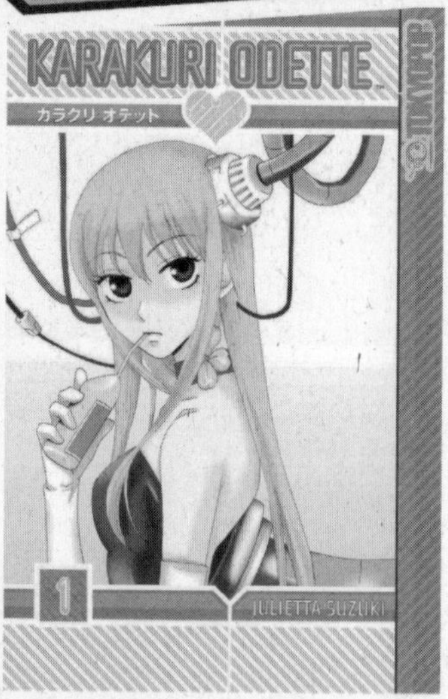
KARAKURI ODETTE
カラクリ オデット
1
JULIETTA SUZUKI

From the creator of *Akuma to Dolce*

Odette is an android created by the young, talented Dr. Yoshizawa. Wanting to find the ultimate difference between humans and androids, she decides to enroll in high school. Follow Odette's adventures, as she ventures through her school's hallowed halls, in search of the true meaning of being a human!

BE SURE TO VISIT WWW.TOKYOPOP.COM/SHOP FOR EVERYTHING YOU COULD EVER WANT!

TOKYOPOP MANGA SUPPLEMENT

D·N·ANGEL

TOKYOPOP
D·N·ANGEL
VOLUME 12 • YUKIRU SUGISAKI

D•N•Angel Returns!

Forbidden love + suave alter egos + romantic adventure = D•N•Angel volume 12

In order to rescue Risa, Daisuke teams up with his longtime rival, Satoshi Hiwatari. Will they be up to the challenge against Argentine's devious plot?!

FANTASY

T TEEN AGE 13+

BE SURE TO VISIT WWW.TOKYOPOP.COM/SHOP FOR EVERYTHING YOU COULD EVER WANT!

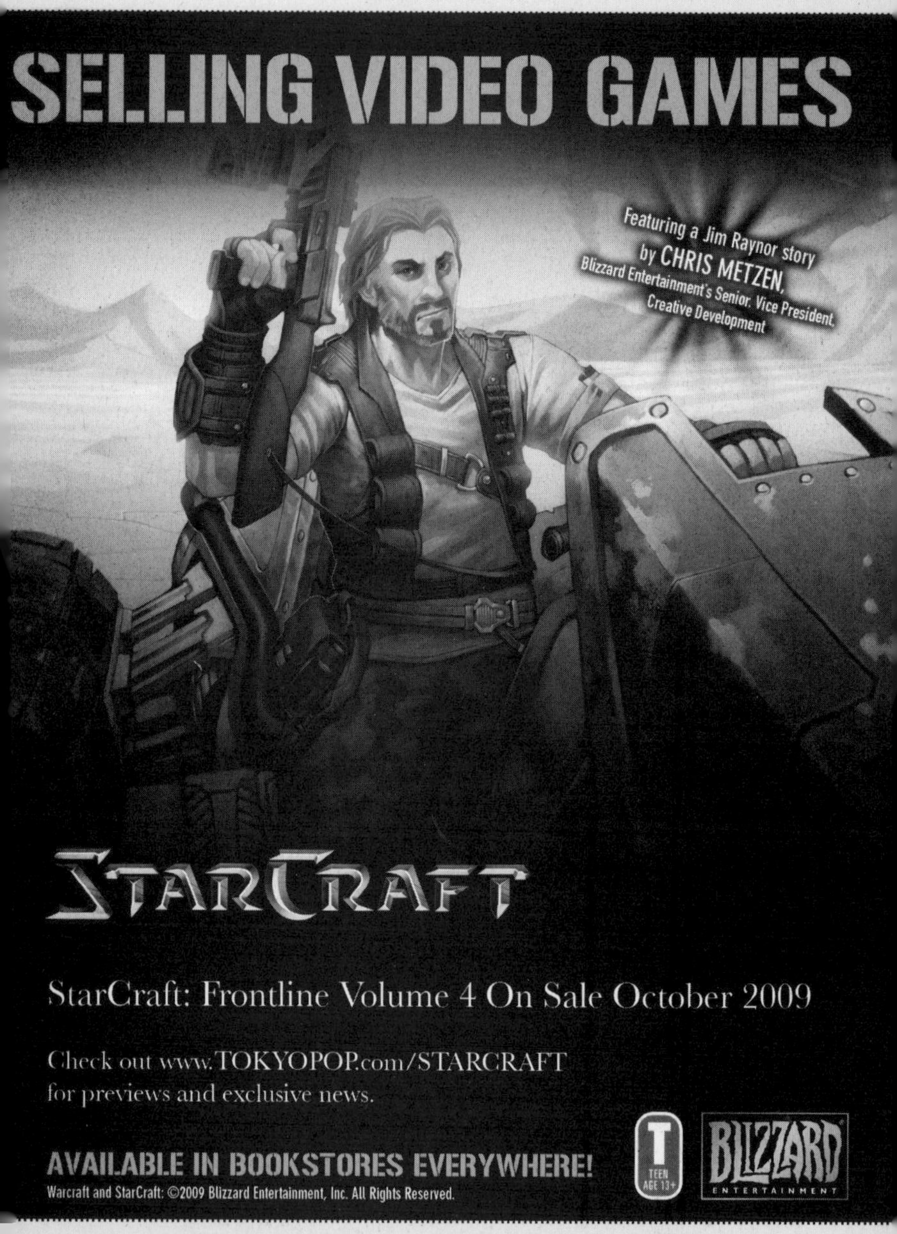
SELLING VIDEO GAMES
Featuring a Jim Raynor story
by CHRIS METZEN,
Blizzard Entertainment's Senior Vice President,
Creative Development
STARCRAFT
StarCraft: Frontline Volume 4 On Sale October 2009
Check out www.TOKYOPOP.com/STARCRAFT
for previews and exclusive news.
AVAILABLE IN BOOKSTORES EVERYWHERE!
Warcraft and StarCraft: ©2009 Blizzard Entertainment, Inc. All Rights Reserved.
T
TEEN
AGE 13+
BLIZZARD
ENTERTAINMENT

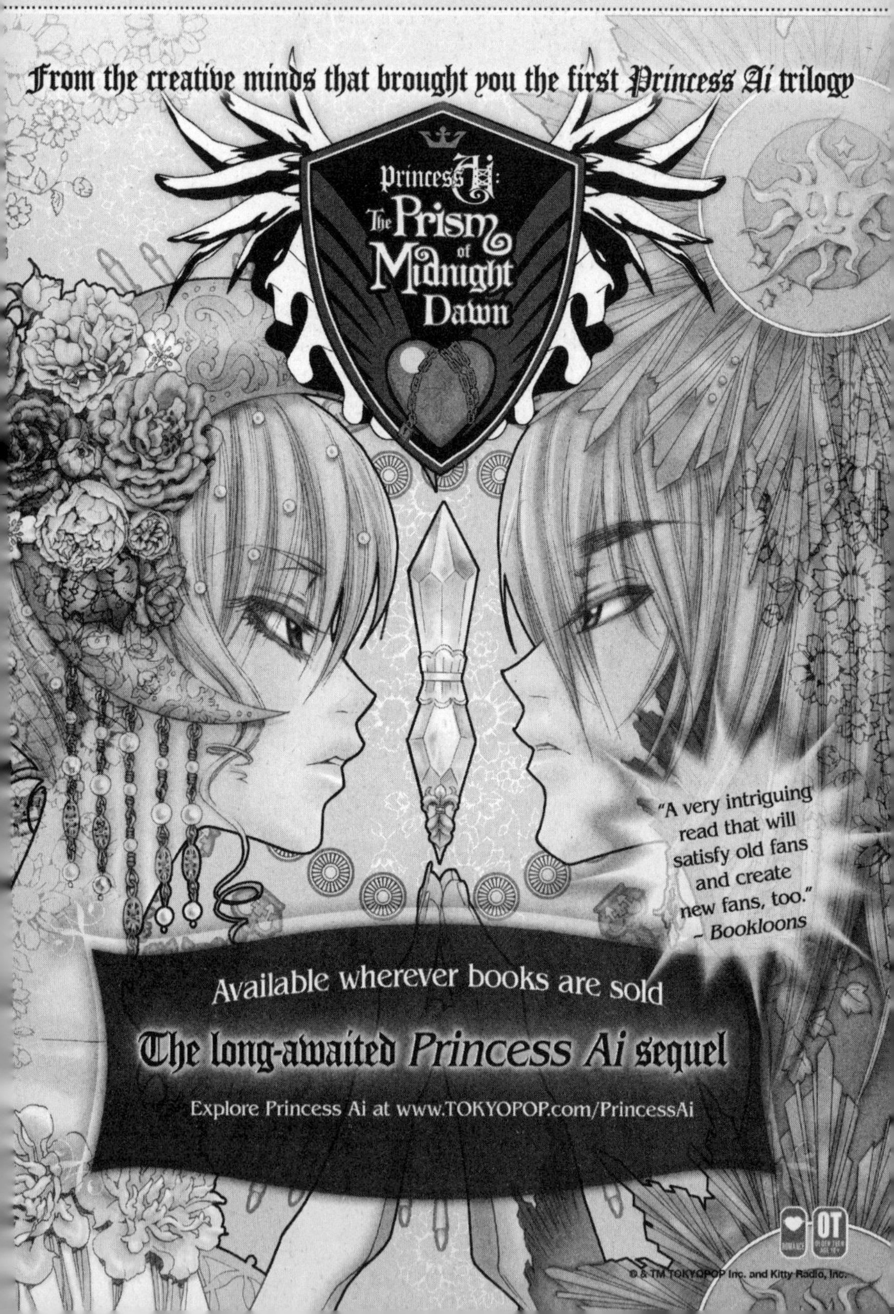
From the creative minds that brought you the first Princess Ai trilogy
Princess Ai: The Prism of Midnight Dawn
"A very intriguing read that will satisfy old fans and create new fans, too."
– Bookloons
Available wherever books are sold
The long-awaited Princess Ai sequel
Explore Princess Ai at www.TOKYOPOP.com/PrincessAi
© & TM TOKYOPOP Inc. and Kitty Radio, Inc.

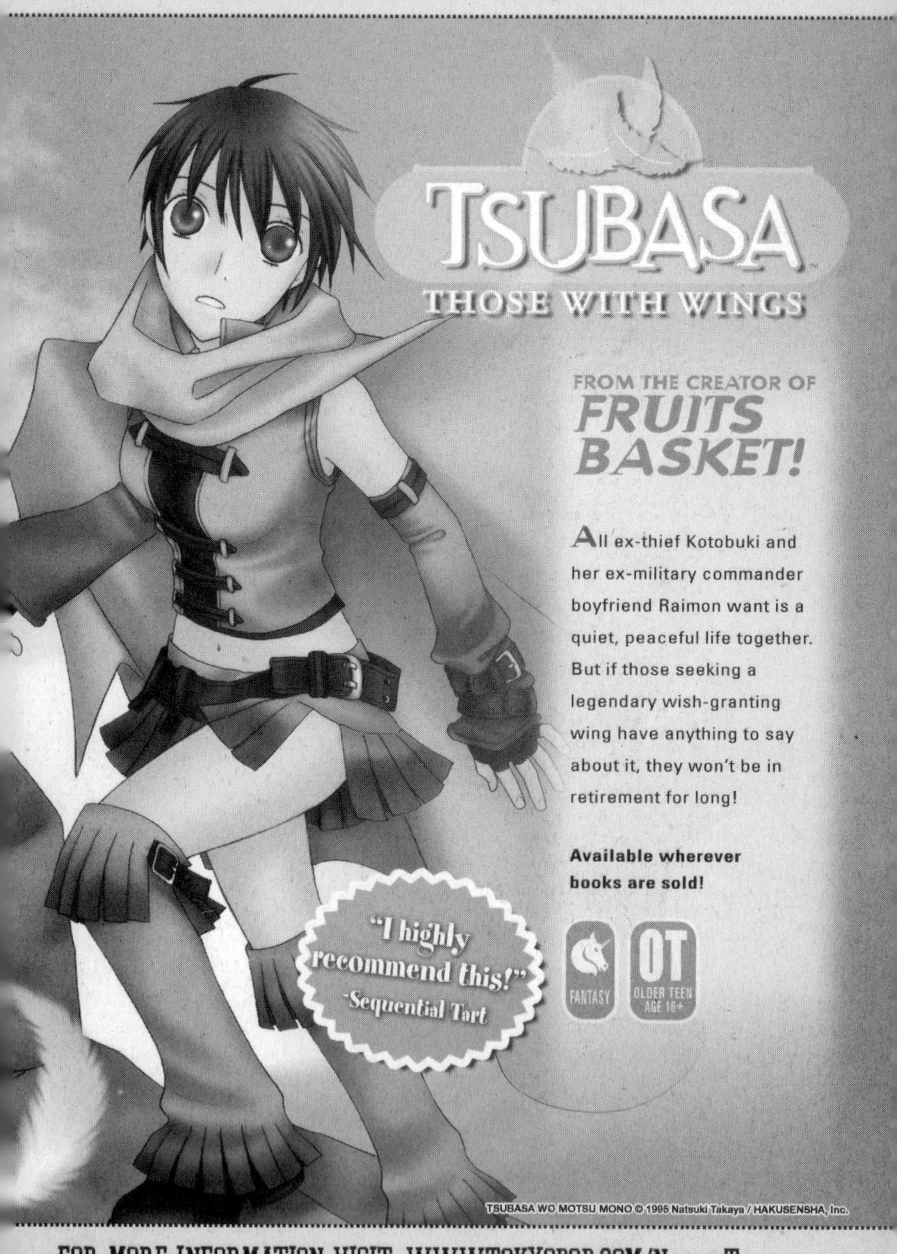
TSUBASA
THOSE WITH WINGS
FROM THE CREATOR OF
FRUITS BASKET!
All ex-thief Kotobuki and her ex-military commander boyfriend Raimon want is a quiet, peaceful life together. But if those seeking a legendary wish-granting wing have anything to say about it, they won't be in retirement for long!
Available wherever books are sold!
"I highly recommend this!"
-Sequential Tart
FANTASY
OT
OLDER TEEN AGE 16+
TSUBASA WO MOTSU MONO © 1995 Natsuki Takaya / HAKUSENSHA, Inc.

STOP!

This is the back of the book.
You wouldn't want to spoil a great ending!

This book is printed "manga-style," in the authentic Japanese right-to-left format. Since none of the artwork has been flipped or altered, readers get to experience the story just as the creator intended. You've been asking for it, so TOKYOPOP® delivered: authentic, hot-off-the-press, and far more fun!

DIRECTIONS

If this is your first time reading manga-style, here's a quick guide to help you understand how it works.

It's easy... just start in the top right panel and follow the numbers. Have fun, and look for more 100% authentic manga from TOKYOPOP®!